The Psychology of Sexual Health

The Psychology of Sexual Health

Edited by

David Miller

and

John Green

**Blackwell
Science**

© 2002 by
Blackwell Science Ltd
Editorial Offices:
Osney Mead, Oxford OX2 0EL
25 John Street, London WC1N 2BS
23 Ainslie Place, Edinburgh EH3 6AJ
350 Main Street, Malden
    MA 02148 5018, USA
54 University Street, Carlton
    Victoria 3053, Australia
10, rue Casimir Delavigne
    75006 Paris, France

Other Editorial Offices:

Blackwell Wissenschafts-Verlag GmbH
Kurfürstendamm 57
10707 Berlin, Germany

Blackwell Science KK
MG Kodenmacho Building
7–10 Kodenmacho Nihombashi
Chuo-ku, Tokyo 104, Japan

Iowa State University Press
A Blackwell Science Company
2121 S. State Avenue
Ames, Iowa 50014–8300, USA

First published 2002

Set in Minion and Stone Sans
by Sparks Computer Solutions Ltd, Oxford
http://www.sparks.co.uk
Printed and bound in Great Britain by
Antony Rowe Ltd, Chippenham, Wiltshire

The Blackwell Science logo is a
trade mark of Blackwell Science Ltd,
registered at the United Kingdom
Trade Marks Registry

DISTRIBUTORS
Marston Book Services Ltd
PO Box 269
Abingdon
Oxon OX14 4YN
(*Orders:* Tel: 01235 465500
           Fax: 01235 465555)

USA
Blackwell Science, Inc.
Commerce Place
350 Main Street
Malden, MA 02148 5018
(*Orders:* Tel: 800 759 6102
                781 388 8250
           Fax: 781 388 8255)

Canada
Login Brothers Book Company
324 Saulteaux Crescent
Winnipeg, Manitoba R3J 3T2
(*Orders:* Tel: 204 837-2987
           Fax: 204 837-3116)

Australia
Blackwell Science Pty Ltd
54 University Street
Carlton, Victoria 3053
(*Orders:* Tel: 03 9347 0300
           Fax: 03 9347 5001)

A catalogue record for this title
is available from the British Library

ISBN 0-632-04979-0

Library of Congress
Cataloging-in-Publication Data
The psychology of sexual health/edited by David Miller and
John Green.
        p.   cm
Includes bibliographical references and index.
ISBN 0-632-04979-0 (alk. paper)
1. Hygiene, Sexual. 2. Sexually transmitted diseases. 3. Sex
(Psychology) I. Miller, David, 1955- II. Green, John, clinical
psychologist.
RA788 .P794 2001
613.9--dc21
                                                    2001043509

For further information on
Blackwell Science, visit our website:
www.blackwell-science.com

To Ruth, Anne and Barbara (DM)

To Jonathan and Abigail (JG)

Contents

List of Contributors

Michael Adler
Professor of Genitourinary Medicine
Royal Free & University College Medical
    School
Department of Sexually Transmitted Diseases
The Mortimer Market Centre
London WC1E 6AU

Ron Alcorn
Lead Consultant Psychiatrist
Maragerete Centre
St James House
108 Hampstead Road
London NW1 2LS

Simon Barton
Consultant in Genitourinary Medicine
St Stephen's Clinic
Chelsea Westminster Hospital
Fulham Road
London SW10 9TH

Robin Bell
Associate Specialist in Genitourinary Medicine
Jefferiss Wing
St Mary's Hospital
London W2 1PD

Andrew Billington
Head of Information Services
Terrence Higgins Trust
52–54 Gray's Inn Road
London WC1X 8JU

Micheline Byrne
Consultant in Genitourinary Medicine
Jefferiss Wing
St Mary's Hospital
London W2 1PD

Michel Carael
Chief, Evaluation
Programme Development and Coordination
UNAIDS
20 Avenue Appia
CH-1211 Geneva 27
Switzerland

Jose Catalan
Reader in Psychiatry
Department of Public Mental Health
Division of Neuroscience and Psychological
   Medicine
Imperial College School of Medicine
Charing Cross & Westminster Campus
1 Nightingale Place
London SW10 9NG

Sarah Chippindale
Head Health Adviser
The Mortimer Market Centre
London WC1E 6AU

Paula Christmas
Clinical Psychologist
Charterhouse Building
Archway Campus
Whittington Hospital
Highgate Hill
London N19 3UA

Linda Cooke
Consultant Clinical Psychologist
Horizon Centre
Farnham Road Hospital
Farnham Road
Guildford GU2 7LX

Oliver Davidson
Consultant Clinical Psychologist
The Mortimer Market Centre
London WC1E 6AU

Françoise Dubois-Arber
Head of Evaluation Unit
SG University Instutute of Social and
   Preventive Medicine
Bugnon 17, 1005
Lausanne
Switzerland

Delia Easton
Hispanic Health Council
175 Main Street
Hartford, CT 06105
USA

Max Elstein
Professor and Executive Director
Institute of Medicine, Law and Bioethics
The University of Manchester
G705 Stopford Building
Manchester M13 9PT

Kevin Fenton
The Mortimer Market Centre
London WC1E 6AU

Paul Fox
Specialist Registrar in HIV/GUM
St Stephen's Clinic
Chelsea Westminster Hospital
Fulham Road
London SW10 9TH

John Green
Chief Clinical Psychologist
Paterson Centre
20, South Wharf Road
London W2 1PD

Sunanda Gupta
Institute of Medicine, Law and Bioethics
The University of Manchester
G705 Stopford Building
Manchester M13 9PT

Janice Hiller
Head of Sexual Health
Redbridge Psychology, Psychotherapy and
    Counselling Service
Goodmayes Hospital
Barley Lane
Ilford
Essex IG3 8XJ

Myra Hunter
Consultant Clinical Psychologist and Lead
    for Clinical Health Psychology
Department of Psychology
Adamson Centre
Block 8, South Wing
Lower Ground Floor
St Thomas's Hospital
London SE1 7EH

Helen Kennerley
Consultant Clinical Psychologist
Psychology Department
The Warneford Hospital
Warneford Lane
Headington
Oxford OX3 7JX

Deborah Lee
Consultant Clinical Psychologist
Camden & Islington CHS NHS Trust
Traumatic Stress Clinic
73 Charlotte Street
London W1P 1LB

Aruna Mahtani
Clinical Psychologist
Medical Foundation Caring for the Victims
    of Torture
Star House
104–108 Grafton Road
London NW5 4BD

Lucia O'Sullivan

Richard Parker

Jenny Petrak
Consultant Clinical Psychologist
Head of Psychology Services
Ambrose King Centre
St Bartholomew's Hospital
London EC1

John Richens
Hon. Senior Lecturer
Royal Free & University College Medical
    School
Department of Sexually Transmitted Diseases
The Mortimer Market Centre
London WC1E 6AU

Peter Scragg
Lecturer in Psychology
Sub-Department of Clinical Health
    Psychology
University College London
Gower Street
London WC1E 6BT

Anne Walker
Senior Lecturer
University of Aberdeen
Health Services Research Unit
Foresterhill
Aberdeen AB25 2ZD

Shamil Wanigaratne
Head of Clinical Psychology
Addictions Directorate
Addictions Resource Centre
Maudsley Hospital
63–65 Denmark Hill
Camberwell
London SE5 8RS

Jim Watson
Professor and Head
Department of Psychotherapy and General
 Psychiatry
Ling's College London
University of London
5th Floor, Thomas Guy House
Guy's Hospital
London SE1 9RT

Preface

Over the last 25 years sexual health has become one of the most important areas of health care across the world. A global pandemic of HIV, the rapid worldwide spread of other sexually transmitted diseases, and an increasing awareness of sexual health issues by the public globally have all increased enormously the needs of those dealing with sexual health problems to have access to information on theory and practice that can help them address the diversity of issues they now face. Central to sexual health is an understanding of its psychology, how people behave, how they relate to their sexual partners, the steps they take to protect themselves against sexual health risks, their attitudes, beliefs and knowledge about sex and what is effective in helping them to reduce their sexual health risks and the impact of sexual health problems on their lives.

Understanding the psychology of sexual health means building on the foundations of academic psychology, on cognitive–behavioural and other traditions in psychological medicine, and on psychosexual, feminist, gay and transcultural psychologies. These are all areas in which there has been tremendous progress in recent years. A lot of the impetus has, of course, come from the HIV/AIDS pandemic. However, there have been enormous strides made in our understanding across a wide range of sexual health issues.

Despite these advances, there has been no unifying text that draws together the diverse advances in knowledge base and clinical practice across the sexual health field. That has been our objective in editing this book. We hope that this book will prove useful to those whose work is primarily in sexual health and to those who may not be specialists in the area but who find sexual health issues coming up in their everyday work.

Although the book is primarily a clinical text, we have tried to set the psychology of sexual health in a broader context than is possible by simply focusing on disease and its management. Doing so makes good clinical sense. As an example, a very significant proportion of attendees at genitourinary medicine services present with issues not associated with having a disease or infection but, rather, with sexual health issues relating to behaviour, prior experience, relationships, and cultural context. Practitioners in other fields of sexual health find their own work requires them similarly to address a potentially vast range of diverse issues.

We have also tried to set clinical issues in a theoretical and research base. The book has two parts. The first ('Lessons of History and Context') aims to provide a context in which the evolution of psychological thinking in a variety of sexual health settings is covered. It is not exhaustive, but identifies some of the key imperatives in the development of sexual health awareness. The second ('Practical Applications in the Psychology of Sexual Health') is primarily composed of clinical management chapters reflecting much of the range of issues that come up in sexual health clinical management settings.

No book can cover all the issues and we acknowledge that this one is just a first step in bringing together some key issues in the psychology of sexual health. However, we hope it may be a start in drawing together a number of areas where cross-fertilisation of ideas is likely to prove very fruitful indeed.

Our thanks go out to all our colleagues who so kindly agreed to contribute to this book. We salute their often pioneering work in legitimising and developing the psychology of sexual health as it manifests in clinical and cultural development. Thanks also to all at Blackwell Science for their patience and support in bringing this project together, particularly Antonia Seymour and Rupal Malde.

David Miller
John Green
July 2001

Part 1

Lessons of History and Context

Chapter 1

Introduction: the Meaning of the Psychology of Sexual Health

David Miller and John Green

'Fear of the pox is the beginning of wisdom.'

Psychological approaches to sexual health have arisen more or less independently in a variety of different contexts. So, ideas and concepts about the psychology of reproductive health have developed separately from ideas and concepts about the psychology of sexually transmitted diseases. We believe that bringing together psychological approaches to different aspects of sexual health provides an opportunity to look at the ways in which these approaches are similar and different. There is obvious scope for cross-fertilisation of ideas between different fields and, ultimately, a single individual in the population might find that any or all the areas covered in this book would apply to them. The implication of this must be that it should be possible to move towards integration into an overall psychological approach to sexual health. Clearly we are a long way away from that at the moment, but the impetus must be there.

In 1975, the World Health Organization defined sexual health as:

'... the integration of the physical, emotional and intellectual and social aspects of sexual being in ways that are enriching and that enhance personality, communication and love.'

(WHO, 1975)

If this definition is followed, sexual health implies genital health, reproductive health, psychosocial and emotional health, absence of disease, freedom of reproductive rights and choices, full access to sexual health education, health care and decision-making, recognition of the *meaning* of sex in the lives of those addressed, freedom from the burden of stigmatisation, discrimination and sociopolitical repression, and probably much more. We need to address all of these issues if we are to move towards helping people to achieve optimal sexual health.

Some of the key areas of sexual health are shown in Table 1.1. This is intended to be nei-

Clinical areas	Clinical issues
Reproduction	Fertility control, Menopause
Gender identity	Transsexuality
STD adjustment	Recurrent STDs
Sexual dysfunction	Finding optimal ways to treat psychological dysfunctions, combining drug and psychological approaches
Surgery	Minimising the impact of surgery on sexual self-image and sexual functioning
Psychiatry	Organic and functional syndromes affecting desire and performance
Social issues	Reducing prejudice against alternative lifestyles
Sexual trauma	Preventing sexual assault and managing its aftermath
Somatising	Finding better ways to manage hypochondriasis and dysmorphophobia,
Pain	Better management of genital pain
HIV	Adjustment, bereavement, psycho-neuroimmunology
Health psychology	Communication, compliance with treatment, helping people to protect themselves, maintenance of health
Investigations	Managing clinical investigations to reduce distress to patients, genetic counselling

Table 1.1   A selection of issues in the development of a clinical psychology of sexual health.

ther a complete nor a definitive list but just to illustrate the range and breadth of the challenges we face.

At the same time that we face a large agenda of current psychological issues in which we imperfectly understand how to intervene, the rest of the sexual health field is also moving forward. Other linked areas are advancing and bringing up new psychological issues. So, for instance, the introduction of oral treatments for erectile dysfunction has provided new challenges. Genetic research is advancing rapidly and will potentially allow screening for many damaging recessive alleles which may well have implications for partner choice. Al-

ready a few such alleles are known in conditions like sickle cell disease and cystic fibrosis. There is a strong likelihood that a male 'pill' to control fertility in the male will become available, but what will be the impact of this on sexual behaviour? Can men even reliably take it? It is unusual, to say the least, for one person to take medication to prevent a biological event happening in someone else.

Advances in other areas of sexual health are not always advances in technology or knowledge, sometimes they are changes in the way we use existing technologies. A good example is syndromic management for sexually transmitted diseases, an approach aiming to treat on the basis of symptom complexes rather than the traditional approach of managing – in part at least – on the basis of laboratory tests. This approach obviously has many merits in countries where good laboratory facilities are unavailable.

The syndromic approach to case management classifies the main causative agents by the clinical syndromes to which they give rise. It uses flow-charts which help the service provider to identify the causes of a given syndrome. It treats the patient for all the important physical causes of the syndrome. It ensures that partners are treated, patients are educated on treatment compliance and risk reduction, and that condoms are provided. It includes only those syndromes that are caused by organisms which both respond to treatment and lead to severe consequences if left untreated (viral STDs and dysuria in women are not typically included). However, it does not investigate meaning or focus on psychosocial parameters of STDs, such as power in gender relations, sociocultural contexts of sexual expression and reproduction, and outcomes of initiating changes in such issues.

As Adler (1980) wisely noted:

'If we are to tackle the problem of the sexually transmitted diseases we will need to examine our own attitudes towards them and those who contract them.
The knowledge of why individuals put themselves at risk, how often they do this, and why they behave in different ways after doing so is essential to understanding the spread of disease and its containment and eventual control. The behaviour of the individual must be a component of the research strategy of-

fered by the new academic department [of sexually transmitted diseases].'

Years later, when the true extent of the potential of the nascent global HIV/AIDS pandemic was becoming accepted, Parker and Gagnon (1995) were moved to note:

'Even within the constraints of a concern for AIDS, a narrow view of sexual behaviour may be effective if all we are concerned with is social book-keeping and epidemiological modelling, but it will be inadequate to the task of understanding behaviour in a way that results in behaviour change.'

The history of medicine shows that, although the disease is part of a person, management of patients in health care systems often involves a focus fundamentally on the technology – the tools – of management, at the expense of considering the impact of the disease on the individual, and of the individual on the disease. The shortcomings of this approach are easily seen in the low compliance rates for many forms of medical treatment. We provide treatment to patients; they don't take it, yet we still have only the most rudimentary understanding of why. This failure to engage with the patient has a long history. As one example it typified a lot of the management of syphilis in prior centuries (Quetel 1990). Also lost, often, is the social context of disease. AIDS first appeared in the United States predominantly in gay men. When it came to tackling the disease at the preventative level this was both a strength because of the unparalleled community response which gay men were able to mount and a weakness because many people all over the world were able to write it off as a 'gay disease' at a time when they might have acted early to prevent it gaining a foothold in their communities. Whether they would have succeeded is, of course, another matter – but they denied themselves their best opportunity.

Responding to the psychological issues in disease means understanding the issues and what we can do about them. That means establishing a proper evidence base. Where there is no evidence base prejudice tends to guide people's actions. One of the pioneers of venereology in the UK was pleased to report in his 1862 statement on sexual health management that 'The majority of women (happily for society) are not very much troubled with sexual feelings of any kind' (Acton 1862, cited by Adler 1980).

However not all the problems in developing and applying psychological approaches are external to psychology itself. The field has generated its own internal shortcomings. Ingham and van Zessen (1997) reported how cognitive and social models tend to:

- Incorporate an individualistic bias that places insufficient attention on the relational and wider social and cultural contexts in which sexual activity takes place.
- Are built on an assumption of rationality in that they assume there will be consistent and predictable relations between attitudes, cognitions, intentions and behaviour.
- Are static in that they attribute to individuals (and assume that these can be measured through questionnaires) certain fixed levels of properties such as knowledge, attitudes, perceived risk, perceived severity, and so on.

We know that such assumptions do not reflect reality. However an attachment to existing models, even when we know that they fail to describe or predict human behaviour, has been characteristic of psychological approaches, not just in sexual health. The corpses of dead models, accompanied by pages of damning criticism, litter the standard psychology textbooks. Surely no field of science preserves its dead so reverently, or indeed sometimes fails to see that they are dead at all.

If we are to achieve meaningful and lasting change in behavioural support of an enhanced sexual health of populations, we need to know how individuals' perceptions, their understanding of social norms and their level of desire to comply with them affect their behaviour. Public health therefore requires individual normative understanding and, crucially, an investment in the reality of individual complexity. As noted by Adler et al. (1996) in relation to the STI and HIV pandemics, we

'… need to create a paradigm that is no longer based solely on a medical construct, but takes into account all the elements that contribute to the transmission of STIs and their effective management. Biomedical interventions are only of limited value and the effective control of the epidemic of STIs and HIV requires broad approaches which address and understand in addition the social, cultural, economic and political dimensions of this major health crisis.'

If we appear to have concentrated too much on negatives, barriers and problems in sexual health in this introduction, we hope the book itself will provide a counterweight. There has been tremendous progress in our understanding of the psychology of sexual health and most of it has occurred in the last twenty years. More people are interested in the area than ever before and there is an obvious increase in interest in psychological aspects of sexual health by those many practitioners in the sexual health field who do not regard themselves as having a psychological background. We do believe that it is a field with tremendous potential. We hope that this book reflects some of that potential.

References

Adler, M.W. (1980) The terrible peril: a historical perspective on the venereal diseases. *British Medical Journal*, **281**(6234), 206–211.

Adler, M., Foster, S., Richens, J. & Slavin, H. (1996) Sexual Health and Care: Sexually Transmitted Infections –Guidelines for Prevention and Treatment. Overseas Development Administration, London.

Ingham, R. & van Zessen, G. (1997) From individual properties to interactional processes. In: Van Campenhoudt, L., Cohen, M., Guizzardi, G. & Hausser, D. (eds), *Sexual Interactions and HIV Risk: New Conceptual Perspectives in European Research*. Taylor and Francis, London.

Parker, R. & Gagnon, J. (1995) *Conceiving Sexuality: Approaches to Sex Research in a Postmodern World*. Routledge, London.

Quetel, C. (1990) *History of Syphilis*. Polity Press, Cambridge.

World Health Organisation (1975) *Education and Treatment in Human Sexuality: The Training of Health Professionals* (Techinical Report Series No. 572). WHO, Geneva.

Chapter 2

Epidemiology of Sexually Transmitted Diseases and Sexual Health

Michael Adler

Introduction

The venereal/sexually transmitted diseases are some of the oldest diseases known to man, with references made to them in the Bible. They have always invoked stigma, marginalisation of individuals and groups, and caused considerable anxiety. During the 19th and early 20th century, government reports and legislation in Britain failed to control the venereal diseases (gonorrhoea, syphilis and chancroid) and, if anything, had created more controversy than the illnesses themselves. The Contagious Diseases Acts of 1864 and 1866 required the compulsory registration and police supervision of all prostitutes, plus regular examinations for venereal diseases, and even compulsory hospital detention. The Royal Commission on Poor Laws of 1909 also recommended detention orders for patients with these diseases and the Royal Commission on Divorce in 1912 reported that the passing on of a venereal disease was an act of cruelty second to none as grounds for divorce. Society was happier ignoring the problems of these ill-

nesses and developed suitable defence mechanisms, one of which was to project the blame on to the sufferer. For example, Dr Samuel Solly, President of the Royal Medical and Chirurgical Society giving evidence to a government committee, said of syphilis that it was 'self inflicted, was avoidable by refraining from sexual activity, and intended as a punishment for our sins and that we should not interfere in the matter' (HMSO 1867–68). Even though this was said in 1868, attitudes had not greatly changed by the turn of the century, and some members of the profession still refused to treat patients. It was reported that one doctor had written to a patient as follows: 'you have had the disease for one year, and I hope it may plague you many more to punish you for your sins, and I would not think of treating you' (HMSO 1916).

At the beginning of this century, one third of the total population of the United Kingdom was insured, and in theory entitled to receive medical treatment for venereal diseases, as for any other illness. However, under the rules of most insuring societies, a person suffering from these diseases was suspended from benefits. The National Insurance Commission had the following rule: 'no member shall be qualified for sickness or disablement benefit in respect of injury or disease caused by his own misconduct' (HMSO 1911). The stigma and financial hardship of treatment both in the private sector and under the Insurance Act will have driven large numbers of potential patients to ignore their disease, or turn for treatment to unqualified persons. A government report on the practice of medicine and surgery by such persons, published in 1910, confirmed that in many large towns, treatment of venereal diseases was largely in the hands of lay people (HMSO 1910).

At the beginning of the century, both mortality and morbidity from venereal diseases were high. It is uncertain how high since the existing systems for collecting these data either did not exist as we know them today, or were incomplete and inaccurate. The Registrar General recorded 1639 deaths due to syphilis in adults and 1200 in infants in 1910 in England and Wales. These figures were regarded as a gross underestimate, since many deaths were not certified as syphilis for fear of offending relatives, and a more accurate estimate was thought to be 60 000 deaths instead of the reported number of less than 200 (Osler 1917).

The notification system only began to improve in England and Wales with the setting up of free and confidential services for venereal diseases following a report of the Royal Commission on Venereal Diseases in 1916 (HMSO 1916). It was recommended that there should be the establishment of a free open-access medical service, and that local authorities should be responsible for organising this service within county and general hospitals. The Royal Commission's recommendations were not universally accepted. Many anticipated that the creation of a service would encourage people to contract a disease rather than control them, and lead to immoral behaviour. For example, the most active organisation was called The National Council for Combating Venereal Diseases. One of the driving forces of this organisation was the physician Sir Francis Champneys, who was violently opposed to education and prophylaxis, and believed that 'venereal disease should be imperfectly combatted than that in an attempt to prevent them, men should be enticed into mortal sin' (Champneys 1917). The moral dilemma presented by making services available, and the fear that these would result in the very thing that one was trying to prevent, has been re-run time and time again, more recently in relation to termination of pregnancy, contraceptive advice and society's response to patients with HIV and AIDS.

The most recent sexually transmitted disease epidemic, namely that of HIV infection and AIDS, has illustrated all too painfully how we have not learnt from history. Infectious diseases with high mortality, disability and generating considerable public anxiety, are not new. But our initial responses over the last two centuries, and more recently with AIDS, have often been primitive rather than rational. The responses have not been based on past experience and a realisation that history can teach us lessons without re-running the issues again and losing valuable time that should have been devoted to developing humane and comprehensive control and treatment programmes.

We should have learned that blaming and ostracising groups and trying to lock them up has no place, and that alienating them by accusing them of self-inflicted disease, is no way to engage them in the battle. But all of these have happened in this country. Homosexual men have been blamed for the AIDS epidemic, and interestingly the word *innocent* is only used about haemophiliacs, it is never used for those infected sexually, but who may not have realised that they were being exposed to infection. Those infected with HIV have been ostracised by friends, employers and workmates, and children have been deprived of schooling. In some countries, for example Cuba, infected individuals have been interned. In the UK we have not legislated for compulsory screening and isolation, even though many have called for this. Finally, it is sad that we have had to rehearse the argument once again, that explicit education and freely available condoms will unleash immoral behaviour. It is unfortunate that all the attitudes and postures seen throughout the 19th and first half of the 20th century with regard to STDs, have been unleashed upon those suffering from HIV infection during the early days of the epidemic, and made the control of this infection more difficult than it should have been.

Trends in England

Sexually transmitted diseases (excluding HIV/AIDS)

Whereas previously there were only three designated venereal diseases (gonorrhoea, syphilis and chancroid), it is now recognised that the range of diseases spread by sexual activity have continued to increase. In England, the number of cases seen in sexually transmitted disease clinics (genitourinary medicine clinics) has doubled over the past 20 years, and now amounts to just over 1 million new cases per year. The three commonest sexually transmitted diseases seen in clinics in 1999 (latest figures) are genital warts (113 528), non-gonococcal/non-specific urethritis (93 408) and chlamydial infection (51 083). We have long-standing data only for gonorrhoea and syphilis. Until the middle 1970s there was a considerable increase in gonorrhoea, with a decline since the mid-1980s. However in the last few years we have seen a slight increase in both sexes. For example, between 1995 and 1999 there was a 56% increase (Fig. 2.1). Other conditions also increased recently (Fig. 2.2).

Syphilis is not now a major problem, and the small rise in the incidence of syphilis

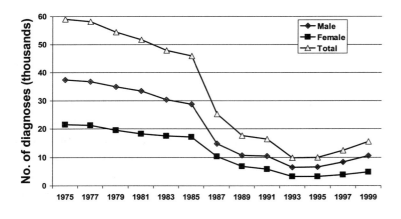

Fig. 2.1 Rates of uncomplicated gonorrhoea: new diagnoses in England, 1975–99.

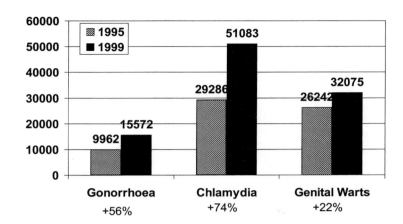

Fig. 2.2 Changes in cases seen in departments of genitourinary medicine/ sexually transmitted diseases, England, 1995–99.

(mainly primary and secondary) in the 1970s and early 1980s has occurred mainly in homosexuals. The decline in the 1980s and early 1990s was probably accounted for by the adoption of safer sex techniques amongst this group, with the advent of HIV infection and AIDS. However, recently there have been outbreaks of syphilis, mainly amongst gay men.

Other conditions which are common are trichomoniasis, pediculosis pubis and genital herpes, all of which can be sexually transmitted. On the other hand, other conditions seen in sexually transmitted diseases clinics, such as scabies and vaginal candidiasis, are not usually acquired sexually. Similarly, sexually transmitted hepatitis A, B and C are becoming more common. But there are a wide variety of other conditions presenting to clinics and requiring specialist investigation and treatment, for example, urinary tract infection, pelvic inflammatory disease, dermatological and psychosexual problems. Chancroid, granuloma inguinale, lymphogranuloma venereum, yaws and pinta are now rare in Britain. Finally, many patients seek reassurance, require counselling or advice and screening for HIV, and want general STD check-ups. All need to be

investigated. The advent of HIV infection in the early 1980s has created a major workload for departments of genitourinary medicine.

HIV/AIDS

The first recognised cases of the Acquired Immunodeficiency Syndrome (AIDS) occurred in the summer of 1981 in America. Reports began to appear of *Pneumocystis carinii* pneumonia and Kaposi's sarcoma in young men, who it was subsequently realised were both homosexual and immunocompromised. The first cases were not seen in the United Kingdom until 1983 and, as in North America, occurred in homosexual men. In the UK, proportionally more homosexual men have been notified with AIDS than in America (67% of cases compared with 48%, respectively) (Table 2.1). More recently, there has been an increase of HIV and AIDS amongst heterosexuals in both the UK and USA. Currently in the USA, 16% of AIDS cases have occurred in women and, although the commonest risk factor amongst females is injecting drug use (44%), the next most common mode of transmission is heterosexual contact (39%). The

Patient groups	USA (June 1999) N	%	UK (June 2000) N	%
Men who have sex with men	334073	48	11227	65
Intravenous drug user	179228	26	1071	6
Men who have sex with men and IV drug user	45226	6	303	2
Received blood/haemophilia	13440	2	820	5
Heterosexual contact	70582	10	3238	18
Mother to infant			367	2
Other/undetermined	60159	8	176	1
Total	702748	100	17202	100

Table 2.1 AIDS – adult patient groups USA and UK.

nature of the epidemic within the UK is changing, with more heterosexual transmission. In the UK, 11% of adult cases of AIDS have occurred in women, 85% of which have resulted from heterosexual intercourse. Year by year the proportion of HIV infection as a result of heterosexual intercourse has increased, and homosexual intercourse decreased. For example in 2000, 44% of all the HIV infection in that year was as a result of men having sex with men, but 53% as a result of heterosexual intercourse. Similar figures, respectively, for 1985 were 94% and 2% (Table 2.2).

Year (to end)	Sexual intercourse Between men	Between men and women	Injecting drug use
1985	94	2	3
1986	84	5	10
1987	78	9	12
1988	75	12	12
1989	73	16	11
1990	71	19	8
1991	66	24	8
1992	62	28	7
1993	62	28	7
1994	61	29	7
1995	58	33	7
1996	63	30	6
1997	57	32	8
1998	54	34	8
1999	46	50	3
2000	44	53	2

Table 2.2 Trends in exposure category distribution (%) of HIV-infected persons (England, Wales, N. Ireland).

The global picture

STDs

Sexually transmitted diseases present a major public health problem and are among the commonest causes of illness and even death in the world, and have far-reaching health, social and economic consequences. Failure to diagnose and treat traditional infections such as gonorrhoea, chlamydia and syphilis can often have a deleterious effect on pregnancy and the newborn, e.g. miscarriage, prematurity, congenital and neonatal infections and blindness. Other complications, particularly in women, such as pelvic inflammatory disease, ectopic pregnancy, infertility and cervical cancer, are large health and social problems. Eighty percent of HIV infection is spread by the sexual route. The recognition that the presence of an STD, particularly genital ulcer disease, can enhance both the acquisition and transmission of HIV by increased shedding of the virus within and from the genital tract, has resulted increasingly in the development of integrated control programmes for HIV and STDs. Both AIDS and STDs have a major demographic, economic, social and political impact, particularly in Sub-Saharan Africa, and increasingly in Asia. In 1993 the World Bank estimated that, for women aged 15–44, STDs excluding HIV were the second cause of healthy life lost after maternal morbidity and mortality (World Bank 1993).

Unlike the United Kingdom, most developing countries do not have an effective control programme and notification system for sexually transmitted diseases. The World Health Organization (WHO) has been responsible for a series of estimates of the size of the problem represented by STDs, and they estimate

an annual total of 333 million new STD infections per annum (WHO 1995). This does not include genital papilloma virus infection, which has in the past been estimated at 30 million new infections per year, herpes at 20 million, and chancroid at 7 million (Table 2.3). The major focus for STDs is South-East Asia, with an estimated 150 million new cases in 1995, and Sub-Saharan Africa with 65 million. The estimated prevalence and incidence of sexually transmitted disease by region shows considerable variation. For example, the difference in prevalence and incidence between Sub-Saharan Africa and Western Europe is 4 and 3-fold, respectively (Table 2.4). Recently there has been considerable concern about the epidemic of sexually transmitted diseases in Eastern Europe, and in particular there has been a noticeable (14-fold) increase in new cases of syphilis in Russia and the Baltic States between 1990 and 1998 (Fig. 2.3). It is unlikely that the epidemic is only occurring in relation to syphilis, and it is highly likely that there is also an epidemic of gonorrhoea and HIV infection hidden behind this surge in syphilis.

The lack of data and notification systems can to some extent be overcome in the de-

Table 2.3 The annual total of sexually transmitted infections (excluding HIV).

Condition	Total (million)
Trichomoniasis	170
Genital chlamydia	89
Gonorrhoea	62
Syphilis	12
Total	*333*

Genital papilloma virus 30 million, genital herpes 20 million, chancroid 7 million.
Source: WHO 1995.

Region	Prevalence per 1000	Incidence per 1000
Sub-Saharan Africa	208	254
South and Southeast Asia	128	160
Latin America and Caribbean	95	145
Eastern Europe and Central Asia	75	112
North America	52	91
Australasia	52	91
Western Europe	45	77
Northern Africa and Middle East	40	60
East Asia and Pacific	19	28
Total	*85*	*113*

Table 2.4 Estimated prevalence and incidence of STIs by region.

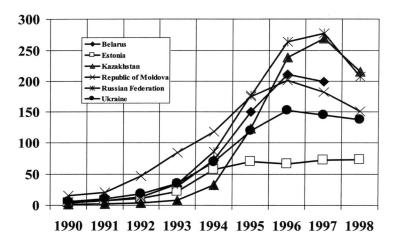

Fig. 2.3 Annual incidence of syphilis in Belarus, Estonia, Kazakhstan, the Republic of Moldova, the Russian Federation and Ukraine, 1990–98 (rate per 100 000).

veloping world by point prevalence studies in particular communities. Such information is useful but limited, since it is not totally representative of the population, as it is obtained from atypical high-risk and usually consulting groups of individuals and/or patients. As expected, high rates are found amongst commercial sex workers and women attending STD clinics and family planning clinics. A lower risk group of women attending antenatal clinics also have high levels of infection (Fig. 2.4).

HIV/AIDS

As with sexually transmitted diseases, the real size of the problem of HIV throughout the world is not fully known. However, the United Nations AIDS Programme (UNAIDS) have calculated that by the end of 2000 there were 36.1 million people living with HIV/AIDS, and that during that year, the number of new HIV infections was 5.3 million (UNAIDS/ WHO 2000). This is equivalent to 16 000 new infections per day, 10% of which are occur-

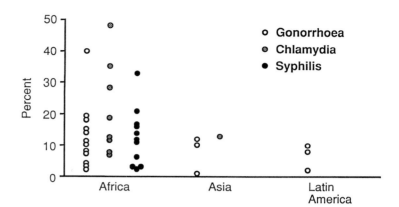

Fig. 2.4 Prevalence rates of gonorrhoea, chlamydia and syphilis in women attending antenatal clinics.

ring in infants. The geographical distribution for HIV infection and AIDS is similar to that for sexually transmitted diseases, with the majority of infections being seen in Sub-Saharan Africa (25.3 million), and South and South-East Asia (5.8 million). In Thailand, it is estimated that one in 50 adults is infected, one in 40 in Sub-Saharan Africa, and in some African countries as many as one in three adults are infected. Globally, currently three out of every five adults living with HIV are men. By early 2000 the gap between the sexes will have narrowed. As infections increase in women, so does the mother-to-child transmission. It is now estimated that there are more than 1.4 million children who have been infected since the beginning of the epidemic. Similarly to STDs, more local accurate data is available from seroprevalence studies performed over time in various groups and countries.

The demographic, economic and social impact of AIDS is far reaching, with considerable effect on individuals, families and countries. It is estimated that up to 50 million uninfected children in Africa will have lost their mothers to AIDS by the end of the century. AIDS threatens the capacity of households to func-

tion as an economic unit, and disrupts and even dissolves the social fabric of family structures. Population growth and death rates will be increasingly affected, and many African countries have shown a marked reduction in life expectancy due to AIDS. For example, in Zimbabwe life expectancy has been reduced by 22 years as a result of AIDS, in the Cote D'Ivoire by 11, and in Burkina Faso by 11.3 (World Bank 1997). This is a major problem for the economic viability of countries, since the major burden of AIDS in terms of premature death and morbidity is in highly productive adults at the peak of their output. This is bound to have a considerable impact on these nations' GDP. It is therefore clear that HIV/AIDS affects individuals and family structures as well as industry, agriculture and whole economies.

The causes

There are a number of factors associated with the acquisition of sexually transmitted diseases and HIV (Table 2.5). The risk of acquiring infection is a function of the number of infected sexual partners to which an individual

Table 2.5 Factors associated with the spread of HIV infection and sexually transmitted diseases.

- Demographic/partner change
- Lack of diagnostic and treatment facilities
- Social unrest and war
- Poverty, urbanisation and migration

is exposed, the extent of this exposure and the level of infectiousness of each infected partner. Young age is an important determinant of STD/HIV transmission since young people have higher rates of sexual partner change. In most resource-poor countries the age structure is substantially bottom-heavy, thus the most sexually active groups represent a much larger proportion of the population than in the industrialised world. Men tend to migrate from rural to urban environments to obtain jobs. Separated from their wives and families they are more likely to have intercourse with commercial sex workers. Social unrest and war bring with them a constellation of risk factors such as population and troop migration, rape, and, with the fear of death, more emphasis on today rather than tomorrow or next week. In developing countries the socio-economic factors related to the acquisition of STDs play a vital role in predisposing to certain risk behaviours due to social dislocation, migration and inadequate control facilities. The complexity of the aetiology of STD/HIV infection makes control extremely difficult. Therefore two approaches need to be put into place. The first is the programme-based approach which attempts to deliver an integrated system for prevention and treatment, and the second is more complex and relates to the infra-structural issues in relation to poverty, social dislocation and powerlessness of women.

Models of control

In the developed world, control programmes for STDs tend to be part of vertical programmes provided through specialist centres with laboratory support based on an aetiological diagnosis. Whatever models and approaches are used, there are certain principles of effective STI control:

- To prevent new infections.
- To treat those with symptoms of infection.
- To identify and treat those without symptoms.
- To motivate health-seeking behaviour among those who may know they are infected but who delay or avoid seeking treatment.

Strategy for control of STDs can theoretically be broken down into primary and secondary prevention.

Primary prevention

The basis of primary prevention is health education/promotion, in an attempt to avoid disease and reduce the risks of contracting infection. Condom promotion, particularly programmes of social marketing, has had a very significant impact on uptake. In Africa there has been encouraging evidence that increased condom use has been accepted by high-risk groups such as commercial sex workers and their clients, and that this has altered levels of infection. Examples of this have also been reported in Africa and South-East Asia. A three-year programme of condom promotion and STD control in Zaire saw an increase in consistent condom use from 0 to 68% amongst commercial sex workers (Laga *et al.*

1994). Social marketing of condoms in that country saw sales increasing from 20 000 to 18 million in a period of 3 years (Kyungu Mormat *et al.* 1992). In parallel with the increased condom use in commercial sex workers, the incidence of gonorrhoea, trichomoniasis, genital ulcer disease and HIV declined. In Thailand, an education programme advocating the use of condoms by commercial sex workers and clients was followed by an increased usage from a baseline of 14%, to 94% (Hanenberg *et al.* 1994). A concurrent decline in bacterial STDs was seen over the same time period.

Social, cultural and economic interventions are difficult to implement, but need to be addressed. For example, often women are so poor and disempowered that they have sex on a commercial basis against their will, and are unable to effectively negotiate the use of condoms. Women need to be taught skills that help them to negotiate safer sex with clients and regular partners. This is particular difficult with the latter, since husbands and regular partners can see such negotiation as a reflection of themselves, at the same time suggesting that the woman has herself had multiple partners. Raising the status of women in the developing world will be a crucial factor in the control of STDs, and can only be achieved through equality in the fields of education and employment.

Secondary prevention

Secondary prevention is concerned with the promotion of healthcare-seeking behaviour and case management. It is a central part of a health education programme to point out the symptoms associated with a possible STD, but also to reinforce the understanding that many diseases are asymptomatic, particularly in women. This knowledge and awareness will encourage more appropriate uptake of treatment and screening services by those with infection or at risk. Case management strategies, as indicated earlier, will vary between countries depending on resources.

Different approaches to diagnosis and management

A theoretical model, originally devised by Fransen and Piot for control of tuberculosis, but now used to give a conceptual idea of STDs, quite clearly indicates that the majority of people who are infected never reach services (Fig. 2.5). Their useful cascade illustrates that only half of the women with an STD symptom recognise its significance and only half of these present for treatment, of whom a further half receive adequate treatment.

Vertical services for STDs

These are services which are specialist and dedicated to the control and provision of accurate microbiological diagnosis and tailored treatment, counselling and partner notification. The disciplines involved in this are specialist-trained doctors, nurses, psychologists, counsellors and health advisors, with laboratory support services, particularly microbiology and virology. The advantages of this type of approach (which is the one that is used for example in the United Kingdom), is that patients are treated by specialists, with accurate laboratory diagnosis, and appropriate treatment can be given. Training of staff can be part of the role of the specialist service, as can monitoring, surveillance and research. The disadvantages of this approach are that it is expen-

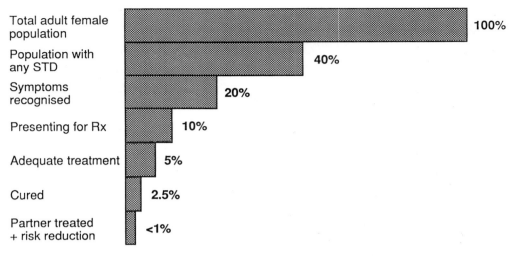

Fig. 2.5   Healthcare-seeking behaviour – women with STDs.

sive, that there can be delays in diagnosis, and the availability of the service may be limited, as may its coverage of the total population. Finally, if a clinic is designated as an STD clinic, this can bring with it an element of stigmatisation.

Integrated services

These are, by definition, services which deliver case management, counselling, education and partner notification through existing-run non-specialist facilities. The disciplines or service outlets included would be primary health centres (PHCs), maternal and child health centres (MCHCs), family planning or outpatient clinics at any hospital. The services are delivered by non-specialist doctors, nurses and health care providers. The advantage of such an approach is that it is problem-orientated and that immediate presumptive diagnosis and treatment can be given on the basis of possible aetiology using syndromic management. The service is provided by non-specialists without laboratory support and there-

fore tends to be less expensive. The disadvantages of this approach, using algorithms, is that it is known that there is a low sensitivity/specificity for cervical gonococcal and chlamydial infection in women. Secondly, asymptomatic infection is not detected, and women who are unaware of their infection may only get treatment on the basis of active partner notification.

WHO has placed increasing emphasis on integrated approaches, especially at primary health care (PHC) level, using a syndromic approach for patient management (WHO 1991). It is particularly advocated in high prevalence areas where there are inadequate laboratory facilities and trained staff. The recent Mwanza study has demonstrated the importance of an integrated STD programme and the impact on HIV incidence. This randomised controlled trial showed that improved STD care, integrated at primary care level, resulted in a reduction of HIV incidence of 42% over the 2-year period of the study (Grosskurth *et al.* 1995). The study confirms the effects of STDs on HIV acquisition and transmission, and that the integrated non-specialist and syndromic approach can be very effective.

The way forward

There is no 'correct' way to control sexually transmitted diseases, but common principles outlined previously should be adhered to in programmes of primary and secondary prevention. The design of control programmes to some extent will be defined and shaped by resources, population dispersion, and the political desire, or otherwise, to develop programmes. It is important that resource-rich countries do not impose their own specialist and expensive models on the developing world, where they are not sustainable and appropriate to local conditions, facilities and resources.

Within the United Kingdom, a specialist-based service which developed after the Royal Commission in 1916 has resulted in comparatively low incidence and prevalence for these diseases compared to many other countries. Population-based studies would suggest that there is not a substantial amount of sexually transmitted disease which is not identified and treated. However, recent prevalence surveys of chlamydia in women attending clinics for family planning and termination of pregnancy would indicate that the levels of this infection are high. The development of urinary-based diagnostic tests using ligase chain reaction and PCR will mean that more widescale screening can take place on a non-invasive basis, and it is likely that in the next 20 years more opportunistic screening in non-special-

ist services will also occur. This is to be welcomed, however, it is important that STDs diagnosed outside specialist services are treated to the same high quality, and that the public health aspects of partner notification and screening of potentially infected partners is still carried out. Experience would suggest that non-specialists who are unused to this approach feel less comfortable doing so, and a marriage between the non-specialist and specialist within the United Kingdom will have to be achieved.

Finally, it is interesting that the evolution of the venereal disease/sexually transmitted disease services in the United Kingdom has now moved on one further step to embrace all aspects of sexual health. Many clinics offer not only screening to asymptomatic individuals who may feel that they are at risk, but also guidance on sexual dysfunction and family planning. This type of one-stop-shopping is the latest development in a holistic approach to patients with sexual health issues.

Conclusion

Sexually transmitted diseases are a major public health problem throughout the world, usually invoking considerable stigma, and marginalisation of groups suffering from them. Public perception and attitudes of these infections have often resulted in their suboptimal control. However, the considerable morbidity associated with untreated infections means that it is much more cost-effective to have good control programmes in place. Perversely, one of the benefits of the HIV/AIDS epidemic has been that people have begun to think more seriously about resources for, and development of, control programmes for sexually transmitted diseases, often integrated with HIV control. Different models have been developed, depending largely on resources and population dispersion. Both integrated and vertical programmes have benefits and disadvantages, but in their own environments are beginning to prove effective strategies for the control of sexually transmitted diseases. The next two to three decades should see the expansion of such programmes, and in some countries a more total approach to sexual health incorporating all aspects of infection and dysfunction.

References

Champneys, F. (1917) The fight against venereal infection. A reply to Sir Bryan Donkin. *Nineteenth Century* **82**, 1052–1054.

Grosskurth, H., Mosha, F., Todd, J., Mwijarubi, E., *et al.* (1995) Impact of improved treatment of sexually transmitted diseases on HIV infection in rural Tanzania: randomised control trial. *Lancet* **346**, 530–536.

Hanenberg, R.S., Rojanapithayakorn, W., Kunasol, P. & Sokal, D.C. (1994) Impact of Thailand's HIV control programme as indicated by the decline of sexually transmitted diseases. *Lancet* (1994) **344**, 243–245.

HMSO (1867–68) Report of the Committee on the Pathology and Treatment of Venereal Disease, with a view to diminish its injurious effects upon the men of the army and navy. *House of Commons Report* **38**(425). HMSO, London.

HMSO (1910) Report as to the practice of medicine and surgery by unqualified persons in the United Kingdom. *Report of Commissioners to the House of Commons.* HMSO, London. (Cmnd 5422).

HMSO (1911) National Insurance Bill to provide for insurance against loss of health and for the prevention and cure of sickness and for insurance against unemployment; and for purposes incidental thereto. *House of Commons Report*, **4**(198). HMSO, London.

HMSO (1916) Royal Commission on Venereal Diseases. *Final Report of the Commissioners.* HMSO, London. (Cmnd 8189).

Kyungu Mormat, E. (1992) Condom and social marketing and mass media in Zaire. In: *Proceedings of Meeting on Effective Approaches to AIDS Prevention.* WHO, Geneva.

Laga, M., Alary, M., Nzila, N., *et al.* (1994) Condom promotion, sexually transmitted diseases, treatment and declining incidence of HIV infection in female Zairian sex workers. *Lancet* **344**, 246–248.

Osler, W. (1917) The campaign against venereal disease. *British Medical Journal* **i**, 694–696.

UNAIDS/WHO (2000) *Report on the Global HIV/AIDS Epidemic.* WHO, Geneva.

World Bank (1993) Investing in health. *World Development Report.* Oxford University Press, New York.

World Bank (1997) Confronting AIDS: public priorities in a global epidemic. *Policy Research Report.* Oxford University Press, New York.

World Health Organization (1991) Management of patients with sexually transmitted diseases. Report of a WHO Steering Group. *WHO Technical Report Series* 810. WHO, Geneva.

World Health Organization (1995) *An Overview of Selected Curable Sexually Transmitted Diseases.* Global Programme on AIDS/STDs. WHO, Geneva.

Chapter 3

Psychological Factors in Sexually Transmitted Diseases

John Green

Arguably no area of medicine brings in more psychological factors than sexually transmitted diseases. Most people who think that they have contracted a sexually transmitted disease are embarrassed and upset. High levels of anxiety are common. If they have never come into contact with sexually transmitted disease services they are likely to be uncertain about the attitude of the health professional they are seeing. They are also likely to be in turmoil over whom they have caught the disease from and apprehensive about who else they may have to tell about their infection, particularly others that they may have infected. Additionally they will probably have to have an embarrassing and intimate examination and answer highly personal and sometimes distressing questions about their recent sexual behaviour. At the end of the process they may be told that they have an infection of which they have never heard or about which they have sketchy, alarming and sometimes grossly misleading information.

The task for health professionals is to try to calm the patient, to obtain the necessary his-

tory, to carry out an examination and to get across accurate information about the disease, its treatment, its prognosis and issues around partner notification. If possible health professionals will also want to get over information about how the individuals can protect themselves against contracting other infections in the future.

In the past the sexually transmitted disease field was a rather fortunate one. Most infections were seen either as major threats to long-term health but curable, like gonorrhoea and chlamydia or (mostly) minor in respect of long-term morbidity like herpes. However the coming of HIV infection has changed all that. Of course what is minor in terms of long-term health for most patients is not necessarily minor in terms of its psychological impact. Probably few infections raise more anxiety than herpes (HSV), the great scare preceding AIDS, and even though the infection can be managed effectively many patients are terrified by an HSV diagnosis.

The exact structures for treating sexually transmitted diseases vary from country to country around the world. In the UK, in places influenced by the UK system and in many parts of Northern Europe specialist sexually transmitted disease clinics provide the bulk of services. Elsewhere much of the work is done by general physicians. In some parts of the world a large part of sexually transmitted disease treatment is carried out in the private sector; in other areas state provision predominates. In the USA sexually transmitted diseases are treated in both the private and public sector (Brackbill *et al.* 1999). In some parts of Europe sexually transmitted diseases have historically been seen as part of dermatology. In parts of North America the sexually transmitted disease system has sometimes been seen as separate from the general run of medicine because of the public health implications of STDs.

However care is being delivered, at the moment we are living at a time of change. New rapid easy-test techniques for a range of sexually transmitted diseases are becoming available that promise to allow any primary care physician to carry out more or less full diagnostic screening in the primary care setting. Ultimately home tests for common sexually transmitted diseases are feasible; indeed some have already been developed, allowing the patient potentially to check themselves for common sexually transmitted diseases at home.

At present, in many countries the diagnosis and treatment of sexually transmitted diseases is carried out predominantly by specialist health care workers who either carry out only STD work, or for whom STD work is a sizeable part of their duties. Such workers tend to be self-selected, have an interest in the area, and get accustomed to dealing with the psychological problems that STDs bring to patients. The future is much more uncertain but it is likely that the range of health professionals dealing with sexually transmitted diseases will increase considerably and patients may start to engage in self-diagnosis.

If the psychological issues around sexually transmitted diseases are to be addressed in a much more diffuse and complex system there is a vital need to find out more about key psychological issues in the area and to develop clear guidelines and protocols for the management of these issues. At present such guidelines only exist in sketchy forms for a few diseases and the evidence base to prescribe optimal psychological management is simply inadequate. Nonetheless these things need to be developed rapidly if patients are to get the best possible care for their condition in the future.

In this chapter I have looked at what is known about the psychology of sexually transmitted diseases other than HIV infection, which is covered elsewhere in this book (Chapter 11).

Why do people catch sexually transmitted diseases?

Oddly it is quite difficult to explain why people behave in a way that allows them to catch sexually transmitted diseases in the first place. It might have been possible in the past to argue that most people catch them through a lack of awareness of their existence or how they are acquired. However, the rise of HIV infection and the response of governments and populations to HIV have severely undermined any such arguments. In the UK in the mid-1980s the government mounted a series of blanket campaigns whose theme was 'Don't die of ignorance', utilising television, radio, newspaper and billboard advertising, and leaflets sent to every home in the country. Their surveys showed high levels of public awareness of HIV and considerable anxiety in the population about the disease. There was a modest decline in rates of bacterial infections as people modified their behaviour to some extent. However, even in the face of high levels of knowledge and high awareness of methods of preventing a potentially fatal infection that many feared, many people still failed to take precautions and many people continued to catch sexually transmitted diseases.

Why they did not take precautions – and continue not to do so – is a subject that has exercised a great deal of research effort. Existing models such as the Health Beliefs Model and the Theory of Reasoned Action identify some of the key factors governing sexual behaviour (Rosenstock 1974; Becker et al. 1975; Ajzen & Madden 1986; Ronis 1992). People are influenced by what they believe about sexually transmitted diseases. While people may be relatively well informed about HIV they are likely to be much less well-informed about other sexually transmitted diseases. Normative influences, our beliefs about what others like us do, are also an important influence. Self-efficacy (Bandura 1977) is also important, the extent to which we believe that we are able to carry out a particular self-protective behaviour like putting on a condom or getting our partner to do so. Indeed it can be difficult for a woman to get her partner to use a condom even if she believes he is putting her at risk. Availability of condoms for prophylaxis is also a factor: if people can't afford or can't get condoms they are unable to use them. However, even where they are cheap and readily available, many people do not use them.

Putting together all the known factors that affect safer sexual behaviour still fails to account for much of the variance in safer sex behaviour (Brian et al. 1998; Adih & Alexander 1999; Sutton et al. 1999; Taylor 1999). In other words there are a lot of psychological factors involved that we do not properly understand. This is easiest to see not in statistical analyses of tests of the various models but in a very simple fact. Many people are inconsistent in their sexual behaviour (Kasenda et al. 1997; Musaba et al. 1998). They use a condom with some partners but not others; and whether they use a condom or not varies over time with the same partner (Green et al. 2000). It is difficult to explain this sort of inconsistency on most existing models of safer sex because they concentrate on factors to do with the individual's internal thoughts, beliefs and perceptions, which might vary over time but would surely not fluctuate wildly in the way that safer sex behaviour appears to.

Undoubtedly partner behaviour is one factor in such fluctuations. Whatever a man or woman may want to happen they are unlikely to be successful in getting a condom used if their partner refuses to use one or they are so anxious about their partner's response that they cannot even bring the issue up. However, I doubt that this is the whole, or possibly even the main, problem.

We carried out a series of qualitative interviews with 100 sexually experienced women asking them about times when they had had safer sex and unsafe sex (Green et al. 2000). What emerged was the importance of the woman's perception of her partner. People do not go to bed with abstract concepts like general risk, they have sex with particular individuals and how they see them is important.

Women who believed that their partner presented them with a risk were likely to use a condom, those who did not weren't. It wasn't the global general risk a woman felt that she had of contracting HIV, and that was the most commonly mentioned STD, it was the risk that one particular partner was perceived as presenting which made a difference. Once a woman was in a long-term relationship she was likely to discontinue condom usage. In part this was probably the result of the fact that condoms are also used for contraception and a woman without a partner may not bother to take, say the contraceptive pill, until she has what she considers a stable relationship. However we also speculated that experience

might be an important factor. If a man or woman has had sex over a period with a partner and nothing bad has happened, and they feel that they have got to know that partner well and can assume a low level of risk, they are likely to discontinue condom usage for prophylaxis. Personal experience of one individual overrides theoretical concepts of population risk. The model we put forward, the individual risk model, is shown in Fig. 3.1.

Certainly other workers have identified perceptions of partners as an influence on sexual risk behaviour (Williams *et al.* 1992). Further evidence comes from one of the most consistent findings in studies of sexual behaviour. People are much more likely to use condoms

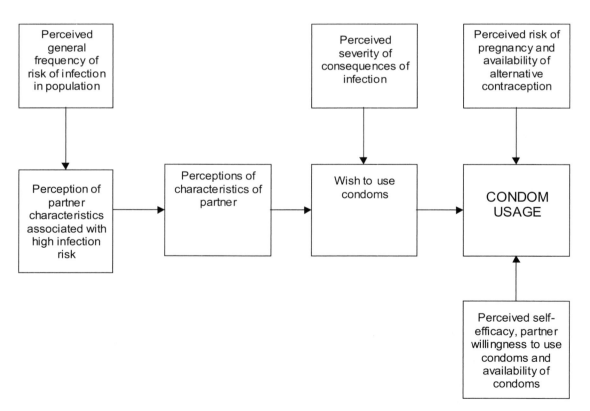

Fig. 3.1   The individual risk model (Green *et al.* 2000; reproduced with permission).

with partners they regard as casual than with partners who they regard as 'regular' (Leonard & Ross 1997; Lansky *et al.* 1998).

It is doubtful if any one factor can explain sexual risks. Sometimes people get drunk and behave unwisely; after all, alcohol can certainly influence risk perception but most occasions of unprotected sex are not caused by alcohol use *per se* (Taylor *et al.* 1999). Others may simply be swept up in the excitement of the moment. There are circumstances under which people put themselves at risk of acquiring a sexually transmitted disease they know their partner has, as in couples discordant for HIV infection (Bedimo *et al.* 1998) or in the many people who embark on, or continue with, sexual relationships with partners with genital herpes. Nonetheless, I suspect that a key element in unsafe sexual behaviour is people's belief that they are able to judge whether a potential partner is a risk to them. Indeed, it is probably not even a judgement as such in many cases – people just don't feel that it is possible that the nice man or woman they have just met could possibly give them a sexually transmitted disease. How sadly wrong they often are.

We probably need to be making much greater efforts in talking to patients to counteract the belief that sexually transmitted infections are a matter of shame and that particular types of dirty promiscuous people contract them. Such beliefs in the population are bound to reinforce any implicit beliefs people have that they are able to identify who does not present a risk of transmitting an infection to them. The truth is that, with the exception of upper respiratory tract infections and food poisoning, sexually transmitted diseases are the most frequent serious infections

of young adults and nice, wholesome, attractive, healthy-looking people catch them just like anyone else.

While knowledge alone is not sufficient to change risk behaviours it is clear that knowledge is necessary for behaviour change to be likely. After all, who will even consider changing their behaviour for a disease, or set of diseases, they are unaware exists? While HIV is famous the world over it is unusual in this respect. Other sexually transmitted diseases are still unfamiliar to most people, until they actually catch them (Vail-Smith & White 1992; Reis & Stephens 1998; Devonshire *et al.* 1999). This is a situation that clearly needs further attention.

Psychological factors in dealing with those with sexually transmitted diseases

The easiest way to explore some of the psychological factors in sexually transmitted diseases is to look at one disease and then to consider the ways in which other diseases are similar or different.

Genital herpes

By far the best researched of sexually transmitted diseases from a psychological perspective other than HIV is genital herpes (HSV). The reasons for the interest in the disease are partly accidental. It is a recurrent disease in many patients and therefore it is possible to look at it longitudinally. It is a common disease so that assembling research samples is relatively easy. The recurrences of the disease also raise the possibility of looking at the impact of psychological factors on immunity, at least in principle, so that there has been a great deal of interest in the impact of stress on recurrences. It has to be said that, although a great deal of effort has been expended on looking for the effect of stress on recurrences, there is little in the way of convincing evidence that stress is an important factor in either the frequency or timing of recurrences (Green & Kocsis 1997). However it is also worth noting that many patients believe that stress impacts on recurrences (Brookes *et al.* 1993).

HSV is caused by one of two viruses, HSV-1 or HSV-2. Although HSV-1 is usually thought of as an infection of the mouth and lips, in most countries it makes up a sizeable percentage of genital infections. HSV-2 infections do occur in the oro-labial area but mainly occur on the genitals. This capacity of HSV-1 to cause genital infections can be a cause of suspicion in couples: I saw one ethnic minority couple, both members with strong religious beliefs, who insisted that neither had ever had sex with anyone else. The woman suddenly developed genital herpes within a few weeks of first intercourse. The man gave a history of frequent cold sores on the mouth and they, rather embarrassed, gave a history of a considerable fondness for cunnilingus. Asymptomatic shedding of HSV-1 into the saliva was thus a potential source of his wife's infection.

HSV infection can occur in the absence of any attack obvious to the patient (Barton & Green 1999). Indeed, inapparent or subclinical attacks are probably not infrequent amongst individuals infected with HSV. Even where there are fairly obvious symptoms the patient may be unaware of them, particularly in men where there may be only a few blisters and levels of pain are often less than in women. If a person

with such attacks transmits the virus to their partner, sometimes after months or even years of a relationship, it can lead to considerable mutual suspicion and recrimination.

It is possible to test for type-specific antibodies against the two strains of HSV, but the crossover between the two viruses in terms of site of infection and the high frequency of HSV-1 infection in the mouth means that diagnosis of genital herpes by blood test alone is often impracticable. Serotesting can be useful in excluding a diagnosis of genital herpes where an individual is HSV-1 and HSV-2 negative. The test can also be of value in, for instance, discordant couples. Where one partner already has, say, HSV-2, then they may have already transmitted it to their partner even though their partner has no obvious symptoms. Given the frequency of the infection in the population, the partner may have acquired it previously from another partner. Either way the couple are freed from concerns about possible transmission of the virus.

HSV (taking both viruses together) usually causes little in the way of serious long-term morbidity except in cases of infection of the neonate during delivery when it can cause disseminated herpes of the neonate (Robertson *et al.* 1989; Forsgren 1990; Roberts *et al.* 1995). This is a condition that can result in serious neurological impairment of the neonate or death. Disseminated herpes of the neonate is usually associated with a primary infection occurring in the last trimester of pregnancy. While this may occur when a transmission suddenly occurs in a long-term stable relationship it is probably more likely to occur when a woman has a relatively new partner. For that reason the incidence of disseminated herpes of the neonate differs widely from country to country and from area to area. Areas where there is social instability – typically poorer areas with disadvantaged populations – tend to have a much higher incidence.

Clearly neonatal herpes has implications for advice to the patient. If a man with genital herpes has an apparently uninfected partner then he should avoid intercourse with her while she is pregnant; or, if the two of them find this unacceptable, at least ensure that all intercourse is protected with a condom and any unprotected genital contact avoided. The advice is most important later in the pregnancy. If a woman has genital herpes attacks she should tell her obstetrician or midwife so the situation can be properly monitored.

Other than disseminated herpes of the neonate the impact of the disease is mainly pain, feelings of ill-health during and perhaps before attacks (malaise is not solely confined to the primary attack as some texts suggest) and a considerable impact on psychological well-being (Goldmeier & Johnson 1982; Goldmeier *et al.* 1986). For someone with very frequent severe attacks the disease can be a major disruptive influence on their life, leading to reductions in performance at work, lack of enjoyment of everyday life and problems with sleep and social life, things in fact very typical of any painful persistent condition (Swanson *et al.* 1995).

The disease initially interferes with sex life even in stable relationships; however, over time people tend to adjust and their sex life probably returns to much what it was before, with the exception that people tend to avoid sex during attacks and also during prodromes – periods immediately before attacks when tingling and odd sensations may warn that an attack is imminent (Brookes *et al.* 1993).

The fear of transmission is probably one of the main problems for people with genital herpes (Silver *et al.* 1986). If their partner does not have the infection, or shows no signs of infection, then they fear that they will transmit the infection to them. In spite of this concern many people with recurrent HSV do not inform sexual contacts of their infection. We carried out in-depth interviews with 50 individuals with recurrent genital herpes looking at their experiences and when and to whom they disclosed their infection (Green *et al.* 2001). Patients were much less likely to tell casual sexual partners about their infection although they were likely to tell long-term partners, usually at the time at which they felt confident both about the strength of the relationship and about the likely reaction of their partner. In fact, many people sought to test out their partner's attitude to herpes before actually disclosing their infection, perhaps by seeking to discuss herpes as a general issue. In telling others, avoiding rejection was a crucial factor.

This problem in telling others is common in other sexually transmitted diseases. Most STD service providers devote considerable effort to trying to get patients to notify partners, or even to tracking down and notifying partners themselves. This has clear health benefits to the person traced, although the extent to which it impacts on the prevalence of sexually transmitted diseases in the population generally is less clear. Low numbers of partners are actually traced in partner notification programmes, regular partners but not casuals tending to be identified by patients (Van de Laar *et al.* 1997; Macke & Maher 1999; Rogstad *et al.* 1999; Gorbach *et al.* 2000). Embarrassment, fear of gossip and fear of rejection and even possible violence from partners are factors. Even in Sweden where public attitudes favour partner notification many individuals report avoiding identifying partners (Tyden & Ramstedt 2000).

Treatment probably plays a very important part in the thinking of people about their HSV infection. It is an unfortunate feature of genital herpes that, in the past, drug trials did not incorporate measures of psychological well-being, using instead clinical end-points. This is particularly unfortunate given that the main reason for antiviral treatment is to decrease distress and disruption to life. As far as we are able to tell from the available evidence it appears that, in common with people with other diseases, not having the symptoms probably allows them to put the disease to the back of their mind. Many patients at first diagnosis are distraught with high levels of anxiety and depression (Goldmeier & Johnson 1982; Goldmeier et al. 1986; Carney et al. 1994). If they do not get a recurrence then these levels fall back to normal. If they do get recurrences then treatment with antivirals, which do not affect the natural history of the disease but suppress the attacks while the patient is taking the medication, appear to reduce adverse psychological reactions and preoccupation with the disease, and to increase quality of life (Carney et al. 1993; Patel et al. 1999). There is some evidence to suggest that these effects may persist even after antivirals are withdrawn.

The whole concept of infectiousness in herpes is particularly difficult. While patients are probably maximally infectious during attacks, they may also shed virus asymptomatically between attacks (Barton et al. 1996). Such asymptomatic shedding is probably a major source of infection of others since people tend to avoid sex during frank attacks (Mertz et al. 1992). In this case asymptomatic shedding and inapparent shedding (where there are lesions on examination or minor symptoms but the patient is unaware of them) amount to the same thing. While there are good theoretical reasons for thinking that antivirals probably reduce infectiousness there is not, at present, actual certainty that this is so, nor evidence about how great a decrement in infectiousness occurs (Barton & Green 1999). However, in our own interviews with patients with herpes it became clear that patients on antivirals assume that their level of infectiousness is low, on the principle that if they have no physical sensations associated with herpes they are unlikely to present a risk.

There is good evidence that, in the long term, most people with recurrent genital herpes adjust to their infection and their lives return to much what they were before (Green & Kocsis 1997). They are no less happy, are able to sustain satisfactory relationships and are able to have satisfactory sex lives. However, a few people are adversely affected in the longer term and find themselves with long-lasting emotional disturbance. The feeling of contamination and the constant reminder of the circumstances under which they contracted the infection (and the person they caught it from if the relationship has ended) can leave a few people with long-lasting feelings of contamination and anger.

Genital herpes shows many of the main psychological features of sexually transmitted diseases:

(1) High levels of distress at the time of diagnosis responding to effective treatment of the underlying condition or at least amelioration of the symptoms.

(2) Feelings of contamination in both men and women, perhaps particularly prominent in women because of cultural values that portray women's genitalia as 'dirty'.

(3) Concerns about the likely attitudes of others if they knew about the infection, not just sexual partners but also friends and family and even employers. Most STD systems in the world go to great lengths to provide the maximum degree of confidentiality possible and not without good reason.

(4) Concerns about the likely attitudes of health care professionals, particularly concerns about being 'judged' for their infection. This is particularly likely in those who have not had previous contact with the sexual health care system.

(5) Fears about transmitting the infection to partners, or about already having done so.

(6) Anxieties about how to tell existing partners and concerns about whether the individual will be able to get another partner in the future.

(7) Fears about long-term consequences of infection for general health. Although genital herpes has little in the way of long-term consequences for most people, alarmist coverage in the media and in some popular books has led many people to view the disease with the greatest fear.

(8) A tendency to assume that if there are no symptoms there is no problem. In other words, people are likely to discount the disease and be less concerned with the risk of giving the disease to someone else, if they have no symptoms.

(9) A tendency to adjust psychologically to long-term chronic conditions.

Genital warts

In terms of course of the disease genital warts are probably the disease most similar to HSV. Genital warts are caused by members of a large family of papillomaviruses. They are highly infectious and there has been a marked upsurge in cases across most of the developed world over the past 20 years. Like genital herpes the use of condoms provides some protection against infection, although this is not perfect (Wen *et al.* 1999).

One of the problems with warts is our lack of a clear understanding of many aspects of the disease. Warts can be removed usually either chemically or through various minor surgical procedures. However, removing the warts themselves does not eliminate the agent that causes warts, which lies in the skin layers and can be found some distance laterally from the site of the wart itself. Warts may recur when removed. Even where they do not recur our understanding of the level of any remaining infectiousness is imperfect. Some clinicians take an arbitrary point, perhaps three months with no recurrences, and reassure patients that they need not take precautions such as using condoms after this point (McClean & Hillman 1997). However, there is little general agreement about the issue and warts do sometimes recur after extended periods. Even the incubation period of warts is difficult to assess, with most people probably developing warts within a matter of weeks of infection but others possibly taking much longer.

There is less hard data on psychological aspects of warts compared to herpes. However, what data is available suggests that the reactions of patients are strikingly similar to those of patients with genital herpes. Both men and women react with emotional disturbance to a diagnosis of warts. Both men and women report that they feel dirty and disgusted by the condition and may report either feelings of self-blame or anger towards the person who they believe infected them. Negative effects on sexual functioning are common and both men and women report a negative impact on their feelings for their partner, particularly if they feel they were infected by them. High levels of anxiety and depression are present at the time of diagnosis. Both men and women are concerned about the possibility of infecting present or future partners. Particularly for those who suffer recurrences or in whom the warts are not easily removed, patients report worries about whether they will ever be cured. Up to a third of patients whose warts have been successfully removed continue to be concerned about the infection. Because of the association of other papillomaviruses with cervical cancer many women are concerned about the long-term impact of the infection on their health and men about the possibility of causing cancer in their partners (Voog & Lowhagen 1992; Persson *et al.* 1993; Clarke *et al.* 1996; Miller & Brodell 1996; Maw *et al.* 1998).

Reitano (1997), in an overview of the area, identifies the paramount need to communicate the facts and uncertainties in warts to patients and to try to involve them as much as possible in decisions about their treatment.

Bacterial infections

Information about the psychological impact of common bacterial infections is even more lacking than information on viral infections. The main reason for this is probably the course of the infection; individuals with chlamydia or gonorrhoea or syphilis are likely to be rapidly and effectively treated. It is known that high levels of anxiety, depression and illness-concern are present in people coming forward for diagnosis of genital discharge diseases (Carney *et al.* 1994). However, what happens to them subsequently is much more difficult to know. The assumption is that once they have been treated they no longer have a problem and therefore they should no longer have psychological difficulties. However, there is a lack of information as to whether this is correct.

If the data from warts and herpes is applicable in this area, as seems a reasonable assumption, then it is likely that the majority of people will indeed experience a resolution of any psychological disturbance after effective treatment. However, some patients are likely to be left with longer-term concerns and with emotional disturbance. It is also likely that infection with a sexually transmitted disease will leave some patients with major relationship difficulties, either because of issues with the partner who they believe infected them or because of issues with partners whom they may have infected in turn, particularly where infidelity is involved. Such situations are not uncommonly seen in genitourinary medicine clinics. Thus the social effects of the infection may persist after the disease itself has been eradicated.

It is difficult to build up a picture of the impact of bacterial infections on the individual over the longer term. People who return with repeat infections are unlikely to be representative of all those who have ever been infected. A large proportion of patients tend not to appear even for test of cure a matter of days after their initial consultation. Many patients will be given treatment on their first visit; for example, in the case of presumed chlamydial infections this may be before laboratory results are available. As a result, by the time that they should be returning for test of cure they have no symptoms and see no reason to return. Attempts to improve test of cure rates have not usually been very successful; they run against the assumption in patients, often but not always correct, that if their symptoms have gone the disease has gone.

Given the problems of recalling any sort of representative population of people with bacterial infections, we are left with a list of characteristics of patients who get gonorrhoea and chlamydia, but little insight into what exactly it is that drives their behaviour. So gonorrhoea and chlamydia are most common in people who are socially and economically disadvantaged, young black men in inner cities being particularly prone to the infection in the UK and North America (Lacey *et al.* 1997; Day *et al.* 1998). What we lack is an understanding of how exactly demographic factors translate into the behaviours and risks of people with those characteristics. While knowing the characteristics of individuals most at risk for a particular infection can allow more efficient targeting of resources and can lead to health gains for individuals at high risk (Han *et al.* 1999) it does not in itself tell us how to optimally promote behaviour change; for that we need to know what is causing the individual to behave in a particular way.

There has been a great deal of interest in the idea of 'core groups' of individuals with bacterial STDs who may possibly have a disproportionate effect on the maintenance of these diseases in the community (Ellen *et al.* 1997). Since both chlamydia and gonorrhoea are frequently asymptomatic, such an idea is attrac-

tive and, assuming their existence, might solve some of the problems in modelling the diseases mathematically. Unfortunately it is not clear whether such 'core groups' exist in the sense of social entities (in contact with each other socially and sharing social norms and behaviours) or whether data pointing towards 'core groups' is just a restatement of the fact that particular subpopulations are at elevated risk of acquiring and passing on sexually transmitted diseases.

Interestingly, women are more likely to claim that they acquire the infection mainly from regular partners while men have a tendency to claim that they have acquired the infection from casual partners. Both men and women tend to identify a low number of contacts. Modelling the data suggests that gonorrhoea should have disappeared under such circumstances or at least that very small changes should eradicate it (Garnett *et al.* 1999). In part this probably reflects the importance of asymptomatic cases in the population in the dynamics of bacterial sexually transmitted diseases, but one might cynically suggest that patients who have contracted a sexually transmitted disease do not perhaps always tell researchers the absolute truth about their sexual behaviour. It is worth recalling that in population sex surveys the aggregate numbers of partners reported by women is almost universally considerably less than the aggregate numbers of partners reported by men, a mathematical and practical impossibility.

General considerations

General embarrassment about sexually transmitted diseases is one of the main enemies to controlling and adequately treating them. As noted above, patients are reluctant to inform sexual partners, particularly casual ones and, it is to be suspected, reluctant to identify partners to health professionals so that they can contact them. There are good grounds for suspecting that patients may not always tell the truth about their sexual behaviour to health professionals; concerned that they may be viewed as promiscuous or irresponsible they edit their sexual history to make it more, as they see it, acceptable. Embarrassment even gets in the way of patients seeking treatment in the first place. They delay seeking treatment for sexually transmitted diseases out of embarrassment and in the hope that they will go away (Hook *et al.* 1997; Maw *et al.* 1998).

It is hard to see how this problem can be entirely overcome. Looked at objectively there is no reason why a sexually transmitted disease should be any different from food poisoning acquired by eating in a restaurant. In many, perhaps most, cases the acquisition of a sexually transmitted disease does not involve any infidelity which might lead to embarrassment. With few exceptions most people do not set out to catch a sexually transmitted disease, they simply have sex, a very human and natural desire. On the other hand society does not usually make moral judgements about food poisoning but it does make moral judgements about sex.

The increasing tendency for specialists in sexually transmitted diseases to be invited to talk in schools and colleges is perhaps the best hope. If we can get over the fact that STDs should not be a matter of shame at an early age then we have a better chance that people will take precautions and, if they are unlucky enough to acquire an STD, will seek early and effective treatment. As noted above such an approach also has the advantage that, if we can 'normalise' sexually transmitted diseases, in the sense of getting them seen as another set of infectious diseases that you can protect yourself against and get treated for, then it will be much easier to get them under control at the population level.

For older people, those above school or college level, there is quite simply a need to advertise. Relatively few sexually transmitted disease services anywhere in the world have made great efforts to advertise their services. In the UK things have improved since the days when STD clinics attached to hospitals were hardly signed so that you had to know what you were looking for in order to find them. Nonetheless there is a long way to go in most areas to get over to the public the idea that there are good, non-judgmental services available, which can resolve people's concerns.

It is unlikely that any amount of advertising and education will, at least in the short term, reverse the current unsatisfactory situation. There is also therefore a need to increase screening for common conditions like chlamydia and gonorrhoea and to spread the number of services with a capacity to offer STD services in primary care, family planning and general medicine. To that extent, whatever the difficulties, the new generation of rapid easy screening tests that is coming is to be wholeheartedly welcomed. At the same time, however, it is necessary to get over the psychological dimension of sexually transmitted diseases to health professionals who may never have had to deal with them before and to ensure that they have the skills to deal with the problems that STDs present people emotionally and in their relationships with others.

Implications of what we know for practice and research

Sketchy though the information on the psychology of sexually transmitted diseases sometimes is, there are three clear themes that emerge in terms of dealing with patients.

Communication with patients

Clear communication with patients is the cornerstone of good practice in sexually transmitted diseases. A single example shows the sorts of problem that can arise.

Many patients complaining of chronic urethral or prostatic pain will receive antibiotic treatment as a pragmatic treatment at some point even though it has not been possible to identify a clear causative organism. After one, or more usually several, courses of treatment with no effect, the patient may well be told that there is little point in further antibiotic treatment and that they need take no particular precautions in their sex life. Many patients find this approach hard to accept. Having observed the fact that they are being treated with drugs used to treat an infection they naturally assume that they must have an infection. What appears to them to be a sudden change of mind in the doctor can be hard for them to accept, even though from a clinical point of view the advice may well be entirely sensible.

The practice of medicine, in its broadest sense, is a mystery to many patients, governed by a set of rules and unspoken assumptions, which are second nature to most health professionals and yet a complete mystery to most members of the public. As an example, which will be familiar to most health professionals, many sets of symptoms have a range of possible causes. It is usual practice to look for, and to treat for, the most common cause of those symptoms and, if the problem resolves, assume that one has found the right diagnosis. At the same time most physicians will seek to exclude any acute life-threatening causes of the condition by carrying out reasonable tests, reasonable being determined by the probability of a particular cause and the difficulty, unpleasantness, costs to the patient in terms of money and pain, and practicality of tests. If the first treatment does not work they will then go through to carry out further tests and carry out other treatments. However, conversation with patients, or even with one's friends, reveals that this approach is seldom spelt out to patients. So many people will say 'I went to the doctor with X symptoms and he gave me some tablets and it didn't get better, so I think I am stuck with it'.

If there is one area in which we can probably most easily improve our clinical practice with patients, whether in medicine, psychology, nursing or any other branch of health care, it is probably by explaining clearly to patients why we are taking a particular course of action, what the possible outcomes are and what we will do in each case. This does not have to go down to the absurd, like warning every patient who complains of a headache that they may have a brain tumour, but informing every patient as much as possible without raising remote alarming possibilities is a practical strategy that allows patient and health worker to act together to find the best way of tackling the problem. It is also much more likely that someone who knows why they are being asked to do a particular thing will actually comply with treatment.

Getting an appropriate research agenda and developing effective models

Anyone looking at the research literature on sexually transmitted diseases will be able to find hundreds of papers that say exactly the same thing. People with sexually transmitted diseases tend to be younger, disadvantaged socially, don't use condoms regularly and tend to have more sexual partners. There is probably a limit to the number of times that it is worth finding out this information. The challenge is to make the links. Why don't some people use condoms regularly? Why do some people have more sexual partners than others? It is fairly obvious that our current models of sexual behaviour are not delivering the goods in terms of answering these questions. Getting better answers is important in informing behavioural interventions. Unfortunately the pre-eminence of existing models tends to restrict the sorts of questions that we ask because questions tend to be based around parts of the models. We need to think more widely and to make better use of qualitative approaches to inform models, and later quantitative research, if we are to get anywhere in this area.

In terms of caring for our patients more effectively, we need to find out more about normal reactions to sexually transmitted diseases and why some people adjust rapidly to acquiring an STD while others fail to do so or take much longer to do so. Simply measuring distress at diagnosis, or recurrence of chronic viral infections is not in itself going to address this problem. We need to try to relate different reactions to the beliefs and cognitions of patients and to the social situations in which they find themselves.

We also need the answers to some very practical questions. What is the best strategy for telling a partner that you have a sexually transmitted disease? What is the best way to try to negotiate the use of a condom in a sexual relationship? How can we predict which of our patients will adjust psychologically to a chronic disease and which will not? What is the best way to promote adjustment in diseases like herpes and warts? What is the most effective way to get over the necessary information about a sexually transmitted disease and its treatment and about sexual risks generally that allows us to maximise the chances of the patient complying with treatment and avoiding getting infected in the future? What is the best way to reduce the level of embarrassment and distress in our patients?

Patients coming for sexually transmitted diseases are in an unfamiliar situation, they are usually seeking advice about what to do but our ability to offer good advice on practical everyday problems is often constrained by our ignorance about what the right advice is. This sort of practical research is no less valuable than epidemiological surveys or complex transmission studies, yet it is sadly lacking.

Developing ways of delivering psychological care to patients within resource constraints

Most health care providers in most parts of the world I have visited are busy. Large clinics mean short consultations for the patient. Attending to the psychological well-being of the patient is only one of many tasks that the health care professional is going to have to do during that consultation. This is undoubtedly a disappointing situation, but for most health care professionals dealing with most patients it is a fact.

The consequence is simple. We need to identify what really matters about the psychological care of STD patients and we need to develop ways of integrating these into everyday practice in a way that is actually practicable. An effective way of reducing distress in patients with warts that takes eight hours and relies on specialist staff may be practicable in very severe cases, but it is hardly likely to become a part of the general care of patients with warts.

There is clearly a formidable agenda ahead for the study of the psychological aspects of sexually transmitted diseases.

References

Adih, W.K. & Alexander, C.S. (1999) Determinants of condom use to prevent HIV infection among youth in Ghana. *Journal of Adolescent Health* **24**, 63–72.

Ajzen, I. & Madden, T.J. (1986) Prediction of goal-directed behaviour: attitudes, intentions and perceived behavioural control. *Journal of Experimental Social Psychology* **22**, 453–474.

Bandura, A. (1977) Self-efficacy: towards a unifying theory of behavioral change. *Psychological Reviews* **84**, 191–215.

Barton, S. & Green, J. (1999) *The Psychological Impact of Genital Herpes*. Mosby-Wolfe, London.

Barton, S.E., Munday, P.E. & Patel, R.J. (1996) Asymptomatic shedding of herpes simplex virus from the genital tract: uncertainty in its consequences for patient management. *International Journal of STD and AIDS* **7**, 229–232.

Becker, M.H., Kaback, M., Rosenstock, I. & Ruth, M. (1975) Some influences on public participation in a genetic screening program. *Journal of Community Health* **1**, 3–14.

Bedimo, A.L., Bennett, M., Kissinger, P. & Clark, R.A. (1998) Understanding barriers to condom usage among HIV-infected African-American women. *Journal of the Association of Nurses in AIDS Care* **9**, 48–58.

Brackbill, R.M., Sternberg, M.R. & Fishbein, M. (1999) Where do people go for treatment of sexually transmitted diseases? *Family Planning Perspectives* **31**, 10–15

Brian, A.D., Aiken, L.S. & West, S.G. (1998) Young women's condom use: the influence of acceptance of sexuality, control over the sexual encounter, and perceived susceptibility to common STDs. *Health Psychology* **16**, 468–479.

Brookes, J.L., Haywood, S. & Green, J. (1993) Adjustment to the psychological and social sequelae of recurrent gential herpes simplex infection. *Genitourinary Medicine* **69**, 384–387.

Carney, O., Ross, E., Bunker, C., Ikkos, G. & Mindel, A. (1994) A prospective study of the psychological impact on patients with a first episode of genital herpes. *Genitourinary Medicine* **70**, 40–45.

Carney, O., Ross, E., Ikkos, G. & Mindel, A. (1993) The effect of suppressive oral acyclovir on the psychological morbidity associated with recurrent genital herpes. *Genitourinary Medicine* **69**, 457–459.

Clarke, P., Ebel, C., Catotti, D.N. & Stewart, S. (1996) The psychosocial impact of human papillomavirus infection. *International Journal of STD and AIDS* **7**, 197–200.

Day, S., Ward, H., Ghani, A. *et al.* (1998) Sexual histories, partnerships and networks associated with the transmission of gonorrhoea. *International Journal of STD and AIDS* **9**, 666–671.

Devonshire, P., Hillman, R., Capewell, S. & Clark, B.J. (1999) Knowledge of chlamydia trachomatis and its consequences in people attending a genitourinary medicine clinic. *Sexually Transmitted Infections* **75**, 409–411.

Ellen, J.M., Kohn, R.P. & Bolan, G.A. An investigation of geographic clustering of repeat cases of gonorrhoea and chlamydial infection in San Francisco, 1989–1993, evidence for core groups. *Journal of Infectious Diseases* **175**, 1519–1522.

Forsgren, M. (1990) Genital herpes simplex virus infection and incidence of neonatal disease in Sweden. *Scandinavian Journal of Infectious Diseases* **69** (Suppl.), 37–41.

Garnett, G.P., Mertz, K.J., Finelli, L., Levine, W.C. & St Louis, M.E. (1999) The transmission dynamics of gonorrhoea; modelling the reported behaviour of infected patients from Newark, New Jersey. *Philosophical Transactions of the Royal Society of London* **354B**, 787–797.

Goldmeier, D. & Johnson, A. (1982) Does psychiatric illness affect the recurrence rate of genital herpes? *British Journal of Venereal Diseases* **58**, 40–43.

Goldmeier, D., Johnson, A., Jeffries, D. *et al.* (1986) Psychological aspects of recurrences of genital herpes. *Journal of Psychosomatic Research* **30**, 601–8.

Gorbach, P.M., Aral, S.O., Celum, C. *et al.* (2000) To notify or not notify: STD patients' perspectives of partner notification in Seattle. *Sexually Transmitted Diseases* **27**, 193–200.

Green, J. & Kocsis, A. (1997) Psychological factors in recurrent genital herpes. *Genitourinary Medicine* **73**, 253–259.

Green, J., Fulop, N. & Kocsis, A. (2000) Determinants of unsafe sex in women. *International Journal of STD and AIDS* **11**, 777–783.

Green, J., Ferrier, S., Kocsis, A., Shadrick, J., Ukoumunne, O.C. & Murphy, S. (2001) Disclosure of Genital Herpes (submitted).

Han, Y., Coles, F.B., Muse, A. & Hipp, S. (1999) Assessment of a geographically targeted field intervention on gonorrhoea incidence in to New York State counties. *Sexually Transmitted Diseases* **26**, 296–302.

Hook, E.W., Richey, C.M., Leone, P. *et al.* (1997) Delayed presentation to clinics for sexually transmitted diseases by symptomatic patients. A potential contributor to continuing STD morbidity. *Sexually Transmitted Diseases* **24**, 443–448.

Kasenda, M., Calzavara, L.M., Johnson, I. & LeBlanc, M. (1997) Correlates of condom use in the young adult population in Ontario. *Canadian Journal of Public Health* **88**, 280–285.

Lacey, C.J., Merrick, D.W., Bensley, D.C. & Fairley, I. (1997) Analysis of the sociodemography of gonorrhoea in Leeds, 1989–1993. *British Medical Journal* **314**, 1715–1718.

Lansky, A., Thomas, J.C. & Earp, J.A. (1998) Partner-specific sexual behaviours among persons with both main and other partners. *Family Planning Perspectives* **30**, 93–96.

Leonard, L. & Ross, M.W. (1997) The last sexual encounter: the contextualisation of sexual risk behaviour. *International Journal of STD and AIDS* **8**, 643–645.

Macke, B.A. & Maher, J.E. (1999) Partner notification in the United States, and evidence-based review. *American Journal of Preventative Medicine* **17**, 230–242.

Maw, R.D., Reitano, M. & Roy, M. (1998) An international survey of patients with genital warts, perceptions regarding treatment and impact on lifestyle. *International Journal of STD and AIDS* **9**, 571–578.

McClean, H.L. & Hillman, R.J. (1997) Anogenital warts and condom use – a survey of information giving. *Genitourinary Medicine* **73**, 203–206.

Mertz, G.J., Benedetti, J., Ashley, R.A., Selke, S.A. & Corey, L. (1992) Risk factors for the sexual transmission of genital herpes. *Annals of International Medicine* **116**, 197–202.

Miller, D.M. & Brodell, R.T. (1996) Human papillomavirus infection: treatment options for warts. *American Family Physician* **53**, 135–143.

Musaba, E., Morrison, C.S., Sunkutu, M.R. & Wong, E.L. (1998) Long-term use of the female condom among couples at high risk of human immunodeficiency virus infection in Zambia. *Sexually Transmitted Diseases* **25**, 260–264.

Patel, R., Tyring, S., Price, M.J. & Grant, D.M. (1999) Impact of suppressive antiviral therapy on the health related quality of life of patients with recurrent genital herpes infection. *Sexually Transmitted Infections* **75**, 398–402.

Persson, G., Dahlof, L.G., Krantz, I. (1993) Physical and psychological effects of anogenital warts on female patients. *Sexually Transmitted Diseases* **20**, 10–11.

Reis, J. & Stephens, Y.D. (1998) A discriminant analysis of young adults' knowledge of the human papillomavirus and self-efficacy of condom use. *Journal of Psychology and Human Sexuality* **16**, 71–91.

Reitano, M. (1997) Counselling patients with genital warts. *American Journal of Medicine* **102** (Suppl.), 38–43.

Roberts, S.W., Cox, S.M., Dax, J., Wendel, G.D. & Leveno, K.J. (1995) Genital herpes during pregnancy, no lesions no caesarean. *Obstetrics and Gynecology* **85**, 261–264.

Robertson, D.H.H., McMillan, A. & Young, H. (1989) *Clinical Practice in Sexually Transmissible Diseases.*

Churchill Livingstone, Edinburgh.

Rogstad, K.E., Clementson, C. & Ahmed-Jushuf, I.H. (1999) Contact tracing for gonorrhoea in homosexual and heterosexual men. *International Journal of STD and AIDS* **10**, 536–538.

Ronis, D.L. (1992) Conditional health threats: health beliefs, decisions and behaviours amongst adults. *Health Psychology* **11**, 127–134.

Rosenstock, I.M. (1974) Historical origins of the health belief model. *Health Education Monographs* **2**, 328–335.

Silver, P.S., Auerbach, S.M., Vishniavsky, N. & Kaplowitz, L.G. (1986) Psychological factors in recurrent genital herpes infection: stress, coping style, social support, emotional dysfunction and symptom recurrence. *Journal of Psychosomatic Research* **30**, 163–171.

Sutton, S., McVey, D. & Glanz, A. (1999) A comparative test of the theory of reasoned action and the theory of planned behaviour in the prediction of condom use intentions in a national sample of English young people. *Health Psychology* **18**, 72–81.

Swanson, J.M., Dibble, S.L. & Chenitz, W.C. (1995) Clinical features and psychosocial factors in young adults with genital herpes. *Image: the Journal of Nursing Scholarship* **27**, 16–22.

Taylor, J., Fulop, N. & Green, J. (1999) Drink, illicit drugs and unsafe sex in women. *Addiction* **94**, 1209–1218.

Taylor, S.E. (1995) *Health Psychology* (4th Edn). McGraw Hill, Boston, MA.

Tyden, T. & Ramstedt, K. (2000) A survey of patients with chlamydia trachomatis infection: sexual behaviour and perceptions about contact tracing. *International Journal of STD and AIDS* **11**, 92–95.

Vail-Smith, K. & White, D.M. (1992) Risk level, knowledge and preventive behaviour for human papillomaviruses amongst sexually active college women. *Journal of American College Health* **XX**, 227–230.

Van de Laar, M.J., Termorshuizen, F. & van den Hoek, A. (1997) Partner referral by patients with gonorrhoea and chlamydial infection. Case-finding observations. *Sexually Transmitted Diseases* **24**, 334–342.

Voog, E. & Lowhagen, G.B. (1992) Follow-up of men with genital papilloma virus. *Acta Dermalogica Venereologica* **72**, 185–186.

Wen, L.M., Estcourt, C.S., Simpson, J.M. & Mindel, A. (1999) Risk factors for the acquisition of genital warts, are condoms protective. *Sexually Transmitted Infections* **75**, 312–316.

Williams, S.S., Kinble, D.L., Covell, N.H. *et al.* (1992) College students use implicit personality theory instead of safer sex. *Journal of Applied Sociology and Psychology* **22**, 921–933.

Chapter 4

Behaviour Change for STD Prevention and Sexual Health

Françoise Dubois-Arber and Michel Carael

The very existence of a chapter containing the words 'behaviour change', 'prevention of STDs' and 'sexual health' highlights two recent changes that have been precipitated under the pressure of the HIV/AIDS epidemic:

- There has been a renewed focus on primary prevention in STD prevention – i.e. founded on behavioural change – after a long period with a strong biomedical component during which most of STDs were considered manageable, treatable, and thus more prone to secondary prevention (detection and subsequent treatment). Such secondary prevention included control over certain aspects of sexuality and invasion of privacy (contact notification, compulsory treatment, etc.).
- Sexual health is increasingly treated as a concept meaning more than the absence of disease or problem (e.g. unwanted pregnancy). This concept takes into particular account pleasure, need for intimacy, social interaction and social recognition, and also reminds us that sexual health refers much more to interpersonal or social conditions than to individual characteristics.

In other words the prevention of STDs in an historical view of public health would have dictated individual behaviours using fear of disease as an engine for behaviour change, and blamed those who could not comply. Such an approach might not have been conducive to sexual health. The new approaches are based on the principles of the Ottawa Charter for prevention and emphasise enabling and empowerment as the targets of and precondition for both individually and socially responsible health behaviour. In this context, change of sexual behaviour is not only related to STD prevention but also contains elements of promotion of sexual health (promotion of negotiation capacities, autonomy in sexual choices, life-skills approaches, gender equality, etc.).

Key approaches to behaviour change

Approaches to behaviour change have been viewed along two main axes related to:

- determinants of health – individual lifestyle and behaviour versus social and environmental factors (i.e. targets for intervention) and
- the ways of influencing these determinants – prescription versus participation, top-down versus bottom up approaches.

The different theories of behaviour modification which will be described below contain, in different mixes, elements from both of these axes.

Models with a focus on individuals' psychological processes

These models are all based on the premise that behaviours and behaviour changes are conditioned by a constellation or sequence of knowledge, beliefs, perceptions and attitudes which can be the target of external influence (information, motivation, reinforcement, social norm, etc.).

The *Health Belief Model* (Becker 1974) states that behavioural change in order to avoid a certain disease is a function of several individual factors: perceived susceptibility to the condition, perceived seriousness of the disease, perceived benefits of behaviour change, perceived barriers to behavioural change and the presence of cues to action (Rosenstock 1974; Joseph *et al.* 1987).

The *Social Learning (or Cognitive) Theory* (Bandura 1977) looks at human behaviour as a continuous interaction between cognitive, behavioural and environmental determinants. The main components of the model are self-efficacy – the belief in one's own capability to implement the necessary behaviour – and expectations about outcomes – the belief that expected positive outcomes will outweigh negative ones.

Models inspired of the *Theory of Reasoned Action* are based on the assumptions that human beings are usually quite rational and that they make systematic use of the information available to them. These models give more importance to the context in which behaviour takes place and to the implications on the behaviour in the context (perceived norms and perceived support of behavioural change by significant others). They also consider different steps in behavioural change, with a special emphasis on the intention to perform that behaviour. Such intention would be the most important predictor of behavioural change.

The *Stages of Change Model or Transtheoretical Model* first developed for smoking cessation (Prochaska & Di Clemente 1992; Prochaska *et al.* 1994), defines six successive stages which individuals or groups pass through when changing behaviour: precontemplation, contemplation, preparation, action, maintenance and relapse to any of the previous stages. With respect to condom use, for example, the stages could be described as:

- hasn't considered using condoms (precontemplation)
- recognises the need to use condoms (contemplation)
- considering using condoms in the next months (preparation)
- using condoms consistently for less than 6 months (action)

- using condoms consistently for 6 months or more (maintenance).

This model also assumes that, to be successful, an intervention must target the appropriate stage of the individual or group, in order to help them progress along the stages. Movement between stages depends mainly on cognitive-behavioural processes.

Other models are based on subjective evaluation of risks, and are inspired by the economic *Theory of Expected Utility.* In these models the rational individual acts with the intention of maximising utility or the ratio of benefits to risks. These models imply that individuals will need good information on the probability of risk, but also that subjective preferences regarding the risk/benefit balance might sometimes lead to choices which could at first sight seem to be irrational (e.g. preference for not discussing protection, and for maintaining risky sexual behaviour with a partner because of fear of endangering the romantic nature of the relationship).

Overemphasis on individual behaviour change with a focus on the cognitive level has undermined the capacity of research to understand the complexity of behavioural change. Focus only on individual psychological process ignores the interactive relationship of behaviour in its social, cultural, and economic dimension and thereby misses the possibility of fully understanding crucial determinants of behaviour. While they have contributed to the understanding of the psychological processes individuals go through while attempting to change behaviour, the limitations of the psychological theories of behaviour change have been well described in the literature (Auerbach *et al.* 1994). Most models are based on behaviours which are under intentional and volitional control, ignoring the fact that sexual behaviour involves two people, is often impulsive and is influenced by sociocultural, contextual as well as personal and subconscious factors that may be difficult to influence.

Models or theories with a focus on community

Models or theories that focus on communities go beyond the individual and take into account behaviour in its social, cultural, or economic dimensions. Since they focus less on the forms and stages than on the conditions of behavioural change, they guide reflection towards the means to promote behavioural change.

Many dimensions, in different mixes according to the theories or models, are of relevance regarding the acquisition and maintenance of behaviours:

- social and cultural norms
- social networks, social support
- peer influence/peer pressure
- influence of significant others (community leaders, parents, other role models)
- power structures (such as relations between genders, between customers and sex workers, etc.)
- socioeconomic conditions
- environmental conditions such as elements of lifestyle (scenes, meeting places) or messages and discourse in the media.

Community level theories see human behaviour both as a function of personal characteristics and as the resultant of numerous social relationships and systemic influences as well as considering changes at the community level. Sociological theories assert that society is made up of smaller subcultures, and it is the members of one's immediate surroundings, the peer group with which someone most identifies, that has the most significant influence on an individual's behaviour. Effective prevention efforts, especially in vulnerable communities that do not have the support of the larger society, will thus depend on the development of strategies that can enlist community mobilisation to modify the norms of the peer network to support positive changes in behaviour.

The *Diffusion of Innovation Theory* describes the process of the way in which an idea is disseminated throughout a community. According to this theory, people's exposure to a new idea, which takes place within a social network or through the media, will determine the rate at which various people adopt a new behaviour. The theory posits that people are most likely to adopt new behaviours based on favourable evaluations of the idea communicated to them by other members whom they respect (Kegeles *et al.* 1996). When the diffusion theory is applied to HIV risk reduction, normative and risk behaviour changes can be initiated when enough key opinion leaders adopt and endorse behaviour changes, influence others to do the same, and eventually diffuse the new norm widely within peer networks. When beneficial prevention beliefs are instilled and widely held within one's immediate social network, an individual's behaviour is more likely to be consistent with the perceived social norms (Kelly 1995). Interventions using this theory generally investigate the best method to disperse messages within a community and focus on identifying the leaders able to act as role models to change community norms.

The *Social Influence or Social Inoculation Model* is based on the concept that young people engage in behaviours – including early sexual activity – partly because of general societal influences, but also because of more specific influence from their peers (Howard & McCabe 1990). The model suggests exposing young people to social pressures while at the same time teaching them to examine and develop skills to deal with these pressures. It often relies on role models (such as teenagers slightly older than programme participants) to present factual information, identify pressures, role-play responses to pressures, teach assertiveness skills and discuss problem situations.

The *Social Networks Theory* looks at social behaviour not as an individual phenomenon but through relationships. With respect to sexual relationships, social networks focus on both the impact of selective mixing (i.e. how different people choose who they mix with), and the variations in partnership patterns (length of partnership and overlap). In this model the intricacies of relations and communication within the couple (the smallest unit of the social network) is critical to understanding transmission of HIV/STDs, but the scope and character of one's broader social network (those who serve as reference people), and who sanction behaviour, are key to comprehending individual risk behaviour (Auerbach *et al.* 1994). In other words, social norms are best understood at the level of social networks.

Unlike the psychosocial theories which are essentially gender-blind, the *Theory of Gender and Power* is a social structural theory addressing the wider social and environmental issues surrounding women, such as distribution of power and authority, affective influences, and gender-specific norms within heterosexual relationships (Connell 1987). Using this theory to guide intervention development with women in heterosexual relationships can help investigate how a woman's commitment to a relationship and lack of power can influence her risk reduction choices (DiClemente & Wingood 1995). Programmes using the theory of gender and power would assess the impact of structurally determined gender differences on interpersonal sexual relationships (perceptions of socially prescribed gender relations).

Determinants of sexual behaviour can be seen as a function not only of individual and social but also of *structural and environmental factors* (Sweat & Denison 1995; Tawil *et al.* 1995; Caraël *et al.* 1997; James 1998). These factors include civil and organisational elements as well as policy and economic issues. The earlier concepts of risk and risk-taking behaviour were broadened to include new concepts – such as 'risk situation' and 'vulnerability' – that result from societal factors and that affect adversely one's ability to exert control over one's own sexual health. However linking risk behaviour to social structural change is still problematic in current behaviour change theories (Giddens 1979).

The *Theory for Individual and Social Change or Empowerment Model* asserts that social change happens through dialogue. Such dialogue builds up a critical perception of the social, cultural, political and economic forces that structure reality, and can lead to action against forces that are oppressive (Parker 1996). In other words, empowerment should increase problem solving in a participatory fashion, and should enable individuals to un-

derstand the personal, social, economic and political forces in their lives in order to take action to improve their situations (Israel *et al.* 1994). Empowerment is the process by which disadvantaged people work together to take control of the factors that determine their health and their lives (Werner *et al.* 1997). For this to happen, feelings of powerlessness, which can come from lack of skills and confidence, have to be cast off. Although empowerment can only come from the group itself, enabling empowerment is possible by facilitating its determinants. The common struggle against gender or ethnic oppression, economic exploitation, political repression or foreign intervention is what builds necessary confidence.

A distinction is made between personal, organisational and community empowerment. Personal empowerment has to do with psychological processes, and is similar to self-efficacy and self-esteem. Organisational empowerment encompasses both the processes that enable individuals to increase their control within the organisation and the organisation to influence policies and decisions in the community. An empowered community uses the skills and resources of individuals and organisations to meet their respective needs (Werner *et al.* 1997).

Interventions using empowerment approaches must consider key concepts such as beliefs and practices that are linked to interpersonal, organisational and community change. Intervention activities can address issues at the community and organisational level, such as the central needs the community identifies, and any previous history of organising among community members. The theory would prescribe including community participants in the planning and implementation of activities.

The *Social Ecological Model for Health Promotion* shows how psychological, psychosocial, cultural, social, organisational and political theories can be used to guide the targets of behaviour change at each level of intervention. Intervention strategies range from skills development at the intra-personal level to mass media and regulatory changes at other levels (Laver *et al.* 1988). The theory acknowledges the importance of the interplay between the individual and the environment, and considers multi-level influences on unhealthy behaviour (Choi *et al.* 1998). The importance of the individual is thus de-emphasised in the process of behaviour change.

A number of studies have shown that *socioeconomic factors* have a strong influence on individual sexual behaviour, mostly through poverty and underemployment. Cross-nationally, countries with the lowest standards of living are also the ones with the highest HIV incidence (Tawil *et al.* 1995; James *et al.* 1998). Within both rich and poor countries, poverty is associated with HIV, and HIV intensifies poverty. The proposed mechanisms for the relationship between poverty and HIV include: separation of young married couples which can occur when critical economic situations encourage urban migration, seasonal work and truck driving, sex work. Civil disturbances and war lead to displaced and refugee populations, who not only lose their social and familial support systems but become highly vulnerable to HIV/STDs due to intense social and economic strain in an alien culture (Sweat & Denison 1995). In such situations, sexual health concerns take a very low priority in a risk hierarchy, and any previous or planned ef-

forts for the control of sexual health are disrupted, if not destroyed.

At the level of action these theories (individual or community based) have been used to implement programmes with different philosophies: some are mainly top down (key words are prescription of behaviour and influence on the individual or the populations), others emphasise bottom up or horizontal approaches (key words are participation and the empowerment of the individuals and communities).

Examples of the outcome of theory-driven interventions

Theoretical models that have proven useful in explaining and predicting changes in HIV/STDs related sexual behaviour provide guidance in the design and implementation of prevention programmes (Wingood & DiClemente 1996). Reviews of theory-driven interventions have noted that these interventions emphasise both intra-personal and interpersonal factors, provide skills training, attempt to modify social norms and are thus more effective at reducing risk behaviour among participants (DiClemente & Wingood 1995). Here, we summarise positive outcomes of theory-based interventions concerning four specific population groups: women, sex workers, men having sex with men, and youth.

Women

A review of randomised controlled trials in the United States (Kalichman & Hospers 1997) found that effective interventions for women had a number of common characteristics.

These interventions were guided by the *Social Cognitive/Learning Theory*, provided skills in condom use and sexual communication and emphasised support for continued maintenance of safer sexual behaviour. In addition, all effective interventions were peer-led and addressed gender-related influences such as gender-based power imbalances within the relationship (Kalichman 1998).

In general, successful skills training interventions for women consider cultural factors and attempt to personalise messages (Kalichman 1998). Programmes targeting women in the US, and adolescents in the US and Holland with behavioural skills enhancement have produced positive effects. Kalichman (1997), however, notes that behavioural skills enhancement training has not been tested experimentally outside the US, so it is unclear to what extent it might benefit women in other countries.

Ickovics and Yoshikawa (1998) identified seven types of interventions tried among women globally: small group, community-wide, media, HIV counselling and testing, individual counselling, classroom education and laboratory experiment. Community-wide (12 out of 14) and small-group interventions (13 out of 19) were more likely to show significant results. Several international programmes incorporated peer-led *Diffusion of Innovations* approaches and all reported statistically significant increases in condom use (six studies out of six). According to this review, less effective interventions for women overall were individual counselling (zero out of four) and HIV testing and counselling (three out of six effective as secondary prevention with serodiscordant couples (Ickovics & Yoshikawa 1998).

An intervention among women in a New York City housing project was based on the *Diffusion of Innovation Theory* in combination with community mobilisation. Women were recruited, organised and trained to help develop role model stories of individuals who reduced their risks for the project newsletters. These women were also expected to initiate discussions with their peers regarding HIV prevention. Information was diffused rapidly and seemed to promote discussion and condom use among the housing project women. Reported condom use by female sex partners of intravenous drug users rose from 15% to 45% (Friedman & O'Reilly 1997).

The *Theory of Gender and Power* provided a model for the design of a successful gender-appropriate social skills intervention among African American women in San Francisco. The intervention addressed how to successfully negotiate safer sex and improve partner norms favourable to consistent condom use in comparison to a control group that received similar training in a delayed fashion. The results showed significantly greater consistent condom use, greater sexual self-control, greater sexual assertiveness, and increased partners' adoption of norms supporting consistent condom use in the intervention group (DiClemente & Wingood 1995).

Gender and power imbalances have also been noted in many other studies, pointing to the necessity to build gender constructs into theories, models and interventions (Buunk *et al.* 1998). More generally, studies in the US and in Africa emphasise that the ability to discuss sex and contraception with sexual partners – as well as the imbalance of gender relations – have a potentially significant impact on the capacity to enact changes in sexual behaviour (Edem & Harvey 1998; Van der Straten *et al.* 1998). Such capacities are also affected, especially for vulnerable women, by abusive partners, economic factors, norms within sexual relationships, and societal norms regarding the distribution of roles and power between genders (Bunnell 1996; Kalichman 1998).

The *Stages of Change Model* was used to guide a 6-month longitudinal study among women in drug treatment, housing shelters, and hospital clinics in the US, and showed that women exposed to individual stage-tailored counselling were twice as likely to report consistent condom use with their main partner – at last sex contact – as women receiving free on-site reproductive health counselling and services (Galavotti *et al.* 1998). The stage-based counselling also proved useful at preventing relapse from consistent use further along in the process of change.

Community empowerment has also been a key for behavioural change. As Ulin suggests concerning African women, efforts have been highly successful when interventions have enabled the participants to take part in mobilising and setting goals themselves (Ulin 1992).

Sex workers

Among the numerous studies involving sex workers, only two will be highlighted. A year-long intervention targeting sex workers, brothel owners and clients in Thailand used multiple small group sessions with peer educators who were experienced women and were called 'superstars'. The 'model brothel' aspect of the programme worked with owners to enforce mandatory condom use by sex workers, and clients were also educated to use condoms. Volunteers trained to pose as clients tested sex workers' actual condom negotiation skills. Results indicated that sex workers increased their rate of refusal of sex without a condom from 42% before the intervention to 92% following the programme. The authors concluded that this multifaceted approach (specifically focusing on sex workers, while also acknowledging the importance of working with clients and owners) was critical to their success (UNAIDS 1998).

Another study, guided by the *Health Belief Model* and the *Social Learning Theory* among four groups of female sex workers in Indonesia, found that both increases in knowledge and condom use were related to the number of intervention sessions the women attended (Ford *et al.* 1998). Results reflected the different social context of sexual behaviour of the four groups of sex workers and indicated that the four groups of women had different levels of knowledge about AIDS, different socio-economic levels, different numbers of clients and different self-efficacy. Beliefs about the benefits of condoms were highly predictive of condom use in three of the four groups. In the group with lower knowledge about AIDS, it was perceived susceptibility to other STDs than HIV that was related to condom use. Self-efficacy was highly predictive of condom use in three out of four of the groups of sex workers.

Viewing gender, relationship and context issues as central to sexual behaviour was universally important for the success of these interventions. Using gender-driven theory across cultures might thus prove useful. Peer-led community interventions were more successful overall than individual level interventions. As with other populations, interventions facilitated by peers were often more successful than those using a facilitator from outside the target group.

Men having sex with men

A recent review of interventions with gay men found that studies generally fall into three types: individually based, small-group and community-level (Kegeles & Hart 1998). Controlled studies with men who have sex with men (MSM) have indicated a number of characteristics that have enabled men to change behaviour and maintain safer sex (Kelly 1995):

- eroticising safer sex materials;
- brief training on establishing and maintaining safer sex relationships;
- learning how to negotiate safer sex;
- training on how to reduce stress;
- intensive group counselling.

Behavioural skills enhancement interventions targeting MSM in diverse cultural settings (Kelly *et al.* 1991; Choi *et al.* 1996) have consistently demonstrated increased condom use during anal intercourse, with the greatest changes occurring with non-primary partners (Edem & Harvey 1998).

The *Diffusion of Innovation Theory* has been shown to be effective in changing sexual behaviour of men who have sex with men in a number of different studies in the US. The model was tested in three small Southern cities and results indicated systematic reduction in the population's high-risk behaviour with 15% to 29% reductions from baseline levels (Kelly *et al.* 1992; Kelly 1995; Coates *et al.* 1996).

Youth

A comprehensive international review of 110 outcome evaluations with youth (Peersman & Levy 1998) found that effective programmes:

- focused on understanding social and/or media influences on sexual behaviour in order to strengthen group norms against unprotected sex;
- listened to what young people think and believe in order to ensure that programmes were acceptable and appropriate;
- included modelling and practice of communication or negotiation skills;
- integrated pregnancy and STD prevention with HIV programmes;
- focused especially on disadvantaged youth, providing access to resources and/or services to address their basic needs (health care, legal aid).

The review also suggested that although a clear pattern and full understanding are lacking, *Social Learning Theories* have a greater potential than other theoretical frameworks in changing youth behaviour. Other cross-sectional surveys found that the *Theory of Reasoned Action* and the *Health Belief Model* as well as the *Social Learning Theory* can help understand behaviour of young people. All successful, theory-based interventions for young people have included skills training in addition to information and motivational components (Reitman *et al.* 1996).

Howard and McCabe showed success of the *Social Influence Theory,* using slightly older teenagers to identify peer and social pressures that encourage negative health behaviours, to present factual information, and to teach assertiveness and discuss problem situations (Howard & McCabe 1990).

Taken together, the results of these studies suggest that constructs subsumed in behavioural theory have greatly enhanced our understanding of risk behaviour among youth in varied settings and situations. Skills training, attitudes, norms and self-efficacy have all proven effective in predicting behaviour change among young people. In intervention research, these constructs have been useful in mediating actual risk behaviours.

What are the problems

Each of the models and theories described has been able to predict or explain behavioural change only partially. Each contains interesting elements – not all necessary, not all sufficient – to guide the intervention. None can be identified as *the* model.

Critiques have been addressed to these models:

- Many focus too strongly on *rationality*.
- Many assume a step by step *linearity* of behavioural change. For example the models that focus on the individual and strongly rely on rationality (Health Belief Model in particular) have been criticised for their possible circular causality, i.e. the beliefs can be either causes or consequences of behaviours (Moatti *et al.* 1993).
- They have been conceived mainly in the *Western world*, with probable cultural, social and gender bias (Parker *et al.* 1991).
- The *relative importance of the different elements* of the models in the occurrence of behavioural change is not known: each element appears to have the same 'weight'. This complicates the choice of targets for intervention.
- Behaviours and therefore behavioural change have *many concurrent 'causes'* or are influenced by many concurrent factors. It

has become common sense in prevention to combine interventions that are thought to act on different elements of a model (or even incorporate elements of many models) in the hope of obtaining a mutual reinforcement of different actions. For example an STD prevention programme for adolescents in a community may combine a peer education approach, a mass media campaign for raising awareness in the whole population and a special intervention with role models (actors, etc.). None of the models gives an idea of the ideal mix of interventions at different levels.

Other critiques have addressed the methods used to evaluate the models:

- One of the greatest limitations of interventions and studies assessing these interventions is *short follow-up time*. Lack of follow-up time can undermine an intervention by not allowing positive feedback, not waiting for possible changes in social and cultural norms, and not taking maintenance of behaviour change into consideration.
- *Development of methodologies for implementation and evaluation of community-level programmes has not been sufficiently operationalised.* Assessing effectiveness of these programmes introduces a number of challenging issues such as measuring community level changes, identifying the elements of the intervention to measure, and obtaining large enough sample sizes to detect significance. This makes design of such programmes and the ability to carry them out more complex than individual-based programmes.
- Few studies report on *null findings*. Those that do, however, provide a critical com-

plement to our understanding of the relationships between context, population group, approach, intervention and theoretical background. In some populations behavioural skills training has failed to produce significant differences when compared to control conditions. For example, non-impact of intervention has been shown with inner city African American men and STD clinic patients in the US (Branson *et al* 1996). Other reports of null findings include a randomised controlled trial among STD patients in the UK, in which the intervention was guided by the Social Learning Theory (SLT). Results indicated little difference in self-reported behaviour change (Parker 1996). Another intervention that showed little effect was a brief program based on constructs from the SLT and the Theory of Reasoned Action among youth: the authors suggest a longer intervention that addresses the multiple problems of this group that was drawn from a detention centre and STD clinic (Gillmore *et al.* 1997).

What do we need to know and do

Targeting or tailoring interventions?

There has been much discussion around the issue of targeting interventions. It has been argued that to have an impact on the sexual transmission of HIV and other STDs, and especially early in the epidemic, interventions need to reach those most at risk of acquiring or transmitting the infection (Sepulveda *et al.* 1992). Recent simulation studies have also argued that targeting interventions to priority groups would be an efficient and effective

approach for HIV prevention in developing countries (Morris 1997). When the epidemic spreads into the general population, however, targeting only most-at-risk populations is no longer sufficient to reduce transmission. In addition, too quickly identifying populations at risk and targeting intervention can miss important vulnerable groups, such as happened with male sex workers in Asia (Ford *et al.* 1996).

On the other hand, it has been demonstrated for other public health problems such as smoking or hypertension, that interventions addressed to entire populations (rather than small groups or individuals), by shifting the medium level of risk, bring more to communities than do targeted, more individualised approaches (such as testing and counselling) (Rose 1992). These populational approaches relying mainly on changes in norms and structures are likely to be effective in countries with scarce resources and high prevalences of STDs.

Another concern with regard to targeting is how to operationally define the target group: within one group – for example youth – individuals with high-risk behaviours can be found in very different subsets of this population and may not be identifiable. Targeting populations that are more vulnerable also entails the risk of labelling and stigmatisation. Working with priority groups is important at any stage of the epidemic, but should be combined with other activities to reach a broader population also at risk, even to a lesser degree.

Those in favour of populational approaches and those preferring risk groups approaches generally agree on the necessity of tailoring interventions, i.e. adapting them to the specific context of the population, group or individual. Approaches ought to fit specific language and cultural needs of different communities (Cohen 1992). Even if the principles underlying programmes are the same, tailoring to specific groups in specific settings will make programmes look very different (Kelly *et al.* 1997). Not only should programmes be modified to fit certain cultural settings, but within cultural groups individuals may be at very different stages of readiness to change. Interventions should thus take individual differences into consideration as well. When addressing specific groups such as youth, for example, it has been shown that, to be effective, interventions must look differently at those who have initiated sex and those who have not.

Multilevel, complementary interventions

Although tremendous challenges regarding AIDS/STD prevention still await public health and the social sciences globally, much has been already learned. It has become clear that effective HIV/STD risk reduction interventions extend beyond giving basic information and help: sensitise people to personal risk, improve sexual communication in couples, increase individuals' condom use skills, change social norms, increase social support, reinforce efforts at changing, etc. (Kelly 1995). These principles form the foundation of successful HIV prevention strategies, but differences in individual, social, cultural and economic conditions dictate specific design and implementation of programmes.

An important point stressed in this broad overview of approaches to behaviour change is the need to see the different levels of HIV prevention initiatives as being complementary. Individual approaches have shown im-

pact, but community and structural level programmes are a critical complement to stem transmission on a larger scale. The question remains open as to the respective proportion of resources to be invested in each of these components (the ideal mix of interventions). This question is crucial for developing countries, which have not received their share of the attention and resources allocated to AIDS interventions globally. The countries with the highest prevalence of HIV are those with the least resources and where medical and social support systems are already strained. They do not have the means to develop the needed evaluations of multilevel, multicomponent interventions, yet they are the communities that need them the most urgently.

Acknowledging the model(s) and assumptions guiding the intervention

As has been shown, no one behavioural change model or theory can be considered universal or holistic. This does not mean that such models and theories cannot be used to guide interventions. On the contrary. It is possible to use these models as a whole, to use only some components of a model or to combine elements from different models. Theory based interventions have the advantage of making clear the assumptions underlying the (multiple) causal relationships between different steps or elements involved in behavioural change. They allow explicit and individualised definition of the many components of the intended action, of its targets, goals and milestones, and clarification of the processes of implementation of the intervention. They therefore also provide a good base for sound evaluation and further refinement of interventions.

In this chapter we have seen that the approach to behavioural change regarding sexuality has been viewed – under the influence of HIV/AIDS – mainly from a point of view of health as the absence of disease. It is to be hoped that the control of the epidemic will make possible another approach to sexual health, one based on well-being and on pleasure.

Acknowledgements

The authors would like to acknowledge the important contribution of Rachel King in reviewing the relevant literature and in synthesising the main findings.

References

Auerbach, J., Wypijewska, C. & Brodil, K. (1994) *AIDS and Behavior: An Integrated Approach*. National Academy Press, NW.

Bandura, A. (1977) *Social Learning Theory*. Prentice-Hall, Englewood Cliffs, NJ.

Becker, M.H. (ed.) (1974) *Health Education Monograph, 24*. Special edition on the HBM, reprinted as *The Health Belief Model and Personal Health Behaviour*. Charles Black, NJ.

Branson, B., Ransom, R., Peterman, T. & Zaidi, A. (1996) Randomized controlled trial of intensive group counseling to reduce risk behaviors in high-risk STD clinic patients. *11th International Conference on AIDS*, Vancouver.

Bunnell, R. (1996) *Promoting or paralysing behavior change: understanding gender and high levels of perceived risk of HIV infection in Southwestern Uganda*. Doctoral Thesis; Harvard School of Public Health, Boston, MA.

Buunk, B., Bakker, A., Siero, F., Eijnden, R. & Yzer, M. (1998) Predictors of AIDS-preventive behavioral intentions among adult heterosexuals at risk for HIV-infection: extending current models and measures. *AIDS Education and Prevention* **10**(2), 149–172.

Caraël, M., Buvé, A. & Awusabbo-Asare, K. (1997) The making of HIV epidemics: what are the driving forces? *AIDS* **11** (Suppl. B), S23–S31.

Choi, K., Lew, S., Vittinghoff, E., Catania, J., Barrett, D. & Coates, T. (1996) The efficacy of brief group counseling in HIV-reduction among homosexual Asian and Pacific Islander men. *AIDS* **10**, 81–87.

Choi, K., Yep, G. & Kumekawa, E. (1998) HIV prevention among Asian and Pacific Islander American men who have sex with men: a critical review of theoretical models and directions of future research. *AIDS Education and Prevention* **10** (Suppl. A) (1), 19–30.

Coates, T., Chesney, M., Folkman, S., *et al.* (1996) Designing behavioural and social science to impact practice and policy in HIV prevention and care. *International Journal of STD and AIDS* **7** (Suppl. 2), 2–12.

Cohen, M. (1992) Prevention. In: *AIDS in the World: A Global Report*. (eds J. Mann, D. Tarantola & T. Netter). Harvard College.

Connell, R. (1987) *Gender and Power*. Stanford University Press, Stanford, CA.

DiClemente, R. & Wingood, G. (1995) A randomized controlled trial of an HIV sexual risk-reduction intervention for young African-American women. *JAMA* **274**(16), 1271–1276.

Edem, C. & Harvey, S. (1998) Use of health belief model to predict condom use among university students in Nigeria. In: *Progress in Preventing AIDS? Dogma, Dissent and Innovation. Global Perspectives*. (eds D. Buchanan & G. Cernada). Baywood Publishing, Amityville, NY.

Ford, K., Wirawan, D., Fajans, P., Meliawan, P., MacDonald, K. & Thorpe, L. (1996) Behavioral interventions for reduction of sexually transmitted disease/HIV transmission among female commercial sex workers and clients in Bali, Indonesia. *AIDS* **10**, 213–222.

Ford, K., Wirawan, D. & Fajans, P. (1998) Factors related to condom use among four groups of female sex workers in Bali, Indonesia. *AIDS Education and Prevention* **10**(1), 34–45.

Friedman, S. & O'Reilly, K. (1997) Sociocultural interventions at the community level. *AIDS* **11** (Suppl. A), S201–S208.

Galavotti, C., Gielen, A., Armstrong, K., *et al.* (1998) The effect of a theory-based HIV prevention intervention on condom use with main partners in samples of US women. *12th International Conference on AIDS*, Geneva.

Giddens, A. (1979) *Central Problems in Sociological Theory. Structure and Contradictions in Social Analysis.* Action Press, Macmillan, London.

Gillmore, M., Morrison, D., Richey, C., Balassone, M., Gutierrez L. & Farris, M. (1997) Effects of a skill-based intervention to encourage condom use among high risk heterosexually active adolescents. *AIDS Education and Prevention* **9** (Suppl. A), 22–43.

Howard, M. & McCabe, J. (1990) Helping teenagers postpone sexual involvement. *Family Planning Perspectives* **22**(1), 21–26.

Ickovics, J. & Yoshikawa, H. (1998) Preventive interventions to reduce heterosexual HIV risk for women: current perspectives, future directions. *AIDS* **12** (Suppl. A), S197–S208.

Israel, B., Checkoway, B., Schulz, A. & Zimmerman, M. (1994) Health Education and community empowerment: conceptualizing and measuring perceptions of individual, organizational and community control. *Health Education Quarterly* **21**(2), 149–170.

James, N., Gillies, P. & Bignell, C. (1998) Evaluation of a randomized controlled trial of HIV and sexually transmitted disease prevention in a genitourinary medicine clinic setting. *AIDS* **12**, 1235–1242.

Joseph, J.G., Montgomery, S.B., Emmons, C.A., *et al.* (1987) Magnitude and determinants of behavioral risk reduction: longitudinal analysis of a cohort at risk for AIDS. *Psychology and Health* **1**, 73–96.

Kalichman, S. (1998) *Preventing AIDS: A Sourcebook for Behavioral Interventions.* Lawrence Erlbaum Associates, Mahwah, NJ.

Kalichman, S. & Hospers, H. (1997) Efficacy of behavioral skills enhancement: HIV risk-reduction interventions in community settings. *AIDS* **11** (Suppl. A), S191–S199.

Kegeles, S. & Hart, G. (1998) Recent HIV-prevention interventions for gay men: individual, small-group and community-based studies. *AIDS* **12** (Suppl. A), S209–S215.

Kegeles, S., Hays, R. & Coates, T. (1996) The Mpowerment Project: a community-level HIV prevention intervention for young gay men. *American Journal of Public Health* **86**(8), 1129–1136.

Kelly, J. (1995) *Changing HIV Risk Behavior: Practical Strategies.* Guilford Press, New York.

Kelly, J., Kalichman, S., Kauth, M., *et al.* (1991) Situational factors associated with AIDS risk behavior lapses and coping strategies used by gay men who successfully avoid lapses. *American Journal of Public Health* **81**, 1335–1338.

Kelly, J., Lawrence, J., Stevenson, Y., *et al.* (1992) Community AIDS/HIV risk reduction: the effects of endorsements by popular people in three cities. *American Journal of Public Health* **82**(11), 1483–1489.

Kelly, J., Murphy, D., Sikkema, K., *et al.* (1997) Randomised, controlled, community-level HIV prevention intervention for sexual-risk behaviour among homosexual men in US cities. *Lancet* **350**, 1500–1505.

Laver, S., Van Den Borne, B. & Kok, G. (1988) Using theory to design an intervention for HIV/AIDS prevention for farm workers in rural Zimbabwe. In: *Progress in Preventing AIDS? Dogma, Dissent and Innovation. Global Perspectives.* (eds D. Buchanan & G. Cernada). Baywood Publishing, Amityville, NY.

Moatti, J.P., Beltzer, N. & Dab, W. (1993) Les modèles d'analyse des comportements à risque face à l'infection à VIH. *Population* **5** 1505–1534.

Morris, M. (1997) Sexual networks and HIV. *AIDS*, **11** (Suppl. A), S209–S216.

Parker, R. (1996) Empowerment, community mobilization and social change in the face of HIV/AIDS. *AIDS* **10** (Suppl. 3), S27–S31.

Parker, R.G., Herdt, G. & Carballo, M. (1991) Sexual culture, HIV transmission and AIDS research. *Journal of Sex Research* **28**(1), 77–98.

Peersman, G. & Levy, J. (1998) Focus and effectiveness of HIV prevention efforts for young people. *AIDS* **12** (Suppl. A), S191–S196.

Prochaska, J. & Di Clemente, C. (1992) Stages of change in the modification of problem behaviors. *Progress in Behavior Modification.* (eds M. Hersen, R. Eisler & P. Miller). Sycamore Publishing, Sycamore, IL.

Prochaska, J., Redding, C., Harlow, L., Rossi, J. & Velicer, W. (1994) The transtheoretical model of change in HIV prevention: a review. *Health Education Quarterly* **21**(4), 471–486.

Reitman, D., St. Lawrence, J., Jefferson, K., Alleyne, E.,

Brasfield, T. & Shirley, A. (1996) Predictors of African American Adolescents condom use and HIV risk behavior. *AIDS Education and Prevention* **8**(6), 499–515.

Rose, G. (1992) *The Strategy of Preventive Medicine*. Oxford University Press, New York.

Rosenstock, K. (1974) The Health Belief Model and preventive health behaviour. *Health Education Monograph* **2**, 354–365.

Sepulveda, J., Fineberg, H. & Mann, J. (1992) *AIDS: Prevention Through Education: A World View*. Oxford University Press, New York.

Sweat, M. & Denison, J. (1995) Reducing HIV incidence in developing countries with structural and environmental interventions. *AIDS* **9** (Suppl. A), S251–S257.

Tawil, O., Verster, A. & O'Reilly, K. (1995) Enabling approaches for HIV/AIDS prevention: can we modify the environment and minimize the risk? *AIDS* **9**, 1299–1306.

Ulin, P. (1992) African women and AIDS: negotiating behavioral change. *Social Science Medicine* **34**(1), 63–73.

UNAIDS (1998) *Relationships of HIV and STD Declines in Thailand to Behavioural Change*. UNAIDS 98.2, Best practice material, Geneva.

Van der Straten, A., King, R., Grinstead, O., Vittinghoff, E., Serufilira, A. & Allen, S. (1998) Sexual coercion, physical violence and HIV infection among women in steady relationships in Kigali, Rwanda. *AIDS and Behavior* **2**(1).

Werner, D., Sanders, D., Weston, J., Babb, S. & Rodriguez, B. (1997) *Questioning the Solution: The Politics of Primary Health Care and Child Survival with an Indepth Critique of Oral Rehydration Therapy*. Healthwrights, Palo Alto, CA.

Wingood, G. & DiClemente, R. (1996) HIV sexual risk reduction interventions for women: a review. *American Journal of Preventive Medicine* **12**(3), 209–217.

Chapter 5

Sexualities and Sexual Health/Lessons from History: Emergence of Sexuality as a Sexual Health and Political Issue

Delia E. Easton, Lucia F. O'Sullivan and Richard G. Parker

Introduction

Sexual health can be defined as the capacity to enjoy and control sexual behaviour in line with a personal and social ethic, free from psychological factors that inhibit sexual response and impair sexual relationships, and free from physiological disorders that interfere with sexual function (Mace *et al.* 1974). In general, however, those in the public health and clinical fields have adopted a far more restricted view. Sexual health has been construed primarily as a medical issue with a particular emphasis on functional deficits. In line with this view, the primary driving force behind sexuality research has been a preventive health agenda that views sexuality as a social problem and behavioural risk (di Mauro 1995). Relationality and sociocultural factors are minimised in this conceptualisation, if not overlooked altogether. A growing number of sex researchers are concerned about the dearth of social, cultural, and behavioural research examining the non-dysfunctional aspects of sexual health, including such topics as sexual subjectivity, sex-

ual satisfaction, enhanced interpersonal relations, and adaptive decision-making and coping strategies. But what is left when we eliminate pathology from the study of sexuality? We argue here that the unidimensional focus on biological processes typically adopted by the public health and clinical fields renders sexuality a medical issue or, more to the point, a medical problem, and we suggest that we must reframe our analysis to more adequately account for the social, cultural, political and historical dimensions of human sexual experience.

Historical development

The work of Kinsey and his colleagues is generally considered to be the onset of modern behavioural research in sexuality. Prior to the work of Alfred Kinsey and his colleagues, sexuality research was restricted primarily to case studies and references to historical figures and classical sources (see Bullough 1998; Robinson 1976). It was a field dominated by physicians – one of the few professions whose credibility and qualifications were not seriously challenged by the study of sexual issues. They were concerned with promoting a preventive health agenda aimed explicitly at 'controlling sexuality, particularly masturbation and the spread of disease' (di Mauro 1995).

Popular interest in the early twentieth century followed suit. It turned to sexuality in the form of purity crusades and social hygiene movements and was characterised by zealous reforms to curtail prostitution and to educate the public about the dangers of masturbation and sexually transmitted diseases (Bullough 1998). The preface of the book *Safe Counsel* was 'Fight social diseases with facts, not sentiments; study the problems of venereal (sic) infection for information, not sensation; combat social evils with science, not mystery' (Jefferis & Nichols 1925). This popular book was promoted as a source of information regarding the 'essential facts of sex life in their relationship to human happiness.' These movements grounded associations between sexual health and morality.

Ironically, the purity crusades soon became the basis for scientific research on human sexuality. Recognising the paucity of social and medical information about human sexuality in the United States, the National Research Council formed the Committee for Research in the Problems in Sex with support provided by the Rockefeller Foundation funded Bureau of Social Hygiene (Bullough 1998). The social research of Alfred Kinsey and his colleagues (Kinsey *et al.* 1948, 1953) was originally sponsored by this committee. Kinsey's group conducted over 17 000 individual surveys assessing a wide range of sexual behaviours. Their publications constituted the first widely available detailed source of human sexual data and, in spite of a range of methodological problems, are of considerable scientific value even today.

The published volumes quickly became the subject of much public discourse and debate. Many of the findings from the surveys clashed with normative cultural expectations about 'typical' 'normal' sexual behaviour, forcing a re-examination of public values and attitudes (Udry 1993; Bullough 1998), and exposing the pluralistic ignorance that characterised western societies about issues of sexuality. For instance, Kinsey's findings challenged beliefs about the essential asexuality of women, and the rarity of same-sex sexual experiences and extramarital sexual relations (Bullough 1998). The Kinsey publications forced a demythologisation of sexual behaviour and a social desensitisation to sexual issues. The study of human sexuality essentially 'shifted from the confessional to the research laboratories and clinics' (Bullough 1990, p. 81). Sexuality had become a viable subject of scientific investigation, much to the chagrin and dismay of many. Moreover, the sexuality survey became an important social tool used to quantify disquieting social developments (Clement 1990).

A proliferation of sexuality surveys eventually followed the Kinsey lead, although little funding was provided for research employing national samples or for studies addressing sexual issues directly (di Mauro 1995). The search for universal norms of sexual behaviour was resumed in part by the famous physiological studies of Masters and Johnson in the 1960s. These studies appeared to capture an invariant sequence of physical changes associated with sexual response, largely ignoring the social dimensions of sexual experience (as well as the highly specific social and demographic background of research subjects who were studied) (Tiefer 1996). In the 1960s, the stream of research funding became stronger once again with support for studies assessing premarital sexual behaviour and adolescents, followed by studies assessing fertility issues in the 1970s. The public's interest returned to the study of sexual behaviour in the form of popular surveys sponsored, conducted, and published by women's magazines such as *Cosmopolitan* and *Redbook* (di Mauro 1995). Today, most sexuality research is funded indirectly by survey research on HIV/AIDS or adolescent health. Large-scale research on sexuality outside of the public health context is, for the most part, not supported financially or promoted politically by either the government or private sector, particularly in the United States, where conservative political forces have consistently opposed the allocation of budgetary resources for work related to sexualities.

Social movements and ideologies of sexuality: 1960–1990

Changing perspectives about sexuality in both academic and non-academic circles are invariably linked to broader historical and cultural transformations (Lancaster & di Leonardo 1997; Parker 1999). In the Anglo-European world, beginning in the 1960s, the growing momentum of a series of social movements, spurred in part by changing economics and the growth of technology, generated activism and theoretical discussions about sexuality that have ultimately had a deep and lasting impact on how sexuality is conceptualised in both public and private domains (Lancaster and di Leonardo 1997). In contrast to the wholly biological models of sexuality dominating the first half of the twentieth century, as a result of the sexual revolution, civil and gay rights, and feminist movements of the last three decades, the cultural and political dimensions of sexuality have gradually become more widely and readily acknowledged. The social movements of the 1960s challenged narrow, medical constructions of sexuality, gender, sexual health and sexual abnormality, contending that sexuality can not be understood without 'historical or cultural prejudice' (Tiefer 1996, p. 256).

To begin, feminist theory, based upon cross-cultural anthropological research and Marxist analysis of women's societal roles, challenged traditional ideologies about what constituted women's biological and cultural roles (Vance 1991). Cross-cultural evidence of the diversity of women's roles in different settings refuted beliefs in the inherent correspondence between sexuality and gender roles (see Rubin 1975; 1984). Feminist theory provided the impetus for social constructionist models of sexuality which contend that sexuality is constructed differently according to cultural setting and historical period (Vance 1991). Social constructionist arguments stand in contrast to earlier essentialist models of sexuality premised on the notion of its biological universality. Most importantly the feminist movement sparked new thinking about categories of 'sexuality' and 'gender' by contesting the widely assumed invariable links between female sexuality, traditional gender roles, and reproduction (Vance 1991). Feminist activist groups, for instance, fought to secure the right for the increased accessibility of birth control, and the legality of abortion as a means of increasing women's autonomy. Feminists in academia grappled with the same issue, and in 1984, Gayle Rubin proposed that the idea of sexuality be conceptualised as a concept distinct from gender as part of her larger argument against deeply entrenched western notions of the biological basis and ultimately, reproductive function of female sexuality (Rubin 1984; see also Rubin 1975).

Ironically, while proponents of feminist theory called into question western essentialist models of sexuality, and raised awareness about the male-centred biases in western medical and scientific systems (Jacobus, Keller & Shuttleworth 1990; Vance 1991), reproductive rights advocates campaigning for the legality of abortions and the widespread availability of birth control drew sexuality research and activism further into male dominated medical and legal domains. While the sexual revolution of the 1960s is considered a time of sexual freedom and experimentation for both genders through the lens of popular culture, a retrospective examination of social mores at this time suggests that this revolution was primarily sexually liberating for men (Lancaster & di Leonardo 1997). In contrast, as issues of female reproductive health were seen more frequently as public health considerations, women's sexuality became more legally and medically contested.

By tapping into feminist discourse reconceptualising 'gender' and 'sexuality' as separate categories, and drawing support from sex research that reframed homosexuality as a valid lifestyle rather than a pathological condition, the gay rights movement also began to influence models of sexuality beginning in the 1970s (Lancaster & di Leonardo 1997; Parker

& Aggleton 1999). Manifested through activism, public demonstration and political struggle, the gay rights movement pushed the ideology of feminism further by questioning established notions of 'masculinity' and 'femininity,' broadening the sexual revolution to include same sex couples, and drawing attention to the heterosexist biases of existing medical, scientific and legal discourse and practice. The gay rights movement increased public tolerance for homosexuality and created greater societal awareness about the parameters of what sexual activities, and with which partners, could be considered 'normal' expressions of sexuality. In this way, gay activism helped to invalidate traditional medical and psychological constructs of sexuality, as well as diversify definitions of sexual health.

The political will and mobilisation manifest in the gay rights movement exposed how power differentials between both men and women, and perceived members of the 'dominant' culture and marginalised 'subcultures' are exceptionally significant in the construction and embodiment of sexuality. The politics of sexuality were discussed in both academia – as evidenced by the success and acclaim of Foucault's *The History of Sexuality* (Foucault 1978) – as well as the popular media (see Tiefer 1996; Vance 1991). Academicians addressed the question of the universality of sexual identity as indexed by partner preference and gender, especially in light of a growing body of anthropological work documenting the diversity of expressions of sexuality cross-culturally (see Vance 1991).

The heightened awareness of the heterogeneity of sexuality cross-culturally, and the acknowledgement of the relationship between power and sex, were both ideologies encompassed within the civil rights movement. Ultimately, understanding of the cross-cultural variation of sexuality magnified racial and ethnic stereotypes about sexuality in the US and Europe. To a greater degree than the other social movements preceding it, the civil rights movement illuminated how class differentials influence conceptualisations of sexuality. Considering views of sexuality in the last 30 years, the growing comprehension of power differentials inherent in gender dynamics, class relations and heterosexism, have all contributed to the understanding of sexuality as a cultural construct integrally shaped by larger historical, social, political and economic changes (Lancaster & di Leonardo 1997).

AIDS and medical models of sexuality

Through questioning the legitimacy of previously unchallenged cultural categories such as 'masculinity,' 'femininity,' and 'sexuality,' the theoretical debates arising from the gay rights movement paved the way for the possibility of designing more effective AIDS intervention programmes when the first HIV cases of the early 1980s began to reach epidemic proportions (Carrier 1989; Carrier & Bolton 1991; Daniel & Parker 1993; Parker 1987, 1991, 1994). However, as reflected in both academic and popular writings, the AIDS crisis once again reinvoked and reinforced a biomedical model of sexuality, premised on a presumed universality of sexual norms. Waldby (1996) argues that within the context of AIDS, biomedicine strictly adheres to essentialist models of sexuality as a way of seemingly explaining and containing the virus. For example, the first AIDS epidemiological risk categories put forth

in the US by the Center for Disease Control comprised gay men, IV drug users, haemophiliacs, and Haitians. The early categorisation not only erroneously located the *sources* of risk, but was premised on the idea that the four categories in question were natural, uniform and universally existing groups. In 1992, the CDC's redefined AIDS 'risk groups' as HIV 'risk behaviours' (Mann 1991).

In the past decade, the AIDS crisis has been the impetus behind numerous federally funded medical research projects incorporating aspects of sexuality (Vance 1991). The absorption of sexuality studies under the larger rubric of AIDS research has had both positive and negative consequences for the field. The urgent need to develop effective AIDS interventions, built upon descriptive and diverse data on sexuality and sexual cultures, made obvious glaring gaps in what was known about sexuality, as well as weaknesses in existing models of sex research (Herdt & Boxer 1991; Parker *et al.* 1991; De Zalduondo & Bernard 1995). To a large extent, recognising the paucity of useful information and means of explaining sex behaviour propelled research on a broad range of communities and contexts from anthropological, psychological, and public health perspectives. Beginning in the mid-1980s, there was an impressive increase in research in sexuality cross-culturally, both internationally and domestically. Public health pressure to conduct HIV/AIDS research promoted a political environment supportive of particular types of research on sexual behaviour, and encouraged professional examination of a range of sexuality methods and models (di Mauro 1995). In the US, Great Britain and Australia, for example, social scientists began to study cultures of sexuality in earnest, across a range of variously defined groups and communities, such as drug users, gays and lesbians, heterosexuals, bisexuals, sex workers, Latinos, African Americans, the young and the old (see for example, Day 1988; Alonso & Koreck 1989; Lang 1989; Singer *et al.* 1990; Sufian *et al.* 1990; Carlson & Siegal 1991; Sibthorpe 1992; Dowsett 1996).

Yet in spite of themselves, the majority of sexuality research completed at this time was subsumed under AIDS intervention research and conducted at medical institutions. As such, it adhered to disease prevention agenda, reified traditional medically defined categories of 'normal' versus 'exotic' sexual practices, and was based on medical models (e.g. epidemiological assessment, pharmaceutical development and intervention) of existing knowledge and practice. In light of the biomedical focus of most federally-funded AIDS research projects in the US for example, social scientists became particularly vocal advocates of the need for amassing qualitative, descriptive, and 'experience-near' information about sexuality across cultures and within communities (see Parker *et al.* 1991). Cross-culturally and domestically, anthropologists, in particular, continued to challenge the applicability and meaning of the categories of sexuality, sexual practice and sexual identity that had already been questioned and to some degree, deconstructed as part of the feminist, gay and civil rights movements (Parker 1987, 1989, 1992; Magãna & Carrier 1991; Carrier & Bolton 1991; Farmer & Kim 1991; Bolton 1992a,b; Kane & Mason 1992; Schoepf 1992a,b; Parker *et al.* 1995). For example, ethnographic research showed that in many contexts sexual roles – such as being 'active' or 'passive' – have greater cultural salience than do more west-

ern-defined categories of 'sexual preference' (for example, Alonso & Koreck 1989; Carrier 1989; Parker 1987, 1991). This awareness is clearly crucial to the development of effective AIDS education and intervention programmes.

In addition, the AIDS pandemic has had an indelible impact on how sexuality is perceived and experienced for people worldwide. In the wake of AIDS, sexuality has been associated with immorality, pollution, and most obviously, death (Sontag 1988; Clatts & Mutchler 1989; Douglas 1993). In the west, the fear generated by AIDS initially resulted in a renewed conservatism about sex, inspiring right-wing political groups to intensify calls to return to more traditional values. Indeed, especially in the United States, a highly organised minority with an extreme, conservative social and political agenda continues to effectively thwart efforts to conduct substantive investigations of sexual behaviour and dictate the agenda of primary funding sources. In stark contrast to the values emerging out of the sexual revolution of the 1970s, safer sex campaigns and information about AIDS available in the popular press have to a large extent advocated monogamy and committed sexual relationships as a way of safeguarding against HIV infection. However, the degree to which AIDS education programmes and fear about AIDS have resulted in long-term changes in sexual behaviour remains debatable (Stall & Ekstrand 1990; Dowsett 1993).

Reproductive health and models of sexuality

Attention to the issue of reproductive health

grew out of numerous population and fertility studies of the 1960s and 1970s (di Mauro 1995), the implicit agenda of which was population control. Examining the nature and meaning of sexual behaviour was regarded as irrelevant and, often, controversial. A resurgence of feminist concerns in the 1980s recast previous population control issues as the study of reproductive health, largely driven by reproductive rights movements initially focused exclusively on understanding and promoting women's sexual health. It was at this point, concurrent with the growing abundance of sexuality research conducted in the context of HIV intervention in the 1980s, that researchers in the field of population studies began addressing the paucity of studies devoted exclusively to sexuality and sexual health, specifically exploring the links between how reproductive decisions and behaviours influence the expression of sexuality and sexual health.

By the early 1990s reproductive rights research had grown to encompass male sexuality, and the role of men in sexual and reproductive decision-making, a previously neglected arena of this type of research (Kain 1990; Whitehead 1992; Das 1995; Martin 1995). The new agenda of reproductive health in the 1990s was clarified at the 1994 United Nations International Conference on Population and Development held in Cairo. Here, a formal reproductive health plan integrating several reproductive health topics including sexuality, sexual health, and gender issues, was drawn up for the reproductive programmes of the UN and individual countries for the next 20 years (di Mauro 1995). The formalisation of reproductive health agendas eventually resulted in more money allocated for research on sexuality, considered to be pertinent to reproductive health (di Mauro 1995).

The two separate movements of sexuality research, one encapsulated within AIDS prevention and intervention efforts, and the other inspired through a shifting focus from population control to reproductive rights, clearly share some similar theoretical and practical concerns such as securing funding. Increasingly, these movements have overlapped through the shared agenda of promoting and carrying out more sexuality research (see, for example, Chen *et al.* 1991). Reproductive health research has informed AIDS intervention efforts in various ways. For instance, discussions of gender power differentials brought to the forefront in reproductive health research have underscored the importance of addressing gender power inequities in AIDS intervention designs (Schoepf 1992a, b). The focus brought to gender power differentials was significant since previous attempts to develop effective AIDS programmes were stymied by an inadequate funding to investigate and better understand the full role of gender power relations in women's ability to negotiate sex relations (La Guardia 1991). Further, prior to the AIDS pandemic, the promotion of condoms around the world as a birth control method had previously raised the issue of cross-cultural differences in the acceptability of using condoms for family planning as well as concerns regarding the ethics of population control (Hunter & Mati 1991). Interest in North American women's reproductive health eventually led to greater amounts of research money set aside for women's AIDS and sexuality research (La Guardia 1991), a trend that has increasingly spread worldwide.

A problematic outcome of the overlap between AIDS and reproductive health studies in AIDS research has been the further resurgence of essentialist models of sexuality utilised in much reproductive health literature. Reproductive health initiatives, while theoretically aimed at fostering women's health and sexual autonomy, sometimes have the adverse effect of casting sexuality as a purely biological and medical phenomenon, in the process often restoring traditional and conservative values about sex (di Mauro 1995). At present, this can be evidenced most vividly in federally-funded 'revirginisation' and 'abstinence' programmes in US school systems. In much the same way that AIDS has heightened societal concern with sexual purity and cleanliness (Douglas 1992), the success of these programmes is based on notions of sexual purity and chastity.

More recently, cross-cultural and cross-national sexuality and reproductive health research have emphasised the inadequacy of the study and application of reproductive health outside of an historical, political and cultural context (Ginsburg & Rapp 1995). *Reproductive health* has been defined by the World Health Organization as having four essential features. The first is the ability to regulate reproduction; the second is the right for women to have safe pregnancies and childbirth experiences; the third is the right to have 'successful' pregnancies in terms of both maternal and infant survival; and the fourth is the choice of having sexual relationships free of concern about both disease and unwanted pregnancy (La Guardia 1991). Absent from the WHO definition of reproductive health, however, is an acknowledgement of the daily experiences – shaped by history, politics, community and cultural values – of most women's lives. The

focus instead, apart from the fourth point, is primarily on women as reproductive vehicles (Martin 1987), an ideology emphasised in traditional biomedical conceptualisations of sexuality and intertwined with the concerns of capitalist enterprise (Treichler 1990). Further, in some cultures it remains difficult for women to manage safe, full-term pregnancies or to negotiate disease-free sexual relationships, for example.

So, in light of global world politics and economics, the WHO definition is meaningless without recognition of cross-cultural variation in the values and practices concerning sexuality, pregnancy and childbirth, as well as a perspective incorporating a broader view of sexuality. In the late 1990s, work on reproductive health has started to explore the dynamic between transnational and global processes influencing reproductive technology and knowledge and 'local' interpretations and experiences of reproductive health. Morsy (1995), for example, describes how the neglect of women's health in Egyptian state and government health politics is obscured through cultural values that blame women themselves for poor reproductive health and maternal mortality. Globalisation is likely to continue to expand the conceptualisations of what constitutes reproductive health.

Implications for public health management

Policies to improve sexual health currently involve the design, development, and implementation of public health programmes aimed at treating sexual problems or the negative consequences of sexual behaviour, such as sexually transmitted diseases and infertility. As previously discussed, sexuality research has historically been plagued with chronic problems accessing resources, and so is typically incorporated into research projects addressing HIV/AIDS or adolescent health issues and placed within a public health context.

The topics investigated by researchers interested in human sexuality are also restricted by political vehicles, such as funding agencies and academic tenure systems. In the US for example, the two primary federal funding agencies for sexuality research are the Centers for Disease Control (CDC) and the National Institutes of Health (NIH). Thus federally funded sexuality research occurs within a public health context and continues to reflect the prevailing political climate – one that only favours problem-based, medical models of sexual behaviour.

Prior to HIV/AIDS, the CDC was a strong supporter of community and behavioural interventions during the 1970s and 1980s, and even of national surveys of adolescent sexual behaviour (at least those that addressed reproductive behaviour) (Kantner & Zelnik 1972). In contrast, after AIDS was categorised as a health crisis in the 1980s, the objectives of the sexuality research funded by the CDC focused on identifying the aetiological agent of HIV by means of epidemiological studies in order to inform the public about the routes of HIV infection (Darrow 1996). Once a serological test identifying HIV infection was developed in 1985, counselling and testing became the primary behavioural intervention promoted by the CDC. The fact that the CDC budget through the early 1990s allocated no resources whatsoever for social and behavioural interventions, effectively eliminating almost all

sexuality investigations that fell outside the relatively narrow confines of epidemiological research, once again attests to the continued dominance of biomedical models of sexuality and AIDS prevention.

Despite the political weight provided by federal funds, the allocations of which may be the most reliable index of the political, moral, or social value of a research area, sexuality researchers continue to face considerable political barriers in their practice of what is still perceived as a controversial field. In the United States, efforts to conduct large-scale, nationally representative surveys using public funds have been effectively halted in their tracks to the extent they address sexual issues outside of an explicit public health context (Laumann *et al.* 1994). The most famous example of such interference involved the Secretary of Health and Human Services and the Congress of the United States which stalled an $18 million research project on adolescent sexual behaviour that had been peer-reviewed and approved for funding by the NIH. The politics blocking this survey made the front-page headlines on all major newspapers in the US because of concerns that exposing adolescents to the sexual items of the survey would promote 'sexual licence,' most notably homosexual behaviour, rather than curtail rates of HIV infection amongst adolescents (Udry 1993). This survey was finally funded and conducted after deletion of almost all of the sexual items.

Other studies of human sexuality have been funded by private foundations or university budgets which typically limit the scope and ultimately compromise the quality of the projects conducted (Darrow 1996). Again, these researchers typically restrict their foci to sexual topics addressing public health issues because it is not considered professionally legitimate to contribute to the existing knowledge of normal sexual diversity in the social science disciplines (di Mauro 1995). Those who address broader sexual issues in their research often do so in unfriendly territory, being challenged for taking on such sensitive topics (Sonenschein 1987; Urdy 1993). They are unlikely to assume a primary professional identity of sexual researcher, hence reducing the extent to which this research community has voice (O'Sullivan *et al.* 1998). The primary outcome of imbedding sexuality research in a public health context is that most research essentially addresses risk behaviour. Sexuality researchers are most likely to acquire funding for public health projects that address the severe negative sequelae of sexual behaviour that comprise problems of public health (Frank 1994). These include unwanted pregnancy (particularly for adolescents), sexually transmitted disease, sexual coercion, and infertility. There appears to be little support for projects that do not correspond to the medical model of sexuality, such as preventive or proactive measures that advance sexual agency, healthful decision-making, problem-solving, choice, variety, or tolerance.

Following the focus on sexuality in the wake of the AIDS epidemic and the reproductive health movements, the dearth of research on the wide range of sexual behaviours and experiences has become more apparent. The behaviour of the general population continues to be characterised by extrapolating from dated sources of information, such as the Kinsey interviews. In addition, most research has used individuals or groups labelled as deviant, victimised, dysfunctional, abnormal, or problematic (di Mauro 1995). Baseline data

are simply not available for comparison purposes, or for providing a context within which to interpret findings or understanding the medical, clinical, social, or political implications. Because 'sex-positive' researchers are unable to contribute to sexual science, then the content of what is known about human sexuality continues to be generated by those who regard sex as problematic and normal sexual diversity as deviant (O'Sullivan *et al.* 1998).

In the US, the spiralling rates of sexually transmitted diseases, increased rates of infertility, and continued high rates of adolescent pregnancy indicate that the general public experiences poor sexual health. These trends also indicate that current pathology-based efforts to promote sexual health are failing, especially to the extent that they continue to disregard the sociocultural context of poverty (d'Ardenne 1998). In contrast, North European countries that emphasise vitality rather than pathology in their public health approaches experience comparably low levels of these negative consequences of sexual behaviour (Warren 1992), underscoring the importance of accentuating well-being in campaigns to promote sexual health.

Society is becoming increasingly dependent on sexuality professionals in all fields to provide information about such issues as sexuality education, homosexuality in the military, fertility, and the like (Moglia 1994). Restricting sexual investigations to the arena of public health limits the extent to which sexuality researchers are able to make meaningful contributions to the field. Yet within the realm of public health, there is potential for change in how sexuality is viewed and how sexuality research is conducted. Reference to what is known about human sexuality cross-culturally is the most useful means of providing credible information to the field in a sex-negative culture such as that in the US. Cross-cultural data provides a means of confronting questionable political agendas given that the US privileges scientific knowledge above all other types of wisdom (O'Sullivan *et al.* 1998). Also, given the recent overall shift in public health towards a focus on well-being rather than disease, sexuality may increasingly be framed as integral to physical and psychological health.

Implications for clinical care

Despite being challenged by the social movements of the 1960s and 1970s, essentialist and medicalised definitions of sexual health are perhaps even more apparent in the clinical fields than ever before. Sexuality is still best understood in terms of the myriad of disorders that may be diagnosed or treated. There is a pervasive reference to 'normal' sexual response although clearly little consensus on what such response entails. Those deviating from these standards are considered dysfunctional, or at times, perverse, often in terms expanding far beyond one's sexuality. Indeed, the diagnosis and treatment of sexual dysfunctions as medical and psychiatric disorders has a long history in western societies (Frank 1994).

Although little is known about what constitutes 'normal' sexual response, clinicians have rarely hesitated to liberally apply diagnoses asunder of 'abnormal' sexual response. The terminology employed by clinicians most clearly reflects the sociocultural values and biases steering our modern conceptualisation of sex-

ual health. For instance, alternative terms to 'impotence,' a medical term favoured by urologists which suggests more than the vasocongestive processes involved, have been 'erectile failure' and 'erectile dysfunction'. Relatively few clinicians have replaced the use of the term 'premature ejaculation' with the more physiologically correct 'rapid ejaculation'. The distress experienced by 'patients' also reflects such sociocultural biases in those cases where they cling rigidly to performance-based expectations.

Health care providers are the source of sexual information for the majority of people in western societies, as well as in many developing countries, yet relatively few receive adequate training in sexuality, in counselling others about sexual issues. One review indicated that most of the human sexuality course work offered to health care providers is mandatory and varies considerably in content and quality (Weerakoon & Stiernborg 1996). Moreover, this review indicates that the acquisition of accurate sexual knowledge is given less priority than addressing clinicians' attitudes about treating sexual problems and most information is presented in lecture formats rather than skills-based formats. To compound this problem of inadequate training, health care providers typically receive their sexuality education from educators not formally schooled in human sexuality or education methodology.

Clinics often justify medicalising sexual health in order to attract women and offer counselling and other adjunct services. Before being able to obtain a method of birth control, women have to comply with demands to take a Pap test, and breast and pelvic examinations to check for sexually transmitted diseases and cervical, ovarian, and breast cancers. Men, at risk for prostate cancer, are not encouraged to the same extent or in the same way to submit their bodies to such examinations under the pretext of ensuring sexual health. Women's experiences of objectification in the medical process and the pathologising of normal female functions, such as menstruation, pregnancy, childbirth, breast-feeding, and menopause, have been well documented (Martin 1987; Daniluk 1993).

Following the increasing focus on men's role in reproductive health, men are also being subjected to the medicalisation of their sexual health. There have been revolutionary developments in the field of sexual pharmacology and physical treatment for sexual dysfunctions (arousal, orgasmic, and libidinal), such as intracavernosal injections of vasoactive drugs and orally active medication for treatment of erectile dysfunction (Hirst *et al.* 1996; Guirguis 1998). Comparable pharmacological agents for women are currently in the pipeline (Tiefer 1996). These interventions constitute easy, practical solutions without having to contend with difficult relational or sociocultural issues.

The significance of these pharmaceutical developments can not be understated. Treatment of sexual disorders as sexual health issues is now rapidly shifting from the hand of mental health professionals to medical professionals. The pharmaceutical industry is now also determining research agendas at a time when there has been considerable deregulation of the pharmaceutical industry, thus accelerating the pace of new developments. The focus has shifted full-force from therapy to medical interventions. These interventions are not available for some groups in society, espe-cially the poor, yet traditional sources of aid are becoming more difficult to obtain.

In conclusion, the study of human sexual behaviour reflects the need to adopt a broad perspective to understanding the diversity of sexualities, and the manifestations of sexuality cross-culturally. Although much has been learned about sexuality in the wake of the social movements of the 1960s, the AIDS epidemic, and the reproductive rights movement, there is obviously still much that can be learned. Perhaps more importantly, sexuality research, and the field of sexology, warrants the same respect as other social sciences. Further, essentialist and medical models will increasingly prove to be barriers to fully understanding the plurality of sexualities cross-culturally in a world now characterised by a global flow of ideas, values, and products.

References

Alonso, A.M. & Koreck, M.T. (1989) Hispanics: AIDS and sexual practices. *Differences: A Journal of Feminist Cultural Studies* 1(1), 101–124.

Brandt, A. (1986) AIDS: from social history to social policy. *Law, Medicine and Health Care* 14(5–6), 231–243.

Bolton, R. (1992a) AIDS and promiscuity: muddles in the models of HIV prevention. *Medical Anthropology* 14, 145–223.

Bolton, R. (1992b) Mapping terra incognita: sex research for AIDS prevention – an urgent agenda for the 1990s. In: *The Time of AIDS: Social Analysis, Theory and Method.* pp. 124–158.

Bullough, V. (1998) Alfred Kinsey and the Kinsey Report: historical overview and lasting contributions. *Journal of Sex Research* 35, 127–131.

Carlson, R. & Siegal, H. (1991) The crack life: an ethnographic overview of crack use and sexual behaviour among African Americans in a midwest metropolitan city. *Journal of Psychoactive Drugs* **23**(1), Jan–Mar.

Carrier, J. (1989) Sexual behaviour and the role of AIDS in Mexico. In: *The AIDS Pandemic: A Global Emergency* (ed. R. Bolton), pp. 37–50. Gordon & Breach, New York.

Carrier, J. & Bolton, R. (1991) Anthropological perspectives on sexuality and HIV prevention. *Annual Review of Sex Research* **2**, 49–75.

Catalan, J. (1996) Sex in the time of AIDS. *Sexual and Marital Therapy* **11**, 15–18.

Chen, L.C., Amor, S. & Sheldon, S. (eds) (1991) *AIDS and Women's Reproductive Health.*

Clatts, M. & Mutchle, K. (1989) AIDS and the dangerous other: metaphors of sex and deviance in the representation of diseases. In: *The AIDS Pandemic: A Global Emergency* (ed. R. Bolton), pp. 13–22. Gordon & Breach, New York.

Clement, U. (1990) Surveys of heterosexual behaviour. *Annual Review of Sex Research* **1**, 45–74.

Daniel, H. & Parker, R. (1993) *Sexuality, Politics and AIDS in Brazil.* The Falmer Press, London.

Daniluk, J.C. (1993) The meaning and experience of female sexuality. *Psychology of Women Quarterly* **17**, 53–69.

Darrow, W.W. (1996) Evaluating behavioural interventions for HIV prevention. *AIDS* **10**, 346–348.

Das, V. (1995) A national honor and practical kinship: unwanted women and children. In: *Conceiving the New World Order: The Global Politics of Reproduction.* (eds F. Ginsberg & R. Rapp) pp. 212–233. University of California Press, Berkeley, CA.

Day, S. (1988) Prostitutes, women and AIDS: anthropology. *AIDS* **2**(6), 421–428.

d'Ardenne, P. (1998) Medical solutions for sexual dilemmas. *Sexual and Marital Therapy* **13**, 125–127.

de Zalduondo, B. & Bernard, J. (1995) Meanings and consequences of sexual–economic exchange: gender, poverty and sexual risk behaviour in urban Haiti. In: *Conceiving Sexuality: Approaches to Sex Research in a Postmodern World.* (eds R.G. Parker & J.H. Gagnon), pp. 157–180. Routledge, London and New York.

di Mauro, D. (1995) *Sexuality Research in the United States: An Assessment of the Social and Behavioural Sciences.* The Sexuality Research Assessment Project, The Social Science Research Council.

Douglas, M. (1993) *Risk and Blame: Essays in Cultural Theory.* Routledge, New York.

Dowsett, G. (1996) *Practicing Desire: Homosexual Sex in the Era of AIDS.* Stanford University Press, Stanford.

Farmer, P. & Kim, J. (1991) Anthropology, accountability and the prevention of AIDS. In: *Anthropology, Sexuality and AIDS* (eds G. Herdt, W. Leap & M. Sovine). *Journal of Sex Research* **28**(2), 203–222.

Frank, O. (1994). International research on sexual behaviour and reproductive health: A brief review with reference to methodology. *Annual Review of Sex Research* **5**, 1–49.

Foucault, M. (1978) *History of Sexuality.* Pantheon, New York.

Ginsburg, F. &. Rapp, R. (eds) (1995) *Conceiving the New World Order: The Global Politics of Reproduction.* University of California Press, Berkeley.

Guirguis, W.R. (1998) The future of sex therapy in the era of oral treatment. *Sexual and Marital Therapy* **13**, 129–130.

Handwerker, W.P. (1990) Politics and reproduction: a window on social change. In: *Births and Power: Social Change and the Politics of Reproduction*, pp. 1–39. Westview Press, Boulder.

Herdt, G. & A.M. Boxer (1991) Ethnographic issues in the study on AIDS. *Journal of Sex Research* **28**(2), 171–187.

Hirst, J.R., Baggaley, M.R. & Watson, J.P. (1996) A four-year survey of an inner-city psychosexual problems clinic. *Sexual and Marital Therapy* **11**, 19–36.

Hunter, D. & Mati, J. (1991) Contraception, family, and HIV. In: *AIDS and Women's Reproductive Health* (eds L. Chen, J.S. Amor & S. Segal), pp. 93–125. Plenum Press, New York.

Jacobus, M., Fox Keller, E., & Shuttleworth, S. (1990) Introduction. In: *Body Politics: Women and the Discourses of Science.* (eds M. Jacobus, E. Fox Keller & S. Shuttleworth), pp. 1–10. Routledge, New York.

Jefferis, B.G. & Nichols, J.L. (1925) *Safe Counsel or Practical Eugenics.* J.L. Nichols, Illinois.

Jemmot, J.B., Jemmot, L.S. & Fong, G. (1992) Reduction in HIV risk assessment behaviour among black male adolescents: effects of an AIDS prevention intervention. *American Journal of Public Health* **82**, 372–377.

Kain, E.L. (1990) *The Myth of Family Decline: Understanding Families in a World of Rapid Social Change.*

D.C. Health, Lexington, MA.

Kane, S. & Mason, T. (1992) 'IV drug users' and 'sex partners': the limits of epidemiological categories and the ethnography of risk. In: *The Time of AIDS: Social Analysis, Theory and Method* (eds G. Herdt & S. Lindenbaum), pp. 199–224. Sage Publications, Newbury Park.

Kantner, J.F. & Zelnik, M. (1972) Sexual experience of young unmarried women in the United States. *Family Planning Perspectives* **4**, 9–18.

Keeling, R. (1997) The ecology of sexual science: context and challenge. *Journal of Sex Research* **34**, 115–118.

Kinsey, A., Pomeroy, W. & Martin, C. (1948) *Sexual Behaviour in the Human Male.* Saunders, Philadelphia.

Kinsey, A., Pomeroy, W., Martin, C. & Gebhard, P. (1953) *Sexual Behaviour in the Human Female.* Saunders, Philadelphia.

LaGuardia, K. (1991) AIDS and reproductive health: women's perspectives. In: *AIDS and Women's Reproductive Health* (eds L. Chen, J.S. Amor & S.J. Segal), pp. 17–26. Plenum Press, New York..

Lancaster, R. (1995) 'That we should all turn queer?': homosexual stigma in the making of manhood and the breaking of a revolution in Nicaragua. In: *Conceiving Sexuality: Approaches to Sex Research in a Postmodern World* (eds R.G. Parker & J.H. Gagnon), pp. 135–156. Routledge, New York and London.

Lancaster, R.N. & di Leonardo, M. (eds) (1997) *The Gender/Sexuality Reader: Culture, History, Political Economy.* Routledge, New York and London.

Lang, N. (1989) AIDS, gays and the ballot: the politics of disease in Houston, Texas. *Medical Anthropology* **10**, 203–209.

Laumann, E.O., Michael, R.T. & Gagnon, J.H. (1994) A political history of the national sex survey of adults. *Family Planning Perspectives* **26**, 34–38.

Mace, D.R., Bannerman, R.H.O. & Burton, J. (1974) The teaching of human sexuality in schools for health professionals. *Public Health Papers* **57**. World Health Organization, Geneva.

Magãna, J.R. & Carrier, J. (1991) Mexican and Mexican American sexual behaviour and spread of AIDS in California. *Journal of Sex Research* **28**(3), 425–441.

Mann, J. (1991) AIDS; challenges to epidemiology in the 1990s. In: *AIDS and Women's Reproductive Health* (eds L. Chen, J.S. Amor & S.J. Segal), pp. 11–16. Ple-

num Press, New York.

Martin, E. (1987) *The Woman in the Body: A Cultural Analysis of Reproduction.* Beacon Press, Boston.

Martin, E. (1995) From reproduction to HIV: blurring categories, shifting positions. In: *Conceiving the New World Order: The Global Politics of Reproduction* (eds F. Ginsberg & R. Rapp), pp. 256–269. University of California Press, Berkeley.

Moglia, R. (1994) Sexuality education in higher education in the USA: analysis and implications. *Sexual and Marital Therapy* **9**, 181–191.

Morsy, S. (1995) Deadly reproduction among Egyptian women: maternal mortality and the medicalization of population control. In: *Conceiving the New World Order: The Global Politics of Reproduction* (eds F. Ginsberg & R. Rapp), pp. 162–176. University of California Press, Berkeley, CA.

O'Sullivan, L., Byers E. & McCormick, N. (1998) Notes from the field: research training for the sexuality professional. *Journal of Sex Education and Therapy* **23**, 20–25.

Oakley, A. & Darrow, W.W. (1998). Social, cultural, and political aspects. *AIDS* **12** (Suppl. A), S189–S190.

Parker, R. (1987) Acquired immunodeficiency syndrome in urban Brazil. *Medical Anthropology Quarterly* (New Series) **1**(2), 155–175.

Parker, R. (1989) Youth, identity, and homosexuality: the changing shape of sexual life in Brazil. *Journal of Homosexuality* **17**(3/4), 267–287.

Parker, R. (1991) *Bodies, Pleasures and Passions: Sexual Culture in Contemporary Brazil.* Beacon Press, Boston.

Parker, R. (1994) Sexual cultures, HIV transmission, and AIDS prevention. *AIDS* **8** (Suppl.), S309-S314.

Parker, R. (1989) *Beneath the Equator: Cultures of Desire, Male Homosexuality, and Emerging Gay Communities in Brazil.* Routledge, New York and London.

Parker, R. & Carballo, M. (1991) Human sexuality and AIDS: the case of male bisexuality. In: *AIDS and Women's Reproductive Health* (eds L. Chen, J.S. Amor & S. Segal), pp. 109–119. Plenum Press, New York.

Parker, R, Herdt, G. & Carballo, M. (1991) Sexual culture, HIV transmission and AIDS research. *Journal of Sex Research* **28**(1): 77–98.

Parker, R, Quemmel, R., Guimares, K., Mota, M. & Terto, V. (1995) AIDS prevention and gay community mobilization in Brazil. *Development* **2**, 49–53.

Rubin, G. (1975) The traffic in women: notes on the 'political economy of sex'. In: *Toward an Anthropology of Women* (ed. R. Reiter), pp. 157–210. Monthly Review Press, New York.

Rubin, G. (1984) Thinking sex: notes for a radical theory of the politics of sexuality. In: *Pleasure and Danger: Exploring Female Sexuality* (ed. C.S. Vance), pp. 267–319. Routledge & Kegan Paul, London.

Schoepf, B. (1992a) AIDS, sex and condoms: African healers and the reinvention of tradition in Zaire. *Medical Anthropology* **14**, 225–242.

Schoepf, B. (1992b) Women at risk: case studies from Zaire. In: *The Time of AIDS: Social Analysis, Theory and Methods.* (eds G. Herdt & S. Lindenbaum), pp. 259–286. Sage Publications, Newbury Park.

Shilts, R. (1987) *And the Band Played on: Politics, People, and the AIDS Epidemic.* Penguin Books, London.

Sibthorpe, B. (1992) The social construction of sexual relationships as a determinant of HIV risk perceptions and condom use among IVDUs. *Medical Anthropology Quarterly* **6**(3), 255–270.

Singer, M., Castillo Z., Davison, L., Burke, G., Scanlon, K. & Rivera, M. (1990) SIDA: the economic, social and cultural context of AIDS among Latinos. *Medical Anthropology Quarterly* **4**(1), 72–114.

Sonenschein, D. (1987) On having one's research seized. *Journal of Sex Research* **23**, 408–414.

Sontag, S. (1988) *AIDS and its Metaphors.* Farrar, Straus & Girroux, New York.

Sufian, M., Friedson, S.R., Neaigus, A., Stephenson, B., Rivera-Beckman, J. & Des Jarlais, D. (1990) Impact of AIDS on Puerto Rican intravenous drug users. *Hispanic Journal of Behavioural Sciences* **12**(2), 122–134.

Stall, R. & Ekstrand, M. (1990) Relapse from safe sex: The AIDS Behavioural Research Project. In: *Current Directions in Anthropological Research on AIDS* (ed. D. Feldman). Special Publication No. 1, pp. 10–12. AIDS and Anthropology Research Group, Miami, FL.

Tiefer, L. (1996) *Annual Review of Sex Research.*

Treichler, P. (1990) Feminism, medicine and the meaning of childbirth. In: *Body/Politics: Women and the Discourses of Science* (eds M. Jacobus, E.F. Keller & S. Shuttleworth), pp. 113–138. Routledge, New York.

Udry, J.R. (1993) The politics of sex research. *Journal of Sex Research* **30**, 103–110.

Vance, C.S. (1991) Anthropology rediscovers sexuality: a theoretical comment. *Sociological and Scientific Medicine* **33**(8), 875–884.

Waldby, C. (1996) *AIDS and the Body Politic: Biomedicine and Sexual Difference.* Routledge, New York.

Warren, C. (1992) Perspectives on international practices and American family sex communication relevant to teenage sexual behaviour in the United States. *Health Communication* **4**, 121–136.

Weerakoon, P. & Stiernborg, M. (1996) Sexuality education for health care professionals: a critical review of the literature. *Annual Review of Sex Research* **7**, 181–217.

Whitehead, T.L. & Reid, B.V. (eds) (1992) *Gender Constructs and Social Issues.* University of Illinois Press, Urbana, IL.

Chapter 6

STD Control and the Psychology of Sexual Health in Developing Countries

John Richens

Historical background and early attempts at control

The recognition of sexually transmitted diseases in developing countries goes back many centuries and accounts of common symptoms such as genital ulcer and genital discharge have been identified in ancient texts from countries such as India and China. The recognition of sexually transmitted diseases familiar to Europeans as well as the identification of exotic STDs followed soon after the earliest contacts by European explorers. For example, Captain Cook despite his best efforts was unable to prevent major outbreaks of venereal disease amongst his sailors during his Pacific voyages. The term tropical or climatic bubo was given to the STD now known as lymphogranuloma venereum when epidemics occurred amongst ships' crews visiting prostitutes in the Zanzibar area.

As colonisation proceeded STDs rapidly assumed public health importance, particularly for European doctors charged with medical care of soldiers, sailors and indigenous labour

forces. Early efforts to respond to these infections often focused, as they did in Europe, on the prostitutes. In many places, for instance British and French colonies, more pragmatic campaigners preferred a harm reduction strategy, accepting the impossibility of suppressing prostitution, insisting on the need for young single men to have sexual outlets and proposing regulation and periodic medical examination of prostitutes in order to reduce the spread of infection and the use of 'Lock' hospitals to isolate women found to be infected until recovery. The legacy of this approach is still to be found in countries such as Senegal where licensing of prostitutes is still maintained and the Indonesian system of official brothels where prostitutes are often given monthly injections of penicillin. The success of the famous 100% condom policy in Thailand (Celentano *et al.* 1998) has been in a large measure due to the existence of institutionalised prostitution under a substantial degree of police and government control. The alternative approach to prostitution adopted in many other countries, or, in some cases, alongside some degree of regulated prostitution, was to introduce repressive legislation in the hope of eradicating prostitution. This is seen in its most widespread form in China where large numbers of women have ended up interned in 're-education' camps. In many countries such as India laws against prostitution have resulted in widespread harassment of prostitutes and their families, physical and sexual abuse whilst in custody, extortion by police, and enforced HIV testing (Government of India 1996). There is increasing recognition that repressive approaches are counter-productive for public health as well as infringing human rights.

Box 6.1 describes a particularly interesting example of an STD epidemic precipitated by the clash of Western and tribal culture and brought under control only by sacrificing the unique way of life of one of the most colourful tribes of New Guinea.

Box 6.1 Donovanosis among the Marind-anim in Dutch New Guinea

The Marind-anim were a tribe inhabiting the South-West coast of New Guinea when the Dutch colonised the area in the late 19th century. In 1902, in response to complaints from the Australian administration about incursions into their territory by headhunting raids of the Marind-anim, a government station was built at Merauke with the aid of Australian aboriginal labour. It appears that the aboriginals introduced the tropical STD, donovanosis, into the Marind-anim population and within a short time large numbers of infected tribesmen were noticed by local Dutch missionaries. In common with many tribes in this part of New Guinea, the Marind-anim practised ritual forms of homosexual

and heterosexual group sex. Not understanding the nature of the epidemic that had hit them, their sexual rituals may in fact have intensified in the hope of staving off the epidemic. Instead, the epidemic spread rapidly, affecting 30% or more of the population in some areas. Goaded by local missionaries, the government eventually responded by sending in a husband and wife team of two German doctors who conducted annual clinical surveys of the population, detaining all infected persons in bush hospitals for a month or more of treatment with intravenous tartar emetic which was administered by local Javan bird-of-paradise hunters whose level of education was deemed sufficient for them to be trained as nurses. Alongside the case finding and treatment, legislation was enacted which banned all ritual activity among the Marind-anim and the population was re-settled in new model villages which replaced the traditional system of sexual segregation with family huts. Infected persons were barred from the new villages until they died or were cured and eventually the old villages were destroyed. The epidemic was brought fairly rapidly under control with these vigorous measures at the expense of the local culture which was virtually wiped out. This story serves as a fascinating illustration of the impact of beliefs and behaviour on a sexually transmitted disease, as well as demonstrating the type of response that was considered appropriate by the local colonial power.

Source: Vogel & Richens (1989).

Factors associated with the spread of STDs in developing countries

The incidence and prevalence of STDs in developing countries are typically many times higher than those seen in wealthier nations. Some of the reasons for this are intuitively obvious such as restricted access to good quality health care, but there are a host of less obvious factors that deserve attention. The most fundamental of these is perhaps the marked demographic differences between developed and developing nations. The ageing populations of wealthier countries contrast markedly with those of developing countries where a far higher proportion of the population (typically about 40%) is made up of young, sexually active individuals.

The spread of STDs is determined by the duration of infectiousness, the rate of partner change and the efficiency of transmission per exposure. Each of these factors is in turn influenced by a wide array of socioeconomic, political, geographic, technological and behavioural factors which are discussed below.

Factors promoting high rates of sexual partner exchange

Large-scale surveys of sexual behaviour comparable with the major surveys from France, the UK and USA published in the early 1990s have not been conducted in the developing world. In 1995 Carael et al. published results from cross-sectional household surveys, using face-to-face interviewing in 18 developing countries mainly in Africa and Asia (Carael et al. 1995). Sample sizes varied from 1300 to 6995 and interviewees were aged 15–49. The data was collected between 1989 and 1993. Condom use was very low in most study sites. Men reporting sexual contact outside regular partnerships ranged from 4–47% and those reporting contacts with sex workers ranged from 1–25%. Women were much less likely to report non-marital sex than men. These findings reflect the traditional dominant role of males in sexual relations which renders women powerless to protect themselves, even when they recognise that the behaviour of their male partners is putting them at risk. Polygamy remains important in some more traditional societies and was an identified risk factor for HIV in at least one African study (Carael et al. 1988). The frequency of pre-marital and extra-marital sexual activity is closely linked with factors such as urban migration in search of work, delayed age of marriage, and relaxation of strict religious and moral codes following in the wake of economic development. The long periods of sexual abstinence traditionally required following childbirth in some cultures have been cited as another factor that promotes extramarital sexual activity. The potential influence of ritual sexual behaviour on the transmission of HIV is well illustrated in the case study from Rwanda (Box 6.2).

The large colonies of young, single, male migrant workers to be found in many developing countries provide fertile ground for the growth of prostitution and epidemic spread of STDs. Another key influence on rates of partner change is the low status of women and the poor educational opportunities they are afforded which leaves them ill-equipped for economic survival outside of marriage and means many young single women cannot survive without the exchange of sex for economic necessities.

Box 6.2 Traditional mourning customs in rural Rwanda

In 1994 Bulterys *et al.* described the 'ubwera' purification rite that is performed in Rwanda following a death and can involve sexual intercourse of the widow or widower with a partner (umweza) who takes on the contamination of death to allow the family to resume normal life. Among 19 widowed males, 10 reported unprotected sex with a young unmarried umweza who was given payment. Among 30 women sex with an umweza was reported by only eight, a figure influenced partly by a counselling programme for women. Condom use was reported in 1/26 cases recorded. The authors of this report suggest that actual sexual intercourse is replaced by a symbolic act as is also practised when the surviving spouse is already ill.

Source: Bulterys, M., Musanganire, F., Chao, A., *et al.* (1994) Traditional mourning customs and the spread of HIV-1 in rural Rwanda: a target for AIDS prevention. *AIDS* **8**, 858–859.

Factors tending to prolong the duration of STDs

The duration of STD infections depends on the recognition of symptoms, the motivation to seek treatment or screening and the availability of curative treatment. Continued sexual activity is most likely to occur when infection is asymptomatic. The discovery by the individual of asymptomatic infection is very much dependent on an awareness of STDs and availability of relatively sophisticated medical facilities which have the capacity to screen for asymptomatic infection through laboratory testing. While STD clinics in richer coun-

tries spend an increasing amount of their time screening those who have no symptoms but who are concerned that they may have contracted an infection, this type of activity is seldom seen in poorer countries, leading to much lower rates of STD case-finding among asymptomatic persons. When it comes to those with symptoms, the motivation to seek treatment depends on knowledge and beliefs about the nature of STD symptoms and their importance or significance, as well as views about suitable sources of care and the availability of health care. One of the effects of the HIV pandemic in developing countries has been a growing realisation that successful prevention programmes call for a much greater understanding of what people believe about the origins of STDs, about transmission and prevention and what they believe more generally about health and sickness. There is a small body of ethnographic and anthropological literature that deals with local beliefs about STDs but the picture we have remains scanty and incomplete in many areas.

Table 6.1 lists incorrect beliefs about HIV and STDs described in papers by Nicoll *et al.* (1993) and Field *et al.* (1998). Nicoll *et al.* have commented on how beliefs about AIDS in East Africa among members of the general public, among health workers and policy makers were often incorrect, undermined control efforts and were 'powerful, persistent, and resistant to conventional educational methods' (Nicoll *et al.* 1993).

Continuing sexual activity in the presence of STD symptoms has often been reported from several developing countries and is influenced by factors such as correct identification of symptoms as STD-related, access to health care, whether income is derived wholly

Table 6.1   Examples of incorrect beliefs about HIV, STDs and condoms.

Transmission	• Mosquitoes and bed bugs transmit HIV • HIV can be transmitted by casual contact • You cannot get HIV from fat women, women from rural areas, school girls • Bar girls and prostitutes are resistant to HIV • You can recognise an HIV-infected person • A well-dressed man or woman cannot have HIV or STDs • Women are less likely to catch HIV from uncircumcised men because the foreskin acts as a natural condom • Men cannot get infected and don't need to use a condom if they ejaculate outside their partner and then drink a lot of water in order to pass a lot of urine • Burning urination can be caused by incomplete ejaculation • Genital abscess result from washing in unclean water
Treatment and prevention	• Gonorrhoea can be cured by sex with a virgin • A cure for HIV will soon be widely available • STDs and HIV can be prevented by protective charms, tattoos, traditional vaccination (using herbs in skin incisions)
Condoms (see also Box 6.4)	• Condoms can be dangerous, sometimes vanish inside women and cause blockages • Condoms are impregnated with HIV • Condoms leak bacteria and viruses • The emphasis on condom promotion is an attempt to introduce population control by other means • The integrity of a condom can best be tested by putting it on a finger which has a cut and then placing a pepper sauce on the outside
Origins of HIV/STDs	• HIV originated from a US laboratory • HIV was originally the organism which caused leprosy. Persons with leprosy killed during the war between Tanzania and Uganda in 1979 fell into Lake Victoria, were eaten by fish and the leprosy organism changed into HIV which was contracted by persons around the lake eating the fish • HIV is not the cause of AIDS • STDs are due to sorcery, taboo violation or contamination e.g. STDs are contracted by having sex with an uncleansed widow or a woman who has had an abortion, wearing the clothes of an infected person; urethritis is caught by urinating under a full moon or stepping in infected urine (Green 1992; Hodes 1997; King & Homsy 1997)

or partly from the sale of sex, and the influence of drugs or alcohol. A recent study from Kenya showed women were more likely than men to continue having sex when symptomatic and this applied both to married women and women selling sex (Moses *et al.* 1994a). A study of South African men and women with genital ulcer disease showed that 36% of both sexes continued to have sex after the onset of symptoms (O'Farrell *et al.* 1992).

There is a growing body of information about the health-seeking behaviour of patients with STD symptoms in developing countries. From these studies it is clear that, for many poorer patients struggling for day-to-day survival, symptomatic STDs do not take high priority (Evans *et al.* 1997) and those that do seek treatment tend to turn to pharmacies, traditional healers and other informal sources of care in preference to public health facilities (Benjarattanaporn *et al.* 1997). The impact of user fees on access was vividly illustrated in a well-known Nairobi clinic where the introduction of fees led to a sharp fall in attendance (Moses *et al.* 1992). From studies conducted in Africa and South-East Asia (Moses *et al.* 1994a; Mulder 1994; Benjarattanoporn *et al.* 1997) the following themes repeatedly emerge:

(1) Convenience, affordability and the desire to avoid embarrassment often dictate the choice of treatment site.
(2) A high proportion of patients seek care in the informal sector (e.g. street vendors, pharmacies, traditional healers) or the private sector.
(3) Delay in seeking help for STD symptoms is common.

(4) Continued unprotected sexual activity commonly occurs following the onset of symptoms and prior to seeking medical advice.

In most developing countries one of the main dilemmas facing planners is how to direct effective STD curative services towards a population which mostly prefers to seek treatment for STDs in the informal or private sector in preference to public sector services. Available evidence suggests low standards of STD care tend to prevail in the private and informal sectors where there are few incentives to base treatment on up-to-date scientific evidence (Brugha & Zwi 1998).

The availability of curative services for STDs in developing countries is often poor and has deteriorated with the emergence particularly of penicillinase-producing *Neisseria gonorrhoeae* which requires treatment with more expensive and less available drugs than penicillin. Even where drugs are available health staff may display judgmental and moralising attitudes to STD patients which deter many from seeking treatment, especially women and adolescents. In many countries STD services suffer from underfunding and lack of training although this is beginning to change in response to the HIV pandemic.

Factors influencing transmission efficiency

STD transmission efficiency in developing countries can be influenced by specific cultural factors. Probably the most important of these is circumcision, a practice which shows marked variations in the developing world both between and within countries. Studies reporting transmission of HIV to uncircumcised men increased up to eight times.

Moses *et al.* (1994b) have repeatedly attracted attention and have led to suggestions that circumcision should be encouraged as a specific HIV prevention strategy. It is not understood how this risk-reduction factor operates but it has been suggested that in circumcised men the epithelium of the glans develops a protective keratin layer that acts as a form of natural condom which renders circumcised males less susceptible to genital ulceration or to direct HIV transmission. In addition the absence of a foreskin may improve genital hygiene and allow lesions of the glans to heal more quickly. Circumcision practices show great variation in Africa and it has been suggested that the pattern of the HIV epidemic within Africa with relative sparing of West Africa reflects the lower frequency of circumcision and greater incidence of genital ulcer disease in Eastern and Southern areas.

In Africa the use of vaginal drying agents (Box 6.3) to enhance sexual pleasure has been identified as a possible risk factor for STD and HIV transmission although no definite link has been established (Sandala *et al.* 1995).

The influence of hygiene on STD transmission is seen in the so-called tropical STDs, chancroid, lymphogranuloma venereum and donovanosis. These diseases have always been associated with poverty and poor hygiene and their declining incidence in previously endemic areas in wealthier countries appears to parallel improving hygienic standards. Lymphogranuloma venereum is an interesting example. It is caused by invasive L1-L3 strains of *Chlamydia trachomatis*. In the West this organism is responsible mainly for urethral and cervical infections, whereas in developing countries, in conditions of poor hygiene, the serotypes which cause trachoma and lymphogranuloma venereum are also able to thrive.

Box 6.3 Dry sex

Dry sex refers to the use of drying agents to produce a tight, dry vagina during sexual intercourse and has been reported from Zimbabwe and Zaire. The practice is also used to attract sexual partners and ensure their faithfulness. Women using dry sex have reported reluctance to use condoms for fear of blocking the 'magic' of drying agents and have also reported more frequent condom breakage during dry sex. These observations have obvious relevance for AIDS and STD prevention programmes.

Source: Civic, D. & Wilson, D. (1996) Dry sex in Zimbabwe and implications for condom use. *Social Science and Medicine* **42**, 91–98.

It was established at an early date in the American HIV epidemic that unprotected receptive anal intercourse conferred a particularly high risk of HIV acquisition. In most developing countries homosexuality and anal intercourse are taboo subjects. The link between HIV and homosexuality led to denial in the many developing countries that there was any risk of HIV affecting them. Conversely, once the existence of transmission became irrefutable it was not unusual for campaigns to highlight the risks of gay sex despite overwhelming evidence of predominantly heterosexual transmission. To what extent does receptive anal intercourse contribute to transmission in developing countries? Certainly, many sexual behaviour surveys suggest anal intercourse is rarely practised but on the other hand there is abundant anecdotal evidence that both heterosexual and homosexual anal intercourse are practised by a substantial proportion of the population in many countries. Anthropologists have described communities that practise heterosexual anal sex for contraceptive reasons and authorities such as Hyam have provided extensive evidence of ample opportunities for penetrative anal sex afforded to British expatriates working in British colonies from the seventeenth century onwards (Hyam 1990). An interesting example cited by Hyam of a well established culture of male homosexuality in Africa was the case of the Buganda 'martyrs' in Uganda. Homosexual practices at the Buganda court in the 1880s were opposed by Christian missionaries who persuaded young males to refuse sexual advances from older men. The Kabaka court leadership were so angered by this that over 30 young men were burnt alive for their Christian principles. While the epidemics in most developing countries are clearly driven predominantly by heterosexual transmission, there is increasing recognition that homosexual men constitute a significant group in all countries, often practising high-risk behaviour with other men while remaining largely hidden (often within marriages) because of discrimination, intolerance and the stigma associated with homosexuality.

The use of condoms to act as a barrier to STD/HIV transmission has seen dramatic changes in developing countries in the last 20 years. Condom distribution in sub-Saharan Africa has grown hugely but it remains clear that usage falls far from ideal levels among some vulnerable groups. Box 6.4 lists some beliefs about condoms cited by Nyonyo and

Schapink (1997) that had to be addressed by condom campaigns in Tanzania.

Box 6.4 Obstacles to condom use reported from Africa (see also Table 6.1)

- Popular opinion that says flesh to flesh is the real thing.
- Condom use is associated with disease; if one asks to use a condom it may imply that one is HIV positive.
- Condom use is linked to undesirable social behaviour and sexual practices.
- Condom use is inappropriate in cultures that value fertility highly.
- Women's objections ('I do not want to see the face of a condom entering my body', 'Having sex is good for my skin. It wouldn't work with a condom').
- Men's objections ('You do not eat a sweet with the wrapper on').
- Condoms are impregnated with the HIV virus, condoms leak HIV, a condom can disappear into a woman's body and cause sterility.
- AIDS is linked to witchcraft and a condom cannot protect against witchcraft.

King Homes has summarised the factors that have fostered epidemics of STDs in developing countries during the 20th century as

'... separation of families with male urban migration, low status of women, increasing urban, periurban and interurban prostitution, a demographic transition characterised by growing and destabilising excesses of teenagers and young adults no longer under the regulatory influence of a nuclear or extended family or community, and war, migration, and travel ...'

(Homes 1994)

The challenge of STD control in developing countries

Impact of patients' perceptions about HIV/STDs

The link between genital complaints and sexual activity is not always obvious to individuals and it is possible both to attribute a genital symptom incorrectly to sexual activity e.g. to assume that haematuria due to schistosomiasis has resulted from unprotected sex or to dismiss a genital complaint as not sexually-related, e.g. to assume vaginal discharge is a woman's health problem (which it may be) and not due to an STD (which it may also be). In many cultures the question arises not merely 'how did I catch this illness?' but also 'why did I catch it?' For many individuals the latter question is paramount. The answer will often be sought from a traditional healer and will frequently invoke explanations that relate to sorcery, taboo violation or contamination.

In India disease processes are often explained in terms of hot and cold, wet and dry and the body's relationship with the environment. Lifestyle and diet are considered important. Some diseases are attributed to internal blockages or shifts of internal organs (Evans & Lambert 1997). Clearly these concepts are liable to have considerable influence on patients' behaviours and can frequently explain the popularity of traditional healers in the STD field.

Beliefs about treatment are also important. Evans and Lambert in their study of health-seeking strategies among Calcutta sex workers illustrate the importance of powerful Western medicines to the women they studied but also point out that these medicines are feared for their power. Some women consider they have

a potentially weakening effect and that they should be consumed in the minimal possible dose. Clearly this may have implications for adherence and the development of resistance for medications that cannot be administered as single dose therapies. Certain beliefs relating to treatment have drawn attention because of particularly adverse public health implications. The most notorious among these is the notion described in a number of African countries that gonorrhoea in a male can be cured by sex with a virgin. Closely akin to this is the notion that HIV is best avoided by having sex with very young females.

Beliefs among doctors

Contemporary views in the industrialised countries about best practice in the sexual health field lay strong emphasis on the need for accepting, non-judgmental attitudes to STD patients and openness about sexuality. In many developing countries attitudes displayed towards STD patients reflect the less tolerant views of the local community with the result that patients are made to feel heavily stigmatised by the way in which services are offered and by the unfriendly way they are treated by health staff, conditions which were widespread in sexual health services in affluent countries until quite recently.

An interesting point of debate among clinicians at present centres on the best clinical approach to STD patients in resource-poor settings. The expert view within international bodies such as UNAIDS and the World Health Organization is that the so-called 'syndromic approach' to STD case management offers important advantages over traditional laboratory or clinical diagnostic approaches by offering effective treatment at the first visit without recourse to costly laboratory services. This is achieved by giving a combined treatment that covers all aetiological agents known or believed to be important locally as causes of the main symptom with which the patient presents (e.g. genital ulcer or genital discharge). While this approach has been vigorously promoted by international experts, many clinicians working in developing countries have expressed the view that they are being asked to adopt inferior clinical practices which are not used by the international experts in their own settings. The author recently visited a central Asian republic where the local press carried an article accusing the proponents of the syndromic approach of visiting Nazi-style medical experiments on the local population.

Development of STI services and access to care

The advent of HIV has led to major developments in STD services in developing countries. The most important reason for this has been the recognition HIV is itself predominantly sexually transmitted and that STDs act as co-factors for HIV transmission, but there has also been recognition that STDs have long been neglected and the incidence and prevalence of STDs and their complications has been chronically underestimated with consequent underfunding for detection, case management and prevention.

The main response to this has been a strong push to try and integrate STD case management with primary health care and to train as many health workers as possible in STD case management using the syndromic approach. Integration of STD care in family planning,

maternal and child health clinics is also being advocated although implementation has been slow.

While integration of STD services with primary health care appears to offer one solution to the problems of improving access to STD care, it is recognised that many vulnerable groups, e.g. adolescents and sex workers, still find it difficult to obtain treatment. The problems of providing services for vulnerable groups has been successfully met in many projects by creating special outreach services for sex workers. A good example is the Sonagachi project in Calcutta (Box 6.5).

Box 6.5 The Sonagachi Project

The Sonagachi Project operates in an established red-light area of Calcutta with an estimated 4000 sex workers. The project includes a provision of clinical services from a special clinic sited in the heart of the red-light district which offers general health services as well as screening for STDs. Attendance at the clinic is encouraged by a team of peer educators who often escort women new to the area to the clinic. The project is based on mutual respect and acceptance of sex workers, and securing the trust and co-operation of pimps, police, gangsters and brothel owners proved vital to the success of the project. The project co-ordination involves CBOs, NGOs, local government and foreign donors and lays special emphasis on participation of the target group. Growing independence and organisational capacity among the women suggest the project is moving towards a sustainable future.

Source: Gordon, P. & Sleightholme, C. (1995–96) *Review of 'Best Practice' for Interventions in Sexual Health*. British Overseas Development Administration Health and Population Office, New Delhi.

Linking with traditional health workers

In many developing countries the proportion of STD patients who seek care from appropriately trained health care workers is small, with large numbers of patients having recourse to pharmacies, street vendors, or traditional healers. Many different factors underlying this pattern of health-seeking behaviour have been identified and prominent among them are beliefs about STDs, their causes and treatment, cost of specialist services and attitudes to STDs among health workers. It has been estimated that traditional healers see 70% of African patients with all kinds of ailments (Chipfakacha 1997).

Nations *et al.* report a programme in which Afro-Brazilian Umbanda healers taught 126 fellow healers about safe sex, avoidance of ritual blood behaviours and sterilisation of cutting instruments (Nations *et al.* 1997).

In South Africa 1510 traditional healers recruited through national, formal associations were trained over a 10-month period to advise patients about how HIV is transmitted, how to prevent transmission and how to demonstrate correct condom use. The programme later expanded to recruit healers through indigenous associations of diviner-mediums known as impandes (Green *et al.* 1995). A useful recent review by King & Homsy (1997) reviews African projects to date which have involved traditional healers in AIDS education and counselling.

Problems of surveillance

While there is no country in the world that can boast of complete STD reporting, the problems of incomplete and inaccurate reporting are far greater in developing countries which tend to have a much higher incidence of STDs. It has been estimated in Africa that STDs account for 2.5–15% of all outpatient diagnoses. In most countries statistics are largely derived from public health facilities which will often see a minority of the total case load and frequently lack laboratory facilities to confirm specific diagnoses or to screen for asymptomatic infection. Reporting is minimal from the private and informal sectors which between them often deal with the majority of STD cases. Statistics that are available tend to be incidence data only, whereas for a more comprehensive view of the STD endemicity what is really needed is community-based prevalence data. In recent years many developing countries have conducted small research studies to collect prevalence data (e.g. from antenatal mothers) but it is rarely available on a continuous basis. The introduction of syndromic case management of STDs in many developing countries in primary health care settings has led to the development of syndrome-based reporting systems which can provide useful data on patients attending with common STD symptoms such as genital discharge or ulcer.

There are a number of important and sometimes harmful consequences that follow from the poor quality of STD reporting in developing countries. Firstly the data that is available may be used as the basis of decision-making about resource allocation to STD control, with consequent underfunding leading to a vicious circle of poor services, poor reporting and further cuts in resource allocation. Secondly, misinterpretation of poor quality data can lead to an assumption that either a programme is succeeding when in fact all that is happening is the reporting system has broken down, or that increased investment in STD control is failing to produce results when, in fact, a rise in reported cases is simply due to more complete reporting.

Psychosexual morbidity in developing countries

Wherever treatment for STDs is made available a significant proportion of patients attending may present with concerns about fertility, sexual functioning problems, fear of STD or some of the culture-specific psychiatric syndromes such as dhat in India and koro in Malaysia (Box 6.6). In some countries such patients are exploited by private practitioners advertising themselves as sexologists and often charging high fees for ineffective or inappropriate treatments. If efforts are to be made to make public sector sexual health services more attractive to patients then training must equip health workers to deal more appropriately with the more common psychosexual problems that occur in their community.

Box 6.6

Dhat
Often referred to as prostatorrhoea or 'night fall' by Indian physicians, this condition is bound up with the notion that seminal loss equates with loss of vitality and requires specific medical intervention. Seminal loss is described not only as occurring at night, the more familiar nocturnal emission recognised worldwide, but is also described as occurring during or after defaecation or that vital semen is being passed in the urine. Patients often complain of accompanying fatigue, weakness and palpitations.

Koro
This is a delusion that the penis is shrinking into the body and will eventually cause death. It has been described principally in South East Asia either in epidemic form or individual cases. An outbreak in northeastern Thailand in November 1976 involved at least 200 patients attending hospital. Patients complained of acute anxiety, shrinking of the penis. Popular opinion, re-enforced by local media attributed the epidemic to Vietnamese food and tobacco poisoning caused by a conspiracy against the sexual vitality and general health of the Thai people.

Sources
Malhotra, H.K. & Wig, N.N. (1975) Dhat syndrome: a culture-bound sex neurosis of the orient. *Archives of Sexual Behaviour* **4**, 519–528.
Jilek, W. & Jilek-Aall, L. (1977) Massenhysterie mit Koro-Symptomatik in Thailand. *Schweizerische Archiv für Neurologie, Neurochirurgie und Psychiatrie* **120**, 257–259.

Future needs

Major needs in developing countries at present are to gather on a regular basis information about risk behaviour and health-seeking behaviour and its determinants, and to use this information to design interventions appropriate to resource-poor settings and measure their impact. Scientists and doctors in developing countries need support in developing local capacity to design, implement and evaluate national programmes.

A major challenge for many developing countries is to translate successful interventions from individual studies and projects into workable operational programmes country-wide. The much-cited Mwanza study from Tanzania is a prime example of a highly effective intervention specially designed with sustainability in mind. This controlled study, published in 1995, showed a 40% reduction in HIV incidence in rural communities where STD care, using the syndromic approach, was integrated into existing primary health care services (Grosskurth *et al.* 1995). Following publication of the results of the study many national STD control programmes have declared intentions to follow the model described, but successful implementation has proved a difficult task for the overburdened primary health care services of many countries struggling to cope with structural readjustment and heavy indebtedness.

Although many promising intervention projects in sexual health have been set up throughout the developing world, in virtually all cases they are heavily dependent on outside donor input. In most cases only the most tentative steps have been taken to ensure longer-term sustainability. Two critical areas are those of drug financing and condom supplies. Meeting recurrent STD drug costs has proved a major hurdle for many national and local programmes and many projects encounter difficulty because they are unable to create a dependable supply of appropriate antibiotics. Many countries wish to provide drugs at low cost or for free to improve access to treatment but are unable to find sufficient funds to make this workable.

Social marketing of condoms has been hugely successful in many countries but so far the subsidy that supports such initiatives has largely come through foreign aid. One recent discussion on the subject of sustainability talks of 'the burden of unpayable recurrent

costs … reaching a point of crisis' (Walraven *et al.* 1997). Undoubtedly reproductive health care could be improved within many countries by a redistribution of available resources, e.g. from military expenditure towards health care. Current expenditure on health in many countries is inefficient with excessive amounts of money spent on a small number of tertiary institutions and further potential for savings being possible through health sector reform. An important component of health sector reform is to decentralise planning, implementing and evaluating STD/HIV prevention and care to district level. Walraven has called for primary reproductive health care programmes developed with community participation which combine improved woman and child health with safe motherhood, fertility awareness and HIV/AIDS care. This author takes the view that community participation is essential for sustainability but feels that considerable long-term external donor assistance is essential in the short term (Walraven 1996).

References

Benjarattanaporn, P., Lindan, C.P., Mills S., *et al.* (1997) Men with sexually transmitted diseases in Bangkok: where do they go for treatment and why? *AIDS* **11** (Suppl. 1), S87–95.

Brugha, R. & Zwi, A. (1998) Improving the quality of private sector delivery of public health services: challenges and strategies. *Health Policy and Planning* **13**, 107–120.

Bulterys, M., Musanganire, F., Chao, A., *et al.* (1994) Traditional mourning customs and the spread of HIV-1 in rural Rwanda: a target for AIDS prevention. *AIDS* **8**, 858–859.

Carael, M., Cleland, J., Deheneffe, J.C., Ferry, B. & Ingham, R. (1995) Sexual behaviour in developing countries: implications for HIV control. *AIDS* **9**(10), 1171–1175.

Carael, M., Van de Perre, P.H., Lepage, P.H., *et al.* (1988) Human immunodeficiency virus transmission among heterosexual couples in Central Africa. *AIDS* **2**(3), 201–205.

Celentano, D.D., Nelson, K.E., Lyles, C.M., *et al.* (1998) Decreasing incidence of HIV and sexually transmitted diseases in young Thai men: evidence for success of the HIV/AIDS control and prevention program. *AIDS* **12**(5), F29–36.

Chipfakacha, V.G. (1997) STD/HIV/AIDS knowledge, beliefs, practices and experiences of traditional healers in Botswana. *AIDS Care* **9**, 417–425.

Civic, D. & Wilson, D. (1996) Dry sex in Zimbabwe and implications for condom use. *Social Science and Medicine* **42**, 91–98.

Evans, C. & Lambert, H. (1997) Health-seeking strategies and sexual health among female sex workers in urban India: implications for research and service provision. *Social Science and Medicine* **44**, 1791–1803.

Field, M.L., Price, J., Niagn, C., *et al.* (1998) Targeted intervention research studies on sexually transmitted diseases (STD): methodology, selected findings and implications for STD service delivery and communications. *AIDS* **12** (Suppl. 2), S119–126.

Gordon, P. & Sleightholme, C. (1995–96) *Review of 'Best Practice' for Interventions in Sexual Health.* British Overseas Development Administration Health and Population Office, New Delhi.

Government of India (1995–96) *Societal Violence on Women and Children in Prostitution.* National Commission for Women.

Green, E.C. (1992) Sexually transmitted disease, ethnomedicine and health policy in Africa. *Social Science and Medicine* **35**, 121–130.

Green, E.C., Zokwe, B. & Dupree, J.D. (1995) The experience of an AIDS prevention program focused on South African traditional healers. *Social Science and Medicine* **40**, 503–515.

Grosskurth, H., Mosha, F., Todd, J., *et al.* (1995) Impact of improved treatment of sexually transmitted diseases on HIV infection in rural Tanzania: randomised controlled trial. *Lancet* **346**, 530–536.

Hodes, R. (1997) Cross-cultural medicine and diverse health beliefs. Ethiopians abroad. *Western Journal of Medicine* **166**, 29–36.

Homes, K.K. (1994) Human ecology and behaviour and sexually transmitted bacterial infections. *Proceedings of the National Academy of Sciences of the USA* **91**, 2448–2455.

Hyam, R. (1990) *Empire and Sexuality. The British Experience.* Manchester University Press.

Jilek, W. & Jilek-Aall, L. (1977) Massenhysterie mit Koro-Symptomatik in Thailand. *Schweizerische Archiv für Neurologie, Neurochirurgie und Psychiatrie* **120**, 257–259.

King, R. & Homsy, J. (1997) Involving traditional healers in AIDS education and counselling in sub-Saharan Africa: a review. *AIDS* **11** (Suppl. A), S217–225.

Malhotra, H.K. & Wig, N.N. (1975) Dhat syndrome: a culture-bound sex neurosis of the orient. *Archives of Sexual Behaviour* **4**, 519–528.

Moses, S., Manji, F., Bradley, J.E., *et al.* (1992) Impact of user fees on attendance at a referral centre for sexually transmitted diseases in Kenya. *Lancet* **340**, 463–466.

Moses, S., Ngugi, E.N., Bradley, J.E., *et al.* (1994) Health care-seeking behaviour related to the transmission of sexually transmitted diseases in Kenya. *American Journal of Public Health* **84**(12), 1947–1951.

Moses, S., Plummer, F.A., Bradley, J.E., *et al.* (1994) The association between lack of male circumcision and risk for HIV infection: a review of the epidemiological data. *Sexually Transmitted Diseases* **21**(4), 201–210.

Mulder, D. (1994) Disease perception and health-seeking behaviour for sexually transmitted diseases. In: *Prevention and Management of Sexually Transmitted Diseases in Eastern and Southern Africa: Current Approaches and Future Directions.* Network of AIDS Researchers of Eastern and Southern Africa, pp. 83–91.

Nations, M.K. & de Souza, M.A. (1997) Umbanda healers as effective AIDS-educators: case-control study in Brazilian urban slums (favelas). *Tropical Doctor* **27** (Suppl. 1), 60–66.

Nicoll, A., Alukamm, J.U., Mwizarubi, B., *et al.* (1993) Lay health beliefs concerning HIV and AIDS – a barrier for control programmes. *AIDS Care* **5**, 231–241.

Nyonyo, V. & Schapink, D. (1997) Condom promotion and distribution. In: *HIV Prevention and AIDS Care in Africa. A District Level Approach.* KIT Press.

O'Farrell, N., Hoosen, A.A., Coetzee, K.D. & van den Ende, J. (1992) Sexual behaviour in Zulu men and women with genital ulcer disease. *Genitourinary Medicine* **68**(4), 245–248.

Sandala, L., Lurie, P., Sunkutu, M.R., *et al.* (1995) 'Dry sex' and HIV infection among women attending a sexually transmitted diseases clinic in Lusaka, Zambia. *AIDS* **9** (Suppl. 1), S61–68.

Vogel, L.C. & Richens, J. (1989) Donovanosis in Dutch South Now Guinea: history, evolution of the epidemic and control. *Papua New Guinea Medical Journal*, **32**, 203–218.

Walraven, G. & Ng'weshemi, J. (1997) Integration and sustainability. In: *HIV Prevention and AIDS Care in Africa. A District Level Approach.* (eds J. Ng'weshemi, T. Boerma, J. Bennett & D. Schapink), pp. 371–386). Royal Tropical Institute, Amsterdam.

Walraven, G.E. (1996) Primary reproductive health care in Tanzania. *European Journal of Obstetric Gynecology and Reproductive Biology* **69**, 41–45.

Chapter 7

Race and Cultural Issues in Sexual Health

Oliver Davidson, Kevin A. Fenton and Aruna Mahtani

Introduction

Sex is a universal component of human experience. Its influence stretches across all cultures and societies, and helps define who we are and how we came to be. Sexuality is a significant theme in understanding human psychology, regardless of the way in which people behave in relation to their sexual drives. Culture, on the other hand, is as intricate as it is varied. The manner in which culture impacts upon sexual experience is therefore of great significance. Our particular culture governs what we learn about sexuality and sexual health. It governs how we learn this, and how we behave in response.

This is not a simple process. Sexual pleasure, passion and morality, along with guilt, fear, and shame can be intense emotions. Sexual development, sexual behaviour, fertility and pregnancy, along with sexual abuse, sexually transmitted infections (STIs), HIV/AIDS, and STI/HIV-related death are all capable of being profound experiences. Clearly, cultural variables such as ethnicity, nationality, religion, politics, geography and language combine with age, gender, education and socio-economic status in a way that greatly influences these experiences.

The focus of this chapter is on race, culture and ethnicity. Although these all play a very significant role, it is important to remember that these will also be influenced by subcultural factors such as sexual orientation and personal lifestyle. The chapter begins by defining the key concepts of race, culture and ethnicity and explores how these are related to sexual health and the access and utilisation of sexual health services. It will then explore ways in which an individual's cultural background influences the nature of the psychological interaction from the client's and clinician's perspectives. It also reviews some of the difficulties which may arise in this interaction. Finally we look at strategies to deal with cross-cultural working, focusing specifically on transcultural psychology, but including other techniques.

Key definitions: the concepts of race, culture and ethnicity

Race is often defined as referring to unalterable traits in an individual's genetic and biological make-up (Wyatt 1991). In social science research, race membership is commonly defined by shared similar physical characteristics, most commonly skin colour, hair texture, or facial features. These traits may contribute to health or behaviour patterns under study. It is often assumed that these traits will have some hereditary link, thereby accounting for shared behaviours or experiences noted within the group. Race is often described within categories such as Black, White and Asian, based on physical characteristics as assigned to a person by either that person or by someone else (e.g. a researcher). This categorisation however is limited by the criteria of group classification, the effect of inter-racial mixing, and the role of the dominant culture with which an individual may identify. Some authors (e.g. Miles 1989) view race and racism as contested concepts of little analytical value. They argue that race refers to nothing objective, but is an ideological concept whose use emerged in Europe only after the initiation of (and indeed to rationalise the practice of) African enslavement by the Europeans (Miles 1993). Since its inception, a variety of groups beyond blacks (e.g. Jews, Irish, Muslims and Asians) have become racialised and accordingly subjected to racially derogatory treatment. Thus, far from being explanatory principles, racialisation and racism require explanation. 'Race' then becomes a category of inclusion or exclusion that undertakes to naturalise the social formation that it characterises.

Ethnicity describes cultural or learned factors which distinguish groups and implies that an individual's socialisation is part of a collective identity that is socioculturally based.

> 'An ethnic group is a segment of a larger society whose members are thought, by themselves or others, to have a common origin and to share important segments of a common culture and who, in addition, participate in shared activities in which the common origin and culture are significant ingredients.'
>
> (Yinger 1994)

Ethnicity in sexual research allows the examination of the overall context of sexual interactions, cultural mores and values as passed between generations. These cultural values may influence an individual's sense of self in relation to others, their perceptions of the world, and in turn their patterns of behaviour. Ethnic categories used within research are often broad and the group members may often not share an identical racial background, spiritual beliefs, cultural values, attitudes towards health and health histories. It has been suggested that the broad terms should not be used unless the accompanying statements can be generalised to all the subgroups included, whose composition need to be specified.

It is perhaps difficult, if not dangerous, to look at particular aspects of an individual's behaviour in isolation, disregarding the sociopolitical context in which they occur, and how these in turn influence the behaviour. In the past research was geared more towards descriptive studies which served to highlight differences between cultural groups without the benefit of describing the context in which these differences occur. The essential question of whether these differences are hereditary or acquired remains unanswered.

The role of racism and its effect on the delivery and access of health care remains an area for further exploration. Defined as 'the predication of decisions and policies on considerations of race for the purposes of subordinating a racial group and maintaining control over that group', racism has been examined as a factor promoting the disparities in health care among ethnic groups, several studies having shown that racism is perceived as a major obstacle to health service usage by black and ethnic minority peoples. Racism in the wider context affects education, occupation and social opportunities and becomes an indirect but critical factor causing morbidity and mortality.

Key issues in ethnicity and sexual health

Ethnic inequalities in reproductive and sexual health have been described in many western industrialised states (Fenton 1997; Ross 1998). In the United States, disproportionately high rates of gonorrhoea (CDC, 1994; Ellerbrock et al. 1991), syphilis (Webster et al. 1993) and HIV/AIDS (Neal et al. 1997) have been described among African Americans, particularly those resident in inner city areas (Otten et al. 1994). A recent syphilis epidemic in south-eastern United States was confined largely to poor, rural Black American groups (Maruti et al. 1997). Young Black and Hispanic women are increasingly affected by HIV/AIDS in the US with rates 30 to 40 times those of similarly aged white women (Rosenberg & Biggar 1998). In Europe, similar evidence is emerging to suggest that resident Black African communities have been disproportionately affected by heterosexually acquired HIV/AIDS (Del Almo et al. 1996).

In the UK there has been an absence of ethnicity information in routine surveillance of HIV and sexually transmitted infections data, due in part to the concern over possible misinterpretation, misuse and controversy that the publication of such epidemiological information may precipitate (Fenton & Johnson 1997). Similar disparities in sexual health have been described among Britain ethnic minority communities. AIDS surveillance data have identified that Britain's Black African communities have been severely affected by the UK HIV/AIDS epidemic (PHLS AIDS Centre and the SCIEH, 1995). In July 1998, 30% (3541/11768) of all newly diagnosed HIV infections reported to the PHLS AIDS and STD Centre were attributed to transmission through sex between men and women. The majority (63%) of these however occurred in people from or who had spent time in countries in sub-Saharan Africa, where heterosexual transmission is common. Most (67%) ethnic minority cases probably acquired their infection through heterosexual intercourse with a partner from a high incidence country (Bhatt 1995). Although ethnicity data has been poorly recorded in the past, recent reports argue that the age-adjusted relative risk for reported cases of AIDS in the UK for 1994–95 was 20 times greater for African adults in the UK and 355 times greater for African children in the UK, compared to non-Africans living in the UK (De Cock & Low 1997).

Emerging evidence from GUM clinic and community-based surveys demonstrates the relationship between ethnicity, sexual attitudes and lifestyles, and STD prevalence. However, a few reports are now being published that attempt to document the influence that ethnicity may have on STI incidence in the UK. One study reported that the incidence of gonorrhoea in south London was found to be over eight times higher in 'Black' populations compared to 'White' populations. These findings were independent of age and gender, and the differences persisted after adjustment for socio-economic status using Jarman indices (Low *et al.* 1997). Although the study attempted to collect ethnicity data in accordance with the 1991 census categories, inconsistencies in ethnic monitoring within the GUM clinics forced the authors to use only three broad categories (White, Black, other and unknown). The authors therefore caution against making distinctions within the ethnic categories, but nonetheless assert that large inequalities in STI incidence do exist between ethnic groups, and that these need to be taken seriously by the communities themselves.

The only nationwide study to examine sexual attitudes, behaviours and lifestyles was the national sexual attitudes and lifestyles survey (NATSAL) carried out by Johnson *et al.* (1994). There were very few respondents from Black and minority ethnic backgrounds in this research, but this has been addressed in the next version of the survey carried out in 1999. Preliminary work directly aimed at sexual health and minority ethnic people in the UK has only been developed recently. Examples include the qualitative ExES Study (Exploring Ethnicity and Sexual Health) which examined sexual attitudes and lifestyles of five minority ethnic groups in central London (Elam *et al.* 1999), the Mayisha Study which assessed HIV-related knowledge, attitudes and behaviour in five African communities in central London (e.g. Fenton *et al.* 1999), and a study by Mahtani *et al.* (1999) which examined the medical and psychological priorities of minority ethnic attenders at a London GUM clinic.

Ethnicity data needs to be collated and utilised in a sensitive and responsible manner (Bhopal 1997). However, this must be balanced by the growing need to assertively override the fear of sensationalist misuse that such data gathering attracts (e.g. De Cock & Low 1997). Information can and must assist the people being studied, not solely be held against them.

There is a complete lack of ethnicity data in the epidemiology of psychosexual problems related to HIV, STIs and sexual dysfunction in the UK. This relates to the overall lack of ethnicity data for sexual health in general, as discussed above, but also probably reflects the relative lack of priority given to psychosexual problems in the past. While there are many anecdotes and clinical impressions regarding psychosexual problems in different ethnic groups, none have been tested through NHS service monitoring systems or, more importantly, through community-based prevalence surveys.

Modes of intervention: theory, issues and working models

A transcultural framework

Psychological models have their concepts embedded historically in western, that is, European and North American culture. Katz (1985) demonstrates a clear link between the components of western therapies and values and beliefs of white culture such as the emphasis on individualism, action orientation, self-disclosure, goal orientation, and western-style talk therapy. These values permeate the way in which clinicians offer therapy to clients from all ethnic backgrounds. It is only since the 1980s that the UK literature has reflected the growing concerns and limitations of these western models when working with clients from minority ethnic communities (for example, d'Ardenne & Mahtani 1989). There has been a shift from blaming the culturally different client when therapy does not work to trying to understand the interface between the client's different culture and western models. For example, a white clinician working with a migrant Bangladeshi couple will have to consider how to deal with the husband speaking on behalf of their sexual problems, and the wife's embarrassment and lack of practice with talking about herself as a sexual being to a stranger. The clinician here has a starting point of awareness, but the skill lies in keeping an open enough mind not to be bogged down with stereotypes that all Bangladeshi people behave in one way. Bangladeshi people's behaviour varies widely in just the same way as British people's behaviour does.

A transcultural model of working locates the responsibility for working through cultural differences and the effects of racism on the clinician. The clinician has to develop the skills to be able to disentangle their own values and beliefs as well of those of their models when working transculturally. All of us hold subjective views and stereotypes about 'other' groups which can subtly affect our interac-

tions. Training and supervision about these issues are essential in transcultural work. Gaining some knowledge of the client's culture through reading as well as asking the client directly about their culture in a respectful manner is also necessary. In the field of sexual health this can be difficult and embarrassing for both. The clinician can explain to the client how sexual therapy works and elicit the client's reaction to the model. They can then both work together towards changing and refining the model to suit the client's needs. The clinician also has to be aware of how the reality of the client's external world affects their relationship with the clinician. For example, if an African Caribbean man has had many racist encounters with white authority figures, he may well be suspicious of his white clinician's approach to him.

The most important clinical issue to remember is that psychologists should never assume anything about a service user, merely on the basis of their ethnicity. There are no rules governing the manner in which a service user's attitudes towards sexual issues are predetermined by their ethnicity, religion, gender, sexuality, politics or country of origin. We can not assume anything about the degree to which a health service user is influenced by their cultural background. Service users should be considered individually, in the context of their own separate systemic influences. Although their ethnic background may well have significantly influenced their psychological development, we can not presume in what manner. People may choose to interpret such backgrounds in whatever manner they choose. Ethnic stereotypes are in no way useful when considering the psychological concerns of an individual service user.

It has been argued that there is a history of racist research and teaching surrounding ethnicity and health, including sexual health. There have been many attempts to demonstrate racial variations in disease states (amongst other things), but there is a growing demand towards the responsible use of ethnicity and health research to provide an assessment of the needs and inequalities of different ethnic groups and to help guide practical resource allocation to help act upon any inequalities (Bhopal 1997; Fenton & Johnson 1997).

Recent data suggest that there are significant differences in the incidence of HIV and STIs across different ethnic groups in the UK, and although many of these differences can be attributed to confounding variables such as age, sex, or socio-economic status, strong trends remain even after these factors are taken into account.

Potential cultural factors

An individual's cultural belief can influence the attitudinal relationship between sexual response and psychological well-being. A number of issues may be relevant when working on sexually related issues with service users from different cultures.

1 The family as a social unit

In comparison with contemporary western society, many cultures do not hold the individual as the most important social unit, and the concerns of the extended family hold priority over the individual when decisions are being made regarding a particular individual's behaviour. This could be especially relevant when issues related to sex, sexual function-

ing, STIs, and reproduction are concerned. The importance of an individual's attitudes towards these sexual issues may therefore be surpassed by the concerns of the whole family and its reputation in the community. For example, an individual who is asked by the health service to contact recent sexual partners following the diagnosis of HIV (or even an STI) may place the reputation of their family in higher regard than their responsibility towards their own health or that of their partners.

Another implication is that when an extended family lives together, perhaps in a small dwelling, the close proximity of sleeping and accommodation may impact upon a couple's ability to enjoy privacy and sexual intimacy.

Sex can be constructed in terms of personal enjoyment or fulfilment in some cultures. However, sex can also be viewed more in terms of reproduction potential, given the social status that fertility and children can possibly bring upon an individual or family. This was, of course, traditionally an important issue in European societies, and in some cases still is, but it has also been argued that the industrial revolution, the development of contraception technology, and the changing role of women have all influenced the meaning of sex in developed countries.

There can be a number of factors associated with arranged marriages that impact upon a sexual relationship. Such relationships are often as much an issue of developing a relationship between two extended families. Sexual attraction can not be assumed to occur in such relationships; indeed, one of the arguments in favour of these arrangements is that they avoid many of the adverse developmental complications of passionate relationships. The woman may be expected to have never had sex before, and to therefore have very different sexual expectations relative to a sexually experienced woman. Given the pragmatic approach to such marriages, the man's ability to sire a child may be immediately under close scrutiny, especially by the family of his new wife, a situation that can help develop a performance anxiety around his sexual functioning.

2 Sources of information and expertise

Information and knowledge regarding the physiology of the human sexual response can vary greatly across different groups, depending upon education and experience. Awareness of sexual biology and sexual physiology can vary widely, with equally differing understandings of what is going on when things go wrong.

Although medicine has become the strongest provider of sexual health information and care in the developed world, it is fair to say that this power base has become lessened through the humanisation and accountability demanded of the medical profession by the public. Nonetheless, many people still look towards physicians for advice and guidance on sexual health matters. As distinct to the medical doctor or nurse, the spiritual or *folk healer* can also play an important role in the treatment of psychosexual problems (e.g. Muslim *hakim,* Hindu *vaid,* and European *naturopath*). The re-emergence of *alternative therapies* in the west provides a good example of this. Whatever the case, authority figures such as healers or doctors can play an important role in the 'top down' treatment of sexual health concerns, especially if an expert opinion is required.

3 Gender power issues

There have been many social constructs involving the importance of gender power across time and culture. If the service user comes from a context where the male is expected to play a dominant role in marriage, there may be significant concerns if it is felt that he is unable to fulfil that role. For example, male potency can be seen as very important in providing a sense of male identity and power. If not involved in procreation, male ejaculation can sometimes be considered to drain the mind as well as the body. Consequently, masturbation and nocturnal emissions (wet dreams) can be construed in a very negative light, and in a manner that sometimes seems to hold very little physiological evidence. Examples include:

- *koro syndrome:* a fear sometimes expressed by people of Chinese ethnicity that masturbation, wet dreams, and excess sex will cause the penis to retract into the abdomen and cause death.
- *dhat syndrome:* a fear sometimes expressed by people of Hindu and Muslim ethnicity that semen loss is harmful and causes debility and weakness (e.g. Malhotra & Wigg 1975; Paris 1992). Ayurvedic medical systems consider that semen production occurs in the bone marrow, and some rural traditional cultures in and around the Indian subcontinent attribute significant distress to any unnecessary semen loss (emissions, masturbation, excessive sex).
- *blindness*: a fear sometimes expressed by people of Christian or European ethnicity, particularly male adolescents, that masturbation can result in blindness.

Across all cultures, women and men can have very different roles to play in personal, sexual and family decisions. For example, females may be expected to play a submissive role in some cultures, including decisions over sex and family planning. This continued to be the case in western society, prior to the relatively recent development of feminist thinking and power. In many Islamic cultures it can be considered inappropriate for women to express interest in or knowledge about sexual matters. It may also be very inappropriate for a woman to talk to a man about such issues. Within a relationship it may be considered inappropriate for women to discuss sex or negotiate a change in a couple's sexual behaviour.

Female genital mutilation (FGM) can be a firmly entrenched practice endorsed by both men and women within a number of African cultures, including Somalia, Ethiopia and Sudan. Organised dissent from such practices is becoming widespread in these countries, and the WHO is assisting national and international organisations to eradicate this practice, while the UK has formally outlawed the practice through its Prohibition of Circumcision Act (1985). The Northwick Park Institute for Medical Research set up an African well woman clinic in the UK in 1993, believed to be the first such clinic to address FGM issues in the western world.

Such is the concern over female power of sexuality, that in many cultures male extramarital sexual desire can be attributed to the deliberate seductiveness of women, rather than to the individual responsibility of the male. This was also the case in many European cultures and, some would argue, still is.

On the other hand, in some east African cultures the paternal aunts have a very dominant and powerful role over decision-making with respect to a family's children, including sex education and guardianship. They are usually brought in to provide sexual education and an understanding of sexual relationships when daughters reach puberty, and they can have automatic guardianship rights over the children of a deceased brother.

Models

Issues such as those outlined above can significantly influence the ability for contemporary western health models to provide culturally appropriate psychological assessment and treatment services for sexual health concerns. Eurocentric, individual-focused clinical psychology models applicable to sexual health concerns tend to focus on personal empowerment and psychological well-being through the enhancement of individual self-efficacy and internalised locus of control. Such models may not be the most relevant, however, when dealing with people whose culture does not share such individualistic views.

The possibility that people from Black and other minority ethnic groups may not want to utilise services based on such Eurocentric models is an empirically important one. Some preliminary data suggests that some service users from these groups may still want to access sexual health services, and that they may still want to deal with some of the emotional issues associated with their sexual health concerns in the NHS clinic setting (e.g. Mahtani *et al.* 1999). It is interesting to consider the way in which Jehu's 'PLISSIT' model of psychosexual therapy may still assist in the delivery of a psychology service for sexual problems across a number of different cultures. This stage model of psychosexual service delivery (whereby different types of therapeutic intervention are administered hierarchically, as required, beginning with 'Permission', and followed by 'Limited Information', 'Specific Skills', and 'Intensive Therapy') still opens itself to a number of questions when applied across different cultural settings. For example, what actually is permissible sexual behaviour within a certain cultural context?; what types of sex education are appropriate for informing different people?; can specific skill training like Masters and Johnson Sensate Focus work with people who do not share the internal locus of control premise (some argue that it is possible; see d'Ardenne 1996); and how appropriate is intensive therapy across different cultural settings?

However, the systemic model clearly lends itself well to this area. Such a model addresses many of the incongruencies outlined above, by asking questions such as: What is the context under which the problem is occurring? What are the expectations of the service user? What existing resources can be brought to bear within the service user's life to assist in the problem?

Clinical and service recommendations

While cultural background issues help shape the aetiology and impact of any individual's sexual health concerns, they also significantly influence the manner in which the same individual accesses services such as the NHS in order to address these concerns. Outlined below are some of the process issues relevant to service provision.

Some service users may express serious concern over the level of confidentiality governing any information they provide to health staff, both within and outside of the NHS workplace. This may especially be the case with information regarding sexually intimate behaviour or potentially seriously infectious diseases such as HIV, hepatitis, and tuberculosis. Services must therefore clarify the influence of the VD Act (last amended 1974) which places confidentiality of service users as a priority, and ensure staff adherence to this.

While NHS staff may view sexual health status as important, many service users may feel they have other concerns that take more immediate priority; these include their asylum status, financial and accommodation problems, the safety of family still living abroad, and the health and welfare of family and friends in the UK.

Individuals or couples from cross-cultural marriages (religion, nationality, ethnicity, social class, education, etc.) may experience particular problems related to their different expectations regarding gender roles and sexual behaviour (e.g. Clulow 1993). Such differences may manifest themselves in the way that the individual or couple access and utilise the service, and the issues that are raised. Psychologists need to keep this in mind when developing and administering services.

Services also need to consider the impact on staff following disclosure by service users of certain cultural sexual practices, in order that staff continue to provide non-judgmental professional services following the disclosure. Examples from some African cultures include female and male circumcision occurring at puberty, along with labia pulling, wife inheritance by a brother following the death of the husband, polygamy, and so on. Such practices may invoke strong personal feelings in health staff, given the strong differences in practice that they themselves may have experienced and learnt. However, it is one of the aims of a health service to provide a non-judgmental health service, and to delineate when it is appropriate to intervene in a cultural practice (e.g. when there is physical/psychological damage, perhaps in accordance with British law), and when not to intervene (e.g. if a service user communicates satisfaction with the practice).

In general, psychological assessments are best conducted with a systemic framework in mind. What does the presenting problem mean to the service user and their family? What are their explanations? What would they normally/traditionally do to assist with the problem? What is available in their community to assist in the problem?

There are few sources of cultural, ethnic and religious information relevant to health service users in the UK with sexual (and other health) concerns from Black and minority ethnic backgrounds. Although these may be of assistance in attempting to appreciate some of the broader aspects of how culture interacts with sexual health, they are forever in danger of making global estimates and hence guide the clinician into making generalised assumptions. It is impossible for a clinician to attempt to keep up to date on all details of every cultural subgroup; attempting to do so will be frustrating and ultimately unsuccessful. Clearly, service users themselves are the best source of information regarding their own specific cultural issues relating to sex. The meaning of sexual health to the individual service user is the most important concern. Ask them. They are the expert.

The use of interpreters for interviews by a clinician unfamiliar with the language of the service user needs to be arranged with care. Service users may be particularly concerned about confidentiality, especially if the interpreter comes from the same discrete ethnic community. If the service has the freedom to provide choice, the service user should be consulted on whether or not they would prefer a male or a female interpreter and whether or not they would like the interpreter to come from their own ethnic background.

Rather than imposing a Eurocentric psychology on service users with significantly different views of psychosexual issues, it may be best to arrange liaison with culturally appropriate individuals, groups and organisations that already exist in the service users' community. These individuals or groups can in turn work in conjunction with health services, if appropriate. If it is difficult to access such resources, then a more community-based approach may be appropriate. For example, a service can develop the formation of focus/support groups amongst the service user peers with similar concerns, who can in turn inform the statutory bodies the manner in which services can best be developed to maximise equity of access across key groups.

It is probably even less appropriate for psychology sexual health staff to be discussing and working on sexual issues with minority ethnic service users of a different gender. For this reason, it is usually best if gender matching of therapist to service user is offered.

The use of advocates (peers of the service user who have more familiarity with the service) may be useful in the sexual health setting. These tend to come from community-based organisations, and a minimal degree of professionalism is essential regarding confidentiality, treatment options, etc.

Clearly, race and culture are key components to understanding and working with any individual, especially in the area of sexual health. Such social influences weave through any biological or psychological template that determines an individual's behaviour. The urges may be powerful, the attitudes well formed; but people are driven to extreme situations that are constructed around pervasive social normative processes; within religious orders, in urbanised club culture, through socially condoned genital alterations, and so on. There is much importance in a clinician or researcher attempting to accommodate the social, cultural and ethnic context of an individual's sexual health concern. Such thinking can assist both the understanding and the management of sexual health problems.

References

Bhatt, C. (1985) *HIV and Black Communities: A Report of the African HIV Working Group*. The HIV Project and the New River Health Authority Health Promotion Department, London.

Bhopal, R. (1997) Is research into ethnicity and health racist, unsound, or important science. *British Medical Journal* **314**, 1751–1756.

Clulow, C. (1993) Marriage across frontiers: national, ethnic and religious differences in partnership. *Sexual and Marital Therapy* **8**(1), 81–87.

d'Ardenne, P. (1996) Sexual health for men in culturally diverse communities – some psychological considerations. *Sexual and Marital Therapy* **11**(3), 289–296.

d'Ardenne, P. & Mahtani, A. (1989). *Transcultural Counselling in Action*. Sage, London.

De Cock, K.M. & Low, N. (1997) HIV and AIDS, other sexually transmitted diseases, and tuberculosis in ethnic minorities in UK: is surveillance serving its purpose.

British Medical Journal **314**, 1747–1751.

Del-Amo, J., Petruckevitch, A., Phillips, A.N., Johnson, A.M. & Stephenson, J.M. (1996) Spectrum of disease in Africans with AIDS in London. *AIDS* **10**, 1563–1569.

Elam, G., Fenton, K., Johnson, A., Nazroo, J. & Ritchie, J. (1999) *Exploring Ethnicity and Sexual Health*. SCPR, London.

Ellerbrock, T.V., Bush, T.J., Chamberland, M.E. & Oxtoby, M.J. (1991) Epidemiology of women with AIDS in the US, 1981 through 1990. A comparison with heterosexual men with AIDS. *Journal of the American Medical Association* **265**(22), 2971–2975.

Fenton, K. & Johnson, A.M. (1997) Race, ethnicity and sexual health: can sexual health programmes be directed without stereotyping. *British Medical Journal* **314**, 1698–1699.

Fenton, K., Davidson, O., Mudari-Chinouya, M. & Miller, D. (1999) The Mayisha study: engaging African communities in sexual behaviour research. *10th Conference on the Social Aspects of AIDS*, London.

Johnson, A.M., Wadsworth, J., Wellings, K. & Field, J. (1994) *Sexual Attitudes and Lifestyles*. Blackwell Scientific Publications, Oxford.

Low, N., Daker-White, G., Barlow, D. & Pozniak, A.L. (1997) Gonorrhoea in inner London: results of a cross-sectional study. *British Medical Journal* **314**, 1717–1723.

Mahtani, A., Davidson, O., Kell, P. & Miller, D. (1999) Psychological and medical priorities of ethnic minority attenders at a London sexual health clinic: a pilot needs assessment. Paper presented at *1999 MSSVD Conference*, Edinburgh.

Malhotra, H. & Wig, N. (1975) Dhat syndrome: a culture-bound sex neurosis of the orient. *Archives of Sexual Behaviour* **4**, 519–528.

Maruti, S., Hwang, L.Y., Ross, M., Leonard, L., Raffel, J. & Hollins, L. (1997) The epidemiology of early syphilis in Houston, Texas, 1994–1995. *Sexually Transmitted Diseases* **24**, 475–480.

Miles, R. (1989) *Racism*. Routledge, London.

Miles, R. (1993) *Racism after "Race Relations"*. Routledge, London.

Neal, J.J., Fleming, P.L., Green, T.A. & Ward, J.W. (1997) Trends in heterosexually acquired AIDS in the United States, 1988 through 1995. *Journal of Acquired Im-*

mune Deficiency Syndrome and Human Retrovirology **14**, 465–474.

Otten, M.W. Jr, Zaidi, A.A., Peterman, T.A., Rolfs, R.T. & Witte, J.J. (1994) High rate of HIV seroconversion among patients attending urban sexually transmitted disease clinics. *AIDS* **8**, 549–553.

Paris, J. (1992) Dhat: the semen loss anxiety syndrome. *Transcultural Psychiatric Research Review* **29**, 109–118.

Public Health Laboratory Service AIDS Centre and the Scottish Centre for Infection and Environmental Health. (1995) *AIDS/HIV Quarterly Surveillance Tables*. No. 28: Data to end June 1995.

Rosenberg, P.S. & Biggar, R.J. (1998) Trends in HIV incidence in different transmission groups in the United States. Presented at *XI International Conference on AIDS*, Vancouver, July 7–12, [Abstract Tu.C572].

Ross, M. (1998) Race and ethnicity in STD analysis. *Sexually Transmitted Infections* **74**, 2–3.

Webster, L.A., Berman, S.M. & Greenspan, J.R. (1993) Surveillance of gonorrhoea and primary and secondary syphilis among adolescents, United States – 1981–1991. *Morbidity and Mortality Weekly Review* **42**(SS-3), 1–11.

Wyatt, G.E. (1991) Examining ethnicity versus race in AIDS related research. *Social Science and Medicine* **33**, 37.

Yinger, J. (1994) *Ethnicity. Source of Strength? Source of Conflict?* State University of New York Press, Albany.

Chapter 8

Regulation of Fertility

Sunanda Gupta and Max Elstein

Introduction

Rapid population growth can be threatening to the environment and compromises long-term health. Personal regulation of fertility helps women realise their reproductive goals allowing opportunities for career aspirations, and improves maternal health by reducing the risk of pelvic inflammatory disease (PID), associated ectopic pregnancy, morbidity and mortality of illegal abortions and their complications. Regulation of fertility also promotes better health for children and reduces the strain on environmental and community resources. When such a broad concept of reproductive health care is endorsed and recognised it improves the quality of life.

Sub-Saharan Africa has high fertility rates but paradoxically also has the highest incidence of infertility due to sexually transmitted infections (STI). Infertility can be a major cause of ill-health especially in those societies where the worth of a woman is related to her reproductive potential, often resulting in disastrous emotional and psychological seque-

lae. Provision of reproductive health care has a dual role in enhancing the quality of life and impacting on population control policies and demographic targets.

The WHO definition of reproductive health care

The International Conference on Population and Development (ICPD) in Cairo (United Nations 1994) and the United Nations World Conference on Women (Beijing 1995) has apportioned global priority to reproductive health. The ICPD document defines reproductive health care as 'the constellation of methods, techniques and services that contribute to reproductive health and well-being through preventing and solving reproductive health problems'.

The WHO defines reproductive health as a 'state of complete physical, mental and social well being and not merely the absence of disease or infirmity in matters related to the reproductive system and to its functions and processes'. Thus, it also includes sexual health, the purpose of which is enhancement of life and personal relations and not merely counselling and care related to reproduction and STI. This holistic approach is important in the promotion of gender-sensitive and woman-centred health.

The 12 pillars of reproductive health care (Dicfalusy 1995) include adolescent reproductive health and sexual behaviour, the status of women in society, family planning, maternal care and safe motherhood, abortion, reproductive tract infections, HIV/AIDS, infertility, reproductive organ malignancies, nutrition, infant and child health and environmental and occupational reproductive health.

The role of community gynaecologists and reproductive health care doctors in the UK is to manage the provision and delivery of such services, to oversee and co-ordinate school sex education, co-ordinate screening for sexually transmitted infections, deliver contraceptive and legal abortion services, screening for breast and cervical cancer and management of psychosexual dysfunction and menopausal problems. This transition from providing only family planning services to delivering a package of integrated and comprehensive reproductive health care across the boundaries of disciplines is gaining momentum.

Early pioneers and famous names in contraception

In the UK, Thomas R. Malthus (1798) condemned the prevention of conception by artificial means and was of the opinion that anything which hindered the 'generation of off- spring' as a result of the carnal act is a sin (Finch & Green 1963). People were called upon to practise 'moral restraint' but contraceptives were not advocated. The real founder of the British birth control movement was a London-based tailor, Francis Place (1771–1854), who maintained that conception should be prevented until it was convenient. By 1900 the idea of birth control became a subject of interest but still faced fierce controversy on religious and ethical grounds.

Margaret Sanger in the United States and Marie Stopes in the UK were both devoted to the promotion of birth control ideals and shared a similar philosophy. They promoted birth control as a fundamental human right and as a means of offering freedom, sexual satisfaction and joyful motherhood (Wood & Suitters 1970) to save women from the bondage of unwanted pregnancy. Margaret Sanger's efforts led to the American birth control movement which was fiercely opposed, and thereafter also to the international movement.

Meanwhile in England in 1921 the first British birth control clinic was opened in Holloway by Dr Marie Stopes (a distinguished palaeobotanist), whose book *Married Love* focused on managing the sexual needs of couples. She was aided by Dr Helena Wright in London who in 1939 helped form the Family Planning Association (FPA) in the UK with its network of clinics which were integrated into the National Health Service in 1974.

To the four essential freedoms identified by Franklin D. Roosevelt in his address to the nation at the time of World War II – freedom of speech and expression, freedom from fear and freedom of every person to worship God in his own way – Dugald Baird from Aberdeen added a fifth freedom – freedom from the tyranny of excessive fertility (Baird 1965).

Changing role of women in society

The most powerful determinant of reproductive health is the status of women in society. In many developing countries (Sub-Saharan Africa, India, Pakistan) women have low social status and may not be in a position to negotiate safe sex. Victorian women were expected not to have sex for gratification but to dutifully fulfil the needs of their husbands. Worldwide, women also suffer domestic violence (Jejeebhoy & Cook 1997) and abuse (Roberts 1996). The physical consequence of violence often remains hidden but can be profound. Additionally, about 100 million women suffer from genital mutilation every year (Khanna 1997).

The role of women in present-day society is rapidly changing beyond a primary domestic, reproductive and subservient role to a more productive role. The two World Wars (1914–18) and (1939–45) saw a major positive impact on the status and health of women in Britain with resulting freedom in sexual relationships. Women now recognise their right to sexual fulfilment (Sapire 1990) and expect to participate in decisions about family size, sexual harmony and health. However, in some parts of the world, family planning policies are slow to apportion women the new independence they desire.

Adolescent sexuality and reproductive health

In 1964, Helen Brook set up Brook advisory clinics in London, Bristol and Birmingham. The NHS Family Planning Act (1974) permitted local authorities to give advice on birth control without regard to marital status and clinics became empowered to advise the unmarried. However, young women who were most in need continued to have difficulty in accessing reproductive health care in the UK. This was ameliorated to some extent by the 'Gillick ruling' of the Law Lords which allowed doctors to advise young girls under the age of 16 if certain criteria were met (BMA 1991). Nevertheless, reproductive health care services for young people are for the most part inadequate in the UK compared with the Netherlands.

Sex education was introduced in the UK secondary school national curriculum in 1994. However, parental support and dissemination of programmes at a young age is required. Parents should encourage teenagers first to self identify and value themselves and thereafter to develop sexual freedom. In these circumstances, youth are able to exercise restraint and generally make responsible choices. The UK Sexual Attitudes and Lifestyle survey showed that the first sexual act is often unpremeditated and unprotected and sexual activity begins at the much earlier age of 17 (Wellings *et al.* 1994) instead of 21 (Farrel 1978).

Sarrell (1981) considers the initial sexual experience as crucial to sexual health with a reduced chance of psychosexual dysfunction in later life. It is important to reiterate here that early sex education does not lead to an increase in sexual activity and young people who have had sex education are less likely to have unplanned pregnancies (Balda *et al.* 1993).

In Holland, parental pragmatism motivates children to be assertive and develop responsibility in relationships. Dutch sex education programmes are followed through at school and incorporate open recognition and discussion of sexuality as something of special importance and separate from reproduction (Doppenberg 1993). The early reproductive years are a time of learning about sexual relationships and contraception (Belfield 1992). Well-structured school sex education programmes and positive 'double Dutch' messages (integrated information on pregnancy and prevention of STI) promoted by sensitive, non-judgmental and accessible youth advisory services help the foundations for the future. To the young, delivery of contraceptive services is of secondary importance to imparting, without moralising or censoring, an understanding of the full implications, risks and consequence of early sexual activity.

Pregnancy in teenagers is usually unwanted. Teenage pregnancy is an important health and social problem in Britain and continues to grow in proportions that could be considered epidemic. The teenage pregnancy rate in Britain is 9.6/1000 births (Holland 4/1000 births) and the highest rate of female attendances at STI clinics is in the 16–19 age group (1992). Starting a family as a child is likely to perpetuate a cycle of financial and emotional disadvantage and imposes serious health risks to

the mother and the child. Very few teenagers are psychosexually developed before the age of 20 (Sapire 1990) and unwanted pregnancy needs to be avoided at any cost. The RCOG Working Party report (Royal College of Obstetricians and Gynaecologists 1991) has highlighted these issues.

Methods of regulating fertility

In the UK, just over 50% of women use reversible contraception and 24% of couples have undergone sterilisation (HMSO 1995). The use of condoms has steadily increased from 17% in 1993 to 25% in 1995 reflecting heightened awareness of STDs (Durex Report 1997). Both injectables and IUDs are underused (1% and 5%, respectively) and only 1% of couples use diaphragm/cap and natural family planning methods (See Table 8.1).

Combined oestrogen–progestogen methods

Combined oral contraceptive pill (COC)
More than 70 million women worldwide use the combined oral contraceptive pill (IMAP 1995). The pill is the main contraceptive method in Britain with 25% of women aged 15–49 using it (HMSO 1995). It is simple, reliable,

Oral contraception	25% (COC 18%, minipill 6%)
Condoms	17%
Sterilisation	24%
Non users	29%
Injectable method	1%
Safe period and withdrawal	1% and 3%
Diaphragm/Cap	1%
IUD	5%

Table 8.1 Contraceptive usage in Great Britain in women aged 16–49.

safe and reversible. The efficacy of the combined pill is user dependent with a failure rate of 0.5/100 woman years with optimal use and up to 5–8/100 woman years with sub-optimal use.

Benefits

The non-contraceptive health benefits of the pill are considerable and need emphasising (see Table 8.2). The combined pill inhibits ovulation and thus indirectly reduces the incidence of follicular ovarian cysts (Vessey *et al.* 1987). Progressive decrease of oestrogen and progestogen in dosage formulations raises the question of whether such benefits will continue to be manifest (Elstein 1994).

- The pill effects a 50% protection against the occurrence of epithelial ovarian cancer for up to 15 years after discontinuation (Centers of Disease Control and the National Institute of Child Health and Human Development 1987) and a decline in mortality of ovarian cancer in women (Vessey & Painter 1995).
- A similar protective action also applies to endometrial cancer with reduction in risk of 50% for up to 15 years after stopping the pill (Cash 1983).

- The risk of PID is reduced by 50% (Vessey *et al.* 1981) – the cervical mucus becomes thick and impenetrable to the sperm thus indirectly blocking the entry of pathogenic organisms into the upper genital tract. The menstrual flow in women taking the pill is light with less likelihood of alteration in the normal acidity of the vagina creating a less favourable medium for bacterial growth. This effect is of particular benefit to sexually active women, but should not negate the practice of using barriers where appropriate to minimise the risk of sexually transmitted infection.

An increased rate of cervical infection with chlamydia is reported in users of the combined pill. This has been attributed to an association of the pill with cervical ectopy and exposure of the columnar epithelium to the vagina thus increasing the risk of infection (Moss *et al.* 1991). Notwithstanding this, the pill does appear to protect the upper genital tract against the incidence and severity of infection by *Chlamydia trachomatis* and other sexually transmitted organisms (Walner Hanssen *et al.* 1990). The use of the pill, however, does not appear to influence the risk of HIV transmission (Tattel & Kafrissen 1995).

Table 8.2 Non-contraceptive benefits of oral contraceptives.

Condition	% reduction in risk
Epithelial ovarian cancer	50%
Endometrial adenocarcinoma	50%
Menorrhagia and dysmenorrhoea	50%
Benign breast disease	50%
Pelvic inflammatory disease	50%
Ectopic pregnancy	90%
Fibroids	17%

- The pill reduces the incidence of ectopic pregnancies by 90% (Franks *et al.* 1990).
- The pill effects a reduction in benign breast disease of 50% and fibroids of 17% (Ross *et al.* 1986).
- Dysmenorrhoea (Milsom *et al.* 1990), premenstrual tension (Larsson *et al.* 1992), and menorrhagia are improved in pill users.
- Use of the COC may reduce the prevalence of severe disabling rheumatoid arthritis (Spector & Hochberg 1990).

Risks

Cardiovascular disease. The absolute risks of the combined pill among healthy young women who do not smoke are small. Past use and duration of use are not associated with risk of myocardial infarction (MI) (Croft & Hannaford 1989), the small underlying risk being confined to current users over 35 years and particularly in smokers, the relative risk varying from 2.4 (95% confidence interval 1.4–3.9) (Lewis *et al.* 1997) to 5 (95% confidence interval 2.5–9.9) (WHO 1997). The evidence from angiographic studies suggests that the mechanism may be an alteration of blood coagulability as opposed to coronary atherogenesis (Engel 1989).

The presence of other cardiovascular risk factors such as diabetes mellitus, hypertension, dyslipidaemias, obesity and age strongly influence the risk. However the major associated factor is smoking, which is synergistic with the use of the combined pill to considerably increase the risk, so that heavy smokers who take the COC have 20 times the risk of MI (Croft & Hannaford 1989). It is interesting to note that, while the incidence of MI increases with age, there is no convincing evidence that the relative risk of MI among current users of oral contraception differs with age. Current users of oral contraception with a history of hypertension and those who have not had their blood pressure checked prior to use have higher risk of MI than current users whose blood pressure had been checked (Croft & Hannaford 1989; Lewis *et al.* 1997; WHO 1997). There are insufficient data to assess the risk of myocardial infarction in users of low-dose oral contraceptives by the type of progestogens, and the suggestion that users of low-dose combined pills containing gestodene or desogestrel may have a lower risk of MI than users of low-dose formulations containing LNG remains unproven.

Stroke. Current use of the pill increases the risk of thrombotic stroke by 1.5 fold (WHO 1996a) compared with non-users if they are not hypertensive or do not smoke. In women aged under 35 years who do not smoke or have high blood pressure, the risk of haemorrhagic stroke associated with use of the pill is not increased (WHO 1996b). Current users of COC with hypertension have a 10-fold increased absolute risk of haemorrhagic stroke and a 3-fold risk of thrombotic stroke when compared with current users without hypertension, and the risk in women who smoke is twice that in non-users. Similarly, the incidence of ischaemic stroke is increased in women with severe migraine or migraine with aura, in whom the pill should be avoided. Past use, duration of use and the type of the oestrogen or progestogen of the COC does not modify the risk of stroke in COC users.

Venous thromboembolism (VTE). All current COC users have an increased risk of VTE 3–6 fold that of an individual of thrombophatic predisposition. This persists until discontinuation and drops rapidly after use. If the oestrogen content of the pill is < 50 μg, the risk is unrelated to the dose of oestrogen. In October 1995, the Committee on Safety of Medicines in the UK alerted doctors to the findings from new epidemiological studies (WHO 1995) showing a doubling of the differential in the small risk of VTE between pills containing third generation progestogens (desogestrel/gestodene) and those containing levonorgestrel/norethisterone.

VTE is a condition with a low case fatality of about 2%. This puts the excess mortality from VTE associated with third generation pills around one in a million women annually. The absolute risk of VTE associated with the use of the pill rises with risk factors (See Tables 8. 3 and 8.4).

Breast cancer. Every woman is at risk of breast cancer whether or not she takes the pill. The Collaborative Group of Hormonal Factors in Breast Cancer analysed 54 studies from the developed and developing countries and found a small additional risk of breast cancer in women during and for up to 10 years after stopping the pill (WHO 1996c). Risk is not affected by type of pill and duration of use and the cancers diagnosed. In women who have used the pill, breast cancer is clinically less advanced than in those who have never used the pill and is less likely to have spread beyond the breast.

Liver cancer. Benign hepatocellular adenomas can be produced by the oestrogen component of the pill. This has become extremely rare since the advent of low-dose pills. No increase in mortality from liver cancer has been noted since the introduction of the pill in the 1960s.

Cervical neoplasia. Use of the COC may be a marker for unacknowledged high-risk behav-

Table 8.3 Risk factors for arterial and venous disease.

Arterial disease	Venous disease
Smoking (age > 35)	Genetic predisposition
Coagulopathies	Acquired predisposition, e.g. Antiphospholipid syndrome)
Diabetes mellitus	Immobility/trauma
Hypertension	Dehydration
Hyperlipidaemia	Obesity (BMI > 30)
Android obesity	Extensive varicose veins
Family history of coronary artery disease	Family history of VTE

Table 8.4 Risk of non-fatal VTE in COC users.

Background risk	5–11/100 000 users
Risk in pregnancy	60/100 000 users annually
Risk in desogestrel/gestodene users	30/100 000 users annually
Risk in levonorgestrel users	15/100 000 users annually

iour. The incidence of human papillomavirus (HPV) and cervical intraepithelial neoplasia (CIN) has been shown to be higher among COC users, although this may merely reflect the pattern of sexual behaviour and number of partners. A small elevation (1.6 fold) in the risk of squamous cervical cancer (WHO 1985) is seen in long-term COC users but studies need to be interpreted with caution, as other confounding variables of sexual behaviour, for example smoking, age of first intercourse, number of sexual partners (some of whom may harbour HPV) and less likelihood of use of barrier methods, may not have been considered. A history of cervical intraepithelial neoplasia does not contraindicate the use of hormonal contraception.

Combined injectable methods (CIM)
The combined injectables contain both an oestrogen and a progestogen and are administered deep intramuscularly at monthly intervals, but require more evaluation before they can be safely recommended. The two combined injectable formulations are Cyclofem which contains 25 mg of medroxyprogesterone acetate and 5 mg of oestradiol cypionate and Mesigyna containing 50 mg norethisterone oenanthate and 5 mg of oestradiol valerate. The main mechanism of action is suppression of ovulation and the progestogen has effects on the cervical mucus and the endometrium. The combined injectables have fewer side effects than the progestogen-only injectables but there can be logistic problems with provision of monthly injections.

Vaginal rings
A disposable vaginal ring releasing 15 μg oestradiol and 120 μg etonogestrel for cyclic

use has recently been made available and leads to complete inhibition of ovulation. The other progestogens that have been used in rings are LNG, megesterol acetate, medroxyprogesterone acetate, norethisterone acetate, nesterone and natural progesterone.

Progestogen methods

The progestogen-only pill (POP)
is an alternative method of contraception for women intolerant of or with sensitivity to oestrogens and for lactating women. The failure rate is 0.3–4/100 woman years. Efficacy may be lower in younger women and those over 70 kg weight. The progestogen thickens the cervical mucus making it relatively impenetrable to sperm (Toth *et al.* 1982) and indirectly bacteria cannot ascend the upper genital tract. The thickening of the cervical mucus itself is a major protective factor for sexually transmitted infections (Toivenen *et al.* 1991).

As the therapeutic window of efficacy is rather narrow it is important that this pill is taken regularly at the same time each day. A new version of the POP (Cerazette) is due out soon. There is an apparent increase in the prevalence of ectopic pregnancies although this pill prevents intrauterine pregnancy more effectively. Due to partial suppression of follicular development, there is an increase of follicular ovarian cysts in 30% of POP users. Progestogen-only contraceptive vaginal rings designed to release 'minipill' dosages of various progestogens have been marketed for some years in Chile.

Progestogen-only injectable contraception
Depo Provera (depot medroxyprogesterone acetate DMPA) and Noristerat (norethisterone

oenanthate) are long-term, reversible, highly effective and safe progestogen-only contraceptive methods licensed for first-line use since 1995 and have been marketed in over 70 countries for some time without restriction, unlike the initial case in the UK. DMPA is given at 12-week intervals and Noristerat every 8 weeks.

Health benefits

Women report reduction in symptoms of premenstrual tension, menorrhagia, dysmenorrhoea, endometriosis and iron deficiency anaemia. The risk of endometrial cancer is reduced. It is of particular benefit to mentally retarded women in that they develop amenorrhoea with prolonged use. Haematological improvement has been noted in sickle cell disease (WHO 1991; De Ceuler *et al.* 1982) with DMPA. The effects on the cervical mucus help to reduce the risk of STI, but the 'double Dutch' approach is a good recommendation where appropriate. The protective effect of DMPA against endometrial cancer continues for up to eight years after user discontinuation.

Undesirable effects

Women can suffer unwanted side effects like prolonged and breakthrough bleeding, weight gain, mood changes and depression. About 50% of women using DMPA for one year or more report amenorrhoea (Belsey 1988). Long-term amenorrhoea in DMPA users has been shown not to be detrimental to bone density (Gbolade *et al.*1998). No harmful effects on lactation have been observed. Concerns over the safety of DMPA arose on the possible risk of breast cancer in beagle dogs and endometrial cancer in monkeys, but the beagle is now considered an inappropriate model for testing carcinogenic risks associated with progestogens. The return to fertility may be delayed for up to a year to 18 months. Use of DMPA in contraceptive doses does not increase the risk of congenital anomalies.

Recent WHO data indicate that the use of DMPA is not associated with an increase in the risk of cancer of the breast, endometrium, ovary, liver, or cervix (WHO 1991a, b, c).

Progestogen implants

Implants are a valuable addition to the range of contraceptive methods. Norplant is a six-rod Levonorgestrel (LNG) implant introduced in the UK in 1993 as an alternative method of long-term contraception. An essential feature of this method is its provision by providers skilled in insertion and removal (Fraser *et al.* 1998). The 5 years cumulative pregnancy rate is approximately 1/100 woman years and the ectopic pregnancy rates are low (0.3/100 woman years). Norplant prevents pregnancy by inhibition of ovulation in most women and prevention of normal sperm transport through the female genital tract, particularly the cervix. In implant users in whom ovulatory activity continues, luteal insufficiency and endometrial effects are the ancillary contraceptive mechanisms. Due to the effect on cervical mucus there is a reduced risk of PID. Hoechst Marion Roussell has stopped marketing it now.

A single-rod formulation with 3-keto desogestrel (Implanon) and a contraceptive lifespan of three years has greater ease of insertion and removal and initial data suggest high efficacy. New second generation implants are to be marketed soon, which should reduce some of the problems of insertion and removal of six-rod implants. There are the two-rod LNG implants which have a similar duration of action and efficacy to Norplant and single-rod formulations with the progestogens.

Risks and benefits

There are no data on the risk of reproductive tract cancers in women using implants. Long-term studies of bone mineral density in adolescents and women aged 20–45 have shown an increase in bone mineral density of the lumbar spine and distal forearm at 2 years after insertion (Naessen *et al.* 1995). Twenty per cent of users develop functional ovarian cysts which are managed expectantly.

Side effects

Menstrual changes are the most common side effects and irregular bleeding is more marked during the first year of use. 30% of Norplant users note changes in mood, body weight, headaches, and acne. Appropriate counselling is therefore essential.

Barrier methods of contraception

These are non-hormonal methods where efficacy depends on age, motivation, consistency and skill of the users. The user should be informed of alternative effective methods of contraception and the need for emergency contraception if their chosen method fails.

Latex condoms applied prior to genital contact and used consistently have shown protection of both men and women against gonorrhoea, and non-gonococcal urethritis (Cates & Holmes 1996) and HIV transmission (De Vincenzi 1994). Use of condoms reduces the total HIV risk between unprotected sex and complete sexual abstinence by 70% (Cates

1996). Worldwide programmes and public education emphasise the use of condoms as part of an STD/HIV strategy. A spermicide used in conjunction with a barrier method (Kirkman & Chantler 1993) maximises protection against both unwanted pregnancy and STIs.

Polyurethane female condoms (Femidom) are an alternative to male condoms but have been described as noisy, costly (Bounds *et al.* 1992), unattractive and not very popular, with failure rates of 15% at 12 months. *In vitro*, the Femidom is impermeable to HIV, cytomegalovirus (CMV) and hepatitis B infections. *In vivo*, it has been shown to prevent trichomoniasis. At present there are no *in vivo* data on protection against HIV infection by female condoms, but the potential is there if the method is acceptable.

Diaphragms and cervical caps are non-hormonal methods under the control of women and do not interfere with the sensation of either partner. The failure rate is 2/100 woman years with careful use and 15/100 woman years when it is used less consistently (Bounds 1994). Several studies have shown protection against cervical gonorrhoea and other STI rates are reduced by about 50% (Cates & Stone 1992). However, women may be allergic to the spermicide in the latex. There is also an increase in the risk of urinary infection and bacterial vaginosis (Hooton *et al.* 1989). Diaphragms have not been shown to prevent HIV transmission as they cover only the cervix and transmission can occur through the vaginal walls, vulval epithelium and penis (Howe *et al.* 1995).

Spermicides

Most commonly used spermicides in the UK

and USA use Nonoxynol 9 as the active ingredient. Spermicides provide limited protection against pregnancy (failure rates as high as 10–20%) and are not recommended as the only method of contraception. Nonoxynol 9 has a direct detergent-like action on the lipid components of the spermatozoa, disrupting the cell membrane, and may possess a virucidal action. The dual action on the spermatozoa and the microorganisms suggests a role in the sexual transmission of herpes simplex virus (Singh *et al.* 1976) and prevention of other STIs (*Chlamydia trachomatis* and gonorrhoea) (Cutler 1977). Nonoxynol 9 inactivates HIV *in vitro* at concentrations well below those expected to be present in the vagina (Hicks *et al.* 1985). The point of crucial importance is that there is no evidence that spermicides act against HIV *in vivo* (Bird 1991). High doses of spermicides may result in epithelial disruption and alteration of the vagina and/or cervix (Niruthisaard *et al.* 1991) which could contribute to HIV transmission.

Natural family planning and fertility awareness

Natural methods play an important part in the overall regulation of fertility but have a limited application, particularly in the prevention of STI as users of this method tend to be at lower risk of PID. They are non-hormonal methods with no physical side effects and can be taught by non-medical personnel. The disadvantages are a high degree of shared responsibility (Flynn 1980), commitment and sustained motivation and interference with sexual spontaneity. Good teaching and enthusiasm is essential to the success (WHO/BLAT 1982). Data showing life table probabilities of prefer-

ence during typical use show a range of overall optimal method effectiveness of 97.5% to 80% where less favourable conditions prevail (Trussell & Grummer Strawn 1990; Lambrecht & Trussell 1997).

The underlying principle is to predict the timing of ovulation and identify the fertile and infertile phases by changes in the cervix, quality and quantity of the cervical mucus, and basal body temperature. Sexual intercourse is avoided during these fertile days. The calendar method involves determining the fertile period based on cycle monitoring for 12 months but the failure rate can be high. Over-the-counter commercial kits are available to detect LH surge.

Persona Contraceptive Device

Persona was launched in the UK in 1996 by Unipath. It is a hand-held computer device designed to detect urine oestrone 3 glucouronide reached at a level 5–6 degrees below ovulation that defines ovulatory peak and LH using urine test sticks. The information is entered onto a computer database in the device. Efficacy is approximately 93–95% (WHO 1981). It is unsuitable for women taking tetracyclines, women who have irregular cycles and breast-feeding women, women taking COC and HRT and women with polycystic ovaries.

Lactational amenorrhoea method (LAM)

Prolonged breast-feeding is of major global importance in the control of fertility and women who do not breast-feed regain ovulatory status 3–5 weeks after delivery. LAM provides highly efficient contraception (98% efficacy) provided there is lactational amenorrhoea in the mother with a fully breast-fed infant under 6 months old (Perez *et al.* 1992).

The main mechanism of ovarian suppression during lactation is the suppression of release of serum FSH and LH. Suckling determines the impulses to the hypothalamo-pituitary axis and stimulates prolactin levels. Prolactin inhibits the release of FSH/LH.

IUD

Modern IUDs are long-term, non-hormonal, convenient, safe and reversible methods of contraception offering contraceptive efficacy at least as good as and possibly better in use effectiveness than that of the combined pill: 0.5–1.4/100 woman years (WHO 1990). IUDs appear to be underused in Britain (5%) (Tait *et al.* 1997). Long-term use of the IUD does not increase the risk of PID (Fairley *et al.* 1992) if women are carefully selected prior to IUD fitting. Infection is most likely to occur up to three months after insertion (Fairley *et al.* 1992) and unnecessary re-insertions should be avoided. While IUDs offer little protection against STDs because they do not affect the cervical mucus, they are safe in a mutually monogamous relationship. IUD use has not been proven to cause infertility in women who may otherwise not be at risk of STI. The prevention of intrauterine and ectopic pregnancy is significantly better with new IUDs containing $> 350\,mm^2$ of copper (Sivin 1991). Modern IUDs do not increase the risk of ectopic pregnancy (Sivin 1991) and are not contra-indicated in women with a high risk of ectopic pregnancy if the exposed surface of copper is more than $350\,mm^2$ of copper. The IUD is not recommended for HIV positive women as immunodeficiency may enhance the risk of PID. Counselling of HIV infected couples should include correct and consistent use of condoms for disease prevention when they choose a method other than condoms for the prevention of pregnancy.

Actinomyces-like organisms (ALOs) are common microaerophilic vaginal commensals present in small numbers. They are found on cervical smears in 30% of women wearing a plastic IUD and the rate increases with the duration of use. If these are found on cervical cytological smears, the Faculty of Family Planning and Reproductive Health Care in the UK (Faculty of Family Planning and Reproductive Health Care 1998) advises women to come back for a full clinical assessment. Relevant swabs for infection are taken and, if signs and symptoms of pelvic infection are present, the device is removed, sent off for a microbiological assessment and treatment instituted. A new copper-containing device is replaced after the infection subsides. If the woman is asymptomatic informed choice is appropriate and the IUD can safely be left in. If an IUD user becomes pregnant, the risk of a spontaneous abortion is about 50% and removal of the IUD is recommended if threads are accessible in the first trimester, preferably if the IUD has been demonstrated to be below the conceptus on ultrasound examination.

Levonorgestrel releasing IUS (Mirena)
Mirena was first marketed in the UK in May 1995. The silastic capsules on the vertical stem release approximately 20 µg of levonorgestrel daily into the uterine cavity. The progestogen increases the viscosity of the cervical mucus and may protect against ascending genital tract infection. It is a highly effective contraceptive method and also reduces average menstrual blood loss by 90% (Andersson & Rybo 1990), producing amenorrhoea by direct ac-

tion on the endometrium in 2 out of 10 women (Andersson & Rybo). In the early months of use, acne, headaches, depression and irregular bleeding can occur.

Emergency contraception

Awareness of and easy access to effective back-up methods to prevent unwanted pregnancy after an unprotected episode of sexual intercourse or if a barrier contraceptive method fails is important. Revised guidelines have recently been issued by the Faculty of Family Planning and Reproductive Health Care (Kubba & Wilkinson 1998) on emergency contraception. The standard licensed regime is the Yuzpe method – 100 μg of ethinyl oestradiol and 500 μg of levonorgestrel (2 PC4 tablets) repeated 12 hours later and started within 72 hours of unprotected intercourse or current method failure/inadequacy. However, nausea and vomiting occur in up to 50% and 20% of users, respectively. The failure rate per 100 women treated per cycle is 1–5% (Yuzpe et al. 1982; WHO Task Force 1998).

An equally effective alternative is the Ho and Kwan method (Ho & Kwan 1993) comprising two doses of levonorgestrel (LNG) 0.75 mg (25 tablets of the POP product – Microval, Norgeston) taken 12 hours apart, the first dose being administered within 48 hours of unprotected intercourse. However, the new WHO LNG regime (WHO Task Force 1998) (i.e. with an extended time of up to 72 hours) is better tolerated, has a lower incidence of nausea and vomiting (6%) and is more effective (1.1% failure) than both the Yuzpe (Finch & Green 1963; Ho & Kwan 1993 Cornelison et al. 1997; Jejeebhoy & Cook 1997) and Ho and Kwan (Wood & Suitters 1970; Dicfalusy 1995)

regime (Office for National Statistics 1997). A copper-containing IUD can be used post-coitally any time in the cycle within 5 days of the earliest episode of unprotected intercourse or within 5 days of the earliest calculated date of ovulation (i.e. up to day 19 of a 28-day cycle) or up to day 15 after prolongation of the pill-free interval. It is highly effective and can be used to provide long-term contraceptive protection thereafter.

Female sterilisation

In Britain, almost 50% of women aged 35–44 have been sterilised or have a partner who has been sterilised. Sterilisation is a highly acceptable, effective and safe operation. The first year failure rates are 0.1–0.8% and the 10 years cumulative probability of pregnancy with clips (Cornelison et al. 1997) is 3.6% and of ectopic pregnancy is 7.3/1000 procedures (Peterson et al. 1997). The risk of ectopic pregnancy is higher in women under 30 and those sterilised by bipolar coagulation as opposed to clips. Simultaneous abortion and sterilisation increase the failure rate by at least three-fold, and may increase regret and requests for reversal. Female sterilisation procedures may have a protective effect against ovarian cancer (Cornelison et al. 1997). Successful reversal of tubal sterilisation performed with clips is more likely than reversal of vasectomy procedures, particularly if performed within five years of the primary procedure.

Abortion

In England, Wales and Scotland termination of pregnancy is controlled under the Abortion Act 1967 as amended in 1990 by the Human

Fertilisation and Embryology Act. The abortion rates are 13/1000 in the age group 14–49 years (Office for National Statistics 1997). Recourse to abortion may be required when a woman's chosen contraceptive method fails and she has had difficulty in personal regulation of fertility. However, the practice by some women to regard it as a method of contraception should be discouraged.

Provision of legal abortion services is variable in the UK and, though gynaecologists in theory agree to abortion, in practice provision can be difficult due to constraints on the system by general gynaecology workload. Efficient and fast referral systems for abortion which aim to streamline the availability of early medical and surgical abortion linked with counselling and family planning services are important. Medical abortion is simple and requires fewer medical and other resources, can be run by suitably trained nurse practitioners with supervision by doctors and increases choice for women. As post-abortion infection is well documented, screening and assessment for chlamydia and bacterial vaginosis, treatment of positive cases and follow-up and treatment of contacts has been recommended (Blackwell *et al.* 1993). The RCOG (UK) recommends prophylactic antibiotics to prevent or reduce the likelihood of infection. A woman's request for abortion if handled sympathetically will lead to more returns for further sexual health and contraceptive advice.

Infertility

Infertility constitutes a failure to achieve a pregnancy after a year of actively trying to conceive and can affect 15% of couples. The level of infertility may be related to the incidence of STIs. The common causes of infertility are preventable – tubal disease (STI, post-abortion and post-partum infections). The other causes are male factor disease, ovulatory disorders, peritoneal factors, e.g. PID and endometriosis, cervical factors and failure of implantation.

General measures of counselling, reassurance and advice on frequency and timing of intercourse are helpful. Couples may feel stigmatised with a sense of inadequacy and powerlessness and their psychological needs should be handled with empathy. Investigations for semen analysis, for ovulation, cervical mucus, tubal status and hormone profile if indicated are useful. Ovulation disorders respond to medical induction in 70–80% of cases. Tubal damage requiring surgery achieves success rates of approximately 40% according to the underlying pathology.

Many sub-fertile couples have benefited from assisted conception procedures like *in vitro* fertilisation (IVF), gamete intrafallopian transfer (GIFT) and intracytoplasmic sperm injection techniques (ICSI).

Male participation in fertility regulation

Lack of choice in male methods and attitudes of men to participating in fertility regulation are significant obstacles to the use of family planning by men. Hence, much of the burden of regulating fertility falls on women. However, the modern man is more ready to accept a fair share in the options for family planning.

Vasectomy

Vasectomy is a simple, irreversible and minor surgical procedure more widely practised in the UK and the developed world as opposed to the developing world. Local anaesthesia is the anaesthetic of choice. Most studies report failure rates of less than 1% (Trussell & Kost 1987), the efficacy being similar to laparoscopic female sterilisation. Haematoma formation occurs in 2% of men and sperm granulomas are common. Vasectomy has no impact on sexual function and does not cause atherosclerosis (Peterson *et al.* 1990), testicular cancer (Henrick *et al.* 1994), prostatic cancer (Zhu *et al.* 1996) or osteoporosis (Byrne *et al.* 1997). Three out of 10 men suffer from post-vasectomy pain syndrome and should be adequately counselled about this. Psychogenic erectile dysfunction may follow if the procedure is not well accepted (Ahmed *et al.* 1997). Reversal of vasectomy can be expensive and may result in restoration of fertility in 50–60% of cases.

References

United Nations (1994). Programme of action of the United Nations International Conference on Population and Development (ICPD), Cairo, Chapter VIII C. *Women's Health and Safe Motherhood Action* 8.25. UNFPA, New York.

Ahmed, I., Rasheed, S., White, C., *et al.* (1997) The incidence of post vasectomy chronic testicular pain and the role of nerve stripping of the spermatic cord in its treatment. *British Journal of Urology* 79(2), 269–270.

Andersson, K. & Rybo, G. (1990) LNG IUD in the treatment of menorrhagia. *British Journal of Obstetrics and Gynaecology* 97, 690–694.

Baird, D. (1965) A fifth freedom? *British Medical Journal* 2, 1141–1148.

Balda, M., Aggleton, P. & Slutkin, G. (1993). Does sex education lead to earlier or increased sexual activity in youth? *WHO Global Programme on AIDS*, Geneva.

Belfield, T. (1992) The problems of compliance in contraception. *British Journal of Sexual Medicine* 19, 76–78.

Belsey, E.M. (1988) Vaginal bleeding patterns among women using one natural and eight hormonal methods of contraception. *Contraception* 38, 181.

Bird, K.D. (1991) The use of spermicides containing 9 nonoxynol in the prevalence of HIV infection. *AIDS* 5, 791–796.

Blackwell, A.L., Thomas, P.D., Wareham, R., *et al.* (1993) Health gains from screening for infection of the lower genital tract in women attending for termination. *Lancet* 342, 206–10.

BMA, GMSC, Brook Advisory Centres, FPA & RCGP. (1991) *Confidentiality and People Under Sixteen*. BMA, London.

Bounds, W. (1994) Diaphragm study. *British Journal of Family Planning* 26, 66–72.

Bounds, W., Guillebaud, J. & Newman, G.B. (1992) Female condom. A clinical study of its use, effectiveness and patient acceptability. *British Journal of Family Planning*, 18, 36–41.

Byrne, P.A., Evans, W.D. & Rajan, K.T. (1997) Does vasectomy predispose to osteoporosis? *British Journal of Urology* 79(4), 599–601.

CASH Study of the CDC and NICH (1983). Oral contraceptive use and the risk of endometrial cancer. *Journal of the American Medical Association* 249, 1600.

Cates, W. Jr., & Stone, K.M. (1992) Family planning, STD and contraceptive choice – a literature update. *Family Planning Perspectives* 24, 75–84.

Cates, W.J. & Holmes, K.K. (1996) Condom efficiency against gonorrhoea and non gonococcal urethritis. *American Journal of Epidemiology* 143, 843–844.

Cates, W.J. (1996) Contraception, unintended pregnancies and sexually transmitted diseases: Why isn't a simple solution possible? *American Journal of Epidemiology* 143, 311–318.

Centers of Disease Control and the National Institute of Child Health and Human Development (1987) Cancer and steroid hormone study of the reduction in the risk of ovarian cancer associated with the use of the combined pill. *New England Journal of Medicine* **316**, 650.

Cornelison, T.L., Natrajan, N., Piver, M.S., *et al.* (1997) Tubal ligation and the risk of ovarian cancer. *Cancer Detection and Prevention* **21**(1), 1–6.

Croft, P. & Hannaford, P.C. (1989) Risk factors for acute MI in women: evidence from the RCGP oral contraceptive study. *British Medical Journal* **298**, 65–68.

Cutler, C.J. (1977) Vaginal contraceptives as prophylaxis against gonorrhoea and other sexually transmitted diseases. *Advances in Planned Parenthood* **12**, 45.

De Ceular, K., Hayes, R., Gruber, C., *et al.* (1982) Medroxyprogesterone acetate and homozygous sickle cell disease. *Lancet* **2**, 229.

De Vincenzi, I. (1994) A longitudinal study of HIV transmission by heterosexual partners. *New England Journal of Medicine* **331**, 341–346.

Dicsfalusy, E. (1995) From population policy to reproductive health: numbers, rates or human beings. In: *From Contraception to Reproductive Health Care* (ed. M. Elstein), pp. 15–39. Parthenon, Carnforth.

Doppenberg, H. (1993) Contraception and STI: what can be done? Experience and thoughts from the Netherlands. *British Journal of Family Planning* **18**(4), 123–125.

Durex Report (1997) D97 London International House, Herts.

Elstein, M. (1994) Consensus paper. Low dose formulations – is further education in steroid design justified? *Advances in Contraception* **10**, 1–4.

Engel, H.J. (1989) Angiographic findings after myocardial infarction of younger women: role of oral contraceptives. *Advances in Contraception* 1991, **7** (Suppl. 3), 235–243.

Faculty of Family Planning and Reproductive Health Care (1998) *Advice on IUDs and ALOs on Smear.*

Fairley, T.M.M., Rosenberg, M.J., Rowe, P.J., *et al.* (1992) IUDs and PID: perspectives from a large international database. *Lancet* **339**, 785–788.

Farrel, C. (1978) My mother said: The way young people learn about sex and birth control. In: *Contraception and Sexuality in Health and Disease.* (ed. McGraw Hill), 48 pp. Routledge, London.

Finch, B.E. & Green, H. (1963) Famous names in contraception. In: *Contraception Through the Ages.* pp. 136–145. Helmreich & Blair, Aberdeen.

Flynn, A. (1980) Natural methods of family planning. *British Journal of Family Planning* **6**(1), 9–14.

Franks, A.L., Beral, V., Cates, W., *et al.* (1990) Contraception and ectopic pregnancy risk. *American Journal of Obstetrics and Gynecology* **163**, 1120.

Fraser, I.S., Tutinen, A., Affandi, B., *et al.* (1998) Norplant consensus statement and background review. *Contraception* **57**, 1–9.

Gbolade, B., Ellis, S., Murby, B., *et al.* (1998). Bone density in long term users of depot medroxyprogesterone acetate. *British Journal of Obstetrics and Gynaecology* **105**, 790–794.

Henrick, M., Knudsen, L.B. & Lynge, E. (1994) Risk of testicular cancer after vasectomy; cohort study of over 73,000 men. *British Medical Journal* **309**, 295–299.

Hicks, D.R., Martin, L.S., Getchell, J.P., *et al.* (1985). Inactivation of HTLV III infected cultures of normal human lymphocytes by 9 non oxynol *in vitro*. *Lancet* **2**, 1422–1423.

Ho, P.C. & Kwan, M.S.W. (1993) A prospective randomised comparison of LNG with the Yuzpe regime in postcoital contraception. *Human Reproduction* **8**, 89–92.

Hooton, T.M., Fihn, S.D., Johnson, C., *et al.* (1989). Association between bacterial vaginosis and acute cystitis in women using a diaphragm. *Archives of Internal Medicine* **149**, 1932–1936.

Howe, J.E., Minikoff, H. & Duerr, A. (1995) Contraceptives and HIV. *AIDS*, **8**; 861–871.

IMAP (1995) Statement on steroidal oral contraception. *IPPF Medical Bulletin* **29**(4), 1–7.

Jejeebhoy, S.J. & Cook, R.J. (1997) State accountability for wife beating; the Indian challenge. *Lancet* **349**, 5110–5112.

Khanna, I. (1997) The global burden of reproductive health. *Progress in Human Reproduction Research* **42**, 2–4.

Kirkman, R.J.E. & Chantler, E. (1993) Contraception and the prevention of STI. *British Medical Bulletin* **49**(1), 171–181.

Kubba, A. & Wilkinson, C. (1998) Recommendations for clinical practice; emergency contraception. *British Journal of Family Planning* **23**, 4.

Lambrecht, V. & Trussell, J. (1997) Natural family planning effectiveness: evaluating published reports. *Ad-*

vances in Contraception **13**, 155–165.

Larsson, G., Milsom, I., Lindstedt, G., *et al.* (1992) The influence of a low dose COC on menstrual blood loss and iron status. *Contraception* **46**, 327.

Lewis, M.A., Heinemann, L.A.J., Spitzer, W.O., *et al.* (1997) For the trans-national research group on OCs and the health of young women. The use of oral contraceptives and the occurrence of acute MI in young women. Results from the trans-national study of OCs and the health of young women. *Contraception* **56**,129–140.

Milsom, I., Sundell, G. & Andersch, B. (1990) The influence of different combined oral contraception on the prevalence and severity of dysmenorrhoea. *Contraception* **42**, 497.

Moss, G., Lemetson, D. & D'Costa I., *et al.* (1991) Association of cervical ectopy with heterosexual transmission of HIV. *Journal of Infectious Diseases* **164**, 588–591.

Naessen, T., Olsson, S.E. & Gudmundsson, J. (1995) Differential effects of bone mineral density of progestogen only methods for contraception in premenopausal women. *Contraception* **52**, 35–39.

Niruthisaard, S., Roddy, R.E. & Chuitvangse, S. (1991) The effects of frequent Nonoxynol 9 use on the vaginal and cervical mucosa. *STD* **18**, 176–179.

Office for National Statistics (1997) *POP and health monitor.* Series AB, no 22, ONS, London.

OPCS (1993) *General Household Survey: 1993 series.* GHS No. 24. HMSO, London.

Perez, A., Labbock, M. & Queenan, J.T. (1992) Clinical study of the lactational amenorrhoea method of family planning. *Lancet* **339**, 968–970.

Peterson, H.B., Huber, D.H. & Belkar, A.M. (1990) Vasectomy: an appraisal for the obstetrician and gynaecologist. *Obstetrics and Gynecology* **76** 3:(2), 569.

Peterson, H.B., Xia, Z., Hughes, J.M., *et al.* (1997) The risk of ectopic pregnancy after tubal sterilisation – A collaborative review of sterilisation. *Working Group for the New England Journal of Medicine* **336**(ii), 762–767.

RCGP (1989) Oral contraceptive study. *British Medical Journal* **298**, 165–168.

Roberts, R. (1996) Forensic gynaecology and sexual assault. In: *The Year Book of RCOG.* (ed. J. Studd), pp. 79–88.

Ross, R.K., Pike, M.C., Vessey, M.P., *et al.* (1986) Risk factors for uterine fibroids: reduced risk associated with oral contraceptives. *British Medical Journal* **293**, 359–362.

Royal College of Obstetricians and Gynaecologists (1991) *Working Party Report on Unwanted Pregnancy.* Chamelion Press, London.

Sapire, K.E. (1990) Sexual health. In: *Contraception and Sexuality in Health and Disease.* (Adapted by T. Belfield & J. Guillebaud), pp. 327–30 & 456. McGraw Hill, Maidenhead.

Sarrel, L.J. & Sarrel, P.M. (1981) Sexual unfolding. *Journal of Adolescent Health Care* **2**, 93–99.

Singh, B., Postic, B. & Cutler, J.C. (1976) Virucidal effect of certain chemical contraceptives on Type 2 Herpes viruses. *American Journal of Obstetrics and Gynecology* **126**, 422–425.

Sivin, I. (1991) Dose and age dependant ectopic pregnancy risks with intrauterine contraception. *Obstetrics and Gynecology* **78**, 291.

Spector, T.D. & Hochberg, M.C. (1990) The protective effect of the COC on rheumatoid arthritis: an overview of the analytic epidemiological studies using meta analysis. *Journal of Clinical Epidemiology* **43**, 1221.

Tattel, H.F. & Kafrissen, M.D. (1995) A review of combined pill use and the risk of HIV transmission. *British Journal of Family Planning* **20**, 112–116.

Templeton, A. (ed.) (1996) Recommendations arising from the 31st Study Group on The Prevention of Pelvic Infection. In: *The Prevalence of Pelvic Infection.* RCOG Press, London.

Toivenen, J., Luikainen, T., & Allonen, H. (1991) Protective effect of intrauterine release of levonorgestrel on pelvic infection. A three year comparative experience of levonorgestrel and copper releasing IUDs. *Obstetrics and Gynecology* **77**, 261–264.

Toth, A., O'Leary, W.M. & Ledger, W. (1982) Evidence for microbial transfer by spermatozoa. *Obstetrics and Gynecology* **59**, 556–559.

Trussell, J., & Grummer Strawn, L. (1990) Contraceptive failure of the ovulation method of periodic abstinence. *Family Planning Perspectives* **22**, 65.

Trussell, J. & Kost, K. (1987) Contraceptive failure in the United States: A critical review of the literature. *Studies in Family Planning* **21**, 237–283.

Vessey M.P., Metcalfe, M.A., Wells, C., *et al.* (1987) Ovarian neoplasms, follicular ovarian cysts and the combined pill. *British Medical Journal* **294**, 1518–1520.

Vessey, M.P. & Painter, R. (1995) Endometrial and ovarian cancer and oral contraception – findings in a large cohort study. *British Journal of Cancer* **71**, 1340–1342.

Vessey, M.P., Yeates, D. & Flowel, R. (1981) PID and the IUD: findings in a large study. *British Medical Journal* **282**, 855–857.

Walner Hanssen, P., Eschenbach, D.A., Paavonen, J. *et al.* (1990) Decreased risk of symptomatic chlamydial pelvic inflammatory disease associated with oral contraceptive use. *Journal of the American Medical Association* **263**, 54–59.

Wellings, K., Johnson, A.M. & Wadsworth, J. (1994) *Sexual Attitudes and Lifestyle Survey*. 92 pp. Blackwell, Oxford.

WHO (1981) Prospective multicentre trial of the ovulation method of natural family planning II The effectiveness phase. *Fertility and Sterility* **36**, 591–598.

WHO (1985) Collaborative study of neoplasia and steroid contraceptives (1985). Invasive cervical cancer and the combined pill. *British Medical Journal* **292**, 961–965.

WHO (1990) Collaboratory special programme of research development and research training in human reproduction. The CuT 380A, CuT 220c, Multiload 250 and Nova T IUD at 3, 5 and 7 years of use. *Contraception* **42**(2), 141–158.

WHO (1991a) Collaborative study of neoplasia and steroid contraceptives. Breast cancer and depot-medroxyprogestrerone acetate: a multinational study. *Lancet* **338**, 833–838.

WHO (1991b) Collaborative study of neoplasia and steroid contraceptives. Depot medroxyprogesterone and risk of endometrial cancer. *International Journal of Cancer* **49**, 186–190.

WHO (1991c) Collaborative study of neoplasia and steroid contraceptives. Depot medroxyprogesterone acetate (DMPA) and risk of liver cancer (1991). *International Journal of Cancer* **49**, 182–185.

WHO (1995) Collaborative study of CVS disease and steroidal hormones. VTE and the COC: results of an international multicentre case control study. *Lancet* **346**, 1575–1582.

WHO (1996a) Collaborative study of cardiovascular disease and steroid hormone contraception. Ischaemic stroke and COCs: results of an international multicentre case control study. *Lancet* **348**, 498–505.

WHO (1996b) Collaborative study of cardiovascular disease and steroid hormone contraception. Haemorrhagic stroke and COCs: results of an international, multicentre case control study. *Lancet* **348**, 505–510.

WHO (1996c) Collaborative Group on Hormonal Factors in Breast Cancer. Breast cancer and hormonal contraceptives: collaboration and analysis of individual data from 54 epidemiological studies. *Lancet* **347**, 1713–1727.

WHO (1997) Collaborative study of CVS disease and steroid hormone contraception. Acute MI and combined oral contraceptives: results of an international MC case control study. *Lancet* **349**, 1202–1209.

WHO Task Force (1998) A post ovulatory method of fertility regulation. Randomised controlled trial of LNG vs the Yuzpe regime of combined Levonorgestrel contraception for emergency contraception. *Lancet* **352**, 428–433.

WHO/British Life Assurance Trust (BLAT) (1982) *A Resource Package for Teachers of Natural Family Planning Methods.* Centre for Health and Medical Education, Family Fertility Education, London.

Wood, C. & Suitters, B. (1970) The fight for acceptance. In: *History of Contraception*. Medical and Technical Publishing, Aylesbury.

Yorkshire Regional Health Authority. (1992) *Working Party Report on Teenage Sexual Health*. YRHA, Yorkshire.

Yuzpe, A.A., Smith, R.P. & Radmaker, A.W. (1982) A multicentre clinical investigation employing ethinyloestradiol combined with norgestrel as a postcoital contraceptive agent. *Fertility and Sterility* **37**, 508–513.

Zhu, K., Stanford, J.L., Daling, J.R., *et al.* (1996) Vasectomy and prostate cancer; a case control study in a health maintenance organisation. *American Journal of Epidemiology* **144**, (8), 717–722.

Part 2

Applications in the Psychology of Sexual Health

Chapter 9

Taking a Sexual History

James Watson

Introduction

The task of any clinician who sees people with problems is to do their best to understand these problems in such a way as to respond professionally in the appropriate way. This is so whether the clinician is a nurse, doctor, psychologist, or indeed anyone in a professional role who expects and is expected to offer informed help for personal difficulties. How this is best done varies to some extent with the setting in which the consultation occurs, and the clinician needs to be aware of this. For instance, helpseeker–clinician meetings may differ, sometimes in important ways, between primary care (general practice) and specialist (secondary care, including hospital) settings; between public (national health) and private practice settings; in relation to what the referrer has or has not said to the person(s) referred; and the standard of the physical facilities used. Every environment has 'demand characteristics' which frame what happens within the setting. Despite these effects, gen-

eral principles apply to the basic clinical task, wherever it takes place.

Procedure: general outline

The clinician should have a clear idea of how the consultation is to proceed before they meet the patient (this term will be used for convenience, even though many clinicians prefer to refer to helpseekers as 'clients' or sometimes by other designations). The clinician should know how long the meeting is to last, and how they plan to shape what happens during the time. When they first meet the patient, and have invited them to sit comfortably, they can with advantage share this outline with them. For instance:

Thank you for coming. We will have about one hour for this meeting. It would be helpful to me if we could begin with your telling me, in your own words, what are the problems you would like us to discuss, and then go on to say something about when and how they developed.

At first meeting, it is often helpful to make statements rather than ask questions, and to make statements self-referring (e.g. 'it would help me.'). It is good practice to begin an interview with a new patient this way. The patient should have time to tell their views of the evolution of their difficulties in their own words. By the end of this initial phase, the clinician should have a reasonably clear idea of the nature of the problems which the patient has. This will involve the clinician in detailed enquiry of a kind which may not come naturally, since detailed accounts are required of what may have happened in the past and what the patient hopes will happen in the future, and many people speak naturally more broadly, in generalities. For instance:

> The exasperated wife may say to her husband 'you are hopeless'. The husband might agree or protest; if the wife seeks behavioural change, she must specify behaviours which she wants the husband to stop doing or to start, such as 'please bath three times a week; place your clothes tidily on a chair not on the floor when you undress; and kiss me every day before you leave for work'.

In a system where patients see specialists after referral from another (e.g. 'primary care') clinician, the specialist already has ideas about the problem before the patient begins to tell their story to them. As this unfolds, the clinician develops more ideas which may support the initial suppositions, or suggest that a modified view is needed. In seeking to clarify such possibilities, the clinician tends to guide the later parts of the interview more than the initial phase by asking specific questions or drawing attention to particular points. For example:

> You have told me that you sometimes experience the feeling of ejaculation but no fluid comes out as you would expect. Tell me, if you pass urine after sexual intercourse, is the urine cloudy? (This question is directed at the specific possibility of retrograde ejaculation, in which ejaculation occurs into the bladder; the condition is common after the operation of prostatectomy.)

After the patient's general account of current problems has been supplemented by more detailed enquiries, the interviewer will usually need information about the patient's biography, including family and personal history. In addition, when patients complain of sexual problems, questions *always* arise concerning the close relationships in which the patient is involved or in which they would like to be involved. Often, some attempt to assess the patient's current relationship(s) will be needed. Hence, a joint meeting with a partner (or sometimes past partner or prospective partner), or involving patient and partner in separate individual meetings, should always be considered. When – as happens not infrequently when sexual difficulties are at issue – patient and partner have been referred jointly as a couple, the initial interview will usually be with both people together. This situation is considered briefly later in the chapter.

Sexual symptoms

Complaints to clinicians about sexuality form three categories: the *frequency* of sexual activity; its *type*; and its *quality*.

Frequency problems

These include complaints that the amount of sex taking place is more, or less, than is wished. The referred patient may complain that too much sex is occurring, or is sought, or (more commonly) that too little sex is taking place. A discrepancy between the patient and their partner's evaluation of current sex frequency is commonly found (one thinks enough sex is taking place, the other wishes there to be more, or less).

Sometimes, complaints referable to sexual frequency are framed in terms of sexual desire or interest (e.g. *I don't feel like it any more, the urge has gone, I don't get 'turned on'*), implying the wish to re-establish sexual activity that is once more satisfactory. In fact, complaints of lost (or increased) sexual drive justify detailed exploration, since different people mean different things by 'drive' or 'urge'. Sometimes 'drive' refers to the initiation of sexual activity, or satisfaction from sex, rather than the frequency of sexual activity. The experience of 'sexual drive' varies between males and females, and with age in both genders, usually being experienced as less 'urgent' after age about 35.

The experience of sexual drive also varies with properties of the relationship with the sexual partner, including the degree and nature of the attachment between them. Very commonly, the urge for sexual activity so dominant in early passion, and reliant on immediate sensory (predominantly visual and tactile) cues, subsides with continuing familiarity and growing domestic and occupational commitments. 'Sexual drive' in many long-term relationships is sustained without reliance on the immediate 'feeling turned on' of the initial 'falling in love' encounter. A detailed enquiry into complaints of lost sexual drive is always necessary.

On occasion, patients complain of *more frequent* sexual activity, or the urge to it, on their own partner's account. Such sexual activity may be within the relationship, or outside it – in which case the relationship behaviour of the patient(s) should be explored, since there are obvious implications for trust and affectionate attachment between the partners. Sometimes, complaints about sexual frequency are accompanied by difficulties with the *type* of sexual activity, as for instance when a man married for many years develops a passionate homosexual liaison. Both men and women may complain about the frequency of masturbation, an activity often regarded very negatively.

As part of the assessment of sexual problems, it is often helpful to check the desired frequency of sexual activity, to see if both partners agree, and to judge if the aims are reasonable in relation to the individuals' health, age, and past sexual experience. As elsewhere in clinical sexology, it is important not to jump to conclusions about what sexual behaviour is desired, since an individual may have very particular views; explicit enquiry is always advisable. Sometimes, patients seek a complete absence of sexual urge or sexual expression; for example, this occurs in some gender reassigning individuals and in some paraphilic patients tormented by impulses experienced as ego-dystonic and as difficult-to-resist urges to unwanted dangerous or illegal acts.

Complaints about type of sexual activity

These may refer to any variety of sexual behaviour, including masturbation, heterosexual coitus, homosexual lovemaking, and paraphilic behaviours. Sexual activity is a function of the nature of erotic stimulation effective in a particular person, and of the integrity of the individual sexual arousal and response cycle. The range of erotic stimuli to which an individual may respond with sexual arousal is their 'sexual preferences'; this is often surprisingly narrow and tends to be relatively fixed throughout adult life. In the arousal and response cycle, physiological and psychological arousal leads successively to a plateau phase of sexual excitement, orgasm, the reduction of sexual arousal, and a refractory phase. It is important to remember that the *form* of the sexual response cycle is the same, whatever the nature of the arousing stimulation. In its temporal parameters, a person's sexual response cycle varies from time to time with aspects of their general condition which determine their *arousability*, capacity to respond to increments of erotic stimulation.

The most frequent complaints about 'type' of sexual activity concern heterosexual lovemaking, including behaviours which precede and follow coitus as well as sexual intercourse itself. Very commonly, the complaint in an established relationship is that sex has become perfunctory, the 'foreplay' abandoned. Also very commonly, patients complain of inefficiencies in the sexual arousal and response cycle. The so-called 'sexual dysfunctions' can be understood in these terms. Failure of geni-

tal lubrication in the female, and of erection in the male, are referable to the arousal phase; and orgasmic failure in the female, and premature or failure of ejaculation in the male occur in the plateau and orgasm phases. Vaginismus is often classified with these problems as a sexual dysfunction, but is not a disorder of the sexual response cycle, since a woman may experience sexual arousal and orgasm even though their involuntary pelvic muscle contractions may prevent vaginal penetration.

Complaints about erections are the commonest sexual symptoms of all. The history-taker should remember to enquire about three points in particular: the nature of the difficulty; its manner of onset; and its variability from time to time and place to place. Complaints about erections are most commonly of loss of penile rigidity, which may not necessarily make penetrative sex completely impossible; sometimes, complaints turn out to be of changes in penile sensation, or involve ejaculatory problems which may have antedated erectile changes. With respect to onset, the distinction between gradual and acute onset is extremely important, since physically (medically) caused erectile failure usually has a gradual onset, and acuteness suggests a psychological onset. Variability of erectile performance also bears on the question of causation, since a significant physical contribution is unlikely if the sexual response cycle is efficient *under some circumstances at least*.

In women, complaints of having lost sexual interest are common and may reflect loss of inclination to engage in sexual activity, and/or reduced responsiveness, manifest by lack of vaginal lubrication during arousal, failure to achieve orgasm, or both. Particularly sensitive interviewing may be needed to elicit these difficulties, of which women may be very ashamed and which may be consequences of abusive childhood experiences. In such instances, women patients often prefer to see female clinicians.

Homosexual individuals and couples may similarly complain of difficulties referable to the *type* of sexual activity in which they are engaging. Homosexual men are liable to the same erectile and ejaculatory dysfunctions as are heterosexual men; as noted, the sexual response cycle has the same form for all sexual preferences. Heterosexual clinicians who may deal with homosexual individuals and couples should ensure that they inform themselves about the normal behaviours of couples whose sexual activities differ from their own.

In dealing with patients with sexual difficulties, it is important to be clear whether or not any particular behaviour under discussion is *ego-syntonic* or *ego-dystonic*; that is, whether the behaviour is experienced as compatible with the person's overall view of how they themselves think they would like to be, or as not in keeping with this self-view, in which case there may be a sense of conflict within the self about the sexual tendencies. People with ego-dystonic tendencies may come for help personally. Ego-syntonic behaviours are more likely to be labelled as problematic by family, friends, or society at large. *Paraphilic behaviours* may be complained of in either of these ways, by self or others; details are outside the scope of this chapter.

The quality of sexual behaviour

This may also be the focus of symptoms. Of course, complaints about the *type* of sexual activity (when the desired forms of sexual behaviour become unattained, as for example with erectile impotence or premature ejaculation) usually also involve a sense of poor quality; complaints about failing to achieve orgasm are also evaluations of behaviour, estimates of quality. However, on occasion, people complain about the quality of sex which appears to be efficient. Sometimes, people sustain the ability for coitus through the mediation of private fantasy during it. Transsexual people, whose body (before any medical or surgical intervention) appears of one gender but who experience themselves as of the other, may also engage in what a 'third party' might observe to be normal sexual intercourse, while at the time imagining themselves to belong to the desired gender.

A model applicable to sexual problems

The taking of a sex history provides the clinician with information which may be extensive and detailed. There is no point in eliciting information for its own sake; interviewing must be for clearly defined purposes. The patient comes with something which is wrong, and they seek advice as to how it can be put right. They expect or hope that the clinician has some sort of expertise which will achieve this. This expertise begins with a model of how things work and how they can go wrong and be put right. After the first part of the assessment of the interview, in which the patient is encouraged to tell the story of their difficulties, in their own words, the clinician's enquiries are guided by the 'explanatory model' which they use to try and make sense of patients' complaints.

We can indicate the processes involved by considering in outline the application of a 'biopsychosocial' model to sexual dysfunctions, for example erectile impotence. Efficient sexual function requires intact *biological* systems (anatomical, neurological, vascular, hormonal) responsible for genital performance. Genital function may be impaired by disease processes which affect these systems, or the coordination of biological systems which are actually intact may be at fault, resulting in the *inhibition* of bodily functions. The inhibition is predominantly neurally mediated, from the brain via spinal pathways to the genital area. The inhibition originates from the neural effects of *psychological* factors, including feeling states (including pain, anxiety, sadness, etc.), troubled thought patterns (including 'worrying' about current concerns, and having intrusive thoughts about the possibility and expectation of sexual failure), and the present activation of relevant past memories. These experiential states develop in response to *social* factors, including inanimate and personal aspects of the immediate environment (who is in the room, what the room is like, competing concerns for children, domestic worries, work issues, etc.). A clinician using this model would check physical systems, seek to identify inhibitory psychological factors, and evaluate these in relation to the social context and the personal relationship(s) in which sexual problems may have declared themselves.

The model guiding a clinician is useful to the extent that it proves to make sense of clinical problems and point to interventions which prove helpful. The biopsychosocial model as outlined is helpful in most cases of sexual dysfunction occurring in stable, continuing, relationships, but is less satisfactory when problems of affection or hatred impinge on sexual attraction and performance. For this, a concept like the *lovemap* of J Money (1986) is useful. The 'lovemap' is the representation in the brain established in childhood of the properties of the person (or parts or representations of people, or substitutes for them) to which the individual would be able to form erotic attachments. In the process of development, various problems may impair lovemap development in various ways, which have in common some sort of disjunction between sex and affection, genital performances and close affectionate relationships.

Biographical history

The ways in which, and the extent to which, the clinician will seek information about the patient's family of origin, individual development through school to the world of adult occupation, and current situation, will be framed by the general model being used. As full a personal biography as possible is important to clinicians who think current problems can only be fully understood through knowledge of their evolution through and since childhood. Or a clinician following an approach which emphasises the correction of problematic current interaction patterns might, to begin with, need relatively little information about early development. Notwithstanding this principle, *some* information about these matters is needed in most circumstances.

A good principle is to adopt what might be called an 'interview screening' method. This includes a general question about each major aspect of the individual's past life, without expecting at an initial meeting to go into any of them in great detail unless the initial query points to an important problem area. (It is important not to leave the agenda entirely to the patient as important areas may be omitted by the patient on their own as not being recognised as such, or as being very painful to disclose; an important example is the experience of some victims of domestic violence who are not able to complain about this, either because they think doing so might trigger more violence, or because they think they deserve it, or that it is 'their lot in life'.)

In the *Family History* it is useful to know whether parents are presently alive or dead, were together or separated, and the number and ages of siblings or other important family members. An overall evaluation of relationships in the family is helpful, since at least some positive relationship experience in childhood greatly increases the chances of relationship success in adulthood. A history of significant health and relationship problems in family members should be sought, because chronic illness or relationship breakdown during a person's childhood greatly colours later views about these aspects of family life.

The *Personal History* should include a summary of educational attainment – school until what age and qualifications, and whether evaluated generally positively or otherwise. It is often helpful to ask people what they were good at, not where the problems were, since people who have problems severe enough to lead to specialist consultation have often so focused on difficulties and negative points that they have almost forgotten they have had achievements, interests, or successes. It is helpful to remember that there is a one-way relationship between educational attainment and basic intellectual ability: if a person has at-

tained more than three or four A grade GCSE passes, then they have at least average intelligence, but not reaching this level does not mean that the person does not have this level of ability.

An outline of the person's life arrangements after leaving school is valuable. A successful transition from childhood to adult life implies reasonable success in the two great areas of occupation and personal friendships, which together take up so much of an individual's waking time. Of course, occupational adaptation must be assessed in relation to job opportunities in particular localities, and to domestic commitments. In the field of relationships, enquiry into the patient's experience of 'falling in love' is helpful, and into descriptions of different sorts of relationships, such as 'friendships'. While it is very common for people to have difficulties with *some* kinds of relationship, for instance potential sexual involvements, it is most unusual for people to have trouble coping with *all* kinds of relationship. Confusion is common between interaction ('social') skills being absent and their being present but inhibited. The latter is much more common than the former, especially as a manifestation of common mood disorders, notably depression. A history of reasonable success in relationships and occupation in adulthood is evidence against the presence of serious personality problems; the absence of such success does not necessarily indicate the presence of such difficulties.

The history should also include enquiry into alcohol and illicit drug use, medical and psychiatric problems, and any prescribed drugs, since all these factors may adversely affect sexual function. Medical and psychiatric examination may be needed if preliminary enquiries suggest the presence of illness of either sort. In addition, of course, previous sexual and close relationship experience will affect present experiences in both sex and relationship domains and some enquiry into this area is helpful during an interview. Clinicians need to learn the difficult skills needed to allow hearing and talking about aversive sexual and relationship experiences, and to sensitively elicit information in this area, which involves some of the most painful experiences anyone may have. If patients report sexually abusive childhood experiences, it is reasonable to suppose that these may have played some part in later or current sex or relationship difficulties. However, it is important not to jump to conclusions, since no particular form of sexual abuse leads inevitably to any particular sort of adult difficulty.

It is important to develop a sense of the moral values, religious beliefs, and attitudes to sex and relationship issues which govern the patient's approach to these aspects of life. These are of cultural origin to a significant degree and the interviewer needs to try and understand the views and practices concerning sex and relationships of the social, religious, and ethnic groupings in which the patient and their relatives are involved. Experience has shown that much of the 'sex therapy' approach which began in the USA with Masters and Johnson in the 1970s is 'culture bound' and inapplicable to people from many groups worldwide. Attitudes also vary greatly about homosexual interests and practices and about gender reassignment. Jurisdictions vary to some extent about what varieties of sexual behaviour are illegal, but *some* sexual behaviours are illegal everywhere. The interviewing process must acknowledge any legal, religious, or moral constraints on sex and relationship behaviour.

An example of a detailed individual interview format is provided in Table 9.1 (Carnwath & Miller 1986).

Formulation

History taking should provide enough information to allow at least a provisional formulation. This should include a summary of what the patient's problems are, and their genesis and development; and of relevant points from the family and personal history. An attempt can be made to combine these aspects of the case into an explanatory account, which should inform advice and action. For example:

> A businessman aged 45, married for the second time, has erectile dysfunction of gradual onset over two years, worse during the last six months. He has high blood pressure treated with medication, and also drinks about 30 units of alcohol every week. Six months ago, his wife discovered that he had been having affairs with two other women whom he meets when he travels abroad on business. (In this case, multiple physical and psychosocial factors are plausibly causative of the presenting sexual problem, and it might be difficult to disentangle their relative importance.)

It is good practice to attempt to understand the problem with which the patient presents, defining it in detail as outlined. However, the interviewer should always consider whether a

Table 9.1 The individual interview (from Carnwath & Miller 1986).

(1) The precise nature of the problem
- As the patient experiences it, and the referrer see it
- Frequency, timing, duration, onset, course, situational influences, modifiers
- Cognitive factors – sexual thoughts and attitudes, especially towards the problem(s), expectations of sexual activity and response, levels of spontaneous sexual interest

(2) The history of the sexual problem
- Aetiological circumstances – physical, situational, cognitive and emotional
- Maintaining factors
- Consequences of the problem – emotional, interpersonal, attitudinal, physical, domestic

(3) The nature of the relationship
(where a partner is involved)
- Extent of any discord
- Partner's response to sexual difficulty
- Partner's attitude(s) to sex, and the relationship, including motivation and likely cooperation
- Other circumstantial influences – work commitments, family commitments and pressures, financial pressures

(4) Family and personal background
- Quality of interaction with parents, siblings, relatives
- Ethnic and religious influences
- Friendship patterns
- Parental attitudes and behaviours towards sexuality
- Educational and occupational history
- Current domestic circumstances

(5) Personal sexual history
- Early (pre-pubertal) experiences
- Sex education
- Menstrual and pubertal history, and associated difficulties
- Development of first sexual involvements
- Masturbation history and fantasies
- First sexual intercourse and subsequent experiences (prior to and in addition to present relationship(s))
- Honeymoon experiences
- Contraceptive history and experiences – any discomfort, embarrassment, side effects
- Pregnancies, terminations, pregnancy fears – attitudes and experiences
- Homosexual experiences
- Experiences with sexual variations – paedophilia, voyeurism, fetishism, sadomasochism, bestiality, bondage, etc.
- History of rape or other traumatic sexual experiences

(6) Medical and psychiatric history
- History of illness and treatments – drugs, surgery, hospitalisation, aftercare
- Existence of current conditions and impairing physical disabilities
- Anxiety, depression and other psychiatric conditions

(7) Attitudes towards intervention
- Expectations of intervention
- Desired outcome
- Level of motivation
- Other reasons for seeking intervention – impending litigation or separation, attention seeking, fears of failure, etc.

reformulation is needed. This idea is based on the notion that the patient arrives at specialist help with their 'current best guess' about what

their problem is. But, this view might not be the most useful way of looking at the matter. In the case of sexual complaints (excepting only the rare cases when people complain that they cannot masturbate properly), at least one other person is *always* involved; it cannot be assumed that they have the same view of what the problem is. For example, the partners of some men who complain of erectile problems sometimes regard relationship issues as more problematic than the specifically sexual ones on which the man wishes to concentrate. The interviewer may need to raise the possibility with the patient that 'another view' of the problem might be more helpful.

Whenever a relationship issue coexists with a sexual problem, the question arises as to the advisability of a joint interview with the partner. Of course, this will not occur if the relationship issue is that the patient feels difficulties in establishing sexual relationships and has no current partner. Nor is it likely if a current relationship is breaking down. Nevertheless, whenever a patient with a sexual prob-

lem is in a close relationship which is, was, or might become a sexual one, the possibility of a joint meeting with patient and spouse should be raised. Methods of interviewing couples under these circumstances are outside the scope of this chapter, but always include concern about communication between partners, and their mutual commitment.

Reference

Carnwath, T. & Miller, D. (1986). *Behavioural Psychotherapy in Primary Care: A Practice Manual.* Academic Press, London.

Further reading

Bancroft, J.H.J. (1989) *Human Sexuality and Its Problems,* 2nd edn. Churchill Livingstone, London.

Chapter 10

Issues and Principles in the Assessment and Management of Psychosexual Disorders in Sexual Health Settings

Janice Hiller and Linda Cooke

Introduction

Clinicians in sexual health settings today are working in a cultural climate that differs considerably from that of the 1970s when the new sex therapies were introduced. In that decade the combination of behavioural techniques with psychodynamic formulations of relationship factors (Kaplan 1974, 1979) provided an important contrast to Masters and Johnson's (1970) innovative directive methods for couples with sexual problems. Since then the range of psychological therapies applied to psychosexual dysfunctions has extended to include a behavioural-systems approach (Crowe & Ridley 1990), cognitive techniques (Spence 1991) and object relations therapy (Scharff & Scharff 1991).

At the same time as therapeutic interventions have developed, a different range of clients now seek professional help. With the emergence of HIV and AIDS in the 1980s, the clinical population has grown to include same-sex partnerships and individuals facing the immediate and longer term consequences of a positive diagnosis. Fears of disease progression, of social stigmatisation and the possibility of transmitting the virus are associated with negative perceptions of sexuality and with sexual dysfunctions (Dupras & Morisett 1993).

A further thread in the management of sexual disorders in the 1990s has been the introduction of effective pharmacological approaches to restore erectile function. A range of products is available including intracavernosal injections and more recently an oral drug, sildenafil (Viagra). A number of other oral medications are currently at various stages of development and are likely to be available in the near future.

Psychological factors, however will remain important in the management of erectile dysfunction and indeed all sexual problems, as new drugs become available. For as we know from working with people struggling to integrate sexual behaviour into ongoing relationships, pleasure from physical intimacy consists of far more than a set of physical functions. The psychosomatic nature of human sexuality means that intrapsychic and inter-personal dynamics will always be central to re-warding sexual contact. At almost any point in the sexual response cycle, the intrusion of competing emotional states and unwanted cognitions can disrupt the physiological bal-ance of the autonomic nervous system and lead to impairment in response. Whether the intrusions are conscious or unconscious the inhibition of physical reactions can cause dis-tress to the individual and lead to possible misunderstanding between a couple, partic-ularly if one partner feels vulnerable about being wanted and valued by the other.

The assessment and management of psy-chosexual disorders, therefore, entails attention to the couple relationship and individual needs as well as evaluation of the particular nature of the presenting problem, its history and its maintenance. In this chapter we will describe therapeutic approaches that aim to overcome the psychological and physical barriers to sexu-al pleasure, and consider male and female dif-ficulties at each stage of the sexual response cycle. From the perspective of sexuality as a psy-chosomatic response that needs full integra-tion into psychic structures for healthy expres-sion, our focus will be on integrative aspects in treatment. The interface between individual and couple therapy, psychological and medical techniques, cognitive, behavioural and psy-chodynamic approaches will be illustrated in the case material and theoretical discussion.

Classification and assessment of psychosexual disorders

Given the many psychosocial and physical fac-tors influencing sexual responses, the assess-ment procedure requires sensitivity and thor-oughness. The aim is to classify the dysfunc-tion, provide a practically oriented formu-lation, and develop a coherent explanation that is meaningful to the individual or cou-ple. Since 1980 the underlying physiology of the sexual response cycle has been the basis for the classifying of sexual disorders. Thus, a syn-drome is assessed as one of motivation (de-sire), arousal (excitement) or orgasm depend-ing on which of the three phases of the indi-vidual's sexual response is impaired.

The *desire phase* disorders were added to the previous system, in which problems were divided into those of arousal or orgasm only (Kaplan 1979). Phobic reactions to intimacy were at that time not related to a particular as-pect of sexual function and neither were dys-pareunia (painful intercourse) or vaginismus. More recently though, Kaplan (1995) has clar-ified the conceptual framework by subdivid-ing the desire phase into hypoactive sexual de-sire (low or absent motivation for sexual inter-action), and sexual aversion disorders, defined as extreme aversion and phobic avoidance of all genital contact with a partner (DSM IV 1994). This group has been renamed as prob-lems associated with the dysregulation of sex-ual motivation, and a six-point scale ranging from hyperactive sexual desire to sexual aver-sion has also been suggested (Kaplan 1995). Hypersexual behaviour patterns, in which a compulsive sexual appetite interferes with the individual's working life and puts pressure on relationships, has not, however, been recog-nised by the DSM IV committee as a motiva-tional difficulty: instead it is classified as a 'dis-order not otherwise specified'.

The *arousal phase* disorders are currently described as erectile difficulties for men and the inability to maintain adequate lubrication/ swelling for women.

In the *orgasm phase*, men complain of distressingly early (premature) ejaculation or male orgasmic disorder, presenting as delayed or absent ejaculation. For women, orgasmic dysfunction is defined as the absence of orgasm after adequate stimulation.

Thus the commonly assessed sexual disorders are all included in this system apart from dyspareunia and vaginismus, which are classified as either disorders associated with genital muscle dysfunction or sexual pain (Kaplan 1995) or placed in the 'other' category in lCD-10 (Hawton 1995). However if we consider in more detail the physiological underpinnings of sexual arousal in women, the essential changes in the vaginal passage that enable penile penetration and containment without discomfort are not only lubrication and swelling, but also inner expansion (ballooning) and uterine elevation. Without a full genital response the internal organs are at risk of buffeting during thrusting and considerable pain may result from stretched support ligaments (Black 1988).

In the light of the link between failure of genital response and painful intercourse (Bancroft 1989) it has been argued elsewhere that in the absence of an organic basis for coital pain, deep dyspareunia should be more accurately conceptualised as a female arousal disorder, comparable to erectile difficulties in men (Hiller 1996). Moreover the involuntary muscle spasm of vaginismus which leads to closure of the vaginal passage can also be viewed as a failure of genital response, preventing penetration despite desire, lubrication and orgasm in some women. It is this aspect of the female response, the creation of an inter-

nal space, that is central to full arousal and is the distinguishing feature of female potency.

From this perspective, the female arousal disorders should include lubrication, dyspareunia (non-organic) and vaginismic problems, while the male arousal disorders would remain as difficulties attaining and maintaining an erection. The classification system proposed here is more comprehensive than previous concepts and is consistent with describing sexual difficulties according to underlying physiological mechanisms. It also gives fuller recognition to the complexities of the female arousal response, which has been less well investigated than that of the male (Bancroft 1989) despite its centrality in pleasurable and procreative sexual interactions.

For accurate classification and assessment, specific questions are posed concerning every aspect of the problem: current and historical antecedents, previous sexual experiences, attitudes to, and ideas about, sexuality, family of origin issues, etc., to decide on appropriate individualised intervention. Whilst the focus in this chapter is on psychological approaches, awareness of physical factors is essential. Details of organic conditions and the impact of medication on sexuality are well documented (Kaplan 1974; Hawton 1995; Bancroft 1989) and will not be repeated here. We would only point out that although loss of interest and orgasmic problems may be associated with medical conditions and their treatment, it is particularly in the assessment of erectile disorders and coital pain that physical causes need to be evaluated and, if present, integrated into psychological approaches. There is a paucity of research into the relative influences of organic and psychogenic causes in dyspareunia but studies of erectile difficulties indicate that around 30% are the result of organic factors (Segraves *et al.* 1987). Whereas classification of a disorder tends to remain stable over time, individual and relational variables alter in such a way that new material emerges; re-formulation of goals is therefore a continuing theme throughout the process of therapy.

Therapeutic models

Psycho-educational

Many people have limited knowledge of genital anatomy and functioning, particular the role of adequate stimulation in creating sufficient arousal in both partners and the role of competing emotional states like anxiety that may block arousal. Whilst it is easy for men to comprehend their genital parts, the female organs are concealed and internal, except for the vulva, and therefore readily confused or mislabelled. Diagrams and drawings can be helpful, such as those found in Bancroft (1989) and Kaplan (1974), along with explanations of the psychosomatic nature of the three phases of the sexual response cycle. In addition, the susceptibility of interest and desire to anger and fear, the need for unimpeded blood flow for genital engorgement (arousal) and the abandonment to erotic sensations in the orgasm phase, can be discussed as a framework for further therapy. A psycho-educational approach may involve encouraging a woman who is unsure about her body to explore her genitalia, as a link with behavioural exercises with a partner in a fully developed sexual therapy intervention.

Research into the use of instruction manuals and self-help books on their own indicates that 'bibliotherapy' appears useful in the ab-

sence of major relationship problems (Dow 1983), but that contact with the therapist does seem important for successful outcome (Trudel & Laurin 1988).

Cognitive-behavioural

Cognitive-behaviour therapy is based on the proposition that an individual's thoughts, or cognitions, determine emotional states and maintain overt behaviour (Beck *et al.* 1979). Maladaptive thoughts, which tend to become automatic, can result in negative emotions that in turn influence behavioural responses to sexual situations. Whereas behavioural approaches assume that cognitive change will occur as a consequence of behaviour change, cognitive therapy enhances the process by focusing more directly on producing cognitive change. Research into men's assumptions about desirable sexual behaviour has revealed various sexual 'myths', or a fantasy model of sex (Zilbergeld 1983), and that such myths are believed by men with sexual difficulties (Baker & de Silva 1988). Therapy focuses on negative thoughts and misconceptions about what represents sexual fulfilment by challenging the dysfunctional assumptions associated with symptomatology.

In addition to reducing specific attitudes that inhibit sexual functioning, cognitive therapy aims to enhance sexual skills such as the ability to focus attention on bodily sensations and sexual areas, to increase sexual knowledge and to correctly interpret sexual arousal sensations.

This approach emphasises the restructuring of belief systems, with behavioural techniques used for specific dysfunctions (Baker 1993). Spence (1991) has integrated cognitive-behavioural methods for negative cognitions with sexual skills assignments, which are introduced to produce evidence for generating cognitive change.

Object-relations

From an object-relations perspective, sexual difficulties represent earlier developmental conflicts that are re-evoked by intimate relations and sexually demanding situations. In this model particular constellations of internal objects, formed by parent–child interactions and reinforced by aspects of current partnerships, can interfere with sexual expression. Confusing family messages about sexuality, and lack of generational boundaries, lead to genital anatomy and functioning becoming split-off areas, unintegrated with psychosomatic responses. Therapy explores how unconscious sexual and relational anxieties are projected onto the individual's response cycle, thereby causing impairments in sexual functioning. The re-labelling of sexual sensations and physical interactions is an important feature, serving to increase psychosomatic integration and differentiate between past and present reactions. Behavioural tasks are designed to alter current patterns of sexual behaviour and prevent disempowering projections from inhibiting responses to sexual stimuli. Scharff and Scharff (1991) have combined object-relations theory with behavioural methods for couples, and an integrated approach has also been described for women with non-organic dyspareunia (Hiller 1996) and for men with erectile dysfunctions attending without a partner (Hiller 1993).

Behavioural-systems

This is essentially a problem solving approach, combining the behavioural techniques of communication training, reciprocity negotiation and sensate focus exercises with systemic interventions, the latter being used with stuck or intransigent couples and when the problem is one of motivation rather than dysfunction. A hierarchy of alternative levels of intervention acts as a clinical guideline by matching couple characteristics with the various interventions, so that the more rigid and inflexible, in a systemic sense, the couple appears to be, the further up the hierarchy is the chosen method (Crowe 1995). At the top of the hierarchy are the systemic interventions of messages, tasks and timetables, given with a formulation by the therapist after consultation with a team behind the screen.

For couples with incompatible sexual needs a negotiated timetable is suggested, involving the planning of set times for sexual activity, and a compromise frequency agreed by both partners thereby removing the tension from sexual issues (Crowe & Ridley 1990). If a couple seem very rigid in interactional patterns, a paradoxical injunction may be used. Goals of therapy may be scaled down if the system does not seem to shift and behavioural interventions are selected to help adjustment to the presenting problem (Ridley & Crowe 1992).

Behavioural

The first behavioural methods reported in the literature emphasised the central role of anxiety reduction in overcoming sexual fears

(Wolpe 1958) and described the stop-start technique for premature ejaculation (Semans 1956) which was also used by Wolpe and Lazarus (1966). However, it was not until Masters and Johnson (1970) described a series of graded sexual interaction tasks for couples, that directive exercises became the foundation of the new sex therapies. This 'sensate focus' approach was designed as a structured treatment format for conjoint therapy: home-based tasks generally begin with mutual caressing, avoiding genital areas and breasts initially, and progressing in a non-demand way to increasing sexual intimacy. Open communication of needs is encouraged and specific techniques are recommended according to the presenting problem (Kaplan 1974, 1995; Hawton 1995).

Modifications to the content of the assignments have been introduced as theory and practice have evolved. In particular the proscription on sexual intercourse during initial stages of sexual tasks was emphasised by Masters and Johnson (1970), but a more moderate approach to the ban has been suggested to allow some couples to retain flexibility and spontaneity (Lipsius 1987). In cases involving high anxiety levels, involuntary responses, or extreme pressure from one partner, retaining the ban until such factors are modified is useful. Kaplan (1974) has suggested one free lovemaking session per week, apart from systematic exercises, for the treatment of premature ejaculation, and has outlined variations on the stop-start method for men and their partners. In addition, one therapist working alone, as distinct from a co-therapy team as originally recommended by Masters and Johnson (1970), has been shown to be equally effective (LoPiccolo *et al.* 1985).

Ethnic clients respond to modifications in therapy presentation and style that recognise cultural differences, such as the reluctance of women in Sri Lanka to accompany their partners to treatment sessions (de Silva & Rodgrigo 1995). Working with Bangladeshi men in East London, d'Ardenne (1996) used a formal educational model with more drawings, allowing a man to speak for his wife if they both preferred, and engaging other family members to ensure privacy for behavioural exercises. Written guidelines are described for some clients after discussing home-based skills in sessions (Spence 1991). In a book for clients as well as clinicians, Brown and Faulder (1977) describe 25 'sexpieces' to enhance general enjoyment and address particular difficulties.

Behavioural models clearly remain central to psychosexual therapy, yet studies using the traditional Masters and Johnson components have been unable to replicate their high success rates. Halgin *et al.* (1988) suggest that clients with sexual problems seeking help today are more complex and that lack of knowledge and performance anxiety do not adequately explain their difficulties. Rather than applying behavioural techniques in a prescribed way based on the presenting complaint, an individualised approach is required, designed according to the unique parameters of each case and integrated with a cognitive, systemic or object-relations model of therapy for successful outcome.

Psychosexual disorders and HIV

When HIV entered the sexual health arena in the early 1980s, gay men were one of the first identified at-risk groups, although the virus has had an enormous impact on all sexual relationships. Proactive involvement of gay men, many of whom could not access mainstream sexual problem clinics, has resulted in the development of non-judgmental services accepting a range of lifestyles. Genito-urinary medicine or sexual health clinics now offer confidentiality, anonymity and an environment where gay men can comfortably seek help for sexual health concerns and psychosexual disorders.

Sexual problems are more common in HIV positive than comparable HIV negative groups, increasingly so as HIV progresses to symptomatic stages (Tindall *et al.* 1994). This has been demonstrated with different groups including gay men (Catalan *et al.* 1992; Jones *et al.* 1994), haemophiliac men (Jones *et al.* 1994), injecting drug-using women (Meyer Bahlburg *et al.* 1993) and educated middle-class, non-injecting drug-using women infected heterosexually (Brown & Rundell 1990). Catalan *et al.* (1992) found that both HIV positive and HIV negative gay men reported changes in their sex lives related to HIV. In the HIV positive group loss of interest, delayed ejaculation and erectile problems were most frequently reported by the subjects, but only delayed ejaculation was significantly increased in the HIV positive group. Catalan attributes this increased incidence of delayed ejaculation, a usually quite rare presenting problem in clinical samples (Hawton 1982; Renshaw 1988; Spector & Cary 1990), to fears of infecting sexual partners, even when safer sex is being practised. Wilensky and Myers (1987) reported a higher prevalence of delayed ejaculation among gay men generally and pointed to the influence of psychological and interpersonal factors. Although women with an HIV diagnosis report abstinence or decreased frequency of sexual intercourse initially, Hankins *et al.* (1997) found that 84% of the women in their study resumed sexual activity following a period of sexual adjustment, after their HIV positive test result.

Whilst sexual problems in HIV positive people develop for similar reasons to those in the rest of the population, some causal influences are particular to HIV positive clients. These cluster around three distinct themes: adjustment issues, disease progression and on-going sexual risk behaviour. Adjustment to an HIV diagnosis frequently leads to anxiety, stress and depression, all of which interfere with sexual behaviour and therefore need to be the initial focus of therapy, although with medical treatment there is a further possibility of physiological disruption in sexual responding. Disclosure issues also become relevant following diagnosis and can present a real dilemma at a critical time when feelings of vulnerability are high: disclosure of HIV status risks the painful experience of rejection and loss, while failure to disclose engenders guilt and anxiety and fears of infecting a partner. An HIV diagnosis can trigger a distressing examination of sexuality particularly if there is ambivalence and guilt about sexual and lifestyle choices, or if crises concerning previous heterosexual relationship and children are provoked (Sherr 1995). In such instances HIV may be interpreted as a punishment and withdrawal from sexual intercourse or inability to feel comfortable with any further sexual contact is not unusual. The conscious choice of an HIV positive partner is one option for positive gay men, many of whom will be linked into support groups and informal networks of peers. Discordant couples face particular problems (George 1990).

One may lose interest or experience sexual difficulties while the other may feel rejected, frustrated or uncomfortable about continued interest in sex. Guilt may result from sex outside of the relationship.

Progression of HIV disease can significantly influence sexual responses due to both psychological and organic factors. Even if the mechanisms are unclear it is crucial to acknowledge the possible role of organic influences and to set realistic therapeutic goals, without erring on the side of pessimism. If HIV disease progression is accompanied by suppressed immunity, fatigue, weight loss or altered body shape, confidence and self-image are easily undermined. It is particularly difficult to cope with inner feelings of being infected or diseased when manifestations of illness are clearly visible on the external physical body. With some clients then, the aim of psychosexual therapy will be to achieve an improved level of sexual satisfaction, despite the organic factors, without expecting a full return to normal functioning.

Unprotected risky sex continues at quite a high level in both gay and straight communities (Sherr 1992; Dawson *et al.* 1994; McLean *et al.* 1994). Fears of HIV transmission, infection or re-infection can heighten anxiety and directly undermine the sexual response. Prieur (1990) argues that unprotected sex may occur in the context of a search for meaning in people's lives. However, it is clear that precautions are taken depending on the resources at the time of having sex, the situation in which it occurs and the level of information (Donovan *et al.* 1994). Safe sex education is clearly essential, notwithstanding the complexity of the sexual behaviour of gay men and their lives.

Combination therapies are the most recent developments in the fight against HIV. Improved quality of life has brought greater expectations for the future and for sexual relationships, with the result that increasing numbers seek help with sexual difficulties. The influence of combination therapies and other HIV treatments on the sexual response is not yet clear, particularly over the long term, and some drugs used to treat AIDS may actually cause sexual dysfunction (Rice 1995).

Therapeutic interventions developed for straight couples can be adapted and modified for use with HIV positive gay men (Gordon 1986) if additional areas of difficulty such as sexuality and relationships as well as HIV are recognised (George 1990). Appropriately tailored therapy can be helpful for gay couples, men in relationships presenting alone and for those with no regular partner. Some who seek help may have a casual partner or multiple casual partners. Individuals who are not in a relationship can benefit from psychosexual therapy, but attending alone if one is in relationship is not a good prognostic indicator (Hirst & Watson 1997).

The therapeutic context: psychological meanings

Discussing sexual behaviour and needs is a sensitive area for most people, particularly when a relationship is not working and the problems lead to feelings of inadequacy and shame. Frequently the person with the identified problem develops a sense of hopelessness about emotional and bodily responses they cannot understand or control. Even more complicated to manage therapeutically is the hostility between people when one holds the other responsible for a sexual dysfunction that is involuntary, yet is experienced as evidence of not being cared for enough or of involvement in another relationship.

Whether the anger was a contributory factor in the aetiology of the disorder or serves as a maintaining factor, negative reactions to a partner's sexual difficulties threaten to undermine the clinician's attempts to promote change. Instead of believing that the problem means failure, not being loved or a sexual involvement elsewhere, the individual or couple need a therapeutic framework that considers alternative explanations and creates a co-operative context for ongoing work. The elaboration of psychological explanations for blocks to pleasurable sexual activity is not necessarily undertaken to foster insight or to find the causes or reasons for the dilemmas, although this may occur and is often seen as helpful. Rather the aim is to formulate the problem in a way that alters the tendency to experience guilt and blame, and encourages trusting relationships, as a basis for behavioural and affective change.

Moreover, generating different meanings for the unwanted behaviour patterns or symptoms paves the way for an approach that blends individual and conjoint therapy with the directive tasks of psychosexual therapy. Although some authors see a dichotomy between couple and sexual therapy, we agree with those who advocate combining models, in view of the close connection between relational factors and sexual satisfaction (Zimmer 1987; Crowe & Ridley 1990). Furthermore a combined approach enables the clinician to address the emotional, interactional and physiological levels of sexual situations in a flex-ible way that facilitates integration of response modes within the individual and response patterns between two people.

Case examples

Male avoidance of marital sex associated with paraphilic interests: individual and couple therapy, object-relations and psychosexual interventions

Sam and Jill, both in their forties and married for 22 years, were referred by their GP to a sexual health service for Sam's complete avoidance of sexual contact with his partner for the previous 4 years, resulting in her anxiety symptoms and low self-esteem. In the initial couple session Jill was extremely angry about an affair Sam had been involved in, giving him little chance to speak. During the subsequent individual session Sam revealed that the affair had not ended, as Jill believed, but provided an outlet for his need to be punished and dominated sexually by a woman in order to become sexually aroused. When he had tried to explain his needs to Jill she had been very judgmental. As Sam was unsure about remaining in a marriage without the opportunity for sexual fulfilment, a phase of individual therapy was embarked upon, enabling him to express his intense guilt and shame about his predicament.

Individual work explored the link between his paraphilic desires and his early family life in which he felt neglected and abandoned from the age of 2, when his mother was preoccupied with an ill brother who died at 13 months, and then immersed herself in the care of the next baby. Sam experienced his mother as a dominant and punitive figure, while his father remained shadowy and remote. In addition his mother frequently criticised her husband for his inadequacies while creating a sexualised atmosphere with Sam, by confiding her fantasies about an ex-lover who was killed in the war. During his teens Sam's father died and his mother exerted pressure on him to marry Jill, threatening suicide, before remarrying herself.

Sam's current wish for a sexual situation in which he was punished for being bad was viewed as a re-enactment of an internal world in which a useless inadequate man is treated harshly by a dominating and powerful woman who withholds affection but causes pain. Within an object-relations framework his mother's rejection of her own husband and over-involvement with Sam as her confidante in sexual matters, had collapsed generation boundaries and impaired healthy separation and individuation. Sam did not want to repeat an abandonment of his own two children: at the point where he felt able to stop the affair, couple therapy was reinstated with the aim of achieving a relationship where he could talk about his needs without expecting Jill to comply sexually. She knew that individual work had addressed Sam's relationship with his mother but was not informed about the affair.

Psychosexual couple therapy involved progressive stages of physical intimacy, starting with non-genital sensual pleasuring, while many issues of anger, guilt and disappointment were expressed by both partners. Eventually they were able to discuss Sam's need to feel punished sexually and to separate that from their newly formed relationship of trust, tolerance and shared physical and family ties.

Female aversion disorder: fear of penetration (non-consummation): individual object relations and psychosexual therapy
Zara referred herself to a psychosexual therapy service at a community family planning clinic, with a fear of sexual intercourse after 3 years of marriage which had led to tension in the relationship and

anxiety about the possibility of having children. The couple, in their mid-twenties, were able to enjoy foreplay with stimulation to climax, but Zara avoided any form of penetration. She attended on her own due to her partner's work commitments. Initially it was suggested that on the behavioural level the couple could continue mutual pleasuring but refrain from attempting intercourse while the underlying issues maintaining the aversion were explored.

Zara was the oldest of six children born in eleven years to a mother who seemed perpetually stressed by domestic pressures and by an aggressive, violent husband. As she was growing up Zara received many warnings from her mother about the dangers of mixing with boys, letting them have their way and the disgrace of an unplanned pregnancy. There were frequent rows between her parents over sex. Later her mother told her she had been forced into sex too soon after childbirth and that Zara's youngest brother was the result of unwanted intercourse. After the last pregnancy Zara was expected by her family to take on the household chores when her mother became unwell, instead of being with her friends. Zara also had memories of intense fear when her father came into her bedroom in tight underwear to say good night, and of an uncle who pressed his erection against her and tried to kiss her. She grew up thinking penises were too big and fearing being overwhelmed by a man.

From an object-relations perspective it seemed that a close internal bond with a mother who gave negative messages about sexuality was re-activated in Zara's adult life and blocked her ability to create her own sexual bond. Although Zara's partner was tolerant and understanding, unlike her father, she continued to fight him off in identification with a mother who was unable to protect herself from sexual demands. As these links were explored to aid Zara's internal separation from disabling early experiences, she was encouraged to get used to her vaginal passage in gradual stages and eventually to allow her partner to partially insert a finger. Couple exercises were suggested to decrease her anxiety about the erect penis in the absence of pressure for penetration. To address her increasing desire for a baby, she was referred to an infertility clinic where a nurse showed her how to insert a cannula with her husband's sperm. The aim here was to counteract her mother's helplessness by increasing Zara's sense of empowerment over her body's procreative potential. As Zara's fears diminished she moved progressively towards an acceptance of an internal space that could accommodate a penis. Her defences against allowing sensations in her vagina were slowly replaced by an acceptance of pleasurable bodily response, and penile penetration became a part of their sexual interactions.

Individual cognitive behavioural and psychosexual therapy for erectile difficulties with an HIV positive gay man

Tom, a 42-year-old HIV gay man, was referred to the psychology team for erectile problems which had started 3 years ago following his AIDS diagnosis. He had symptomatic illnesses with weight loss and fatigue, his health having recently improved with combination therapy. Tom still had occasional morning erections but had begun to experience secondary loss of interest in the first new relationship since his HIV diagnosis 10 years previously. His partner was also positive with good sexual desire and arousal, and asymptomatic.

There was virtually no contact between Tom and his family who rejected him because of his sexuality. Following the HIV diagnosis his feelings of being unlovable and

diseased had increased: the AIDS diagnosis had exacerbated his expectation of rejection. He imagined his partner would leave if their sexual relationship did not improve. Interpersonal relationships were a struggle in his adult life, along with work, health and drug treatment which added to his difficulties. The erectile problem appeared to be a function of negative self-image, particularly relating to his partner, fear of intimate relationships, self-imposed performance pressure in sexual situations and possibly some organic influences.

Cognitive-behaviour therapy focused on his irrational negative beliefs about HIV, sex and relationships. In parallel Tom was introduced to sensate focus and began exploring sensual pleasuring at home with his partner, who did not attend sessions but was nevertheless supportive and involved. After discussions about intracavernosal injections with his partner Tom had decided not to proceed. He had some moderate success with a vacuum pump which he purchased himself and used in the short term.

Over the course of therapy there was little change in erectile function but Tom described his sexual relationship as much more enjoyable and relaxed. Love-making became considerably less phallocentric and goal-focused and consequently the frequency of sexual contact increased. Tom's level of comfort in the relationship gradually improved.

Following an initial focus on the sexual relationship problems Tom was seen for five sessions of therapy which were used to explore his feelings about his HIV status and some of his fears about coping in the future.

Female primary anorgasmia: individual and couple cognitive-behavioural and psychosexual therapy

Sue attended a sexual health clinic because of primary anorgasmia with a partner or alone, at the suggestion of her current partner of 1 year with whom she described a good general relationship. He interpreted her lack of orgasm as sexual failure in one or both of them and encouraged her therapy.

Sue was 27 and described a family background where religious beliefs were quite strong, sex was never comfortably discussed and parental disapproval of sex before marriage was clearly expressed. She reported late first sexual intercourse and early anxiety about sex, never having explored masturbation although she was aware of it from her late teens.

Following assessment Sue was seen for a few individual sessions. These were used to introduce a range of exercises, cognitive and behavioural, to facilitate sexual growth (Heiman & LoPiccolo 1988) and included information/education, relaxation, exploration of sensual and sexual self-touch to build confidence and knowledge in the absence of performance pressure. Therapy also included cognitive restructuring of thought patterns destructive to sexuality and sexual growth. Self-help reading was used to support this work. Following some initial progress Sue's partner accompanied her to the sessions. He was introduced to the sensate focus exercises and the couple were encouraged to discuss their sexual needs, wishes and expectations. The meaning of Sue's anorgasmia, was explored and re-framed more positively, rather than seeing it as a reflection on the quality of their relationship. Over the course of therapy Sue became increasingly comfortable and familiar with her own sexual response and arousal. The level of communication in the relationship improved as did the level of satisfaction. Sue began to experience orgasms through self-stimulation and masturbation by her partner. Orgasms did not occur during penetrative sexual intercourse but the couple hoped to work towards this over time.

Psychological aspects of physical interventions: two brief illustrations
A man of 27 with erectile difficulties attended a psychosexual therapy service following the end of a two-year relationship. He had tried six months of intra-cavernosal injections which initially produced erections but left his partner feeling she was not needed for his sexual response, and very unhappy with the situation. His medical treatment had consisted solely of the practicalities of the injections. After some individual work on the intrusive emotions and cognitions underlying his impaired sexual response, he persuaded his partner to attend joint sessions, where their current dilemmas, previous experience, cultural expectations, etc. were fully explored. A different pattern of foreplay and improved communications established that he was able to become aroused with direct stimulation, thereby giving his partner a central role and creating a more equal relationship.

A woman of 28 attended a community-based clinic following a vaginal stretch operation to treat non-consummation of her four-year marriage. Her partner had expected immediate change and was disappointed and angry when their attempts at intercourse failed. Couple therapy addressed a range of cultural, emotional and behavioural issues and misunderstandings. Following a gradual approach aimed at increasing her arousal in non-threatening stages, penetration became possible. Although it was not her preferred mode of experiencing sexual pleasure, she had a sense of achievement and relief at being like other women. The anxieties and arguments about having a family that had previously been a feature of their marriage no longer occurred.

Conclusions

As the pattern of service demand has altered, clinicians and researchers have been challenged to modify existing techniques and to look for creative approaches to the widening range of psychosexual disorders presenting in sexual health settings. This chapter presents a case for an elaboration of what LoPiccolo (1994) described as the evolution of sex therapy into a post-modern approach. We include a thorough assessment of relational, behavioural, cultural and intrapsychic components of sexual functioning and a formulation-based integrated model for management issues. Given the ample evidence that successful outcome is not related to any specific theoretical model, no matter how measured (Shapiro 1996), trained clinicians can pursue an orientation to sexual dysfunction that fits with their preferred style of work, with the knowledge that no one theory has a monopoly on facilitating real change.

There is, of course, much still to achieve in the understanding of underlying mechanisms and the application of available therapeutic methods. While the attention given to physical interventions for erectile dysfunction is such that predictions for the 'end of sex therapy' need to be denied (Guirguis 1998), female sexual responding remains under-researched and less well understood. Not only is there a paucity of knowledge concerning the physiological underpinnings of sexual functioning in women but Parkinson and Bateman (1994) suggest that the extent of drug-induced female sexual dysfunction has been seriously underestimated. Read (1995) notes this tendency to focus on the observable part of the male response and to marginalise female sexual be-

haviour. The most commonly presenting female disorder, loss of sexual interest (e.g. Hirst 1996) still shows poorer outcome results and the apparently smaller number of men with loss of desire are equally difficult to help. The hostility and disappointment seen in such couples can be viewed as representing unresolved family-of-origin issues projected into the relationship where they become the focus for anger and thereby undermine desire. This interface between unconscious representations and external behaviour is not easy to access in psychosexual therapy; hence the frequent resistance of desire phase disorders to current treatment practices.

Evidence from another interface, between physical and psychological interventions, poses questions concerning communication between practitioners with powerful surgical and pharmacological tools at their disposal and those whose expertise resides in the language of cognitions, emotions and behaviour patterns. Guirguis (1998), commenting on the effectiveness of sildenafil – an orally active medication for the restoration of erectile response – rightly urges therapists to encompass new treatments rather than feel threatened by them. At the same time it is to be hoped that medical practitioners will not ignore psychogenic and relationship factors. Such an approach is not only clinically unsound but can create further difficulties.

The use of physical treatments for sexual disorders in HIV positive male clients has been controversial as concern has been expressed about the risk of transmission with intra-cavernosal injections when there may be some bleeding at the injection site. The interaction between oral medication and combination therapies for AIDS is an area for further study.

Although life and death issues tend to be the main focus with AIDS clients, the training of non-mental health workers in psychosexual and relationship understanding may allow previously neglected sexual problems to be identified for focused treatment (Sherr 1995). For women though, the spread of HIV infection does not yet appear to have altered referral patterns in psychosexual clinics. Instead the central concern encountered in younger women with motivation and arousal difficulties is the ability to conceive, an anxiety connected with fundamental relationship and generational issues that requires inclusion into therapeutic regimens.

Research into effective outcomes in psychosexual therapy suggested some time ago that the inadequate assessment and treatment of non-sexual issues is one of the most significant predictors of poor results (Chapman 1982). In the approach outlined here there are no issues in the individual or couple's internal or external worlds that are outside the scope of planning a rational treatment strategy. Tiefer (1998) cautions against the medicalisation of sexuality and suggests a perspective that accepts many methodologies as legitimate sources of insight. As practitioners aiming to help our clients make choices about sexual behaviour rather than be driven by anxiety, shame and fear, we need to provide a variety of therapy choices to reflect increasing awareness of the complexities of human sexual behaviour.

References

Baker, C.D. (1993) A cognitive behavioural model for the formulation and treatment of sexual dysfunction. In: *Psychological Perspectives on Sexual Problems* (eds J.M. Ussher & C.D. Baker). Routledge, London.

Baker, C.D. & de Silva, P. (1988) The relationship between male sexual dysfunction and belief in Zilbergeld's myths: an empirical investigation. *Sexual and Marital Therapy* **3**, 229–238.

Bancroft, I. (1989) *Human Sexuality and its Problems.* Churchill Livingstone, Edinburgh.

Beck, A.T., Rush, A.J., Shaw, B.G. & Emergy, G. (1979) *Cognitive Therapy of Depression.* Wiley, London.

Black, J. (1988) Sexual dysfunction and dyspareunia in the otherwise normal pelvis. *Sexual and Marital Therapy* **3**, 213–221.

Brown, G.R. & Rundell, J.R. (1990) Prospective study of psychiatric morbidity in HIV – seropositive women without AIDS. *General Hospital Psychiatry* **12**, 30–35.

Brown, P. & Faulder, C. (1977) *Treat Yourself to Sex.* Penguin Books, England.

Catalan, J. Klimes, I., Day, A., Garrod, A., Bond, A. & Gallwey, J. (1992) The psychosocial impact of HIV infection in gay men. A controlled investigation and factors associated with psychiatric morbidity. *British Journal of Psychiatry* **161**, 774–778.

Chapman, P. (1982) Criteria for diagnosing when to do sex therapy in the primary relationship. *Psychotherapy: Theory Research and Practice* **19**, 359–367.

Crowe, M. (1995) Couple therapy and sexual dysfunction. *International Review of Psychiatry* **7**, 195–204.

Crowe, M. & Ridley, J. (1990) *Therapy with Couples. A Behavioural Systems Approach to Marital and Sexual Problems.* Blackwell, Oxford.

D'Ardenne, P. (1996) Sexual health for men in culturally diverse communities. Some psychological considerations. *Sexual and Marital Therapy* **1**, 9–16.

Dawson, J.M., Fitzpatrick, KM., Reeves, G., *et al.* (1994) Awareness of sexual partner's HIV status as an influence upon high-risk sexual behaviour among gay men. *AIDS* **8**, 837–841.

De Silva, P. & Rodrigo, E.K. (1995) Sex therapy in Sri Lanka – development, problems and prospects. *International Review of Psychiatry* **7**, 241–246.

Donovan, C., Mearns, C., McEwan, K, & Sugden, N. (1994) A review of the HIV-related sexual behaviour of gay men and men who have sex with men. *AIDS Care* **6**, 605–617.

Dow, M.G.T. (1983) *A controlled comparative evaluation*

of conjoint counselling and self-help behavioural treatment for sexual dysfunction. PhD thesis, University of Glasgow (unpublished).

DSM-IV (1994) *The Diagnostic and Statistical Manual of the American Psychiatric Association*, 4th edn. American Psychiatric Press, Washington, DC.

Dupras, A. & Morisett, K. (1993) Couple therapy and sexual dysfunction among HIV-positive gay males. *Sexual and Marital Therapy* **8**, 37–46.

George, H. (1990) Sexual and relationship problems among people affected by AIDS: three case studies. *Counselling Psychology Quarterly* **3**, 389–399.

Gordon, P. (1986) Sex therapy with gay men: a review. *Journal of Sex and Marital Therapy* **2**, 221–225.

Guirguis, W.K. (1998) The future of sex therapy in the era of oral treatment. *Sexual and Marital Therapy* **13**, 29–30.

Halgin, K.P., Hennessey, J.E., Statlender, S., Feinman, I. & Brown, K.A. (1988) Treatment of sexual dysfunction in the context of general psychotherapy. In: *Treatment of Sexual Problems in Individual Couples Therapy* (eds K. Brown & J.R. Field). PMA, New York.

Hankins, C., Gendron, S., Tran, T., Lamping, D. & Lapointe, N. (1997) Sexuality in Montreal: women living with HIV. *AIDS Care* **9**, 261–271.

Hawton, K. (1982) The behavioural treatment of sexual dysfunction. *British Journal of Psychiatry* **140**, 94–101.

Hawton, K. (1995) Treatment of sexual dysfunction by sex therapy and other approaches. *British Journal of Psychiatry* **167**, 307–314.

Heiman, J.K & LoPiccolo, J. (1998) *Becoming Orgasmic: A Sexual and Personal Growth Programme for Women.* Piatkus, UK.

Hiller, J. (1993) Psychoanalytic concepts and psychosexual therapy: a suggested integration. *Sexual and Marital Therapy* **8**, 9–26.

Hiller, J. (1996) Female sexual arousal and its impairment: the psychodynamics of non-organic coital pain. *Sexual and Marital Therapy* **11**, 55–76.

Hirst, J.F., Baggaley, M.K. & Watson, J.P. (l996) A four-year survey of an inner-city psycho-sexual problems clinic. *Sexual and Marital Therapy* **11**, 19–36.

Hirst, J.F. & Watson, J.P. (1997) Therapy for sexual relationship problems: the effects on outcome of attending as an individual or as a couple. *Sexual and Marital*

Therapy **12**, 321–337.

Jones, M., Klimes, I. & Catalan, J. (1994) Psychosexual problems in people with HIV infection: controlled study of gay men and men with haemophilia. *AIDS Care* **6**, 587–593.

Kaplan, H.S. (1974) *The New Sex Therapy.* Baillière Tindall, London.

Kaplan, H.S. (1979) *Disorders of Sexual Desire.* Baillière Tindall, London.

Kaplan, H.S. (1995) *The Sexual Desire Disorders.* Bruner Mazel, New York.

Lipsius, S.H. (1987) Prescribing sensate focus without proscribing intercourse. *Journal of Sexual and Marital Therapy* **13**, 106–116.

LoPiccolo, J. (1994) The evolution of sex therapy. *Sexual and Marital Therapy* **9**, 5–7.

LoPiccolo, J., Heiman, J.R., Hogan, D.K. & Roberts, C.W. (1985) Effectiveness of single therapists versus co-therapy teams in sex therapy. *Journal of Consulting and Clinical Psychology* **53**, 287–294.

McLean, J., Boulton, M., Brookes, M., *et al.* (1994) Regular partners and risky behaviour: why do gay men have unprotected intercourse? *AIDS Care* **6**, 331–341.

Masters, W.H. & Johnson, V.E. (1970) *Human Sexual Inadequacy.* Churchill, London.

Meyr-Bahlburg, H.F.L., Nostlinger, C., Exner, T.M., *et al.* (1993) Sexual functioning in HIV+ and HIV injected drug-using women. *Journal of Sex and Marital Therapy* **19**, 56–58.

Parkinson, M. & Bateman, M. (1994) Disorders of sexual function caused by drugs. *Prescriber's Journal* **34**, l83–184.

Prieur, A. (1990) Norwegian gay men: reasons for continued practice of unsafe sex. *AIDS Education Preview* **2**, 109–117.

Read, J. (1995) Female sexual dysfunction. *International Review of Psychiatry* **7**, 175–182.

Renshaw, D.C. (1988) Profile of 2376 patients treated at Loyola Sex Clinic between 1972 and 1987. *Sex and Marital Therapy* **3**, 111–117.

Rice, B. (1995) Libido in limbo. What to do when your sexual impulses have diminished. *Sidahora* April/May, 37–38.

Ridley, J. & Crowe, M. (1992) The behavioural-systems approach to the treatment of couples. *Sexual and*

Marital Therapy **7**, 19–22.

Scharff, D. & Scharff, J.S. (1991) *Objective Relations Couple Therapy.* Jason Aronson, Northvale, NJ.

Segraves, K.A., Segraves, R.T. & Schoenberg, H.W. (1987) Use of sexual history to differentiate organic from psychogenic impotence. *Archives of Sexual Behaviour* **16**, 125–137.

Semans, J. (1956) Premature ejaculation: a new approach. *Southern Medical Journal* **49**, 353–358.

Shapiro, D.A. (1996) Foreward to *What Works for Whom? A Critical Review of Psychotherapy Research* (A. Roth and P. Fonagy), pp. viii–x. Guilford Press, New York.

Sherr, L. (1992) Safe sex and women. *Genitourinary Medicine* **68**, 32–35.

Sherr, L. (1995) Coping with psychosexual problems in the context of HIV infection. *Sexual and Marital Therapy* **10**, 307–319.

Spector, I.P. & Carey, M.P. (1990) Incidence and prevalence of the sexual dysfunctions: A critical review of the empirical literature. *Archives of Sexual Behaviour* **19**, 389–408.

Spence, S. (1991) *Psychosexual Therapy: A Cognitive-Behavioural Approach.* Chapman & Hall, London.

Tiefer, L. (1998) Masturbation: beyond caution, complacency and contradiction. *Sexual and Marital Therapy* **13**, 9–14.

Tindall, B., Forde, S, Goldstein, D., Ross, M.W. & Cooper, D.A. (1994) Sexual dysfunction in advanced HIV disease. *AIDS Care* **6**, 105–107.

Trudel, G. & Laurin, F. (1988) The effects of bibliotherapy on orgasmic dysfunction and couple interactions: An experimental study. *Sexual and Marital Therapy* **3**, 223–228.

Wilensky, M. & Myers, M.F. (1987) Retarded ejaculation in homosexual patients: A report of nine cases. *Journal of Sex Research* **23**, 85–91.

Wolpe, J.R. (1958) *Psychotherapy by Reciprocal Inhibition.* Stanford University Press, Stanford.

Wolpe, J.R. & Lazarus, A.A. (1966) *Behaviour Therapy Techniques.* Pergamon Press, Oxford.

Zilbergeld, B. (1983) *Men and Sex.* Fontana, London.

Zimmer, D. (1987) Does marital therapy enhance the effectiveness of treatment for sexual dysfunction? *Journal of Sexual and Marital Therapy* **13**, 193–209.

Chapter 11

Psychological Management in HIV Infection

Jenny Petrak and David Miller

Introduction

As we move towards the end of the second decade of the HIV epidemic, medical advance with the introduction of highly active antiretroviral therapy (HAART) has resulted in dramatic decreases in morbidity and mortality from AIDS in the developed world. Popular media has represented the HIV epidemic as being at an end (Sullivan 1997). This has been used in some countries as an argument for cuts in funding and provision of care. Early optimism is now, however, becoming more tempered with a realisation that there are a number of reasons which suggest predicting the end of the epidemic is premature. Globally the HIV epidemic continues to proliferate as it moves into ever more vulnerable populations (UNAIDS 2000a). The costs of HAART prohibit its widespread use such that it is estimated that more than 90% of the HIV-infected will not be able to obtain these medications, while in developed countries, decreasing death rates and increasing numbers of individuals willing to test for the presence of HIV mean greater numbers requiring long-term and complex care.

These medical advances present a number of new challenges for psychological and behavioural research in HIV/AIDS. Critical areas have been identified including developing interventions to assist individuals in coping with complex medical regimes and treatment adherence, and the possible influence of new treatments on risk behaviours (Kelly *et al.* 1998a, b). HIV is increasingly found within vulnerable populations such as those with serious mental illness (Kelly 1997), thereby also presenting new challenges towards psychological management. Some issues have, however, remained depressingly consistent over the last two decades, in particular, the high level of fear, stigma, and discrimination associated with HIV infection (Herek & Capitanio 1993, 1998). Thus, despite the success of new medical treatments, it is within this social climate of public and private fear that mental health issues in HIV continue to abound (Miller & Riccio 1990).

Psychological research and theory has contributed much towards care and management in HIV. Aside from grappling with the medical complexity of a new life-threatening and debilitating disease, early responses were also characterised by recognition of psychosocial needs in those affected. Psychological literature was initially characterised by formulation and description of clinical phenomena in the domains of prevention and intervention. Literature on prevention of transmission included understanding of lifestyle and risk behaviours, while other work considered the mental health impact of HIV infection in those affected. Early work emphasised the importance of including psychosocial interventions as part of good practice in HIV care.

The evidence for psychological models, particularly behavioural-based interventions in the area of primary prevention of STDs and HIV infection, is established (Sweat 1998). The contribution of psychology to primary prevention of STDs and HIV infection is covered elsewhere (Chapters 3 and 4). However, knowledge of what characterises successful psychological interventions in those infected with HIV remains elusive despite increasing requirements for evidence-based models and proofs of outcome. The focus of this chapter is on psychological approaches to HIV infection, including assessment, intervention, and outcome, after a diagnosis of HIV infection and/or disease has been made.

Assessment of psychological need

Factors influencing psychosocial responses to HIV infection

Each person living with HIV confronts uncertainties about their prognosis and personal health. However, the impact of HIV extends beyond individuals at risk or with HIV. The literature also documents the psychological impact of HIV upon diverse groupings including affected loved ones (Miller 1987; George 1990), families (Bor 1992; McGrath et al. 1993), parents (Foley et al. 1994), young people (Melvin & Sherr 1993), care staff (Miller 1996; 2000), communities (e.g. gay men, Neugebauer et al. 1992). It is important that assessment of psychological need in HIV infection includes identification of who else might be affected.

While the majority of persons with HIV infection cope effectively with their condition, unfortunately for some individuals knowledge of infection can result in profound psychological distress. Identification and treatment of psychological distress is important not just in easing suffering but also in reducing risk behaviours, increasing adherence to care and, ultimately, in reducing health care costs (Chesney et al. 1996). Psychological distress in HIV can be transitory or more persistent. A number of factors are implicated in affecting an individual's psychological response to their HIV infection. These may include factors directly associated with HIV (see below) or factors associated with individual and social responses to HIV (e.g. rejection and social isolation, multiple losses, relationship difficulties, ethnicity, and gender). Factors such as availability and quality of social support, previous history of psychiatric disorder, trauma including sexual abuse, personality disorder, low socioeconomic status, maladaptive coping styles, substance misuse, which are implicated in the development and maintenance of psychological morbidity in general are also relevant in

HIV infection (Catalan *et al.* 1995). Assessment of such factors by those who provide care to those with HIV infection is important in early identification of individuals who may have increased psychological vulnerability.

The relationship between psychological morbidity and HIV infection has generated much research. Psychological difficulties have been documented at all stages of HIV infection (Pakenham *et al.* 1995) although the nature and rates of disturbance may be comparable to other chronic and life-threatening conditions. However, the broader imperatives influencing psychological response and characterising HIV disease include issues such as discrimination, social denial, stigma, isolation, lack of disclosure, multiple death and loss, and fear of infection, and the sheer cumulative impact of such stressors may not resemble other conditions. Individuals who develop HIV infection may come from groups who have already experienced social rejection, disadvantage, and poor health. In both developed and developing countries, the link between HIV disease and poverty leading to poorer health and decreased access to health care is firmly established (Mann *et al.* 1992). Multiple deaths within affected families and communities, particularly in developing countries with high rates of heterosexual infection, have led to major changes in family and social structure (Mann *et al.* 1992). It is within this context that the psychological impact of HIV is considered below.

Extent and nature of psychological problems in HIV infection

Consistent research findings suggest that psychological responses are enhanced at different stages of HIV infection. These include around the time of testing for HIV (Perry *et al.* 1993), during the asymptomatic stage (McCann & Wadsworth 1991), when symptoms develop (Pakenham *et al.* 1995), receiving an AIDS diagnosis (Ostrow *et al.* 1991), and when terminal issues become salient (Folkman *et al.* 1996). Other stressful events identified which impact on psychological response include HIV disclosure (Hays *et al.* 1993; Stemple *et al.* 1995), medication and treatment decisions (Miller *et al.* 1991), bereavement (Sherr *et al.* 1992), procreation issues (Reidy *et al.* 1991) and family and relationship problems (Bor *et al.* 1992). The extent and nature of psychological problems in HIV infection will be influenced by all the above factors and can result in adjustment reactions, anxiety and depression, suicidal thoughts and behaviour, relationship and sexual difficulties, substance misuse, and various decision-making dilemmas. In addition, HIV-related brain impairment can result in mild to severe psychological effects which can both prior to and after a diagnosis of encephalopathy cause problems for the individual and their significant others (Kocsis 1996). Each of these psychological phenomena will be considered briefly below; more extensive reviews are available elsewhere (e.g. Catalan *et al.* 1995).

Adjustment reactions

For most individuals, notification of a positive HIV test result will result in transient adjustment reactions which may include expressions of despair, shock, denial, helplessness, hopelessness, grief, guilt, loss of self-esteem, anxiety and depression (Miller & Riccio 1990). Most studies report a reduction in these reactions in the months after diagnosis (Ironson *et al.* 1990). In a UK study of gay men, Pugh *et al.* (1994) found significant reductions in psychological morbidity 6 and 12 months after HIV testing and no differences between those who tested HIV seropositive or HIV seronegative. The spectrum of distress may resemble the reaction to other major life events or disease diagnoses. However, mixed results have been found comparing HIV seropositive gay men with the general population, with higher rates of psychological morbidity reported in the former in some studies (Atkinson *et al.* 1988) and not in others (Williams *et al.* 1991).

Empirical research in this area is fraught with difficulty, not least being the focus on psychopathology as opposed to measuring possible positive mental health outcomes and, notably, a lack of consideration of the contribution of predisposing and situational factors to adjustment reactions apart from the diagnosis. For example, Perry *et al.* (1993) found that low socio-economic status, a history of injecting drug use, and high baseline psychological morbidity were associated with high levels of psychological distress in HIV seropositive and HIV seronegative individuals at 12 months after HIV testing. This association was not found for HIV status. Nevertheless, the extent of psychological need identified in the aftermath of notification of HIV seropositivity has alerted clinicians to consider psychological reactions to diagnoses and to the provision of appropriate psychosocial support.

Anxiety

Anxiety associated with uncertainties related to HIV infection and the future course of the disease is commonly experienced by individuals with HIV infection (Maj 1991; Kalichman & Sikkema 1994). Anxiety may manifest as transient reactions to, for example, illness progression, threat of disfigurement, pain, fears of becoming dependent on others, decision-making around medical treatments, telling others, fears of rejection, infecting others, isolation, and death of friends to AIDS. For some individuals with HIV infection, anxiety may become chronic, although levels may vary from mild to extreme. The prevalence of anxiety in HIV infection is difficult to assess due to the diverse methodologies used and groups studied. Dew *et al.* (1990) reported that 45% of HIV infected persons with haemophilia showed greater anxiety than an HIV negative group with haemophilia. A recent cross-sectional survey of 95 persons with HIV infection reported that 31% and 28% had definite and borderline anxiety as assessed by the Hospital Anxiety and Depression Scale (Doyle *et al.* 1998). Only a minority had accessed any form of pharmacological and/or psychological treatment, suggesting that, despite the extent of psychological literature on the subject, in clinical practice, anxiety may often be overlooked in the face of other concerns in HIV. Anxiety is characterised by a variety of somatic, behavioural, and cognitive symptoms. Somatic symptoms may include shortness of breath, palpitations, chest pain, tension headaches, dry mouth, sleep difficulties, and sweating. Cognitive symptoms include poor concentration and a preoccupation with symptoms. Behavioural symptoms may include avoidance of particular situations or thoughts. Some anxiety symptoms resemble symptoms found in HIV infection and may exacerbate fear and worry if individuals misinterpret these as progressing disease and, in particular, HIV organic brain disease. Fears associated with the prospect of dying may also exacerbate anxiety, and increase with symptomatic HIV disease (Catania *et al.* 1992).

Depression

The number of cumulative psychosocial stressors associated with HIV infection may often lead to symptoms of depression including low mood, hopelessness, sleep disturbance, guilt and low self-esteem, concentration difficulties, loss of libido, lack of pleasure in usual activities, and suicidal thoughts. Depression is both commonly reported and is the most frequently studied amongst responses to HIV infection. Miller (1988) has suggested that depression represents the 'dynamic tension between uncertainty and adjustment to life with HIV', and therefore might be expected in most patients at some time during the course of their diagnosis. Depression may be more prevalent in the early phases of HIV disease, subsiding during asymptomatic periods, and recurring with the onset of symptomatic HIV disease (Kalichman & Sikkema 1994; Lyketsos *et al.* 1996). HIV infected populations including gay men (Rabkin *et al.* 1991), haemophiliacs (Dew *et al.* 1990), and heterogeneous samples (Perry *et al.* 1990; Dew *et al.* 1997) have all been found to have higher levels of depression than HIV negative controls. Other studies provide conflicting results: Gala *et al.* (1993) found levels of depression and other psychopathology to be similar between individuals with HIV infection and non-HIV infected controls, although in their sample intravenous drug users emerged as having significantly higher psychological morbidity than

gay men and heterosexual participants. Factors commonly mediating depression include previous history of psychiatric disorder, lack of social support, guilt or lack of acceptance about sexuality or lifestyle, and lack of an adequate social infrastructure (Miller & Riccio 1990; Siegel *et al.* 1997). Depression may also be complicated by the frequency of bereavement from AIDS-related deaths. Multiple losses have been noted as a predisposing factor for depression in individuals with HIV infection (Markowitz *et al.* 1994). Others have suggested that death has become 'normative' in some communities (e.g. gay men) and note a process of adaptation to multiple loss with decreasing psychological distress over time (Martin & Dean 1993). Other factors correlated with depression in HIV infection include decreased participation in health promoting behaviours, low self-esteem and social functioning, and hopelessness (Ostrow *et al.* 1989; Cleary *et al.* 1993). Some studies have investigated whether depression has a direct effect on the immune system (e.g. Vedhara *et al.* 1997) although numerous methodological difficulties are noted including variability of immune system markers (e.g. CD4 counts) and depression as measured over time.

Suicidal thoughts and behaviour

Depression is also likely to underlie elevated rates of suicidal thoughts and behaviour observed in persons with HIV infection (O'Dowd *et al.* 1993). Suicidal thoughts are probably not uncommon in individuals who suffer serious physical illness and may be seen as a way of retaining control in the face of unpredictability, physical decay, pain, and dependency on others. However, the social and psychological vulnerability associated with HIV disease may increase risk for suicide. Early reports suggested that the relative risk of suicide in men with AIDS was 36 times that of men without the diagnosis (Marzuk *et al.* 1988) although later reports highlight methodological difficulties, for example, in finding matched control samples and determining cause of death in the context of terminal illness, in determining certainty of suicide risk in this population (Catalan *et al.* 1995). Marzuk *et al.* (1997) suggest that HIV serostatus is associated with, at most, a modest elevation in suicide risk. Risk for suicide and suicidal ideation may be particularly elevated when individuals develop HIV-related symptoms (O'Dowd *et al.* 1993). Factors that commonly exacerbate suicidal tendencies among persons with HIV infection resemble predictors of suicide risk in the general population. These include a history of previous affective disturbance and suicidal behaviour, substance misuse, low social support and loneliness (O'Dowd *et al.* 1993; Catalan *et al.* 1995). There is also some evidence to suggest that suicidal behaviour may be elevated in those seeking HIV testing (Perry *et al.* 1990). Cumulative evidence from these studies suggests that suicide risk should be part of routine assessment in persons with HIV infection.

Relationships and social support

Psychological distress not surprisingly has an impact on others in the personal and social networks of the infected individual. Relationship difficulties were reported by 37% of individuals accessing an HIV clinical psychology service in inner London (Hedge & Sherr 1995). Relationship difficulties may include, for example, fear of infection, lack of HIV disclosure, sexual dysfunction, lack of support for carers, and discord related to cumulative chronic stress in HIV. Difficulties in the areas of relationships and the illness of others were identified as being amongst the most significant stressors in HIV and associated with increased psychological morbidity (Thompson *et al.* 1996). Social support may be the most significant buffer in coping with physical illness (Cohen & Wills 1985). Social support has been linked with improved psychological functioning and decreased depression and anxiety in gay men with HIV infection (Kelly *et al.* 1993a; Hays *et al.* 1993). Accessing social support in the context of HIV infection may be complicated, however, by potential negative outcomes of disclosure of diagnosis. Fears of being rejected by partners and families and being dismissed from work following discovery of an individual's HIV infection are a few reasons why disclosure may not happen (Simoni *et al.* 1995). Hays *et al.* (1993) also suggest that concealment of HIV may lead to difficulties in an individual's ability to adhere to health-related behaviours, and may also cause stress in significant others, particularly if disclosure happens when the individual is ill. Low rates of disclosure of HIV to significant others may be particularly marked in heterosexual men and women and ethnic minorities (Simoni *et al.* 1995; Petrak *et al.* 1998).

Sexual difficulties

Sexual difficulties in HIV disease are common and are often due to a complex combination of psychosocial and organic factors (cf. Chapter 10). Sexual difficulties may include erectile dysfunction, ejaculatory difficulties, loss of interest, loss of libido, sexual aversion, sexual phobias, and commonly, communication and relationship discord. Specific sexual difficulties related to HIV infection have been noted including fear of infecting sexual partners, difficulties in negotiating and maintaining safer sex, and low self-esteem related to changes in body image due to illness (Catalan *et al.* 1995). In addition, a proportion of men may experience erectile and ejaculatory difficulties related to HIV organic changes and side effects of medication (Tindall *et al.* 1994). Assessment should include a full sexual history, previous history of sexual and emotional difficulties including sexual abuse, alcohol and drug misuse, current medication and stage of HIV disease. Psychogenic causes of sexual difficulties may be more prevalent in early stages of HIV infection related to adjustment reactions, whereas later onset sexual dysfunction with symptomatic HIV infection or AIDS may be primarily related to organic changes (Tindall *et al.* 1994).

Substance misuse

Reactions to fear of becoming infected, a positive HIV test, illness progression, or other stressful events can include alcohol and drug misuse. Alcohol and drug misuse across various HIV positive cohorts has been estimated at between 22% and 56%, but this may be declining to general population levels with increasing attempts by individuals to maximise personal health (Dew *et al.* 1997). Substance abuse has been associated with high-risk sexual activity (Robins *et al.* 1994), increased psychological morbidity (Gala *et al.* 1993), and reduced adherence to health care and medication (Kelly *et al.* 1998a, b). Individuals with HIV infection may have prior history of alcohol and drug misuse as part of a lifestyle (e.g.

gay men whose social lives centre on pubs/clubs or injecting drug users who are part of drug networks). Psychosocial factors associated with HIV infection may result in difficulties controlling intake or withdrawing from alcohol and recreational drugs. The potency of certain recreational drugs (e.g. Ecstasy, speed) may be enhanced if taken with prescription medications commonly used in the treatment of HIV. Assessing substance misuse and establishing links with drug and alcohol dependency agencies is important in medical and psychological management of HIV infection.

Decision-making dilemmas

Numerous themes emerge as particular stressors for individuals with HIV infection and which may impact on psychological and emotional well-being. Decision-making dilemmas may include issues associated with HIV testing, telling others, relationships, occupation and work, finance, medication and clinical trials, children, pregnancy, and death and dying. All of these dilemmas may be becoming increasingly salient with increased optimism of a longer and improved quality of life with the advent of HAART. For example, individuals with HIV infection are increasingly considering returning to employment (Ezzy *et al.* 1998). Some may not have worked for several years and consequently encounter reluctance and possible rejection from employers, while some individuals may never have had consistent employment due to illness at a young age. In addition, complex medical regimes associated with HAART including timing of taking medication, dietary restrictions, side effects and routine medical monitoring may necessitate frequent absences from work. For a proportion of individuals maintenance of physical health on HAART at some point after their introduction may no longer be achieved, and can result in increased feelings of despair and hopelessness as treatments fail (Kelly *et al.* 1998a, b). For many dilemmas in HIV there are no immediate answers. Adjustment to and coping with uncertainty characterises life for many persons living with HIV.

HIV-related brain impairment

The psychological assessment and management of HIV-related brain impairment is a complex area and will not be covered in depth here (see Price & Perry 1994; Catalan *et al.* 1995; Kocsis 1996; also Chapter 12). Early reports suggested that the prevalence of AIDS dementia was as high as 38% (Navia *et al.* 1986), whereas later studies found a reported rate of 7% (McArthur *et al.* 1993; Meadows *et al.* 1993). Early reports suggest that these figures may decline further with the advent of protease inhibitors and HAART (Fernando *et al.* 1998). Many early symptoms of AIDS dementia resemble those found in, and can complicate the presentation of existing, psychological disorders in HIV. This may include poor attention and concentration, memory difficulties, problems in planning, low motivation, confusion, slowing of thought, increased distractibility, and emotional lability. Many of these symptoms are also found in anxiety and depression, and a formal neuropsychological assessment along with observation, and, where possible, involving significant others, are useful in differential diagnosis. Fear of dementia itself can become a significant problem for HIV infected individuals. The impact of AIDS dementia is extremely distressing for those affected and psychological assessment should include consideration of the support available to significant others including professional care staff.

Models of psychological intervention and evaluative research

Treatment planning for persons with HIV infection depends on the needs of the individual and their carers but typically reflect those interventions most often used in clinical practice with non-HIV infected clients. Accordingly, theoretical models of psychological interventions in HIV also reflect a broad base and may include social-cognitive, cognitive-behavioural, humanistic, psychodynamic, systemic, and social constructionist models. Types of intervention reported in the literature include, for example, counselling, cognitive-behavioural therapies, stress and anxiety management, coping effectiveness training, psychotherapy and systemic approaches. Group therapy approaches are also often used, focusing on a range of issues in HIV infection including stress, bereavement, social support and coping, and relationships. In clinical practice, however, it is often necessary to draw upon a range of therapeutic approaches in the psychological management of HIV infection, as illustrated in the following case example.

Case example

Mr A (36) referred for 'adjustment difficulties and suicidal ideation.'

Assessment

Mr A recently started antiretroviral therapy on his physician's recommendation after developing symptoms and receiving a high viral load result. He was experiencing low mood, anxiety, and thoughts about ending his life since starting drug therapy. He reported no history of suicide attempts or psychiatric difficulties. His long-term partner died of AIDS one year ago after prolonged illness. Mr A reported 'never grieving' and coped by immersing in academic study and weekend drugs/alcohol 'binges'. He tested HIV seropositive four months after the death of his partner.

Formulation
Delayed grief reaction compounded by recency of own diagnosis and rapidity of progressing to symptomatic HIV infection.

Plan
(1) Bereavement therapy;
(2) monitor mental state (refer to psychiatry if no improvement); and
(3) cognitive-behavioural approach towards adjusting to diagnosis and medication, facilitating coping, and planning for the future.

Outcome
Mr A began to disclose his sadness surrounding the death of his partner. He also reported having immense guilt at expressing anger and frustration towards his partner who developed cognitive and personality changes. Psychological therapy facilitated his ability to accentuate the positive aspects of caring for his partner and acknowledge his grief (and relief) as natural and congruent. His mood improved over time. The focus of therapy shifted towards enabling him to cope with his own HIV diagnosis and fears for the future. He began to limit his weekend binges and develop other social contacts. He is currently planning to return to work.

The provision of such treatments is usually dependent on their local availability, usually in developed countries, and may be carried out by a range of practitioners in both the voluntary and statutory sector. As with mental health interventions in many areas of medical care, the development of evidence-based psychological interventions in HIV/AIDS is either lacking or at an early stage. The main therapeutic interventions are reviewed below.

Counselling

In the developed and developing world, counselling is seen as important in psychosocial care in HIV/AIDS. Although several texts exist characterising what HIV counselling can consist of (e.g. Bor *et al.* 1992; Green & McCreaner 1996), in common usage, it is often used ambiguously. Levels of training and qualification may vary enormously in those delivering counselling services. The term is often used in an all-inclusive way reflecting the fact that basic counselling skills, for example, empathic reflection, good listening, information giving, and a non-judgemental approach, might be considered to be important in most interactions in health care. Counselling in HIV infection has centred on prevention activities including risk reduction and HIV testing and support after diagnosis for HIV-infected individuals and their significant others. The lack of theoretical models and consistent methodology across studies reporting the efficacy of HIV counselling makes interpretation problematic. Recent reviews argue that no single counselling approach can address all the tasks of HIV counselling (e.g. relationship building, risk assessment, information giving, behaviour change, and emotional support), although behavioural and cognitive-behavioural approaches were considered to be most relevant (Sikkema & Bissett 1997). It is important that counsellors are able to recognise complex medical and psychological morbidity in HIV infection and identify where they may refer individuals onwards for mental health assessment and intervention.

Cognitive-behaviour therapy

Cognitive-behaviour therapy (CBT) incorporates both a theoretical model and a relatively well defined format and its efficacy has been reported in relation to a wide variety of psychological disorders (Hawton *et al.* 1989). Cognitive therapy may be an appropriate choice in the context of HIV infection because emotional disturbance may often be associated with maladaptive cognitions. For example, individuals may often self-blame after diagnosis, which may include a number of cognitions (e.g. 'How could I have been so stupid'; 'I shouldn't have been so promiscuous'; 'This is my punishment for being gay'; 'I'll never have a relationship now') which they can be facilitated to reframe. Cognitive-behavioural techniques have been used to help patients with cancer adjust to their illness (Greer *et al.* 1992) using a modification of Beck's (1976) cognitive model. The aim of this model is to reduce psychological morbidity, promote a sense of personal control, encourage ventilation of feelings, improve communication between patient and carers, develop coping strategies, and induce a 'fighting spirit' in the person with cancer. However, individuals coping with life-threatening illness live within an actual negative reality, and the model of therapy incorporates correctly identifying realis-

tic fears and sadness from morbid anxiety and depression. An emerging literature documents the efficacy of CBT for persons with HIV infection and in informing prevention strategies. In the context of HIV infection, CBT has been reported as efficacious in working with women (Lamping *et al.* 1993), gay male couples (Ussher 1990), and in group format (Kelly *et al.* 1993a, b; Lutgendorf *et al.* 1998). Presenting difficulties, control samples, and measures to evaluate outcome vary across these studies, although CBT is reported to be effective in decreasing psychological morbidity (e.g. stress, anxiety, depression) and improving coping, social support, and quality of life. It is less clear from the literature where CBT may not be as optimally effective. In a study comparing cognitive-behavioural and support group brief therapies for depressed HIV-infected men, it is interesting to note that both therapies resulted in improvements in functioning compared to a wait list control, although social support groups focused on emotional coping presented greater evidence of change (Kelly *et al.* 1993a, b). Their findings suggest something of the complexity in evaluating therapeutic outcome and the need for differentiating what actually is successful in achieving change in any given therapy.

Other psychoeducational interventions

A number of other interventions in the psychological management of HIV infection have been reported including those using problem-solving techniques, enhancing coping skills, and stress and anxiety management. The available data limits the comparisons that can be made between these interventions although they are all arguably derived from psychoeducational models such as CBT and social cognitive theory. A number of texts provide detailed description of the application of these interventions in HIV infection (e.g. Miller 1987; Green & McCreaner 1996). Few controlled outcome studies have been reported although two recent psychoeducational interventions, *Coping Effectiveness Training* (CET) (Chesney *et al.* 1996) and *Tools for Health and Empowerment Course* (THE) (Igboko *et al.* 1998), suggest the benefit of an eclectic approach towards some of the problems in HIV infection. CET is based on a stress and coping model developed by Lazarus and Folkman (1984) that emphasises the behavioural and cognitive aspects of coping with stressful events. CET comprises of a number of components including training in being able to appraise stressful situations, identifying problem- and emotion-focused coping strategies, use of social support, homework, and maintenance training, which are adapted to be relevant to various problems in HIV infection. Chesney *et al.* (1996), in a study of 149 HIV-infected men, reported greater increases in coping efficacy and decreases in perceived stress and 'burnout' with 10 sessions of CET in comparison to HIV-information support and a waiting list control group. Their findings suggest that support and information alone are not effective in reducing psychological distress, and advocate the introduction of skills-building interventions (Chesney *et al.* 1996).

Tools for Health and Empowerment (THE) course is unusual amongst the majority of psychosocial research in being multi-centred and drug company sponsored, the latter issue being relevant to the choice of outcome measures which included adherence to antiretroviral medication, amongst other behaviour,

health care and quality of life indices. THE course consists of 11 modules targeted to mixed groups of persons with HIV infection and their care partners. It is based on the premise that long-term change in health behaviours can only be produced if knowledge, beliefs, and behaviours are linked to a systematic learning experience (Igboko *et al.* 1998). Initial results are reported including increased self-care, adherence, HIV knowledge and empowerment, and use of effective coping skills in 80% of the immediate intervention group in comparison to delayed groups (Igboko *et al.* 1998). Long-term follow-up is still required for the above studies but, at least, they illustrate the point that for psychosocial interventions to be successful they generally require an approach marked by some theory, complexity, and duration.

Group approaches

Many of the above interventions are conducted in a group format. The reasons for this are probably partially due to recognition of the disruption to social functioning that can occur with HIV infection and also due to large numbers coming through. Support groups for people living with HIV infection are widely available in both community-based AIDS organisations and mental health services. Support groups are widely heterogeneous in structure and format and in the participants to whom they are directed (Kalichman *et al.* 1996). Group therapy may be particularly efficacious in the problems posed by multiple loss and survival problems in HIV infection (Sikkema *et al.* 1995; Maasen 1998) although there are few outcome studies. Sikkema *et al.* (1995) described a pilot study of a cognitive behavioural group intervention to improve coping with AIDS-related bereavement. Their model incorporated recognition of general grief-responses and also those unique to AIDS bereavement. Improved outcomes were noted for depression, grief reactions, demoralisation, intrusive phenomena, and overall psychological distress after the intervention and at 3-month follow-up (Sikkema *et al.* 1995). Other areas where group interventions have been reported are in helping persons living with HIV to change transmission-risk-behaviour practices (Kelly 1998a, b), staff stress and burnout (Miller 1996), drug use (Mulleady 1992), relationship difficulties (Hedge & Glover 1990), and psychological distress (Levine *et al.* 1991; Kelly *et al.* 1993a). Kalichman *et al.* (1996) have attempted to characterise differences between people who attend support groups and those who do not, and found that non-attenders were more isolated, depressed, and inclined to use avoidant coping strategies in comparison to attenders. A group approach to safer sex maintenance is described in Chapter 19.

Family, systemic and other psychotherapies

A number of other specialised psychotherapeutic approaches may be useful in the management of problems in HIV infection. Clinical experience of counselling based on systemic theory (Bor *et al.* 1992), psychodynamic psychotherapy (Rattigan 1993), and group psychotherapy (Levine *et al.* 1991) suggest these approaches can be of value. The impact of HIV on families in both the developed and developing world has more recently become an important focus of research. Families of individuals with HIV infection may include the traditional nuclear family, extended kin net-

works, friends, lovers and drug-related networks. Family therapy can be adapted and may be useful to meet a range of psychological needs within such networks. Models of family psychological support based on systems theory that address relationships, context, developments themes, belief systems, and recursiveness are described (Bor *et al.* 1992). Research on outcome in the above therapeutic approaches is generally lacking.

Specific issues and current challenges in psychological management

Medication issues

Increasing adherence to medications has long been an area towards which psychology has contributed theory and research. Persons living with HIV infection and AIDS are likely to experience numerous medical interventions including taking increasingly complex drug combinations and participating in clinical trials (Besch 1995). Many of the current combination antiretroviral treatments require vigilant adherence to timing, dosage, and dietary restrictions. Individuals may be taking large numbers of different medications and this is often lifelong. Non-adherence to HAART can have profound negative outcomes in causing increased viral load, HIV replication, and is a major cause of treatment failure (Carpenter *et al.* 1997). Consequently, the need to identify factors contributing to non-adherence and the development and evaluation of interventions to increase adherence, particularly in disenfranchised populations, have been identified as key areas for behavioural research (Kelly *et al.* 1998a, b). Preliminary work suggests that factors such as experiencing side effects, the extent to which particular drug regimes interfere with lifestyle patterns, and forgetting are associated with non-adherence (Hedge & Petrak 1998). In the same study, knowledge about the medications and self-perception of adherence were reported to be high. However, more detailed questioning revealed that many individuals took drug holidays and changed the timing of their medications (Hedge & Petrak 1998). Previous factors also identified as associated with low adherence include substance misuse, mental health problems, lack of social support, and socio-economic disadvantage (Samet *et al.* 1992; Freeman *et al.* 1996). Various sociobehavioural models including the health belief model (Becker & Maiman 1975), the theory of reasoned action (Fishbein & Azjen 1975), and cognitive-behavioral theory (Leventhal *et al.* 1984) have been applied to the explanation and prediction of health-care behaviour and adherence. There is a paucity of intervention studies aimed at enhancing adherence to HIV medications although recent work suggests that individualised medication management using problem-solving techniques may be helpful (Sorensen *et al.* 1998).

Bereavement and multiple loss

Whilst the psychological impact of HIV shares some similarities with other medical conditions there are unique consequences, particularly multiple deaths within affected families and communities. Factors identified as distinguishing AIDS and cancer-related bereavement include lower support, stigma, non-disclosure of the cause of death, and a greater number of losses in the former (Kelly *et al.* 1993). Early literature has described AIDS-related bereavement as 'chronic', particularly in

the gay male populations studied. A study of more than 600 gay men had named an average of six men known to have died of AIDS (Dean *et al.* 1988). Similarly in HIV-infected individuals referred for grief therapy in an inner London clinic, an average of twelve deaths per person were reported (Sherr *et al.* 1992). The applicability of traditional models of grief, which are most often based on studies of white, heterosexual populations, can be questioned in the context of HIV and AIDS where the vast majority of deaths have occurred in sub-Saharan Africa and in gay men in developed countries. Klein (1998) describes a 'multiple loss syndrome' in which there may be insufficient time to anticipate the next loss and grieve the prior loss. This can result in a numbing reaction due to emotional overload characterised by social withdrawal, isolation, loneliness, and a sense of loss of control (Klein 1998). Studies have identified factors mediating the effect of AIDS-related bereavement including finding positive meaning in caregiving, obtaining adequate emotional and practical support, and maintaining optimism (Folkman *et al.* 1996; Rosengard & Folkman 1997). Conversely predictors of depression in caregivers postbereavement have been identified including the use of behavioural escape-avoidance coping, self-blame, longer relationships, and HIV seropositivity (Folkman *et al.* 1996). While grief is a universal human experience and may have positive aspects, it can be helpful for individuals with HIV infection to engage in a psychological therapy. A distinction is usually made between normal, uncomplicated grief and pathological grief which will underpin psychological management. Grief counselling may help facilitate the former whereas behavioural interventions (e.g. guided mourning) may be useful towards resolving chronic grief. Brief, supportive, group psychotherapy for AIDS-related bereavement has also been advocated (Goodkin *et al.* 1996; Maasen 1998).

Survival

Recent medical advances suggest that death may no longer be inevitable after infection with HIV or may follow years of chronic infection. In the US a decline of 48% in deaths from AIDS and 12% in new AIDS cases was reported in 1997 largely attributable to the introduction of combination antiretroviral treatments. The impact on populations psychologically braced to die and who have already faced huge losses is yet to be determined. Studies monitoring long-term progression in HIV and AIDS may be helpful in understanding the impact of treatment advances. Particular dilemmas faced by HIV-infected individuals are reported including how to regain employment and economic self-sufficiency, whether to plan new romantic relationships or pregnancy, and whether the beneficial effect of medication will be maintained. Individuals may experience psychological distress including 'survivor guilt' if an individual maintains good health while the same disease has resulted in the death of loved ones, partners, family members and many close friends (Kelly *et al.* 1998a, b). In addition, the impact of HAART in reducing the saliency of maintaining safer sex with partners is also reported (Elford *et al.* 1998; Kelly *et al.* 1998a, b). There is little current knowledge on the prevalence of the above psychological coping issues and the amenability of existing stress and coping intervention models in HIV infection in their psychological management. The impor-

tance of psychological intervention studies not limiting outcome solely to mental health measures but also including public health and medical management outcomes is emphasised (Kelly *et al.* 1998a, b).

Carer burnout and support

There is growing awareness that the edifice of HIV/AIDS care is vulnerable so long as the pressures on and the needs of those providing the care are unattended. The complexity of caring – and the very significant consequences of doing so – are increasingly well documented, both for formal health care staff and for volunteers, including family and community workers (Miller 2000; UNAIDS 2000b). For example, recent surveys of HIV/AIDS clinic and hospital staff have revealed rates of psychological morbidity above 40%, comparable with staff stresses in complementary fields of health care (Miller 2000). While volunteer staff must be presumed to have similar if not higher rates of stress associated with caring for chronically ill loved ones (e.g. Claxton *et al.* 1993; Maslanka 1996; Blinkhoff *et al.* 1999), far more empirical data are needed in this context.

HIV/AIDS carers experience work stress and burnout for many reasons, including those identified in Table 11.1. Additionally, for community-based volunteers, the stresses include the pressures of financial hardship, living with secrecy and fear of disclosure of status, inadequate training and support for their work, and problems associated with living with HIV/AIDS in families, particularly in discussing this with children (UNAIDS 2000b).

The consequences of work overload resulting in stress and burnout have similarly been summarised (Table 11.2).

Table 11.1 Causes of HIV/AIDS carer stress and burnout (from Miller 2000).

(1) Staff fears
- Anxiety over safety of care procedures for carers
- Fears of HIV contagion

(2) Issues of association
- Intense, long-term relationships with patients
- Self-identification with people with HIV/AIDS (PLHA)
- Managing distressed loved ones and relatives of PLHA
- Grief and bereavement overload
- Boundary problems between staff and PLHA
- Problems with conflicting motivations to work in the field of HIV

(3) Professional and role issues
- The context of care
- Professional role expansion
- Intensity of HIV/AIDS work
- Discomfort in addressing issues of sexuality
- Neurological management difficulties
- Professional inadequacy
- Role ambiguity and conflicts across professions
- Inadequate training
- Absence of a cure
- Working with uncertainty while encouraging PLHA to hope
- Pressures associated with volunteer work

(4) Stigma, discrimination and ethical issues
- Social contagion
- Homophobia and prejudice against IDUs and commercial sex workers
- Ethical dilemmas
- Poor social support because of social pressures and discrimination

Table 11.2 Reported symptoms of carer stress and burnout (from Miller 2000).

(1) Physical
- Physical exhaustion
- Lingering minor illnesses
- Headaches and back pain
- Sleeplessness
- Gastrointestinal disturbances
- Malaise

(2) Behavioural
- Readiness to be irritated
- Proneness to anger
- Increased alcohol and drug use
- Marital and relationship problems
- Inflexibility in problem-solving
- Impulsivity and acting out
- Withdrawal from non-colleagues

(3) Cognitive/affective
- Emotional numbness
- Emotional hypersensitivity
- Over-identification with patients/PLHA
- Grief and sadness
- Pessimism and hopelessness
- Boredom and cynicism
- Indecision and inattention
- Depression

The development of work stress and burnout in HIV/AIDS has been subjected to significant recent discussion, and the discussion is entering a new, conceptual phase (see Miller 2000, for a detailed discussion). However, the need for effective models of intervention remains. Models of intervention suggested to date include:

(1) *Professional supervision*, involving case reviews, professional monitoring and skills assessment.

(2) *Emotional support*, providing opportunities for ventilation of stresses, emotional support, team-building and restoration.

(3) *Stress management and reduction*, including relaxation strategies, seminars and training in time management, team-building, etc.

(4) *Context management*, including attentive management of hours worked, successes achieved, increased autonomy over tasks and decision-making, recognising and normalising the experience and expression of loss, ensuring a pleasant working environment, and providing opportunities for skills development.

Only with investment in carer support and empowerment will the sustainability of care strategies be assured.

Future directions

The last two decades have seen a rapid expansion of psychological knowledge in the area of health care in general. The contribution of psychology in HIV infection and AIDS in applying theory and intervention towards improving quality of life, psychological well-being, and coping may provide impetus in the behavioural management of other medical conditions. It might also be the case that as AIDS comes to resemble other life-threatening, chronic but potentially manageable diseases there may be much gained by other health behaviour approaches on issues such as adherence and coping with survival. Although much information has been gained towards an evidence-based approach towards psychological management in HIV, it will be crucial

for future studies to incorporate treatment and disease-related outcomes. Theory-based psychological interventions are perceived to be expensive and it is essential that studies can demonstrate their efficacy in reducing overall health-care costs. Towards this aim, clinical practitioners need to extend beyond an individualised approach to delivery of services but must actively participate in the creation and evolution of an integrated and psychologically informed health care system. HIV and AIDS is a rapidly changing field of health care and it is important that the psychological knowledge gained is not now lost in the optimism surrounding medical advances in the field. There is also an urgent need to find innovative ways of minimising the negative impact of the disease in the developing world, where poverty, oppression, and lack of availability of medical treatment suggest that the HIV pandemic is far from over.

'The biggest AIDS gap of all is the gap between what we know we can do today, and what we are actually doing.'
Peter Piot, UNAIDS 1998

References

Atkinson, J., Grant, I., Kennedy, C., *et al.* (1988) Prevalence of psychiatric disorder among men infected with HIV – a controlled study. *Archives of General Psychiatry* **45**, 859–864.

Beck, A.T. (1976) *Cognitive Therapy and the Emotional Disorders*. Hoeber, New York.

Becker, M.H. & Maiman, L.A. (1975) Sociobehavioral determinants of compliance with health and medical care recommendations. *Medical Care* **13**, 10–24.

Besch, C.L. (1995) Compliance in clinical trials. *AIDS* **9**, 1–10.

Blinkhoff, P., Bukanga, E., Syamalevwe, B. & Williams, G. (1999) *Under the Mupundu Tree (Strategies for Hope, No. 14)*. Actionaid, Oxford.

Bor, R. (1992) The impact of HIV/AIDS on the family. *AIDS Care* **4**, 453–456.

Bor, R., Miller, R. & Goldman, E. (1992) *Theory and practice of HIV Counselling. A Systemic Approach*. Cassell, London.

Carpenter, C.C.J., Fischl, M.A., Hammer, S.M., *et al.* (1997) Antiretroviral therapy for HIV infection in 1997: Updated recommendations of the International AIDS Society – USA Panel. *Journal of the American Medical Association* **277**, 1962–1969.

Catalan, J., Burgess, A. & Klimes, I. (1995) *Psychological Medicine of HIV Infection*. University Press, Oxford.

Catania, J., Turner, H., Choi, K.H. & Coates, T. (1992) Coping with death anxiety; help-seeking and social support among gay men with various HIV diagnosis. *AIDS* **6**, 999–1005.

Chesney, M., Folkman, S. & Chambers, D. (1996) Coping effectiveness training for men living with HIV: preliminary findings. *International Journal of STD and AIDS* **7**, 75–82.

Claxton, R.P.R., Burgess, A.P. & Catalan, J. (1993) Motivational factors and psychosocial stress in emotional support volunteers (buddies) for people living with AIDS. Paper presented at *IX International AIDS Conference and III World Congress on STD*, Amsterdam, 18–24 June (unpublished).

Cleary, P.D., Van Devanter, N., Rogers, T., *et al.* (1993) Depressive symptoms in blood donors notified of HIV infection. *American Journal of Public Health* **83**, 534–539.

Cohen, S. & Wills, T.A. (1985) Stress, social support and the buffering hypothesis. *Psychological Bulletin* **98**, 310–357.

Dean, L. & Hall, W. (1998) Chronic and intermittent AIDS-related bereavement in a panel of homosexual men in New York City. *Journal of Palliative Care* **4**, 54–57.

Dew, A., Ragni, M. & Nimorwicz, P. (1990) Infection with HIV and vulnerability to psychiatric distress: a study of men with haemophilia. *Archives of General Psychiatry* **47**, 737–744.

Dew, M.A., Becker, J.T., Sanchez, J., *et al.* (1997) Prevalence and predictors of depressive, anxiety and substance use disorders in HIV-infected and uninfected men: a longitudinal evaluation. *Psychological Medicine* **27**, 395–409.

Doyle, A., Petrak, J., Skinner, C., Smith, A. & Hedge, B. (1998) Mental health and quality of life in an East London out-patient HIV clinic population. Abstract from the *12th World AIDS Conference*, Geneva.

Elford, J., Bolding, G., Sherr, L., Maguire, M. & Elford, J. (1998) New therapies for HIV and sexual risk behaviour among gay men in London, UK. Abstract from the *12th World AIDS Conference*, Geneva.

Ezzy, D.M., Bartos, M.R., de Visser, R.O. & Rosenthal, D.A. (1998) Antiretroviral uptake in Australia: medical, attitudinal and cultural correlates. *International Journal of STD and AIDS* **9**, 579–586.

Fernando, S., van Gorp, W., McElhiney, M., Sewell, M. & Rabkin, J. (1998) Highly active antiretroviral treatment in HIV infection: benefits for neuropsychological function. *AIDS* **12**, F65–70.

Fishbein, M. & Azjen, I. (1975) *Belief, Attitude, Intention, and Behavior: An Introduction to Theory and Research*. Addison-Wesley, Reading, MA.

Foley, M., Skurnick, J.H., Kennedy, C.A., Valentin, R. & Louria, D.B. (1994) Family support for heterosexual partners in HIV-serodiscordant couples, *AIDS* **8**, 1483–1487.

Folkman, S., Chesney, M., Collette, L., Boccellari, A. & Cooke, M. (1996) Postbereavement depressive mood and its prebereavement predictors in HIV+ and HIV− gay men. *Journal of Personality and Social Psychology* **70**, 336–348.

Freeman, R.C., Rodriguez, G.M. & French, J.F. (1996) Compliance with AZT treatment regimen of HIV-seropositive injection drug users: a neglected issue. *AIDS Education and Prevention* **8**, 58–71.

Gala, C., Pergami, A., Catalan, J., *et al.* (1993) The psychosocial impact of HIV infection in gay men, drug users and heterosexuals – a controlled investigation. *British Journal of Psychiatry* **163**, 651–659.

George, H. (1990) Sexual and relationship problems among people affected by AIDS: three case studies. *Counselling Psychology Quarterly* **3**, 389–399.

Goodkin, K., Feaster, D.J., Tuttle, R., Blaney, N.T., Kumar, M., Baum, M.K., Shapshak, P. & Fletcher, M.A. (1996) Bereavement is associated with time-dependent decrements in celllar immune functioning in asymptomatic HIV-1 seropositive homosexual men. *Clinical and Diagnostic Laboratory Immunology* 3, 109–118.

Green, J. & McCreaner, A. (eds) (1996) *Counselling in HIV Infection and AIDS*. Blackwell Science, Oxford.

Greer, S., Moorey, S., Baruch, J., *et al.* (1992) Adjuvant psychological therapy for patients with cancer: a prospective randomised trial. *British Medical Journal* 304, 675–680.

Hawton, K., Salkovskis, P.M., Kirk, J. & Clark, D.M. (1989) *Cognitive Behaviour Therapy for Psychiatric Problems*. Oxford University Press, Oxford.

Hays, R.B., McKusick, L., Pallack, L., Hilliard, R., Hoff, C. & Coates, T.J. (1993) Disclosing HIV seropositivity to significant others. *AIDS* 7, 425–431.

Hedge, B. & Glover, L.F. (1990) Group intervention with HIV seropositive patients and their partners. *AIDS Care* 2, 147–154.

Hedge, B. & Petrak, J. (1998) Take as prescribed: a study of adherence behaviors in people taking antiretroviral medications. Abstract from the *12th World AIDS Conference*, Geneva.

Hedge, B. & Sherr, L. (1995) Psychological needs and HIV/AIDS. *Clinical Psychology and Psychotherapy* 2, 203–209.

Herek, G.M. & Capitanio, J.P. (1993) Public reactions to AIDS in the United States: a second decade of stigma. *American Journal of Public Health* 83, 886–891.

Herek, G.M. & Capitanio, J.P. (1998) AIDS stigma and HIV-related beliefs in the United States: results from a national telephone survey. Abstract from the *12th World AIDS Conference*, Geneva.

Igboko, E., Hardy, D.W., Rice, M.M.L., *et al.* (1998) THE (Tools for Health and Empowerment) course: a unique disease management program. Abstract from the *12th World AIDS Conference*, Geneva.

Ironson, G., LaPerriere, A., Antoni, M., O'Hearn, P. & Schneiderman, N. (1990) Changes in immune and psychological measures as a function of anticipation and reaction to HIV-1 antibody status. *Psychosomatic Medicine* 52, 247–270.

Kalichman, S.C. & Sikkema, K.J. (1994) Psychological sequelae of HIV infection: review of the empirical findings. *Clinical Psychology Review* 14, 611–632.

Kalichman, S.C., Sikkema, K.J. & Somlai, A. (1996) People living with HIV infection who attend and do not attend support groups: a pilot study of needs, characteristics and experiences. *AIDS Care* 8, 589–599.

Kelly, J.A. (1997) HIV risk reduction interventions for persons with serious mental illness. *Clinical Psychology Review,* 17(3), 293–309.

Kelly, J.A., Murphy, D.A., Bahr G.R., *et al.* (1993a) Factors associated with severity of depression and high risk sexual behavior among persons diagnosed with human immunodeficiency virus (HIV) infection. *Health Psychology* 12, 310–319.

Kelly, J.A., Murphy, D.A., Bahr, G.R., *et al.* (1993b) Outcome of cognitive-behavioural and support group brief therapies for depressed, HIV-infected persons. *American Journal of Psychiatry* 150, 1679–1686.

Kelly, J.A., Otto-Salaj, L.L., Sikkema, K.J., Pinkerton, S.D. & Bloom, F.R. (1998a) Implications of HIV treatment advances for behavioral research on AIDS: protease inhibitors and new challenges in HIV secondary prevention. *Health Psychology* 17, 215–219.

Kelly, J.A., Hoffman, R.G. Rompa, D. & Gray, M. (1998b) Protease inhibitor combination therapies and perceptions of gay men regarding AIDS severity and the need to maintain safer sex. *AIDS* 12, F91–F95.

Klein, S.J. (1998) *Heavenly Hurts: Surviving AIDS – Related Deaths and Losses*. Baywood, Amityville, NY.

Kocsis, A. (1996) AIDS dementia – counselling issues. In: *Counselling in HIV Infection and AIDS* (eds J. Green & A. McCreaner). Blackwell Science, Oxford.

Lamping, D.L., Abrahamowicz, M., Gilmore, N., *et al.* (1993) A randomized controlled trial to evaluate a psychosocial intervention to improve quality of life in HIV infection. Abstract from the *IXth International Conference on AIDS,* Berlin.

Lazarus, R.S. & Folkman, S. (1984) *Stress, Appraisal, and Coping*. Springer, New York.

Leventhal, H., Zimmerman, R. & Gutmann, M. (1984) Compliance: a self-regulatory perspective. In: *Handbook of Behavioral Medicine* (ed. W.D. Gentry). Guilford, New York.

Levine, S.H., Bystritsky, A., Baron, D. & Jones, L.D. (1991) Group psychotherapy for HIV-seropositive patients with major depression. *American Journal of Psychotherapy* 45, 413–424.

Lutgendorf, S.K., Antoni, M.H., Ironson, G., *et al.* (1998) Changes in cognitive coping skills and social support during cognitive behavioural stress management intervention and distress outcomes in symptomatic human immunodeficiency virus (HIV)-seropositive gay men. *Psychosomatic Medicine* **60**, 204–214.

Lyketsos, M.D., Hoover, D.R., Guccione, M., *et al.* (1996) Changes in depressive symptoms as AIDS develops. *American Journal of Psychiatry* **153**, 1430–1437.

McArthur, J.C., Hoover, D.R., Bacellar, H., *et al.* (1993) Dementia in AIDS patients: incidence and risk factors. *Neurology* **43**, 2245–2252.

McCann, K. & Wadsworth, E. (1991) The experience of having a positive HIV test. *AIDS Care* **3**, 43–53.

McGrath, J.W., Ankrah, M.E., Schumann, D.A., Nkumbi, S. & Lubega, M. (1993) AIDS and the urban family: its impact in Kampala, Uganda. *AIDS Care* **5**, 55–70.

Maasen, T. (1998) Counselling gay men with multiple loss and survival problems: the bereavement groups as a transitional object. *AIDS Care* **10**, S57–63.

Maj, M. (1991) Psychological problems of families and health workers dealing with people infected with HIV-1. *Acta Psychiatrica Scandinavica* **83**, 161–168.

Mann, J., Tarantola, D. & Netter, T. (ed.) (1992) *A global report: AIDS in the world.* Harvard University Press, Cambridge, MA.

Markowitz, J., Rabkin, J. & Perry, S. (1994) Treating depression in AIDS patients. *AIDS* **8**, 403–412.

Marks, G., Bundek, N.I., Richardson, J.L., Ruiz, M.S., Maldonado, N. & Mason, H.R.C. (1992) Self-disclosure of HIV infection: preliminary results from a sample of Hispanic men. *Health Psychology* **11**, 300–306.

Martin, J.L. & Dean, L. (1993) Effects of AIDS-related bereavement and HIV-related illness on psychological distress among gay men: a 7-year longitudinal study, 1985–1991. *Journal of Consulting and Clinical Psychology* **61**, 94–103.

Marzuk, P.M., Tierney, H., Tardiff, K., *et al.* (1988) Increased risk of suicide in persons with AIDS. *Journal of the American Medical Association* **259**, 1333–1337.

Marzuk, P.M., Tardiff, K., Leon, A.C., *et al.* (1997) HIV seroprevalence among suicide victims in New York City, 1991–1993. *American Journal of Psychiatry* **154**, 1720–1725.

Maslanka, H. (1996) Burnout, social support and AIDS volunteers. *AIDS Care* **8**(2), 195–206.

Mason, H.R.C., Marks, G., Simoni, J.M., Ruiz, M.S. & Richardson, J.L. (1995) Culturally sanctioned secrets? Latino men's nondisclosure of HIV infection to family, friends and lovers. *Health Psychology* **14**, 6–12.

Mason, H.R.C., Simoni, J.M., Marks, G., Johnson, C.J. & Richardson, J.L. (1997) Missed opportunities? Disclosure of HIV infection and support seeking among HIV+ African-American and European-American men. *AIDS and Behavior* **1**, 155–162.

Meadows, J., Catalan, J., Singh, A.N. & Burgess, A.P. (1993) Prevalence of HIV associated dementia (HAD) in a central London Health District in 1991. Abstract from the *IXth International conference on AIDS*, Berlin.

Melvin, D. & Sherr, L. (1993) The child in the family-responding to AIDS and HIV. *AIDS Care* **5**, 35–42.

Miller, D. (1987) *Living with AIDS and HIV.* Macmillan Education, London.

Miller, D. (1988) HIV and social psychiatry. *British Medical Bulletin* **44**, 130–148.

Miller, D. (1996) Stress and burnout in HIV/AIDS carers. *AIDS* **10** (Suppl. A), S213–219.

Miller, D. (2000) *Dying to Care? Work, Stress and Burnout in HIV/AIDS.* Routledge, London.

Miller, D. & Riccio, M. (1990) Non-organic psychiatric and psychosocial syndromes associated with HIV-1 infection and disease. *AIDS* **4**, 381–388.

Miller, R., Bor, R., Salt, H. & Murray, D. (1991) Counselling patients with HIV infection about laboratory tests with predictive value. *AIDS Care* **2**, 159–164.

Mulleady, G. (1992) *Counselling Drug Users About HIV and AIDS.* Blackwell Scientific Publications, Oxford.

Navia, B.A., Jordan, B.D. & Price, R.W. (1986) The AIDS dementia complex: I. clinical features. *Archives of Neurology* **19**, 517–524.

Neugebauer, R., Rabkin, J., Williams, J., Remien, R., Goetz, R. & Gorman, J. (1992) Bereavement reactions among homosexual men experiencing multiple losses in the AIDS epidemic. *American Journal of Psychiatry* **149** 1374–1379.

O'Dowd, M.A., Biderman, D.J. & McKegney, F.P. (1993) Incidence of suicidality in AIDS and HIV-positive patients attending a psychiatry outpatient program. *Psychosomatics* **34**, 33–40.

Ostrow, D.G., Monjan, A., Joseph, J., *et al.* (1989) HIV-related symptoms and psychological functioning in a cohort of homosexual men. *American Journal of Psychiatry* **146**, 737–742.

Ostrow, D.G., Whitaker, R.E.D., Frasier, K., *et al.* (1991) Racial differences in social support and mental health in men with HIV infection: a pilot study. *AIDS Care* **3**, 55–63.

Pakenham, K.I., Dadds, M.R. & Terry, D.J. (1995) Psychosocial adjustment along the HIV disease continuum. *Psychology and Health* **10**, 523–536.

Perry, S., Jacobsberg, L. & Fishman, B. (1990) Suicidal ideation and HIV testing. *Journal of the American Medical Association* **263**, 679–682.

Perry, S., Jacobsberg, L., Card, C., Ashman, T., Frances, A. & Fishman, B. (1993) Severity of psychiatric symptoms after HIV testing. *American Journal of Psychiatry* **150**, 775–779.

Petrak, J., Doyle, A., Smith, A. & Skinner, C. (1998) Self-disclosure of HIV serostatus to significant others: an examination of gender and cultural differences. Abstract from the *12th World AIDS Conference*, Geneva.

Price, R.W. & Perry, S.W. (eds) (1994) *HIV, AIDS and the Brain.* Raven Press, New York.

Pugh, K., Riccio, M., Jadresic, D. *et al.* (1994) A longitudinal study of the neuropsychiatric consequences of HIV-1 infection in gay men: II psychosocial and health status at baseline and 12 months follow-up. *Psychological Medicine* **24**, 897–904.

Rabkin, J.G., Williams, J.B., Remien, R.H., Goetz, R., Kertzner, R. & Gorman, J.M. (1991) Depression, distress, lymphocyte subsets, and human immunodeficiency virus symptoms on two occasions in HIV-positive homosexual men. *Archives of General Psychiatry* **48**, 111–119.

Rattigan, B. (1993) Psychoanalytic psychotherapy in treatment of patients with borderline or narcissistic personality disorders affected by HIV infection. Abstract from the *IXth International Conference on AIDS*, Berlin.

Reidy, M., Taggart, M.E. & Asselin, L. (1991) Psychological needs expressed by the natural caregivers of HIV infected children. *AIDS Care* **3**, 331–343.

Robins, A.G., Dew, M.A., Davidson, S., Penkower, L., Becker, J.T. & Kingsley, L. (1994) Psychosocial factors associated with risky sexual behavior among HIV-seropositive gay men. *AIDS Education and Prevention* **6**, 483–492.

Rosengard, C. & Folkman, S. (1997) Suicidal ideation, bereavement, HIV serostatus and psychosocial variables in partners of men with AIDS. *AIDS Care* **9**, 373–384.

Samet, J.H., Libman, H., Steger, K.A., *et al.* (1992) Compliance with zidovudine therapy in patients with human immunodeficiency virus, type 1: a cross-sectional study in a municipal clinic. *American Journal of Medicine* **92**, 495–502.

Sherr, L., Hedge, B., Steinhart, K., Davey, T. & Petrak, J. (1992) Unique patterns of bereavement in HIV: implications for counselling. *Genitourinary Medicine* **68**, 378–381.

Siegel, K., Karus, D. & Raveis, V.H. (1997) Correlates of change in depressive symptomatology among gay men with AIDS. *Health Psychology* **16**, 230–238.

Sikkema, K.J. & Bissett, R.T. (1997) Concepts, goals, and techniques of counseling: review and implications for HIV counseling and testing. *AIDS Education and Prevention* **9**, 14–26.

Sikkema, K.J., Kalichman, S.C., Kelly, J.A. & Koob, J.J. (1995) Group intervention to improve coping with AIDS-related bereavement: model development and an illustrative clinical example. *AIDS Care* **7**, 463–475.

Simoni, J.M., Mason, H.R.C., Marks, G., Ruiz, M.S., Reed, D. & Richardson, J.L. (1995) Women's self-disclosure of HIV infection: rates, reasons, and reactions. *Journal of Consulting and Clinical Psychology* **63**, 474–478.

Smith, M.Y. & Rapkin, B.D. (1995) Unmet needs for help among persons with AIDS. *AIDS Care* **7**, 353–363.

Sorensen, J.L., Mascovich, A., Wall, T.L., DePhilippis, D., Batki, S.L. & Chesney, M. (1998) Medication adherence strategies for drug abusers with HIV/AIDS. *AIDS Care* **10**, 297–312.

Stemple, R.R., Moulton, J.M. & Moss, A.R. (1995) Self-disclosure of HIV-1 antibody results: The San Francisco General Hospital Cohort. *AIDS Education and Prevention* **7**, 116–123.

Sullivan, A. (1997) When plagues end. *The Independent on Sunday*, 16 February.

Sweat, M. (1998) Effectiveness of HIV C&T in changing risk behaviors. *Cochrane Collaborative Review Group on HIV Infection and AIDS.* The Cochrane Collaboration.

Thompson, S.C., Nanni, C. & Levine, A. (1996) The

stressors and stress of being HIV-positive. *AIDS Care* **8**, 5–14.

Tindall, B., Forde, A., Goldstein, D., Ross, M.W. & Cooper, D.A. (1994) Sexual dysfunction in advanced HIV disease. *AIDS Care* **6**, 105–107.

UNAIDS (2000a) *Report on the global HIV/AIDS epidemic.* Joint United Nations Programme on HIV/AIDS (00.13E).

UNAIDS (2000b) *Caring for Carers: Managing Stress in Those who Care for People with HIV and AIDS.* Joint United Nations Programme on HIV/AIDS (00.08E).

Ussher, J. (1990) Cognitive behavioural couples therapy with gay men referred for counselling in an AIDS setting: a pilot study. *AIDS Care* **2**, 43–51.

Vedhara, K., Nott, K.H., Bradbeer, C.S., *et al.* (1997) Greater emotional distress is associated with accelerated CD4+ cell decline in HIV infection. *Journal of Psychosomatic Research* **42**, 379–390.

Williams, J., Rabkin, J., Remien, R., Gorman, J. & Ehrhardt, A. (1991) Multi-disciplinary baseline assessment of homosexual men with HIV infection-II: standardized clinical assessment of current and lifetime psychopathology. *Archives of General Psychiatry* **48**, 124–130.

Chapter 12

Psychiatric Issues in the Management of Sexual Health Problems

Jose Catalan

Introduction

The development of the concepts of sexual health and sexual health promotion is to some extent the result of the need to integrate skills and knowledge from a variety of disparate but related disciplines and models of care: from genitourinary medicine to gynaecology, and from contraception to sex therapy. Integration in the health services is not unique to sexual health – pain clinics, diabetic and HIV/AIDS services are examples of this trend, which represents a reaction to the development of super-specialties in medicine. While there is no doubt that the development of specialist areas of expertise has resulted in enormous progress in knowledge and practice, fragmentation of services and, to a certain extent, of the pattern of care of patients themselves, has been one of its unfortunate consequences. A similar parallel process of specialisation and integration is occurring in mental health services, both within the specialty (with greater emphasis on multidisciplinary care), and in relation to other services, such as general practice and the general hospital. Psychological medicine, incorporating liaison psychiatry and health psychology, provides a good example of the advantages for general hospital patients of this integrated approach to care (Royal College of Physicians and Royal College of Psychiatrists 1995). While psychiatrists and other mental health workers have had for some time links with genitourinary medicine and obstetrics and gynaecology departments, amongst others, it is really since the AIDS epidemic that a much closer relationship has developed (Catalan *et al.* 1995).

In this chapter, the nature and prevalence of the main psychiatric syndromes presenting in sexual health care settings will be reviewed, followed by discussion of management issues, including recognition of mental health problems, assessment and provision of further care.

Psychiatric classification and terminology

Mental disorder has been defined as a clinically significant behavioural or psychological syndrome or pattern that is associated with distress or disability, and with increased risk of suffering death, pain or other harm. The syndrome should be outside the range of culturally sanctioned response to events, and should not include political, religious or sexually deviant behaviour, or be merely the result of conflict between the person and society (DSM-IV 1995). While it is sometimes difficult to tell the difference between a normal but unusual psychological response (for example following a bereavement), and a pathological psychological reaction (such as major depression), in most instances it is possible to identify key symptoms or behavioural responses that can help to distinguish between the two, so that a therapeutic plan of action can be formulated.

In recent years there has been a move towards developing operational definitions of psychiatric syndromes to increase the reliability of diagnoses and to allow better communication between practitioners. Examples of these include the International Classification of Mental and Behavioural Disorders (ICD-10 1992) and the Diagnostic and Statistical Manual of Mental Disorders (DSM-IV 1995). Another area of debate and conceptual development concerns the category known as *personality disorder*, which is generally defined as a pattern of behaviours or traits present since the person's adolescence, and causing distress and/or impairment in social and occupational functioning. Personality disorder (or Axis II disorder in DSM terminology) can occur with or without a clinical syndrome (or Axis I disorder). For example, someone with an antisocial personality disorder can also develop major depression. There is a debate about whether a categorical or dimensional model should be used to describe personality disorder. In the categorical model, distinct clinical syndromes are described on the basis of a qualitatively separate picture, such as paranoid, antisocial or borderline. By contrast, a dimensional model will include a variety of traits, such as extroversion, openness, or impulsivity, all of which may be present to a greater or lesser degree. Long-standing personality difficulties and disorders are commonly seen in individuals experiencing emotional problems in health care settings (Casey 1997; Parker 1998; see Chapter 16).

Extent and nature of mental health problems

Psychological distress and frank mental disorder are common in health care settings, and their aetiology is varied, resulting in a range of specific disorders.

Psychological morbidity in health care settings

Psychological distress and problems are common in patients attending health care settings, more than a third presenting with some form of psychological disorder (Royal College of Physicians and Royal College of Psychiatrists 1995). While in the majority of cases the psychological distress is mild to moderate in severity and self-limited in time, in an important minority of patients the disorder is severe and likely to persist, in particular when the person suffers from a chronic, painful or life-threatening condition. Personality disorders are present in possibly up to 15% of individuals in the general population, but are much more common in health care settings, often complicating medical disorders (DSM-IV 1995).

A similar picture is seen in sexual health care settings. Amongst genitourinary clinic attenders, more than a third have been found to be 'psychiatric cases' using standardised instruments to measure psychiatric morbidity (Pedder & Goldberg 1970; Mayou 1975; Catalan et al. 1981; 1988). In obstetric and gynaecological settings, psychological morbidity may be associated with reproductive difficulties, as in cases of infertility or spontaneous abortion (Petersen 1993). As many as half of the women presenting for elective hysterectomy have high levels of psychological morbidity which drops significantly after surgery (Gath et al. 1982). Pelvic pain is also associated with high levels of psychological morbidity (Renaer et al. 1979).

Causes of psychological problems in health care settings

The association between psychological problems and physical disorders is a complex one. Physical disease or symptoms can be directly responsible for the psychological distress, as in the case of a person with a painful genital infection, such as genital herpes, or with a life-threatening disorder, such as advanced HIV infection with serious complications. Fear of disease (e.g. sexually transmitted disease) or of health problems (e.g. threatened miscarriage) can also result in psychological symptoms or frank psychiatric disorder, like depression. Conditions likely to cause organic brain syndromes, such as untreated syphilis or advanced HIV disease, may also lead to secondary psychiatric disorders.

On the other hand, primary psychiatric disorder may present with concerns or ideas about ill-health, as in the case of the person with severe depression who is convinced of being infected with HIV or syphilis, and seeks treatment at a genitourinary department. Personality factors may be relevant: individuals with a hypochondriacal personality, who are prone to misinterpret somatic symptoms of anxiety as symptoms of organic disease and who worry about becoming seriously ill, may seek reassurance from medical staff and attend frequently for further consultations and tests.

Finally, there may be a chance association between physical and psychological disorder. For example, eating disorders like bulimia nervosa are more likely to be seen in young women, and as this is a group frequently seen in genitourinary clinics, it is not surprising to find individuals with such problems. Alcohol and other substance misuse is not unusual in young, sexually active men and women, and so it would not be surprising to find that the prevalence of such behaviours is substantial in sexual health care settings (Catalan et al. 1988).

Specific psychiatric syndromes and problems

Any psychiatric disorder can present in sexual health care settings, and the main psychiatric disorders (Axis I) seen in such settings are listed and described here:

Stress disorders
While stress disorders are usually regarded as a form of anxiety disorder, the fact that they develop as a reaction to a specific psychosocial stressor makes it useful to discuss them

separately. Several syndromes have been described on the basis of their duration and specific characteristics.

- *Acute stress disorder:* lasting no more than 4 weeks after the stressful event, and characterised at first by numbing and emotional unresponsiveness, and later by anxiety and increased arousal, and by reliving of the incident (images, thoughts, dreams), and avoidance of stimuli that remind the person of the traumatic incident.
- *Adjustment disorder:* a similar but longer lasting stress reaction (up to six months), with predominant anxiety, depressive symptoms, or behavioural disturbance.
- *Post-traumatic stress disorder:* following a severe or extreme stress involving personal experience of threatened death or serious injury, or witnessing of one such incident, the person suffers intense fear, helplessness or distress. Subsequently, persistent re-experiencing of the incident occurs, with increased arousal and avoidance of stimuli associated with the trauma. It lasts more than a month, and its onset may be delayed. Post-traumatic stress disorder and its management is discussed in detail in Chapter 14.

Anxiety disorders
- *Generalised anxiety disorder:* excessive anxiety (restlessness, irritability, muscular tension, sleep disturbance) and worry lasting at least six months, and causing distress and social or occupational adjustment.
- *Obsessive–compulsive disorder:* recurrent obsessions (ideas, impulses or images which are perceived as intrusive and inappropriate), or repetitive behaviours (hand washing, counting or checking which reduce distress). These cause distress and are time consuming, interfering with the person's life. Fears of contamination, or concerns about venereal disease or HIV infection, are common themes.
- *Phobic disorder:* fear of specific situations or objects, with associated anxiety when exposed to the feared situation, and leading to marked avoidance. Illness, blood and bodily fluids are common phobic stimuli.
- *Panic disorder:* recurrent panic attacks (episodes of intense fear or distress with palpitations, sweating, chest pains, giddiness, etc., which develop suddenly). It may present together with agoraphobia (anxiety associated with being in situations or places from which escape might be difficult) or without it.

Abnormal health beliefs

A significant minority of individuals attending genitourinary clinics are afraid of having contracted a sexually transmitted disease, often in spite of repeated examination, reassurance, testing and even treatment. Syphilis, herpes, non-specific urethritis and, more recently, HIV infection have been the illnesses most commonly feared. The terminology used to describe these patients has also evolved over the years. 'Venereophobia' was an early term, recently replaced by AIDS-related labels such as 'AIDS-phobia' (Jacob *et al.* 1987), 'pseudo-AIDS' (Miller *et al.* 1985), AIDS panic (Windgassen & Soni 1987) and 'the worried well' (Miller 1986). Interestingly, the meaning of some of these terms has changed over time. For example, 'worried well' was a term applied at the start of the AIDS epidemic to people who had sexual contact with someone who subsequently developed AIDS and who, understandably, were afraid of becoming ill themselves. As they were asymptomatic and no HIV testing was yet available, the term seemed an accurate description of their plight (Forstein 1984; Morin *et al.* 1984). Nowadays, the term is sometimes used to describe individuals with abnormal health beliefs.

Concerns about infection or disease which do not subside after examination, testing and appropriate explanation and advice, should be regarded as a *symptom*, rather than a diagnosis. They may be part of an *anxiety disorder* (see above), *somatisation disorder*, or *hypochondriasis*. They may be delusional in nature, resulting from an *affective disorder*, such as major depression or mania, or from a *schizophrenic illness*. Establishing the diagnosis is essential before deciding how best to help the person (Catalan *et al.* 1995).

Mood disorders

Depressive symptoms are common in sexual health care settings, but severe clinical disorders are relatively rare. However, the fact that such disorders are often associated with suicide risk and their generally good response to treatment make it the more important to identify and manage them effectively.

Major depression

This is a persistent and severe syndrome characterised by low mood, loss of interest and lack of enjoyment in usual activities, feelings of worthlessness, hopelessness, preoccupation with thoughts about death, 'somatic symptoms' (loss of weight and appetite, insomnia, and tiredness), and thinking and concentration difficulties. There may be delusions involving disease or contamination, and hallucinations can occur in severe forms. Major depression can be an isolated event or recurrent. Bipolar disorders are characterised by the presence of both depressive and manic episodes over time.

Dysthymic disorder

This is a milder and more persistent syndrome, lasting at least two years, with brief periods free from depressive symptoms.

Manic episode

This is a persistently elevated mood, often with irritability, and with grandiosity, pressure of speech and flight of ideas, distractibility and insomnia. Increased interest in sex and sexual activity may be present. There may be delusional or hallucinatory symptoms, and it may cause substantial impairment of social and interpersonal functioning. The term hypomania is sometimes used to describe a less severe syndrome of mood elevation without psychotic symptoms (delusions or hallucinations) and minimal impairment of functioning.

Occasional anecdotal reports have drawn attention to manic episodes being a prodromal expression of organic brain disorders in HIV-asymptomatic patients (e.g. Schmidt & Miller 1988), and one review has suggested that manic episodes are very rare in the absence of organic brain syndromes in HIV-infected people (Vogel-Scibilia *et al.* 1988).

Substance misuse disorders

Alcohol and illicit drugs (such as psychostimulants, opiates, hallucinogenic agents and cannabis) are not uncommonly used by the mostly young, sexually active population usually seen in sexual health care settings. Using the CAGE to screen for alcohol misuse in attenders at a genitourinary clinic, Catalan *et al.* (1988) found that about 18% of men and 12% of women were likely to be drinking excessively. Prescribed and over-the-counter medicines (sedatives, anxiolytics and painkillers) can also be involved. Exposure to such substances can lead to a wide range of clinical syndromes and complications which may become apparent during the consultation, including the effects of acute intoxication, withdrawal reactions, and long-term use. Regardless of the substance used, the following disorders can develop:

Substance dependence

Craving, tolerance of increasing amounts to achieve the desired effects, and withdrawal reactions are characteristic features.

Substance abuse or misuse

A maladaptive pattern of persistent use that causes impairment or distress, with problems in social functioning, risk of physical health problems and legal difficulties.

Organic brain syndromes

Frank organic brain syndromes are generally uncommon in sexual health care settings, but sexually transmitted disorders like syphilis and HIV infection on the one hand, and substance misuse on the other, can lead to the development of such syndromes, and individuals suffering from these disorders may present in sexual health care settings.

General paralysis of the insane (GPI)

This is the result of syphilitic infection of the brain, and is now largely of historical interest, but in the nineteenth century when it was first described it represented an important and common health problem. GPI is essentially a dementing syndrome of gradual onset, often characterised by personality changes and labile mood (Lishman 1987). HIV infection can also be associated with the development of cognitive impairment leading to either *HIV-1 associated dementia* or the milder form of *HIV-1 associated minor cognitive impairment* (Maj *et al.* 1994; Catalan *et al.* 1995; Cotter & Everall 1996).

Other brain syndromes include *acute brain disorders* related to acute intoxication with *alcohol* or *illicit substances,* or due to their withdrawal, and *chronic brain disorders,* in particular *alcohol related dementia* and *amnestic syndrome.*

Schizophrenia and related disorders

Schizophrenic disorders are rare in sexual health care settings, although they may present in connection with abnormal health beliefs (see above) or unusual behaviours. Schizophrenic disorders are characterised by delusions and hallucinations (in particular of an auditory nature) and by other symptoms such as disorganised thought and speech, and bizarre behaviour. For the diagnosis of *schizophrenia* to be made, symptoms need to be present for at least 6 months, shorter episodes being known as *schizophreniform disorder* (1 to 6 months duration) and *brief psychotic episode* (up to 1 month).

Sexual problems

A wide range of sexual problems can present

in sexual health clinics, including concerns about sexual performance, anxieties about sexual orientation (Ross 1986), clear-cut sexual dysfunctions, and sexual dissatisfaction problems (Bancroft 1989; McConaghy 1993). While the majority of presenting problems are seen in individuals attending alone, couples can occasionally present. The prevalence of sexual dysfunction in genitourinary medicine settings has been well studied (Catalan *et al.* 1981; Goldmeier *et al.* 1997), suggesting that a substantial minority suffer sexual dysfunctions. As with other problems presenting in health care settings, it is important to remember that, for example, erectile dysfunction is not a diagnosis, but rather a symptom which needs further assessment to clarify whether it is a manifestation of a physical disorder, secondary to relationship problems between the patient and his partner, or the result of individual psychopathology. In recent years there have been important developments in the treatment of erectile disorders with physical methods, such as alprostadil (intrapenile and trans-urethral) and sildenafil (see Chapters 9 and 10 for detailed discussion of assessment and management of sexual disorders).

A history of sexual assault or trauma has been reported in about a quarter of women and about one tenth of men (Keane *et al.* 1995; Petrak *et al.* 1995; Goldmeier *et al.* 1997), and the sexual and psychopathological consequences of such events can be significant (see Chapter 14 for discussion).

Psychiatric management

Effective management of substantial mental health problems in people attending sexual health care settings will require collaboration between professionals and the recognition that while some generic skills, such as listening, provision of empathy, or ability to ask open-ended questions, should be possessed by doctors, nurses and others, more complex abilities in the assessment and management of mental health problems will require specialists or at least adequately trained staff. What form this collaboration should take and what type of specialists to involve will largely depend on the local needs and circumstances.

Levels of mental health care

A *first level of psychological care* can be effectively delivered by nurses and physicians, provided they have a positive attitude towards their patients, are able to listen to their concerns and recognise verbal and non-verbal signs of distress or embarrassment. Sensitive explanation of the significance of symptoms or test results, treatment plan and prognosis will do much to minimise anxiety and prevent further concerns and fears.

Containment of strong emotions expressed during the consultation, such as sadness, anger, distress or tears, may be more difficult to deal with, and this is an area where training and support by senior staff or mental health specialists could be of value.

A *secondary level of psychological care* may be needed for patients experiencing complex and severe psychosocial difficulties or where they are attempting to cope with serious health problems. In some cases, nurses and physicians may be able to fill this role, although more often other staff attached to the centre, such as health advisers, social workers, will become involved, ideally with the possibility of access to mental health specialists for advice or support.

A *tertiary level of psychological care* would require the involvement of mental health specialists, be they psychiatrists, psychologists or psychiatric nurses. Ideally, access to such specialists should be easy and not disrupted by bureaucratic procedures. In some settings the specialist is part of the sexual health team on a part-time or full-time basis, while in others the possibility of referral to a nearby facility may be available. It is likely that only a minority of patients attending the centre will require specialist contact, but they are likely to be those suffering from the most severe or difficult-to-manage problems. Referral to other treatment centres or to in-patient psychiatric care may sometimes be necessary, and so good links with the local psychiatric services are desirable.

Recognition of mental health problems

Severe mental health problems, such as a manic episode or schizophrenic disorder, may be easy to recognise, but more subtle or less severe disorders can be missed in a busy clinic. Some general questions about the person's mood, sleep, ability to cope with the health problem that led to the consultation, relationships, and use of alcohol or other substances, may be all that is needed for some important information to be disclosed that will alert the professional to the need for more detailed assessment. In most cases, the process of inquiring about psychosocial issues need not take long, although sometimes it may be necessary to make arrangements for a more detailed interview or to provide more time.

Obstacles to the recognition of mental health problems can arise. For example, psychological symptoms may be perceived by doctors and others as being only a manifestation of physical disease, leading to over-investigation and inappropriate treatment, as in the case of individuals with hypochondriasis. Another example of obstacles to the recognition of mental disorder can arise when the psychological response (e.g. distress and sadness) is regarded as normal and understandable under the circumstances faced by the patient (e.g. following sexual assault), so that staff fail to recognise its severity and associated features (e.g. suicidal ideas, major depression). Professionals' perceived psychological skills and confidence in their ability to contain distress and cope with people with psychological problems will also influence their likelihood of picking up cues and following psychological leads during the consultation. Finally, the presence or absence of good referral facilities for specialist mental health care will affect the motivation of general staff to identify severe psychiatric disorders.

Assessment of mental health problems

Assessment of mental state includes first, observation of the person's manner and behaviour; second, sensitive listening to spontaneous comments and statements; and finally, close questioning, asking specific questions to clarify particular symptoms.

Skills in the assessment of *mood disorders*, in particular major depression, are the most important. Persistent low mood, with associated loss of hope in the future, lack of enjoyment of pleasurable activities, loss of interest in things, self-blame and guilt about minor misdeeds are typical. Worries about health in spite of reassurance may be volunteered. The presence of suicidal ideas, whether fleeting or well developed, should be a cause for concern. So called 'somatic symptoms of depression' such as sleep disturbance with early morning waking, loss of weight, appetite and interest in sex may be present, but they are less helpful in the context of physical illness, when they may develop in the absence of depression. Elated mood, as in mania, is characterised by infectious, happy mood, hyperactivity, possible irritability, overflowing energy and expansiveness, and a history of uncharacteristic overspending or travel.

Abnormalities of thinking can take many forms. Delusions are false and unshakable beliefs out of keeping with the person's cultural background, and may be present in severe depression, often including ideas about death or serious illness, and in schizophrenic and related disorders. Morbid fears of a non-delusional nature and distressing thoughts or images may be seen in phobic disorders, anxiety disorders like post-traumatic stress disorder or obsessive-compulsive disorder, or in hypochondriasis.

Perceptual abnormalities such as illusions (misrepresentations where the person realises that there has been a perceptual error) may occur in states of heightened anxiety or fear, while hallucinations (false perception but with the qualities of a real one in the absence of an external stimulus) are of potentially more sinister significance: auditory hallucinations can be typical of schizophrenic disorders, and visual hallucinations point to an organic brain disorder.

Cognitive function can be tested in a simple way by assessing orientation (in time, place and person), attention and concentration (asking for the months of the year backwards or for the subtraction of 7 from 100 and to keep repeating the calculation), recent memory (registration is tested by asking to repeat immediately a name and address or a series of digits, and recall is tested by asking again 5 minutes later), and remote memory (asking about well-known historical events or early personal history details). More detailed assessment will require neuropsychological testing by a trained and experienced professional.

Mental health interventions

Having identified the possible presence of significant psychiatric disorder, a preliminary assessment of the nature and severity of the psychiatric problem will help to plan what further care is needed. A decision will need to be made as to level of intervention required (see above), and in particular whether the physician or nurse involved should deal with the problems alone, or whether to discuss with or refer to another professional. Some psychological interventions, such as counselling and supportive therapy, and some forms of psychopharmacological treatment could be provided by staff working within the sexual health care setting, while more specialised therapies, such as cognitive behavioural therapy or complex psychopharmacological regimes, will require the involvement of psychologists and psychiatrists.

Local needs and service provision will vary between settings. Ideally, access to the full range of mental health interventions, with the understandable exception of in-patient psychiatric care, should be available at the centre, so that patients do not have to be referred on and be seen in another clinic or hospital: many patients will find the prospect of attending a general psychiatric out-patient department, for example, unappealing, and treatment adherence may suffer as a result. Sessional involvement of psychologists and psychiatrist may be a good alternative.

Psychological interventions

A wide range of psychological interventions can be applied in sexual health care settings.

Counselling and supportive therapies
These provide an environment where patients can express their feelings, ask questions and explore difficult choices, and can be very valuable to individuals experiencing traumatic events or having potentially serious disorders. Stress and anxiety disorders, some depressive conditions, substance misuse problems, problems of loss and bereavement, and sexual concerns and anxieties can benefit from this form of help, as can do some more long-standing personal difficulties (Woolfe & Dryden 1996).

Cognitive and behavioural therapies (CBT)
CBT is the treatment of choice for many anxiety disorders, severe stress disorders, moderately severe depressive conditions, and some sexual dysfunctions. Clinical psychologists are the professionals likely to deal with these difficulties effectively (Hawton *et al.* 1989).

Other psychotherapies
Psychodynamic, interpersonal, couple and family therapies can be used provided careful selection of patients and problems takes place, so as to match problem and therapy appropriately.

Psychopharmacological treatments

Psychotropic drugs can be very effective in the treatment of psychiatric disorders in sexual health care settings, usually in combination with psychological treatments (see above). However, they need to be used appropriately (the right class of drug for the right disorder), and in the right dosage and for the right duration. While psychotropic drug prescribing should not be restricted to psychiatrists, if non-specialists are to prescribe antidepressants and other medicines, it is important for them to be familiar with their indications, limitations and side effects. It is preferable to use only a few first-line and well established preparations with known efficacy, rather than to prescribe the latest or most expensive drug. Discussion with the local or team psychiatrist would be desirable in more complex or difficult cases (Gelder *et al.* 1996).

Treatment of depression
Antidepressants are the treatment of choice in major depression and also in less severe depressive disorders which fail to respond to psychological and social intervention. They also have a role in some anxiety disorders. Antidepressants need to be taken regularly and beyond the resolution of the depressive disorder that led to their prescription: six months is the usual length of a course of treatment.

Tricyclic antidepressants (amitryptiline, imipramine) are very effective but their side effect profile and risk in overdose has led to their replacement by a new generation of equally effective antidepressants, in particular the selective serotonin re-uptake inhibitors (fluoxetine, paroxetine, sertraline). These are easier to tolerate and safer in overdose. Adverse sexual side effects can be a problem in sexually active patients, although some are free from this side effect (e.g. nefazodone) (Mir & Taylor 1998).

Treatment of mania and other severe disorders

Major tranquillisers (haloperidol, chlorpromazine) are the treatment of choice for the symptomatic treatment of mania and related disorders, and more recently the new generation tranquillisers (risperidone) have become widely used because of their efficacy and better side effect profile.

Treatment of anxiety disorder and insomnia

Psychological interventions are the treatment of choice for anxiety disorders, but in severe forms of anxiety and stress disorders, combination with short-term use of anxiolytic medication can be effective. Long-term use of anxiolytic medication should be discouraged.

Treatment of organic brain syndromes

Treatment of the cause of the syndrome is essential, but in addition symptomatic treatment with major tranquillisers such as haloperidol or risperidone can be very effective in acute brain syndromes. Chronic brain disorders also require aetiologically driven treatment, be it antibiotics (Lishman 1987) or antiretrovirals (Catalan 1998).

References

American Psychiatric Association (1995) DSM-IV: Diagnostic and Statistical Manual of Mental Disorders, 4th edn. APA, Washington, DC.

Bancroft, J. (1989) Human Sexuality and its Problems. Churchill Livingstone, Edinburgh.

Casey, P. (1997) Clinical assessment of personality. Advances in Psychiatric Treatment 3, 182–187.

Catalan, J. (1998) Update on HIV-1 associated dementia and related disorders. AIDS Targeted Information 12, R63–R65.

Catalan, J., Bradley M., Gallway, J. & Hawton, K. (1981) Sexual dysfunction and psychiatric morbidity in patients attending a clinic for sexually transmitted diseases. British Journal of Psychiatry 138, 292–296.

Catalan, J., Day, A. & Gallway, J. (1988) Alcohol misuse in patients attending a genitourinary clinic. Alcohol and Alcoholism 23, 421–428.

Catalan, J., Burgess, A. & Klimes, I. (1995) Psychological Medicine of HIV Infection. Oxford University Press, Oxford.

Cotter, D. & Everall, I.P. (1996) The neuropathology and pathogenesis of HIV brain infection. International Review of Psychiatry 8, 227–335.

Forstein, M. (1984) AIDS anxiety in the worried well. In: Psychiatric Implications of AIDS (eds S. Nichols & D. Ostrow). American Psychiatric Press, Washington DC.

Gath, D.H., Cooper, P. & Day, A. (1982) Hysterectomy and psychiatric disorder: I levels of psychiatric morbidity before and after hysterectomy. British Journal of Psychiatry 140, 335–342.

Gelder, M., Gath, D., Mayou, R. & Cowen, P. (1996) Oxford Textbook of Psychiatry, 3rd edn. Oxford University Press, Oxford.

Goldmeier, D., Keane, F.E., Carter, P., Hessman, A., Harris, J.R.W. & Renton, A. (1997) Prevalence of sexual dysfunction in heterosexual patients attending a central London genitourinary medicine clinic. International Journal of STD and AIDS 8, 303–306.

Hawton, K., Salkovskis, P., Kirk, J. & Clark, D. (eds) (1989) Cognitive Behaviour Therapy for Psychiatric Problems: A Practical Guide. Oxford Medical Publications, Oxford.

Jacob, K., John, J., Verghesse, A. & John, T. (1987) AIDS-phobia. British Journal of Psychiatry 150, 412.

Keane, F.E., Young, S.M., Boyle, H.M. & Curry, K.M. (1995) Prior sexual assault reported by male attenders at a department of genitourinary medicine. International Journal of STD and AIDS 6, 95–100.

Lishman, W.A. (1987) *Organic Psychiatry: The Psychological Consequences of Cerebral Disorder* (pp. 280–284). Blackwell Scientific Publications, Oxford.

Maj, M., Janssen, R., Starace, F., Zaudig, M., Satz, P. & Sughomdhabirom, B. (1994) WHO neuropsychiatric study: cross sectional phase. *Archives of General Psychiatry* **51**, 39–49.

Mayou, R. (1975) Psychological morbidity in a clinic for sexually transmitted disease. *British Journal of Venereal Diseases* **51**, 57–60.

McConaghy, N. (1993) *Sexual Behaviour: Problems and Management.* Plenum Press, New York.

Miller, D. (1986) The worried well. In: *The Management of AIDS Patients* (eds D. Miller, J. Weber & J. Green). Macmillan, London.

Miller, D., Green, J., Farmer, R. & Carroll, G. (1985) A pseudo-AIDS syndrome following from fear of AIDS. *British Journal of Psychiatry* **146**, 550–552.

Mir, S. & Taylor, D. (1998) Sexual adverse effects with new antidepressants. *Psychiatric Bulletin* **22**, 438–441.

Morin, S., Charles, K. & Malyon, A. (1984) The psychological impact of AIDS on gay men. *American Psychologist* **39**, 1288–1293.

Parker, G. (1998) Personality disorders as alien territory: classification, measurement and border issues. *Current Opinion in Psychiatry* **11**, 125–129.

Pedder, J.R. & Goldberg, D.P. (1970) A survey by questionnaire of psychiatric disturbance in patients attending a venereal diseases clinic. *British Journal of Venereal Diseases* **46**, 58–61.

Petersen, J. (1993) Obstetrics and gynaecology. In: *Psychiatric Care of the Medical Patient* (eds A. Stoudemire & B.S. Fogel). Oxford University Press, New York.

Petrak, J.A., Skinner, C.J. & Claydon, E.J. (1995) The prevalence of sexual assault in a genitourinary medicine clinic: service implications. *Genitourinary Medicine* **71**, 98–102.

Renaer, M., Vertommen, H. & Nijs, P. (1979) Psychological aspects of chronic pelvic pain in women. *American Journal of Obstetrics and Gynaecology* **134**, 75–80.

Ross, M.W. (1986) *Psychovenereology.* Praeger, New York.

Royal College of Physicians and Royal College of Psychiatrists (1995) *The Psychological Care of Medical Patients: Recognition of Need and Service Provision.* Royal College of Physicians Publications Unit, London.

Schmidt, U. & Miller, D. (1988) Two cases of hypomania in AIDS. *British Journal of Psychiatry* **152**, 839–842.

Vogel-Scibilia, S.E., Mulsant, B.H. & Keshavan, M.S. (1988) HIV infection presenting as psychosis: a critique. *Acta Psychiatrica Scandinavica* **78**, 652–656.

Windgassen, E. & Soni, S. (1987) AIDS panic. *British Journal of Psychiatry* **151**, 126–127.

Woolfe, R. & Dryden, W. (eds) (1996) *Handbook of Counselling Psychology.* Sage Publications, London.

World Health Organization (1992) *ICD-10: International Classification of Mental and Behavioural Disorders.* WHO, Geneva.

Chapter 13

Partner Notification: the Management of Partners in the Sexual Health Setting

Sarah Chippindale

Partner notification, the process of contacting the sexual partners of patients diagnosed with a sexually transmitted infection (STI) and advising them to attend for screening and treatment, is a vital public health aspect of work in the sexual health setting. However, discussing this issue with patients can be difficult when they are distressed about an infection, feel guilty, or angry, about how the infection was possibly acquired and anxious about the effect it will have on their relationship/s. Individuals diagnosed with an STI are normally seen on a one-to-one basis, and it can be easy to view them in isolation from their everyday lives. In undertaking partner notification work, it is important to consider the effect of that STI not only on the individual, but also on their partner/s and their relationship/s. This chapter will primarily deal with the management of partners in British Sexual Health/Genito-Urinary Medicine Clinics (GUM) but will consider partner management in other countries.

Definitions

Historically the process of notifying the partners of an individual diagnosed with an STI was known as contact tracing. However, with the advent of HIV, the term partner notification* was endorsed by the World Health Organization (1989: p. 2) as:

'the spectrum of public health activity in which sexual and injection equipment-sharing partners of individuals with HIV infection are notified, counselled about their exposure and offered services.'

---

*A UNAIDS/WHO Consultation on HIV Reporting and Disclosure, Geneva, 20–22 October 1999, recommended that the term 'partner counselling' should be substituted for the term 'partner notification' because, in some contexts, partner notification is associated with coercion and pressure. The Centers for Disease Control, Atlanta, Georgia, USA, now uses the term 'partner counselling'.

The term partner notification is now generally used for all STIs, including HIV infection. Partner notification for all STIs (including HIV) remains voluntary in Britain. The patient initially identified with an STI/HIV is referred to as the *index patient*. *Partners/contacts* are the sexual, or needle sharing in the case of blood-borne infections, contacts of the index patient. Partners may be the source of the infection or individuals to whom the infection may have been passed. If a partner is diagnosed with an STI, they then become a new index patient and the partner notification process is repeated. In this chapter, the term partner will be used rather than contact. The term 'partner' may refer to both current ongoing relationships as well those that have ended. Index patients may present with a variety of relationships: long-term, new or more short-term, multiple, and casual or 'one off'. The impact of partner notification on a relationship will usually depend on the strength, 'type' and length of that relationship, the type of STI acquired, as well as the perceptions that the index and partner/s have about the relationship, and about sex and STIs.

Rationale for partner notification

The distribution of an STI within a community depends on the sexual behaviour of individuals within that community (including rate of partner change, the use of barrier contraception and extent of mixing between high and low risk populations), as well as the efficiency of transmission and how long the STI case remains infectious (Hethcote & York 1984). Behavioural and social factors must be taken into account when trying to control

STIs, more so than for other communicable infections (Rothenberg & Potterat 1990). There are various factors that are important in STI control; these include having accessible services for the screening and treatment of STIs, providing health promotion (including health education on prevention of STIs/HIV and distribution of condoms) and carrying out *partner notification*. Partner notification aims to break the chain of disease transmission by promptly identifying and treating those exposed to the infection, and thereby reduce further spread and limit the pool of asymptomatic but infectious individuals (Adler & Johnson 1988). It also aims to prevent complications of untreated infections (e.g. infertility) as well as the re-infection of the index patient. Other objectives include encouraging sustained behaviour change, reaching at-risk populations and influencing community norms (Potterat *et al.* 1991). The notification of 'contacts' is an established public health method for control of many communicable diseases e.g. tuberculosis. In order for partner notification to serve as an infection control measure, the infection requires:

- A defined incubation period.
- An asymptomatic latency period during which time an infected person is infectious.
- The availability of a test to diagnose asymptomatic infections.
- A cure.
- A test of cure (Partner Notification Steering Group, 1994: p. 12).

Clearly, bacterial STIs fulfil the above criteria so partner notification can be seen to benefit not only the individual but also the community. However, the use of partner notification with viral conditions is more debatable as people identified with infection cannot be cured. From an epidemiological point of view it is only worthwhile identifying people with viral STIs if they will subsequently modify their sexual behaviour in order to lessen the chance of disease transmission (Cowan *et al.* 1996).

In countries with well-developed health care systems, partner notification is a well established tool to control STIs (Blaxter 1991); it may be of more limited use in developing countries which lack the infrastructure and resources for effective partner referral (Njeru *et al.* 1995; see also UNAIDS 2000, and UNAIDS/WHO 2000). Partner notification, whilst central to work in GUM, can be carried out in other settings where STIs are likely to be diagnosed and managed, e.g. general practice, family planning and antenatal clinics. Hence, partner notification can involve a variety of health care workers e.g. physicians, public health nurses, social workers and specially trained professionals (e.g. contact tracers, health advisers or disease intervention specialists) (Fenton *et al.* 1998). Although good partner notification is reliant on all the multidisciplinary team within GUM, in Britain it remains predominantly the remit of the health adviser.

Partner notification for HIV infection

The advent of HIV brought great debate on the use of partner notification as a tool to reduce HIV transmission – a debate that does not seem to have been of concern with other STIs. Oxman *et al.* (1994) found that legal and ethical discussions regarding HIV partner notification were numerous, yet there were no comparable discussions with regard to STI control. Ethical debates have centred mainly on the confidentiality of the index patient, the right of partners to know that they have been at risk versus their right not to know, duty of care, the difficulty in ascertaining when someone was infected and thus how far back to trace partners, and the fact that HIV is not curable. In the early years of the epidemic, the question was whether partners should be notified when there was no treatment and testing HIV positive may result in anxiety, stigmatisation and discrimination (Adler & Johnson 1988). In essence the debate has – and continues to be – centred on the inherent tensions between individual freedom versus the rights of society (see UNAIDS/WHO 2000). Historically, public health in Britain has faced problems balancing these two perspectives (Porter & Porter 1988). In terms of HIV, those who represent HIV positive individuals have mostly opposed partner notification, whereas those who represent the public health have supported it (Adler & Johnson 1988; WHO/UNAIDS 2000). In one study, interviews of staff in 20 GUM clinics in England revealed that only 22% of doctors, 18% of nurses and 5% of health advisers thought partner notification for HIV should be carried out. In comparison 67% of doctors, 66% of nurses and 55% of health advisers thought it should be carried out for other STIs (Allen & Hogg 1993). With the advent of HIV, the health advisers' remit has grown to include pre-HIV test discussion, post-test counselling for those diagnosed HIV positive, and counselling for those affected by HIV/AIDS. There has been growing emphasis on patient autonomy and the development of client centred HIV services. There are inevitable tensions between the client centred empowerment approach underlying counselling and the public health ethos (Cowan *et al.* 1996). In addition, confusion has arisen between the moral duty to warn where the doctor knows the details of a person who may be at risk of infection (e.g. a spouse) and traditional partner notification where the details of partners are not known and rely on the co-operation of the index patient (Bayer & Toomey 1992). With the recent treatment and diagnostic advances in HIV infection, and the ability to reduce mother-to-child transmission in pregnant HIV positive women, there has generally been a move amongst health providers in Britain towards encouraging HIV testing (including antenatal screening) and early diagnosis, and towards an acceptance of HIV partner notification as a part of good clinical practice.

There is a difference in emphasis between partner notification for STIs and partner notification for HIV. With STIs, the aim is to identify and test all partners of the index patient to ascertain who is the source of the infection and to whom it has been passed. The pattern is then repeated for each infected partner. In HIV, establishing the onset of the infection can be problematic and so is less important. The main aim is to offer counselling and testing to as many partners as possible (Ramstedt & Giesecke 1993). Countries have responded to the question of HIV partner notification very differently. For example, in Denmark, confidentiality of the index patient has been absolute and there has been opposition to any official partner notification; whereas in Sweden contacts are legally bound to come forward for testing, doctors are mandated to trace contacts and any individual who suspects in-

fection is legally bound to go for testing (Blaxter 1991). In some states in the USA e.g. South Carolina, it is a criminal offence to have sexual intercourse without informing a partner of your status; in New South Wales (Australia) 'the willful transmission of HIV' has been made a crime (Blaxter 1991). In the same vein, legislation criminalising non-disclosure to sexual partners of known HIV infection continues to be proposed in a number of African states, although has rarely been introduced or enacted (UNAIDS/WHO 2000). In Britain, *The Department of Health Guidance on Partner Notification for HIV* (Department of Health 1992) states that partner notification should be part of comprehensive, co-ordinated HIV and STI prevention, care and support programmes, not an isolated activity, and should only be with explicit consent of the individual obtained without due pressure. Similarly, UNAIDS/WHO guidance on this issue has recommended that in view of the stigma and potential harm associated with HIV disclosure in many societies, 'beneficial disclosure' requires that authorities:

- Conduct public information campaigns and community forums aimed at promoting tolerance, compassion, understanding, and the reduction of fear, stigma and discrimination.
- Encourage participation of people living with HIV/AIDS in public information campaigns and in HIV programmes and policy formulation.
- Establish more voluntary counselling and testing services (VCT), including in rural areas and for marginalised groups.
- Support governmental agencies, NGOs and CBOs to make community-based services,

including VCT, family outreach, community support, positive living, support groups, and care options more widely available.

- Encourage the media to report on HIV/AIDS in a responsible, non-discriminatory and non-sensational manner.
- Train health care workers in the management of HIV and universal precautions, in attitudes of non-discrimination, acceptance and compassion, and in the principles of confidentiality and informed consent.
- Train other professionals (social workers, police, lawyers, judges) in attitudes of non-discrimination, acceptance and compassion, and in the principles of confidentiality and informed consent.
- Train key personnel in non-health employment settings, including human resource management in industry, in promoting non-discriminatory practices in the workplace.
- Enact or reform of laws, administrative guidelines and professional codes of conduct to prohibit discrimination and breaches of confidentiality related to HIV status.
- Create legal support services for those who have suffered discrimination based on HIV status.

Historical background of partner notification

In Britain, efforts to control the spread of STIs probably began in the Middle Ages with brothel owners fined for keeping infected prostitutes; methods were generally punitive and included enforced quarantine (Oriel 1994). By the 19th century there was concern over the prevalence of 'venereal disease' in the armed forces which resulted in the *Contagious Diseases Acts* (1864, 1866, 1869). Women named as prostitutes could be taken into police custody, medically examined and, if found to have a venereal disease, confined until treatment was completed (Porter & Porter 1988). The Acts were repealed in 1886 after vigorous campaigning from social reformers, including Josephine Butler, outraged by this treatment of women. The Acts themselves had little effect on reducing the incidence of venereal disease as they were impossible to enforce and only targeted the women rather than all those who were at risk (Oriel 1994). By the beginning of the 20th century concerns over the high prevalence of syphilis and gonorrhoea in London led the government to set up a Royal Commission in 1913. Their report recommended that free, confidential services for the early diagnosis and treatment of venereal diseases should be established with voluntary attendance (Royal Commissioners 1916); these recommendations led to the *Venereal Diseases Regulations* (1917). Currently GUM clinics in the Britain operate under *The National Health Service (Venereal Diseases) Regulations* 1974. These regulations prohibit disclosure of information on patients attending GUM except when it is in the best interests of the individual or for disease prevention (Cowan *et al.* 1996) and allow for communication between GUM clinics on index patients and their partners.

Partner notification, as practised today, was probably started in the early 1930s in America (Wigfield 1972; UNAIDS 2000). Thomas Parran, an epidemiologist, advocated the use of informing, screening and treating all contacts of syphilis (Bayer & Toomey 1992). The USA has continued to focus its STI services primarily on the provision of case investigation and contact services; whereas Britain has focused on the establishment of a strong, decentralised *special clinic* system (Rothenberg & Potterat 1990). However partner notification has grown with the development of these special clinics. In Britain during the Second World War, Defence Regulation 33B was introduced in an attempt to control STIs; this recognised the importance of tracing partners and recommended that specialist staff were employed to carry out this work (House of Lords 1942). Although repealed in 1947, the Ministry of Health did recommend that *contact tracing* procedures should continue (Cowan *et al.* 1996). The Tyneside Scheme, begun in 1944, included the routine serological testing for syphilis in antenatal departments; and the inauguration of a *contact tracing* scheme. Evaluation of the scheme revealed for the first time the social background of STIs as well as the success of getting contacts to attend (Wigfield 1972).

Partner notification in practice

In order for any partner notification strategy to be successful, there must be good means of communication, and easy access to screening and treatment services with specially trained staff. There are three main methods of partner notification:

- *Index (patient) referral* where the index case agrees to notify their partner/s themselves.
- *Provider referral* whereby the health adviser agrees to notify the index's partner/s on their behalf.
- *Contract (conditional) referral* whereby the index undertakes to notify their partner/s within an agreed time frame. If they fail to do so, then the health adviser does it on their behalf.

In Britain, the main tool to assist with partner notification is the use of the *contact slip* although these should *never be used* in HIV infection. Details of the index patient's reference number, date of attendance and diagnosis are recorded on the slip, as well as details of the issuing clinic. The reference number refers to the clinic number of the index patient which is unique and confidential to the GUM clinic. The diagnosis of the index patient is given by the use of standard specific diagnoses codes for each individual STI or related condition. Diagnoses codes for the UK are not applicable elsewhere but World Health Organization codes are available. When the partner has been diagnosed, similar details are recorded on the reverse of the slip and returned to the issuing clinic. Although the contact slip has never been properly evaluated there are some advantages to its use in partner notification for STIs. Contact slips:

- Give anonymity and confidentiality to the index patient – *details of the index or their diagnosis should never be passed to the partner.*
- Enable partners to seek medical advice, screening and treatment – partners can present at any GUM clinic in Britain.
- Give details of the index patient's diagnosis, reference number and date of diagnosis to ensure the partner is screened/treated appropriately.
- Enable cross-referencing, resolution and evaluation of partner notification activity.

Index referral is the most commonly used method in Britain and can be carried out in a variety of ways i.e. face to face, by letter or by telephone. The method chosen by the index is usually dependent on the type of relationship, for example, the index may only have the phone number of a casual partner. The index patient is encouraged to pass a contact slip to each of their partners; he/she is usually also encouraged to tell their partner the exact nature of the STI where possible.

In Britain, provider referral can only take place with the expressed permission of the index patient. The confidentiality of the index patient remains paramount but the index must be made aware that partners notified by a health adviser may still guess their identity although it would never be disclosed to them. Provider referral requires accurate and full details on partners and can be carried out by letter, phone call or home visit. Index referral is simpler and less expensive than provider referral. Provider referral may be appropriate in the developed world where public health systems have the resources and infrastructure for confidential notification of partners but is less feasible in the developing world which lack these resources and infrastructure. Index referral is more feasible but still has inherent difficulties in the developing world where means of communication or transportation are poor, or where discussions of sexuality and disease are culturally sanctioned (Njeru *et al.* 1995).

Partner notification interview

The partner notification interview has a dual focus. It is as important to discuss with the index patient the future primary prevention of STIs, as it is to carry out the secondary prevention of reducing the spread of the infection. Individual counselling has been shown to be useful in reducing the occurrence of STIs and increases knowledge about and use of condoms (Wynendaele *et al.* 1995; Kamb *et al.* 1998), and may well increase the number of partners who present for treatment (Njeru *et al.* 1995). The health adviser firstly clarifies what the index currently understands about their infection. Discussion then includes:

- the nature of the infection and how it is transmitted;
- complications of untreated infection;
- explanation of treatment and the importance of treatment compliance;
- the rationale for avoiding sexual intercourse;
- the rationale for screening/treating sexual and/or needle sharing partners;
- health education/promotion around HIV/STI prevention.

The *notification period* (i.e. how far back to trace partners) will depend on the nature and site of the infection. Detailed questions are asked regarding numbers of partners, types of sexual activity, condom use and relevant partners identified. In most instances the attendance of the regular partner is seen as a priority. The health adviser will ascertain which partners are *traceable* i.e. the index patient believes they will be able to locate the partner, and which are *untraceable* i.e. will not be able to be found. The health adviser also identifies with the index patient which 'referral' method is to be used to notify each traceable partner; contact slips are issued for each traceable partner identified and their use explained carefully. With index referral, time can be spent helping the patient consider ways of informing their partner/s of the infection. For example, role playing can assist index patients in 'practising' how they might go about telling partners; or the index can discuss what they might put in a letter. Partner notification is carefully recorded either in the index patient notes, on computer or on separate cards according to specific clinic protocols.

Health education/promotion is an integral part of the partner notification interview. By definition the index patient is at high risk of repeat STIs and HIV because of their sexual behaviour (Meheus *et al*. 1990). Safer sex/risk reduction, raising awareness of other STIs, including HIV, condom use, unwanted pregnancy and contraception is then discussed with each index patient as appropriate. At follow-up or test of cure, the outcome of partner notification should be recorded for each partner identified. If the index has failed to contact any of the traceable partners, he/she should be re-referred to the health adviser. Details of a partner's attendance and diagnosis are never given back to the index.

The partner notification interview can be extremely difficult. Patients can be distressed, angry, guilty, embarrassed, concerned about the infection and frightened of the damage that might be done to the relationship when the partner is told to attend for screening. It is important that these feelings are acknowledged and explored with the index patient and support given to them as they adjust to the diagnosis and the need for partner notification. The partner notification is reliant on the co-operation of the index patient and an atmosphere of trust needs to be created in order for the index to openly and honestly discuss

such a sensitive subject as sexual/needle sharing partners.

Partner notification for HIV uses similar techniques as for other STIs although there are some important differences. Contact slips should never be issued and, unlike the case with other STIs, the exact nature of the infection *is* disclosed to partners so they can give full consideration to, and informed consent for, HIV testing. The decision to notify partners is usually more problematic in HIV infection both in terms of deciding which partners to tell and the disclosure itself. It is often difficult to ascertain when the index was infected and therefore establish the notification period. In these instances, limiting partner notification to the current partner and other partners within the last year may be most feasible and effective (Fenton *et al*. 1998). With index referral many patients are concerned about disclosing such sensitive information about themselves and are worried that partners may reject them following disclosure or that the partner will break their confidentiality and disclose the diagnosis to family, friends or work colleagues without their consent. Much time may be spent with the index patient discussing which partners may have been at risk, and how they should be informed – role playing can, again, be extremely useful.

As with other STIs, provider referral for HIV should be with the full consent of the index patient and, again, maintaining the index's confidentiality is paramount. The index patient should be kept informed of all partner notification action undertaken but not of the outcomes (Partner Notification Steering Group 1994). The index must be informed that partners will be told they may have been at risk for HIV; that partners may still guess their identity; that health advisers in other clinics may be involved if partners live in other areas. Indeed the index may ask for other centres to become involved where the partner may guess their identity from the location of the clinic. In Britain, the General Medical Council (1995) has declared that there may be grounds for partner notification without the patient's permission if there is a serious and identifiable risk to a specific individual, who, if not informed, would be exposed to the infection. In circumstances where the index patient refuses to notify this individual, then the doctor may consider it their duty to seek to ensure that any sexual partner is informed, in order to safeguard such persons from infection. Any such action would always be discussed with the index patient first, and only taken in circumstances where all other options had been exhausted.

Recently published guidance on this complex and difficult issue by UNAIDS/WHO (2000) has recommended that, in order to ensure beneficial impact, 'partner counselling' without consent of the index patient should only be undertaken when the following conditions have been met:

- The HIV positive person (source client) has been thoroughly counselled as to the need for partner notification/counselling.
- The counselling has failed to achieve the appropriate behavioural changes, including the practice of safe sex.
- The source client has refused to notify, or consent to the counselling, of his/her partner(s).
- A real risk of HIV transmission to an identifiable partner(s) exists.

- The source client is given reasonable advance notice of the intention to counsel by the health care worker.
- The identity of the source client is concealed from the partner(s) if this is possible in practice.
- Follow-up is provided to ensure support to those involved as necessary and to prevent violence, family disruption, etc.

Additionally, this guidance recognises that in order to encourage ethical partner notification/counselling, there is a need 'to create a social and legal environment that promotes and protects principles of non-discrimination, confidentiality, tolerance and compassion'. More specifically, to encourage ethical partner counselling, UNAIDS and WHO recommend the following:

- Develop national policies and public health legislation on partner counselling that protect the principles of confidentiality and informed consent, and provide for the limited and clearly defined circumstances under which partner counselling may take place without consent.
- Develop public health legislation that authorises health care providers to decide, on the basis of each individual case and ethical considerations, whether to counsel partners without the consent of the source client, under certain circumstances.
- Hold consultations among health care providers, government, and affected communities about how to encourage ethical partner counselling and protect people who disclose their status through such counselling.

- Provide training and guidelines for health care providers and counsellors about how to protect confidentiality and informed consent in the context of partner counselling; how to encourage and assist voluntary partner counselling; how to make difficult ethical decisions in cases where there is refusal to counsel partners; and how to counsel partners in ways that harm is minimised and support is provided.
- Promote the establishment of professional ethical codes among health care and social service providers which require respect for confidentiality, and informed consent, in the context of partner counselling, and provide penalties for unethical conduct.
- Establish mechanisms for accountability and modes of laying complaints within health care institutions and within communities when partners are counselled unethically by health care providers and other professionals.
- Support practical legal and social measures that address the vulnerability of people, particularly that of women to stigma, physical violence, and abandonment, including projects in the community which will assist in providing treatment, care, emotional support and protection from discrimination to those involved in partner counselling.
- Promote and support community projects about the responsibility to protect oneself and others from HIV infection, particularly among men and boys (UNAIDS/WHO 2000).

Efficacy of partner notification

The desired outcome of partner notification is to ensure all identified partners have attended for screening and treatment – partner notification activity can then be *resolved*. There are debates as to what standards should be set for successful resolution. In many clinics partner notification is only resolved when a partner is reported as screened and treated; other clinics may include 'partner informed' or all untraceable contacts as resolved. *Verified* or *partner notification verification* refers to when full cross-referencing has occurred (i.e. the clinic number, diagnosis and treatment regimes of both the index and the partner are ascertained). Verification remains the gold standard.

The efficacy of partner notification is usually measured by the number of named partners who are successfully traced, screened and treated. Cowan *et al.* (1996) note that there are many accounts of partner notification which describe the process used and the number of partners reached. For example, in one USA study reviewed, a 'disease intervention specialist' was able to locate 82% of the 13 845 named contacts (of gonorrhoea, chlamydia and related syndromes) over the 6-year study period (Katz *et al.* 1992). Others have considered that efficacy is more correctly measured by the number of partners per index patient that are reached – recent guidelines on chlamydia have suggested that, as a minimum, at least 70% of index patients should have at least one partner attending (Central Audit Group 1997). Other studies have revealed the usefulness of partner notification in the control of outbreaks of antibiotic resistant strains of gonorrhoea and the identification of core groups (Handsfield *et al.* 1989). Evaluation of the Tyneside Scheme estimated that efficient partner notification reduced the rates of STIs by about 20% (Wigfield

1972); the decline in the incidence of local cases of gonorrhoea has also been primarily attributed to partner notification (Talbot & Kinghorn 1985). Oxman et al. (1994) have performed a systematic review comparing the effectiveness of alternate partner notification strategies and have found that only limited, broad conclusions regarding the effectiveness of these various approaches can be drawn. There have been no community based comparison studies which try to evaluate the effectiveness of partner notification in reducing the incidence/prevalence of STIs in the community (Cowan et al. 1996). Partner notification may also be less effective as a means of disease prevention where index patients are having sex in anonymous settings or having multiple partners who are completely untraceable. However, Potterat et al. (1991) suggest that partner notification may still be of value in these cases because individuals are often members of *core* groups. Whilst members of core groups are often only able to notify a small number of their partners, as these groups are generally limited in size and confined geographically, different people frequently have the same partner. Although partner notification may seem unsuccessful in the short term, it may actually reach many of the core group members over time.

As discussed earlier, partner notification for viral STIs is more problematic as there is no cure, and for most viral STIs, apart from hepatitis A and B, immunisation to prevent infection is not possible. However partners can still be screened for concomitant bacterial infections, and perhaps undiagnosed viral conditions (Cowan et al. 1996). For example, one study found that 33.5% of male partners of women with initial genital herpes either

had signs of initial herpes themselves, gave a history or had signs of recurrent genital herpes or were asymptomatic with herpes isolated on screening (Wooley 1991). Moreover, as behaviour change is vital in order to reduce the spread of viral STIs, partners can benefit from education on risk reduction on an individual and/or a couple basis.

Fenton and Peterman's (1997) review of the effectiveness of partner notification for HIV notes that some studies have suggested that behavioural change occurs after partner notification although follow-up studies have rarely been done. One evaluation of a partner notification programme in Southern Carolina (USA) found that the mean number of named sex and needle sharing partners per 6-month period decreased by 80% in HIV positive people and by 50% in HIV negative people after partner notification during the 30-month study period (Wykoff et al. 1991). Other studies, on serodiscordant couples, that were reviewed, indicate that informing partners about their exposure may result in reduced transmission by the index case as both partners negotiate safer sex and modify their sexual behaviour (Kamenga et al. 1991; Allen et al. 1992; Padian et al. 1993). In reviewing studies on partner notification, Fenton and Peterman (1997) note that, in general, between 50% and 100% of notified partners will accept HIV counselling and testing; and 10–35% of locatable partners will test HIV positive for the first time. The seroprevalence amongst all traceable partners is higher as these figures do not include those contacted who already know themselves to be HIV positive. Fenton and Peterman (1997) also note that the effectiveness of partner notification is constrained by the limited information provided by some index patients and the fact that the identity or where-abouts of many partners is not known. There is often, therefore, a large discrepancy between the number of partners identified, the number who appear to be traceable and the number eventually notified. Thus, the authors note, HIV partner notification may have limited potential as a tool to reduce the incidence of disease in the wider community. Pavia *et al.* (1993) found, in their study of 2 years of a statewide notification programme in Utah, that one fifth of index patients refused to name any partners. Moreover, HIV partner notification was less successful in white homosexual and bisexual groups. Whether this is due to distrust of authorities or whether this group are more likely to choose to notify partners without assistance is unclear; thus, the authors conclude, partner notification for HIV was most successful amongst populations who may be difficult to reach with other interventions. A randomized control trial in North Carolina compared index and provider partner notification for HIV; 50% of partners in the provider referral group were notified compared with only 7% in the index referral group. This was despite North Carolina law requiring that partners be notified (Landis *et al.* 1992). Oxman *et al.'s* (1994) review also revealed that there was moderately strong evidence to suggest that provider referral for HIV is more effective than index referral.

Impact on relationships

Acquiring an STI can be emotionally devastating; people are often shocked, tearful and can feel negative about sex, their sexuality and body image. In many cases the degree of upset will relate to the nature of the infection, when and how it was acquired and the impact it has on their relationship(s). For example, genital herpes occurring in a long-term monogamous relationship can cause major relationship problems. However, when the couple are informed of the latent period of the disease, asymptomatic shedding and how herpes is transmitted it may help them deal with the situation more easily as reassurance can be given that it does not mean a third party has been involved, or that one partner has knowingly infected the other. A woman in a monogamous relationship acquiring chlamydia after an unprotected casual affair may be very fearful of the repercussion to her relationship. Men who have had sex with prostitutes (protected and unprotected at home or abroad) may be terrified that they have caught HIV and are often wracked with guilt over the actual act of 'betrayal'. Many feel unable to use condoms or abstain from sex during the 3-month window period for HIV as this would 'raise suspicion' and yet are 'so scared of transmitting HIV' to their partner. For gay men, the acquisition of one STI can raise acute concerns as to their risks for HIV.

Oxman *et al.* (1994) found no studies that attempted to measure the ethical consequences of alternate partner notification strategies (such as perceived impact on autonomy); or to measure psychosocial impacts on either the index patients or partners. One qualitative study of eight clinic attenders found participants expressing anxiety about the effects of a diagnosis of an STI upon current and future relationships. Issues were raised about the acquisition of the infection, blame, and who, when and how to tell (Holgate & Longman 1998). Stronks *et al.* (1993) looked at 27 patients with genital herpes and a control group of 12 patients with gonorrhoea, and found that patients felt more anxious, more sexually inhibited, more bitter towards their partners and had more psychological complaints during the infection than before. Although these studies are small, the issues raised are common. It takes great skills to sensitively elicit information from index patients who are angry or distressed. Various factors may contribute to difficulties in the index disclosing an STI to partners – lack of information about STIs, lack of awareness and understanding of the need for partner notification, anxiety about undertaking partner notification and their partners' reaction, and their partners' actual reaction (Lindemann 1989). The partner notification interview aims to address most of these areas and support the index with the partner notification process. However the index patient may still feel unable to notify partners. Reasons for failure include the reluctance of patients to face their partners, selective notification (denial that 'nice' partners can be involved); failure to convince partners (partner denial); and lack of interest in the partner notification process (Potterat *et al.* 1991).

A diagnosis of genital herpes is often particularly distressing to patients. Common emotional responses are disbelief, distress, anxiety and altered body image. Patients with herpes often talk of feeling 'dirty', 'marked', 'punished' for being sexually active or see themselves as unfairly infected because they are not 'promiscuous', feel they can 'never have sex again' because of fears of infecting partners or feel anger towards and 'blame' partners for the infection. These feelings can be compounded by the issue of asymptomatic shedding. Those diagnosed with herpes can have particular fears

around telling current or future partners that they have herpes. Common reasons for not telling partners are fear of rejection, fear of false assumptions about past sexual behaviour, fear of gossip and fear that their partner will not understand (Mindel & Carney 1991). Yet social support from a partner (as well as cognitive coping strategies) appear to assist with adjustment (Aral *et al.* 1988).

Making and sustaining relationships in this group can also be problematic. One study showed that those with herpes reported herpes had negatively affected sexual activity and enjoyment and felt depressed and feared rejection (Catotti *et al.* 1993). Moreover 69% were afraid of rejection by a new partner, 89% were concerned about transmitting the virus and 76% felt herpes affected their behaviour with new partners. Brookes *et al.'s* (1993) questionnaire-based study of 90 people with genital herpes (average time since diagnosis was 6 years) found significant differences between the sexes. Women with herpes reported significantly greater reductions in how desirable they felt sexually, in their self-confidence, felt more dirty and reported a greater decrement in their general health since getting herpes, and were more likely to worry about future recurrences than the men. However, the authors found that most subjects reported functioning at the same level as they had prior to contracting herpes, were as sexually active as before and enjoyed and functioned well in sex. There was no evidence to show that, in most of the subjects, herpes had influenced the way they saw themselves, their relationships with partners or their feelings of attractiveness and most people appear to come to terms with their herpes diagnosis, given time.

Those diagnosed with herpes can benefit from time being spent discussing how they might tell current partners and how they might raise the issue of herpes with new partners. Offering to see a couple together to discuss the diagnosis and transmission issues can also be beneficial.

Partners commonly express anger and anxiety over their need to attend regardless of the infection they have been in contact with. In cases where the index partner has not revealed the nature of the infection, these feelings can be exacerbated and partners often find the commitment to index confidentiality difficult to understand. Again partners' reactions are often dependent on their individual feelings about sex and sexuality, the type of relationship and the nature of the infection and how it was acquired. The way a couple cope with an STI within their relationship can be dependent on a number of factors, including their own relationship dynamics. Not all partners who attend will be found to have acquired the particular STI; some partners will refuse to attend despite the best efforts of the index and/ or clinic staff. Often index patients and partners will not be honest with one another about having an infection, how it was acquired and attendance at a clinic. This can often place great burden on clinic staff in their efforts to maintain confidentiality, avoid collusion, fulfil the public health nature of their work, and give honest and factual information to all clinic attendees.

There is more, although often conflicting, data available on the impact of HIV partner notification on relationships. Certainly the risks of domestic violence after HIV partner notification have been documented (North & Rothenberg 1993). Moreover stress, stigmatisation and discrimination may result for partners (Rodgers & Osbourne 1991). The repercussions for the index may be particularly serious in low prevalence communities or in communities where discussing HIV is still taboo. The fear of rejection is often paramount in the index patient's mind. Nabais *et al.* (1996) found that disclosing HIV status was frequent in their sample of 50 HIV positive individuals but despite individuals' beliefs, results indicated that this did not result in separation or disruption of the relationship. In one study of HIV serodiscordant couples in Zaire, nearly 11% of the serodiscordant couples encountered acute psychological distress initially and required intensive counselling. The presence of children appeared to protect against relationship breakup and only 6% of relationships ended in divorce (Kamenga *et al.* 1991).

However White *et al.* (1997) argue that the disruptive effects of HIV infection on family life are immense. Their review of 132 cases of families referred to a paediatric HIV service revealed concordancy of 32.6%, serodiscordancy of 21.5% and, in 46%, the status of the father was unknown either because he was unavailable or untested. Relationship conflict and breakdown was high in both the concordant and serodiscordant group. Actual separation was higher in the discordant group although not statistically significant. Price and Murphy's (1996) review of 24 HIV positive women found that 53% of those in relationships broke up in the months following diagnosis. The fact that relationships ended whether or not the partner was informed suggests that the burden of seropositivity stresses relationships.

Studies of serodiscordant couples also indicate that there are benefits to disclosure with the adoption of safer sex strategies and counselling to reinforce risk-reducing behaviours. Kamenga *et al.* (1991) found that less than 5% of couples had ever used condoms before diagnosis of serostatus, whereas 70.7% of couples reported condom use after serodiscordancy was determined. At 18-month follow-up, 77.4% of the couples still being followed reported continued use of condoms for all episodes of sexual intercourse. In terms of acceptability, one study sent questionnaires to partners who had been traced for HIV partner notification and asked if that had been the right thing to do – 87% said yes and 92% felt the department of health should carry on notifying partners exposed to HIV. Responses were the same for gay and straight men, injecting drug users, men and women, white and black responders (Jones *et al.* 1990). However, the contacted partner may present with a variety of reactions such as anxiety, fear or even aggression and may tell no one that they have been notified and thus become isolated and frightened (Ramstedt & Giesecke 1993). Others may react quite calmly, having already thought that they may have had an HIV positive partner. With current partners, the index patient may well feel guilty if their partner tests positive and blame themselves (or be blamed) for passing the infection on although this may not be the case. In serodiscordant couples, fears of sexual transmission can affect sexual relationships. In Kamenga *et al.'s* (1991) study of serodiscordant couples, there was a statistically significant correlation between the increase in the number of episodes of intercourse/month and the increase in time since notification of HIV status. These changes were similar in serodiscordant couples, whether it was the male or female partner who

was positive. Certainly, it suggests that most couples, given time, will adjust to the situation, although in some cases frequency of sexual intercourse does not return to the level pre-HIV diagnosis. If the partner tests HIV positive near the time of the index patient's diagnosis, then both may face adjustment difficulties concurrently which may overburden the relationship. Conversely, a partner testing negative may give rise to feelings of relief, guilt and even isolation and may negatively affect the dynamics between the couple. In some instances, partners have 'wanted to become infected' so that the HIV can be 'shared' and are disappointed by a negative result or feel burdened by ongoing fears around possible infection. Some couples may also have the added burden of dealing with the HIV positive diagnosis of their children, and/or issues around having a family in the future. All such studies point to the crucial need for support for those needing to negotiate disclosure and behaviour change following diagnoses of HIV and/or STDs, and to the potential usefulness of encouraging couple counselling and testing in HIV diagnostic settings.

In conclusion, partner notification – the management of partners – is a crucial public health aspect of work within the sexual health setting. Partner notification is as important as screening and treatment, in preventing the spread of STIs, reinfection and the complications of untreated infections. In most sexual health settings, individuals are interviewed/screened/treated and partner notified in isolation from their sexual and needle-sharing partners. However, the impact that this need for partner notification has on an individual's relationship(s) outside the clinic must not be ignored. Couples should always be offered the opportunity to be seen together to discuss a specific infection; and for information on safer sex. Counselling and psychology services should be available to see couples with adjustment issues, relationship difficulties and/ or sexual problems (including issues with safer sex) since STI/HIV diagnosis. Although emphasis may be placed on the individual index patient, they should always be seen within the context of their relationships outside of the clinic as well as within the public health remit.

References

Adler, M.W. & Johnson, A.M. (1988) Contact tracing for HIV infection. *British Medical Journal* **296**, 1420–1421.

Allen, I. & Hogg, D. (1993) *Work Roles and Responsibilities in Genitourinary Medicine Clinics*. Policy Studies Institute.

Allen S., Tice J., Van-de-Perre, P. *et al.* (1992) Effect of serotesting with counselling on condom use and seroconversion among HIV discordant couples in Africa. *British Medical Journal* **304**, 1605–1609.

Aral, S.O., Vanderplate, C. & Magder, L. (1988) Recurrent genital herpes: What helps adjustment? *Sexually Transmitted Diseases* **15**(3), 164–166.

Bayer, R. & Toomey, K.E. (1992) HIV prevention and the two faces of partner notification. *American Journal of Public Health* **82**(8), 1159–1164.

Blaxter, M. (1991) *AIDS Worldwide Policies, Problems.* Office of Health Economics, London.

Brookes, J., Haywood, S. & Green, J. (1993) Adjustment to the psychological and social sequelae of recurrent genital herpes simplex infection. *Genitourinary Medicine* **69**, 384–387.

Catotti, D.N., Clarke, P. & Catoe, K.E. (1993). Herpes revisited. Still a cause for concern. *Sexually Transmitted Diseases* **20**(2), 77–80.

Central Audit Group in Genito Urinary Medicine (1997) *Clinical Guidelines and Standards for the Management of Uncomplicated Genital Chlamydia Infection.* Health Education Authority, London.

Cowan, F.M., French, R. & Johnson, A.M. (1996) The role and effectiveness of partner notification in STD control: a review. *GenitoUrinary Medicine* **72**(4), 247–252.

Department of Health (1992) The Department of Health Guidance on Partner Notification for HIV. [PL/CO (92)] DOH, London.

Fenton, K.A. & Peterman, T.A. (1997) HIV partner notification: taking a new look. *AIDS* **11**(13), 1535–1546.

Fenton, K.A., Chippindale, S.J & Cowan, F.M. (1998) Partner notification techniques in dermatologic clinics. In: *Sexually Transmitted Diseases* (eds D. Freedman & B.H. Thiers) Volume 16, No 4, pp. 669–672. WB Saunders, USA.

General Medical Council (1995) *HIV and AIDS: The Ethical Considerations.* GMC, London .

Handsfield, H.H., Rice, J.J., Roberts, M.C. & Holmes, K.K. (1989) Localised outbreak of penicillinase-producing *Neisseria gonorrhoea*: paradigm for introduction and spread of gonorrhoea in a community. *Journal of the American Medical Association* **261**, 2357–2361.

Hethcote, H.W. & York, J.A. (1984) Gonorrhoea: transmission dynamics and control. *Biomathematics*; **56**, 1–105, quoted in Cowan F.M., French, R. & Johnson, A.M. (1996) The role and effectiveness of partner notification in STD control: a review. *Genito Urinary Medicine* **72**(4), 247–252.

Holgate, H.S. & Longman, C. (1998) Some people's psychological experiences of attending a sexual health clinic and having a sexually transmitted infection. *Royal Society of Health* **118**(2), 94–96.

House of Lords Parliamentary Debate (1942) Official Report 125, No 435. HMSO, London.

Jones, J.L., Wykoff, R.F., Hollis, S.L., Longshore, S.T., Gamble, W.B. Jr. & Gunn, R.A. (1990) Partner acceptance of health department notification of HIV exposure, South Carolina. *Journal of the American Medical Association* **264**(10), 1284–1286.

Kamb M.L., Fishbein M., Douglas J.M. Jr., *et al.* (1998) Efficacy of risk-reduction counselling to prevent human immunodeficiency virus and sexually transmitted diseases: a randomized controlled trial. Project RESPECT Study Group. *Journal of the American Medical Association* **280**(13), 1161–7.

Kamenga, M., Ryder, R.W., Jingu, M., *et al.* (1991) Evidence of marked sexual behaviour change associated with low HIV-1 serostatus: experience at an HIV counselling centre in Zaire. *AIDS* **5**(1), 61–67.

Katz, B.P., Caine, V.A. & Jones, R.B. (1992) Evaluation of field follow up in a sexually transmitted disease clinic for patients at risk for infection with *Neisseria gonorrhoea* and *Chlamydia trachomatis*. *Sexually Transmitted Diseases* **19**, 99–103.

Landis, S.E., Schoenbach, V.I., Weber, D.I., *et al.* (1992) Results of a randomised trial of partner notification in cases of HIV infection in North Carolina. *New England Journal of Medicine* **326**, 101–106.

Lindemann, C. (1989) Counselling issues in disclosure of sexually transmitted disease. *Journal of Social Work and Human Sexuality* **6**(2), 55–69.

Meheus, A., Schulz, K.F. & Cates Jr., W. (1990) Development of prevention and control programs for sexually transmitted diseases in developing countries. In: *Sexually Transmitted Diseases*, 2nd edn. (eds K. King *et al.*) Chapter 86, pp. 1041–1046. McGraw Hill, USA.

Mindel, A. & Carney, O. (1991) *Herpes: What it is and How to Cope*. Macdonald Optima, London.

Nabais, J., Goncalves, G., Ouakinin, S. & Figueira, M.L. (1996) Disclosure of HIV infection to sexual partner: implications in relationship. *Presented at XI International Conference on AIDS*, Vancouver, July 1996 [abstract M.C. 4631].

National Health Service, England and Wales (Venereal Disease) Regulations (1974), No 29, (H334), HMSO.

Njeru, E.J., Eldridge, G.D., Ngugi, E., Plummer, F.A. & Moses, S. (1995) STD Partner notification and referral in primary level health centres in Nairobi, Kenya. *Sexually Transmitted Diseases* **22**(4), 231–235.

North, R.L. & Rothenberg, K.H. (1993) Partner notification and a threat of domestic violence against women with HIV infection. *New England Journal of Medicine* **329**, 1194–1196.

Oriel, J.D. (1994) *The Scars of Venus. A History of Venereology*. Springer-Verlag, London..

Oxman, A.D., Scott, E.A.F., Sellors, J.W., *et al.* (1994) Partner notification for sexually transmitted diseases: an overview of the evidence. *Canadian Journal of Public Health* (Suppl.) **1**, S41–47.

Padian, N.S., O'Brien, T.R., Chang, Y., Glass, S. & Francis, D.P. (1993) Prevention of heterosexual transmission of human immunodeficiency virus through couple counseling. *Journal of Acquired Immune Deficiency Syndrome* **6**, 1043–1048.

Partner Notification Steering Group (1994) *Partner Notification Protocol and Manual*. Version 2.

Pavia, A.T., Benyo, M., Niler, L. & Risk, I. (1993) Partner notification for control of HIV: Results after 2 years of a Statewide Program in Utah. *American Journal of Public Health* **83**(10), 1418–1423.

Porter, D. & Porter, R. (1988) The enforcement of health: the British debate. In: *AIDS: The Burdens of History* (eds E. Fee & D. Fox) pp. 97–120, University of California Press, Berkeley.

Potterat, J.J., Meheus, A. & Gallwey, J. (1991) Partner notification: operational considerations. *International Journal of STD and AIDS* **2**, 411–415.

Price, G. & Murphy, S. (1996) HIV Seropositivity and the breakdown of heterosexual relationships in North West London. *International Journal of STD and AIDS* **7**, 146.

Ramstedt, K. & Giesecke, J. (1993) Partner management. In: *AIDS and the Heterosexual Population* (eds L. Sher *et al.*) Harwood Academic, USA.

Rodgers, D.E. & Osbourne, J.E. (1991) Another approach to the AIDS epidemic. *New England Journal of Medicine* **325**, 806–808.

Rothenberg, R.B. & Potterat, J.J. (1990) Strategies for management of sex partners. In: *Sexually Transmitted Diseases*, 2nd edn (eds K. King *et al.*) Chapter 91, pp. 1081–1086. McGraw Hill, USA.

Royal Commissioners on Venereal Diseases (1916) *Final Report of the Commissioners* (Cmnd 8189). HMSO, London.

Stronks, D.L., Rijpma, S.E., Passchier, J., Verhage, F., Van der Meijden, W. & Stolz, E. (1993) Psychological consequences of genital herpes, an exploratory study with a gonorrhoea control group. *Psychological Reports* **73**(2), 395–400.

Talbot, M.D. & Kinghorn, G.R. (1985) Epidemiology and control of gonorrhoea in Sheffield. *Genitourinary Medicine* **61**, 230–233.

UNAIDS (2000) *The Role of Name-Based Notification in Public Health and HIV Surveillance*. UNAIDS, Geneva. (00.28E).

UNAIDS/WHO (2000) *Opening Up the HIV/AIDS Epidemic: Guidance on Beneficial Disclosure, Ethical Part-*

ner Counselling, and Named HIV Case Reporting. UNAIDS/WHO, Geneva (00.42E).

White, J., Melvin, D., Moore, C. & Crowley, S. (1997) Parental HIV discordancy and its impact on the family, *AIDS Care* **9**(5), 609–615.

WHO/UNAIDS (2000) *Questions and Answers on Reporting, Partner Notification and Disclosure of HIV and/or AIDS Serostatus, Public Health and Human Rights Implications.* WHO/UNAIDS, Geneva.

Wigfield, A.S. (1972) 27 years of uninterrupted contact tracing. 'The Tyneside Scheme'. *British Journal of Venereal Disease* **48**, 47–50.

Woolley, P.D. (1991) Value of examining the sexual partners of women suffering from genital herpes. *International Journal of STD and AIDS* **2**, 105–109.

World Health Organization (1989) *Consensus Statement from Consultation on Partner Notification for Preventing HIV Transmission.* WHO/GPA/INF/89.3, Geneva, 11–13 January 1989.

Wykoff, R.F., Jones J.L., Longshore S.T., *et al.* (1991) Partner notification of the sexual and needle sharing partners of individuals with human immunodeficiency virus in rural South Carolina: 30 month experience. *Sexually Transmitted Diseases* **18**, 217–222.

Wynendaele, B., Bomba, W., M'Manga, W., *et al.* (1995) Impact of counselling on safer sex and STD occurrence among STD patients in Malawi. *International Journal of STD and AIDS* **6**, 105–109.

Chapter 14

The Psychological Management of Rape and PTSD: Clinical Issues, Assessment and Treatment

Deborah Lee

Introduction

Rape is a serious, life-threatening and traumatic event that can have a devastating impact on the victim's emotional, mental and physical well-being. The misinterpretation of rape as merely unwanted sex has adversely affected reporting rates, attitudes towards victims and availability of appropriate forms of treatment for the victims (Resick 1993). Rape still holds a social stigma and many victims feel they will be blamed by family, friends and society and so choose not to report the crime or use social support networks available to them. Rape may put individuals' sexual health at risk. Yet some individuals may be too ashamed by the rape to seek screening and treatment.

Rape is not an uncommon event (Kilpatrick *et al.* 1985), although it is difficult to obtain accurate statistics as it is widely accepted as under-reported in both women and men. Rape is also a diverse experience. Most people hold the belief that rape is committed by strangers; however, stranger rape is only one type of rape. Prevalence studies in the United States suggest that stranger rapes account for only the minority of rapes (Russell 1984).

Most people do not appreciate that the majority of rapes involve people who are acquainted. The fact that the rapist is known to the victim makes the experience no less horrific and distressing (Allison & Wrightsman 1993). Indeed it can present more difficulties for the victim as issues of trust are shattered. Also victim-blaming in these circumstances may be more common. Prevalence rates of acquaintance rape are hard to establish as victims are reluctant to report the attack to the police. Koss (1985) found that only 5% of victims of this type of rape reported it to the police. Koss also found that women were reluctant to label themselves as victims of rape when the attacker was an acquaintance (Koss 1985). It was only recently that the 'marital rape exemption', the idea that rape could not occur between married partners, was abolished in British law. However, as with acquaintance rape, spousal rape is heavily under-reported and many victims do not consider themselves to be victims of rape.

In recent years changing attitudes within society have led to a greater understanding of the psychological impact of rape. Most studies have found that, following the experience of rape, victims experience an acute and intense psychological reaction that lasts for a few months.

Acute traumatic stress reactions have been observed in victims of many different types of traumatic events, in the early days following the event, and are considered normal and understandable. The experience of a traumatic event such as rape is overwhelming and extremely distressing to most victims. A period of adjustment, reconciliation of the experience and a disruption to normal functioning is thus expected and it can take several months before premorbid functioning is resumed. The clinician can expect to see a gradual decline in symptoms over the months post-assault in many cases.

However, for some individuals, the experience can devastate their lives and rape has one of the highest reported incidences of post-traumatic stress disorder when compared to survivors of other traumatic events such as physical assault, car accidents, bombings and hold-ups.

Post-traumatic stress disorder and rape

Research has shown that post-traumatic stress disorder (PTSD) is the most common post-rape trauma psychopathology. PTSD has been defined by the DSM IV (DSM IV; APA 1994) as consisting of: (a) exposure to an event in which the person experienced, witnessed, or was confronted with actual or threatened death or serious injury, or threat to physical integrity of self or others and in which the person's response involves intense fear, helplessness and/or horror; (b) symptoms of re-experiencing of the event; (c) symptoms of avoidance of related stimuli and/or numbing of responsiveness; (d) symptoms of increased physiological arousal.

Symptoms of re-experiencing the event

Individuals frequently suffer distressing and intrusive recollections of the attack, nightmares and flashbacks, when the event is vividly relived in the mind (Burgess & Holmstrom 1979; Nadelson *et al.* 1982). It is not uncommon for victims to experience vivid flashbacks during sexual activity, gynaecological examinations or menstruation. This can lead to avoidance of these activities and this has obvious implications for sexual health screenings. Intrusions can be spontaneous thoughts or triggered by reminders of the event. Within PTSD, stimulus generalisation is typically observed and many triggers that resemble the traumatic event stimuli can develop anxiety-eliciting properties. Thus is not uncommon for women to develop fear reactions to men who look like the rapist.

Symptoms of avoidance of related stimuli and/or numbing of responsiveness

Avoidance of stimuli that remind the victim of their experience is common. Women who are raped at work are sometimes fearful of returning to their job; they may avoid going out at night, being alone and sexual intercourse. Fear and mistrust of men in general are common (Burgess & Holmstrom 1979). Other types of psychic avoidance have been noted: for example, dissociation, diminished responsiveness or feelings of detachment and estrangement, loss of interest in significant activities, lack of energy (Burgess & Holmstrom 1979).

Symptoms of increased physiological arousal

The experience of rape typically involves intense fear and heightened physiological arousal. Chemtob *et al.* (1988) suggest that features such as hyper-alertness, excessive startle responses and focused concentrations emerge from a 'survival mode' of functioning which is adaptive during the trauma but persists when the trauma is over. Such symptoms are frequently observed in victims of rape; 'nervousness', 'jumpiness', 'always on the look out' are commonly reported. Other features of increased arousal are memory and concentration problems and sleep disturbances.

The course of the disorder

Several prospective studies have followed the early reactions of victims of rape. One notable study looked at 95 victims of rape weekly for 12 weeks post-assault. At one week post-crime 94% met the symptom pattern for post-traumatic stress disorder and were clinically depressed. At three months post-crime, 47% still met the full criteria for PTSD. Of particular note was that those women who went on to develop chronic PTSD showed little improvement (on all of the symptom scales used) after the first month. Those women who went on to recover continued to show gradual improvements over the three-month assessment period (Rothbaum *et al.* 1992).

Resick (1988) studied reactions in victims over an 18-month period. She found that fear, depression and other mood states, sexual problems, self-esteem problems and problems with social adjustment tended to be quite severe in victims at 1 month post-assault but began to show improvements by 2–3 months post-rape. Particularly issues with fear, anxiety, self-esteem and sexual dysfunction seemed to remain elevated when compared to other non-victim comparison groups at one year post-assault.

Another study assessing the long-term impact of rape found significant long-term problems of fear, difficulties with social adjustment, depression and sexual dysfunction in women who had been raped 6 years previously (Kilpatrick *et al.* 1985; 1987). Fear and anxiety are perhaps the most commonly observed symptoms following rape.

Other psychological reactions following rape

Resick (1993) has compiled a comprehensive review of studies investigating the psychological impact of rape. Several of the key findings from this paper are summarised in this section.

Depression

Comorbidity with PTSD and depression has been found to be very frequent. Studies investigating the prevalence of depression in rape victims have shown inconsistent findings. Some studies have shown that symptoms of depression reduce within a few months post-assault while other studies show that depressive symptoms continue in victims for many months after the assault. Frank and Stewart (1984) found, within a sample of 90 rape victims, that 56% fell into the moderate to severe range on the Beck Depression Inventory (Beck *et al.* 1961), and 43% of women were diagnosed with major depression on a semi-structured interview. They found that the depression diminished by three months post-crime. However, Kilpatrick and Veronen (1984) found differences between victims and non-victims on measures of depression for a year after the crime. Resick (1988) also found significant differences on depression measures between robbery and rape victims at 1, 2, 6, and 18-month sessions on a cross-sectional analysis. However Resick found no differences on depression measures in a smaller sample using a longitudinal design.

In clinical settings, it is not uncommon to find elevated levels of suicidal ideation in victims of rape. Surviving a rape is not just about 'living or dying' but about the quality of life thereafter for the victim. Many victims find their quality of life significantly affected and their emotional well-being greatly reduced. Some victims report feeling that it would have been easier to die during the attack than to live with the psychological aftermath of the attack. Research has shown that rates of suicidal behaviour are significant if not very high in the first month after the attack. For example, Frank *et al.* (1979) found a rate of 2.9%

in their sample. However, Ellis *et al.* (1981) found that 50% of their sample had considered suicide.

Low self-esteem

In clinical settings, anecdotal evidence suggests that victims of rape with chronic PTSD often have issues with low self-esteem. Self-esteem problems have also been substantiated in the research although, as with depression, the findings are equivocal. In her longitudinal comparison of rape and robbery victims, Resick (1988) found differences on self-esteem measures for 1 year post-crime. Furthermore at 1 and 3 months post-assault rape and robbery victims continued to have greater self-esteem than victims who were both raped and robbed, particularly on dimensions of physical self, social self and identity. Schnicke and Resick (1990) found that attributions of self-blame predicted higher self-criticism scores on the Tennessee Self Concept Scale (Fitts 1965), in a treatment-seeking group of rape victims.

Sexual dysfunction

Problems with sexual functioning have also been observed in clinical settings in women who have been raped and such findings are substantiated by research. Resick (1993) suggests that sexual dysfunctions are probably among the most long-lasting problems experienced by rape victims, the most common being avoidance of sex. Becker *et al.* (1986), in a large study of 372 victims of sexual assault, investigated the frequency and types of sexual dysfunction. They found that 59% of the sexual assault victims had at least one sexual dysfunction compared to 17% of the comparison group. In a sub-sample of women who blamed the assault for the development of sexual problems, the majority reported problems with fear of sex, arousal dysfunction and desire dysfunction.

Social functioning

Social problems have also been documented in research. Nadelson *et al.* (1982) in a study of 41 rape victims found that, up to 30 months post-assault, over half the victims reported a restricted social life. Another study found that victims' social adjustment recovered, except in the area of work functioning, by 4 months post-assault (Kilpatrick *et al.* 1979; Resick *et al.* 1981).

Obsessive–compulsive behaviour

It is also worth noting that Resick (1988) and Kilpatrick and Veronen (1984) both found higher levels of obsessive–compulsive symptoms in rape victims (as measured by the Symptom Checklist (Derogatis 1977), than either robbery victims or non-assault victims. Anecdotal clinical evidence also suggests that some women develop extensive cleansing rituals, often to rid themselves of feelings of 'dirtiness', as well as safety rituals after the assault.

Theories and treatment approaches

This section will review the main cognitive/behavioural theories and treatment approaches with proven efficacy in treating PTSD. As a general theoretical framework, it is helpful to see PTSD as the symptomatological indication of a failure in emotional processing (Rachman 1980). Emotional processing is the mechanism whereby emotional experiences, which may be extraordinary, are absorbed into the psyche. Successful emotional processing is associated with a return to normal functioning, whereby emotional experiences no longer cause distress and disturbance to everyday functioning. In this model unsuccessful emotional processing is indicated by persistent intrusive activity, for example repeated entry of traumatic material into the mind via the conscious and/or unconscious (Rachman 1980; Horowitz 1986). In this sense, PTSD indicates that the traumatised individual has been unable to integrate or absorb their experience in a successful way which allows them function normally in their everyday life. Incongruent information, which is not readily processed, forms the basis of intrusive activity (Rachman 1980; Horowitz 1986). Intrusive phenomena, in the context of unresolved trauma, are typically associated with an emotional experience of severe intensity such as fear, shame, guilt and anger. These emotional states arise out of psychological processes such as cognitive appraisal and attribution of causality (Weiner 1986; Joseph *et al.* 1993). The presence of these emotions is indicative of the evaluation of meaning in relation to the self, world and others. For example, if a victim blames themselves for the attack they may experience intense feelings of guilt and/or shame. Thus the resolution of such meanings is the central therapeutic recovery process in traumatised populations (Horowitz 1990; Janoff-Bulman 1992; Janoff-Bulman & Frantz 1997). Intrusive activity is the pathway for the clinician to assess prominent emotional states and their associated meaning.

Cognitive processing therapy (CPT) for rape victims

Resick and Schnicke (1992), drawing on information-processing models, have developed an efficacious treatment package for rape victims. The treatment package is described in a published treatment manual (Resick & Schnicke 1993).

Although PTSD is currently classified as an anxiety disorder, Resick and Schnicke argue that PTSD is much more than just fearful memories. They point out that intrusive memories may be activated by other strong affects and beliefs such as anger, disgust, humiliation, guilt and conflicts between pre-existing schemata (including beliefs about the world, self and others), and the actual event (Resick & Schnicke 1992; 1993).

They suggest that when a rape experience conflicts with prior beliefs, the victim is less able to reconcile (or emotionally process) the event and has greater difficulty recovering. Indeed research supports the notion that schema discrepancies experienced during victimisation are associated with severity of psychological reactions (Schepple & Bart 1983; Frank & Stewart 1984). In order to explain how an individual deals with conflicts between new information and prior schemata, the authors use the concepts of *assimilation* and *accommodation*. According to Hollon and Garber (1988), when an individual is exposed to schema-discrepant information, one of two things normally happens. First, information can be altered to fit into the existing schemata (assimilation); e.g. *'it must have been something*

that I did to make this happen to me so it wasn't really rape'. Thus, they suggest that flashbacks and other intrusive memories may be attempts at integration when assimilation fails (Resick & Schnicke 1992). Second, existing schemata may be altered to accommodate new incompatible information (accommodation), and an example of this might be, *'the world is an unpredictable place and sometimes bad things happen to good people'.*

Hollon and Garber (1988) have suggested that assimilation usually happens more readily than accommodation, since it appears easier to alter one's perception of a single event than to change one's view of the world. Resick and Schnicke (1992) proposed that accommodation is a goal of therapy, but pointed out that over-accommodation can occur when accommodation happens without good social support or therapeutic guidance. An example of over-accommodation might be *'the world is always a dangerous place and I am never safe.'*

In terms of cognitive content, Resick and Schnicke (1992) have drawn on the work of McCann *et al.* (1988), who proposed five areas of major functioning which become disrupted by victimisation: safety, trust, power, esteem and intimacy. Each of these areas are further divided into two loci – schemata relating to self, and schemata relating to others. McCann related each of these ten areas of functioning to specific symptoms if pre-existing positive schemata are disrupted or pre-existing negative schemata are confirmed by victimisation.

In terms of treatment of PTSD in rape victims, Resick and Schnicke (1992) propose that systematic exposure (to the traumatic event) is important in altering the feared memory structures, to the extent that threat cues are restructured and habituated, and indeed perceptions of fear and danger may be altered (Foa & Kozak 1986).

However, they suggested that such exposure will not necessarily alter other emotional reactions without *specific* confrontation of conflicts, misattributions and expectations. Thus, victims may still blame themselves, and feel anger and shame. All such emotions may be sufficiently intense to elicit intrusive memories and avoidance reactions. Thus, without elicitation, the individual may still continue to suffer symptoms of PTSD.

Cognitive processing therapy (CPT) assumes that symptoms of intrusion, avoidance and arousal are caused by conflicts between new information received from the trauma and prior schemata. Within CPT, it is proposed that such new information is typically assimilated into prior schemata in such a way that it blocks attempts at integration and is associated with intense emotions; intrusive memories are evidence of failed integration when assimilation fails. It does not assume that the trauma of rape elicits previously existing dysfunctional thinking patterns – as proposed by Beck *et al.* (1979) in Beckian cognitive therapy. CPT emphasises the eliciting and expression of frequently intense emotions associated with PTSD (Resick & Schnicke 1992).

However, anecdotal clinical evidence suggests that chronic PTSD sufferers often exhibit underlying core maladaptive schemata. These schemata are often associated with intense affect such as shame and guilt especially if they carry meaning about the self as *inadequate, unworthy* or *unlovable.* Once activated (in the context of a traumatic event), they become the dominant mode for processing information and understanding the meaning of the event.

Thus, if present they present difficulties for the individual in ascribing an adaptive meaning to the traumatic event. In these cases schema-focused therapy or cognitive therapy aimed at challenging underlying maladaptive beliefs may be necessary in the first stages of therapy before resolution of the traumatic event can take place (Lee, Scragg & Turner, in preparation).

Fear network model of PTSD

Perhaps the most influential theory of fear and PTSD has been that of Foa and Kozak (1986). They argue that the concept of meaning (not incorporated into the traditional learning theories) is essential and indeed central to the understanding of the human experience of trauma. They have put forward a model for PTSD, which incorporates both Lang's (1977; 1979) work on fear structures and Rachman's theory of emotional processing (Rachman 1980). They proposed that the emotional experience (fear) generated by the traumatic event is represented in the memory as a *fear network.* Thus the emotional experience is encoded in organised semantic networks that contain three types of information: (a) information pertaining to the feared stimulus situation; (b) information about verbal, physiological and overt behavioural responses; and (c) interpretative information about the meaning of the stimulus and response elements of the fear structure. This information structure is perceived as a programme for escape or avoidance behaviour (Lang 1977).

They argue that if the fear structure is indeed a programme for escape behaviour it must purvey a meaning of danger. They illustrated this point by using a case scenario of a delayed reaction of PTSD in a rape victim who only developed symptoms of PTSD when she was given the information that her attacker had killed his next rape victim (Kilpatrick *et al.* 1987). With this additional information, she interpreted the rape situation as life-threatening and developed an information structure which included 'changed interpretative information' to do with threat. Further evidence to support this essential meaning element is found in the work of Kilpatrick *et al.* (1987) who found that rape victims who perceived their situation as life-threatening were more likely to develop PTSD than those who did not. These violations of safety concepts led to the perception of the world as unpredictable and uncontrollable.

The fear/trauma network has properties of coherency, stability and generalisation which differentiate it from fear structures associated with phobias. As a result of higher order conditioning and stimulus generalisation. the trauma/fear network is readily activated and brought to conscious mind. Given the size, complexity and easy accessibility of the trauma network, activation does not lead to exposure under optimum conditions as not all aspects of the trauma network are brought to the conscious mind. Thus the individual is repeatedly exposed to the traumatic material under poor exposure conditions which serves to perpetuate the fear response.

From this theoretical framework they propose that in order to change the fear structure two steps are required. Firstly, the fear structure has to be activated in its entirety under optimal conditions for exposure. This is most effectively achieved with prolonged imaginal exposure, where by the individual recounts the traumatic event in great detail, in the first person present tense. (*N.B. Imaginal exposure is a very powerful therapeutic technique and should not be attempted unless the clinician is fully competent and trained in this technique.*) Secondly, new information needs to be incorporated into the activated fear structure, which is incompatible with some elements already present, thus allowing for changes in the meaning of the event. For example, via imaginal exposure the meaning of the feared memory may be changed so that it no longer means *near death*. The introduction of new incompatible information and changes in meaning structures can be achieved with cognitive restructuring techniques based on cognitive behavioural therapy.

The efficacy of exposure based treatments for PTSD has been demonstrated in several studies (Johnson *et al.* 1982; Fairbank *et al.* 1983; Keane *et al.* 1989; Foa *et al.* 1991; Foa & Meadows 1997). Details of the treatment approach with rape victims are available elsewhere (Foa & Rothbaum 1998).

Theories based on socio-cognitive models

There are a number of other prominent theories for PTSD. Although they do not specifically address PTSD in rape victims, they offer useful theoretical frameworks of PTSD in general. Horowitz (1986) offers a psychodynamic perspective on the processes involved in the integration of information from a traumatic event. Information received from a traumatic event is stored in the individual's memory and continually brought to the conscious mind or repeated in the mind. The traumatised individual is inevitably faced with an overwhelming and negative experience, which is associated with a negative emotional response. Working through the event to establish harmony is needed if the individual is to successfully process the experience. This task involves integrating huge changes in his/her schemata in order to achieve harmony, which is achieved by repeated presentation of this new information (received from the event) into the conscious mind. Such repeated recollection is associated with powerful negative emotional responses and forms the basis of intrusive activity.

Various defence mechanisms (inner inhibitory control systems) come into operation to prevent the individual being overwhelmed by these negative emotional responses. These mechanisms control the presentation of information into the conscious mind and thus allow for gradual assimilation of traumatic information. These mechanisms can operate at a conscious level (suppression), or at a subconscious level (repression).

In this model PTSD is viewed as result of an individual's inability to successfully integrate a traumatic experience into their cognitive schemata. Avoidant symptoms (denial of the event, numbness and avoidance) arise when inner inhibitory mechanisms predominate over the repetition of information into the conscious mind (intrusive symptoms). Similarly, at other times, intrusive symptoms are dominant over the avoidance state. Completion of the working through phase is associated with a cessation of intrusion and denial.

Like Horowitz, Janoff-Bulman (1985; 1992), suggests that trauma creates a mismatch between inner models or pre-existing assumptions about the world and the new information received from the traumatic event. She argues that PTSD arises from the *shattering of basic assumptions* about personal invulner-

ability, the world as meaningful and the self as worthy. Thus beliefs such as 'bad things happen to bad people' are common and are thought to be formed in childhood. Other researchers have emphasised the role of cognitive appraisal at the time of trauma, and the individual's previous schemas for seeing the world. The way individuals make attributions to explain external events is also thought to be important in the response to trauma.

Assessment issues

This section will highlight some of the general psychological and pragmatic principles in the assessment of rape victims. We have covered the issues around assessment in greater detail than is possible here elsewhere (Turner & Lee 1998).

Pragmatic considerations

Assessing traumatised people is a lengthy and complex process. A good first assessment session will greatly aid the establishment of trust and safety which have usually been shattered by the experience of rape. The clinician should expect the first session to last at least two hours. The assessment session is often very intense emotionally for the patient and the clinician and it is important that the patient does not leave the session in a distressed state and feeling overwhelmed with emotions. It may also be necessary for the clinician to debrief with colleagues after an emotionally distressing session. Consideration of the setting is also important and the interview room should feel safe and peaceful, free from loud noises and dark entrance-ways (Turner & Lee 1998).

Consideration should be made about the sex of the assessing clinician. Sensitivity to the wishes of the patient on this matter should be respected. Clinicians should also be sensitive to issues such as shame, humiliation and fear of judgement in victims. Attention to body language is important in gauging the patient's emotional responses. Empathy, trust, respect and knowledge are important aspects in the clinician's approach.

General interview schedule

We have set out a suggested general assessment framework for working with rape victims as well as more detailed guidance on carrying out the assessment in the Trauma Interview Schedule (Turner & Lee 1998). Briefly, we believe that the following areas need to be covered in an assessment:

- Present complaints
- Psychological health
- Physical health including advice on sexual health screening
- Interpersonal relationships:
  Sexual dysfunction
  Social support
- Occupation (impact of trauma)
- Accommodation/practical welfare/finance
- Assessment of PTSD symptoms, depression, suicidal ideation, anxiety, OCD
- Family background:
  Family structure
  Family support
  Family history of emotional difficulties
- Personal background:
  - Developmental experiences
  - Pre-morbid personality
  - Previous trauma

- Belief systems – view of self, world, others (see below)
- Pre-morbid beliefs about rape
- Religious and spiritual beliefs
- The rape experience (see below)
- The post-trauma reaction
- Alcohol, drugs and medication.

In addition to the general assessment process and as part of the therapeutic intervention, in most cases it will be necessary to gain an in-depth picture of the rape experience in order to aid emotional processing of the event.

Assessing the psychological impact of rape

An important part of the psychological assessment and therapeutic process is the recounting of the traumatic event. This may be the first opportunity the person has had to talk about what actually happened in a systematic and detailed way. This may form part of later exposure therapy. Practically this involves asking the person to go through what happened to them in as much detail as possible. As judged by the clinician this should be done at the appropriate point in the therapy process, which could be in the second session or indeed at a later stage. In rare cases it may not be beneficial clinically to go through the event. It is not uncommon for people to say that they have talked about the event with many people and now just want to forget it. The reality is often that they have talked about it in a disjointed fashion, focusing on salient moments or perhaps not mentioning the most disturbing or shameful part of it. This can lead to distortions in memories and faulty information processing.

Some people are very keen to have the opportunity to share their experiences with the clinician. However others are extremely reticent about doing so for fear of how they might be judged and/or because they are experiencing high levels of shame and guilt. Anecdotal evidence suggests that shame is one of the greatest barriers to talking about their experience. Research has also shown that people who blame themselves for events that have a negative outcome are less likely to think it is appropriate to seek help from friends and family and are more likely to withdraw from social support. Given this it is understandable that a person who blames themselves in some way for the attack may be very reluctant to share their thoughts with the clinician. Under these circumstances, it may take several sessions of trust-building before the person feels enough trust to divulge what happened to them.

The clinician must strike a fine balance between encouraging the person to recount their story in a way that allows them a sense of control over the process whilst not coming across as too probing, prying or confrontational. This requires great sensitivity, skill and respect for the person's experience. Traumatised people are very precious about their experiences and sharing of this experience is a very profound process for them and should be treated with the utmost respect by the clinician. A successful recounting of the traumatic event phase sets up a strong therapeutic bond.

As well as establishing a strong therapeutic bond, the purpose of this phase is to allow the clinician to make a comprehensive assessment of what actually happened, what thought processes were in operation, what decisions were made and what emotional states were experienced. By identifying key thought processes, such as self-blame, over-developed sense of responsibility or hindsight reasoning, the clinician can gain insight into the blocks in emotional processing.

There are three core parts to recounting the event:

- *Setting the scene.* The person recounts details of what happened before the event occurred. For example this may include what they were doing half an hour before the attack. This helps to put the event into a context.
- *Experience of the traumatic event.* The person recounts details of what actually happened to them. Careful attention should be paid to eliciting **D**ecisions made, **E**motional reactions, **B**ehaviours, and **T**houghts (mnemonic: **DEBT**). This allows the clinician the opportunity to identify faulty thinking processes and issues such as self-blame which may underpin the blocks to emotional processing of the event. These blocks are indicators for areas of therapeutic intervention using cognitive therapy strategies.
- *Immediate aftermath of the event.* The person recounts details of what happened in the immediate aftermath of the event. For example, how did it end? Who came to their aid? How were they treated by police, medical staff, family, and friends?

Assessing the meaning of the event

The experience of rape affects victims in a variety of profound and different ways. 'Underneath' the recognised symptoms of PTSD lies a labyrinth of psychological processes at work in *a person-specific* way, to give rise to a psychological *trauma reaction profile*. An analysis of these psychological processes is needed before a *meaningful* formulation can be made of the individual's difficulties in the aftermath of the rape. A thorough psychological formulation is a necessary precursor for effective therapeutic interventions.

In the context of PTSD any intrusive imagery, which is associated with negative affect, is an indication of failure in emotional processing. For the clinician, the central question is *what is blocking successful integration of this event?* What are the stuck points or blocks in the cognitive processing that give rise to emotionally charged intrusions? Images in themselves are not harmful. It is the affect associated with the image which causes psychological upset, and it is the *meaning* ascribed to the image that gives rise to that affect.

Similar traumatic events affect people in a variety of different ways – their developmental and life experiences are unique to them as is their psychological interpretation of their experiences. Such life experiences serve to create a framework of reference for the self, the world and others which makes the world meaningful. All experiences, including traumatic events, are emotionally processed and made meaningful by referencing them to this extensive framework.

Hence it is the analysis of the meaning of the traumatic event for the individual, in terms of how it fits or indeed *does not fit* into their systemic framework of the self, world and others, which allows the clinician to identify the barriers to emotional processing. The *trauma reaction profile* is shaped by the meaning ascribed to the individual's experience of a traumatic event.

This point is illustrated in the following example.

A woman involved in a rape perceives the experience as very frightening because she could have died. Every time she thinks about the rape, she experiences intense feelings of fear/anxiety and shame and she is reminded that she could have died. The affect is experienced as distressing and she is motivated to reduce this feeling by avoiding all stimuli which provoke intrusive thoughts. She displays symptoms of distressing intrusive imagery and avoidance behaviour. The intrusive imagery is an indication that she is 'stuck' in her emotional processing of this event.

But what is it that gives rise to this block? If we refer to her framework of self, world and others, we find that prior to the event she held the belief that *'women bring rape on themselves and only bad women are raped'*. Thus she knew rape happened to other people but only *'to those who brought it on themselves'*. The experience of rape *does not fit* into her pre-existing framework of herself, as she did not perceive herself as 'bad'. The shameful feelings arise as the woman attempts to assimilate the information received from the rape, via faulty information processing, which leads to the formation of the meaning of the event, *'I must be bad and have brought this on myself'*. In this case fear/anxiety is associated with the meaning *'I am vulnerable, I could have died.'*

Thus part of the assessment process requires careful analysis of prior beliefs about rape as well as pre-existing beliefs about the self, world, and others. With respect to the latter, Janoff-Bulman's (1985) work on *Shattered Assumptions* sheds further light on previously held beliefs about the self, world and others which are thought to be shattered by the experience of trauma. These include: (i) *The world is a safe, just and predictable place.* This carries the implication that bad things do not happen to good people and that as long as you play by 'the rules' you will be safe and life will be predictable. (ii) *Other people are benevolent.* This carries the assumptions that other people will not cause you harm (*how could they do those things to me?*), that other people are kind and caring in times of crisis (*how could they just walk by and completely ignore my cries for help?*). (iii) *The self as invulnerable and worthy.* This carries the assumptions that no harm will come to you as you are invincible (*I can't believe I nearly died, I could have died, I've never thought that I could die, these things happen to other people*). (iv) That you would always behave in an honourable way in a crisis (*I feel so bad that I trod on that man in the scramble to save myself from the fire*).

It is important to remember that, as well as challenging pre-existing belief systems, traumatic events can also reinforce pre-existing beliefs. For example an adult survivor of childhood sexual abuse may experience a rape in adulthood as consistent with the meaning element 'I am unworthy, I deserved to be abused'. In this instance, this event fits into previous experiences of herself and her world.

It is often the case that people are not willing to disclose their pre-existing beliefs for fear of being judged. For example, as in the case illustration above, a woman who holds the belief that 'anyone who gets raped has done something to deserve it', may believe that '*other people must think that I did something to deserve it as that is what I thought about them before I was raped*' (other people will judge me as I have judged them).

Conclusions

For many people rape is a life-shattering experience. It can have far-reaching consequences which affect the victim's psychological, emotional and physical well-being. A significant number of victims of rape recover to normal functioning after a short period of disruption. Those that do not recover often develop psychological difficulties which may include post-traumatic stress disorder, depression, sexual dysfunction, social problems, feelings of fear, anxiety, shame and guilt. A sensitive, respectful and thorough assessment of the difficulties faced by the victim is essential if they are to engage in psychological treatment. Such an assessment should include a thorough investigation of the meaning the event holds for the individual and how it challenges or confirms pre-existing beliefs about the self, world and others. Clinicians should pay particular attention to feelings of self-blame and shame which could present barriers in disclosing information and lead to treatment drop-out.

Treatment studies have demonstrated efficacy in approaches that utilise cognitive behavioural approaches such as imaginal exposure, cognitive restructuring and cognitive processing therapy. However clinicians should be competent and trained in these therapy techniques before employing them with victims of rape.

Finally, working with victims of rape can be emotionally intense and distressing for the therapist and the patient. Secondary traumatisation and compassion fatigue are recognised hazards when working with trauma (Figley 1995). The clinician is advised to use supervision and peer support to debrief when working with traumatised individuals in order to reduce the secondary effects of trauma.

References

Allison, J.A & Wrightsman, L.S. (1993) *Rape: The Misunderstood Crime.* Sage, CA.

American Psychiatric Association (1994) *Diagnostic and Statistical Manual of Mental Disorders,* 4th edn. (DSM-IV). APA, Washington, DC.

Beck, A.T., Ward, C.H., Mendolsohn, M., Mock, J. & Erbaugh, J. (1961) An inventory for measuring depression. *Archives of General Psychiatry* **4**(86), 1–865.

Beck, A.T., Rush, A.J., Shaw. B.F. & Emery, G. (1979) *Cognitive Therapy for Depression.* Guilford, New York.

Becker, J.V., Skinner, L.J., Abel, G.G. & Cichon, J. (1986) Level of postassault sexual functioning in rape and incest survivors. *Archives of Sexual Behaviour* **15**(3), 7–49.

Burgess, A.W. & Holmstrom, L.L. (1979) Rape: Sexual disruption and recovery. *American Journal of Orthopsychiatry* **49**, 648–657.

Chemtob, C., Roitblat, H.C., Hamada, R.S., *et al.* (1988) A cognitive action theory of post traumatic stress disorder. *Journal of Anxiety Disorders* **2**, 253–275.

Derogatis, L.R. (1977) *SCL-90-R Manual.* Johns Hopkins University Press, Baltimore.

Ellis, E.M., Atkeson, B.M. & Calhoun, K.S. (1981) An assessment of long-term reactions to rape. *Journal of Abnormal Psychology* **90**, 263–266.

Fairbank, J.A., Gross, R.T. & Keane, T.M. (1983) Treatment of posttraumatic stress disorder: evaluation of outcome with a behavioral code. *Behaviour Modification* **7**, 557–568.

Figley, C.R. (1995) *Compassion Fatigue.* Brunner/Mazel, New York.

Fitts, W.H. (1965) *Manual: Tennessee Self-Concept Scale.* Counselor Recordings and Tests, Nashville, TN.

Foa, E. B. & Kozak, M.J. (1986) Emotional processing of fear: exposure to corrective information. *Psychological Bulletin* **99**, 20–35.

Foa, E.B. & Kozak, M.J. (1991) Emotional processing of fear: theory, research and clinical implications for anxiety disorders. In: *Emotion, Psychotherapy and Change* (eds J.D. Safran & L.S. Greenberg), pp. 21–49. Guilford Press, New York.

Foa, E.B. & Meadows, E.A. (1997) Psychosocial treatments for post-traumatic stress disorder: a critical review. In: *Annual Review of Psychology* (eds J. Spence, J.M. Darley & D.J. Foss), Volume 48, pp. 449–490. Annual Reviews, Palo Alto, CA.

Foa, E.B. & Rothbaum, B.O. (1998) *Treating the Trauma of Rape: Cognitive-Behavioural Therapy.* Guilford Press, New York.

Foa, E.B., Rothbaum, B.O., Riggs, D.S. & Murdock, T.B. (1991) Treatment of post-traumatic stress disorder in rape victims. *Journal of Consulting and Clinical Psychology,* **59**, 715–723.

Frank, E. & Stewart, B.D. (1984) Depressive symptoms in rape victims. A revisit. *Journal of Affective Disorders* **1**, 269–277.

Frank, E., Turner, S.M. & Duffy, B. (1979) Depressive symptoms in rape victims. *Journal of Affective Disorders* **1**, 269–277.

Hollon, S.D. & Garber, J. (1988) Cognitive therapy. In: *Social Cognition and Clinical Psychology: A Synthesis* (ed. L.Y. Abramson), pp. 204–253. Guilford Press, New York.

Horowitz, M.J. (1986) *Stress Response Syndromes.* Jason Aronson, Northvale, NJ.

Horowitz, M.J. (1990) Post-traumatic stress disorders: psychological aspects of the diagnosis. *International Journal of Mental Health* **19**, 21–36.

Janoff-Bulman, R. (1985) The aftermath of victimisation: rebuilding shattered assumptions. In: *Trauma and its Wake. The Study and Treatment of Post-Traumatic Stress Disorder* (ed. C.R. Figley), pp. 15–35. Brunner/Mazel, New York.

Janoff-Bulman, R. (1992) *Shattered Assumptions: Towards a New Psychology of Trauma.* Free Press, New York.

Janoff-Bulman, R. & Frantz, C.M. (1997) The impact of trauma on meaning: from meaningless world to meaningful life. In: *The Transformation of Meaning in Psychological Therapies: Integrating Theory and Practice* (eds M. Power & C.R. Brewin), pp. 9–10. John Wiley, Chichester.

Johnson, C.H. Gilmore, J.D. & Shenoy, R.Z. (1982) Use of feeding procedure in the treatment of stress-related anxiety disorder. *Journal of Behavior Therapy and Experimental Psychiatry* **13**, 235–237.

Joseph, S., Yule, W. & Williams, R. (1993) Post-traumatic stress: attributional aspects. *Journal of Traumatic Stress* **6**, 501–513.

Keane, T.M., Fairbank, J.A., Caddell, J.M. & Zimering, R.T. (1989) Implosive (flooding) therapy reduces symptoms of PTSD in Vietnam combat veterans. *Behavior Therapy* **20**, 245–260.

Kilpatrick, D.G. & Veronen, L.J. (1984) Treatment of fear and anxiety in victims of rape. Final grant report (Source: Resick, P.A. (1993) The psychological impact of rape. *Journal of Interpersonal Violence* **8**(2), 223–255.

Kilpatrick, D.G., Veronen, L.J & Resick, P.A. (1979) The aftermath of rape: recent empirical findings. *American Journal of Orthopsychiatry* **49**, 658–669.

Kilpatrick, D.G., Best, C.L., Veronen, L.J., *et al.* (1985) Mental health correlates of criminal victimisation: a random community survey. *Journal of Consulting and Clinical Psychology* **53**, 866–873.

Kilpatrick, D.G., Saunders, B.E., Veronen, L.J., Best, C.L. & Von, J.M. (1987) Criminal victimisation: lifetime prevalence, reporting to the police, and psychological impact. *Crime and Delinquency* **33**, 479–489.

Koss, M.P. (1985) The hidden rape victim: personality, attitudinal and situational characteristics. *Psychology of Woman Quarterly* **9**, 193–212.

Lang, P.J. (1977) Imagery in therapy: an information processing analysis of fear. *Behavior Therapy* **8**, 862–886.

Lang, P.J. (1979) A bio-informational theory on emotional imagery. *Psychophysiology* **16**, 495–512.

Lee, D.A., Scragg, P. & Turner, S.W. The role of shame, guilt and fear in the development of chronic PTSD. A clinical model (in preparation).

McCann, I.L. & Pearlman, L.A. (1990) *Psychological Trauma and the Adult Survivor: Theory Therapy and Transformation.* Brunner/Mazel, New York.

McCann, I.L., Sakheim, D.K. & Abrahamson, D.J. (1988) Trauma and victimization: a model of psychological

adaptation. *Counselling Psychologist* **16**, 531–594.

Nadelson, C.C., Notman, M.T., Zackson, H. & Gornick, J. (1982) A follow-up study of rape victims. *American Journal of Psychiatry* **139**, 1266–1270.

Perloff, L.S. (1983) Perceptions of vulnerability to victimisation. *Journal of Social Issues* **39**, 41–61.

Rachman, S. (1980) Emotional processing. *Behaviour, Research and Therapy* **18**, 51–60.

Resick, P.A. (1993) The psychological impact of rape. *Journal of Interpersonal Violence* **8**(2), 223–255.

Resick, P.A. & Schnicke, M.K. (1990) Treating symptoms in adult victims of sexual assault. *Journal of Interpersonal Violence* **5**, 488–506.

Resick, P.A. & Schnicke, M.K. (1992) Cognitive processing therapy for sexual assault victims. *Journal of Consulting and Clinical Psychology* **60**, 748–756.

Resick, P.A. & Schnicke, M.K. (1993) *Cognitive Processing for Rape Victims.* Sage, Newbury Park, CA.

Resick, P.A. Calhoun, K.S., Atkeson, B.M. & Ellis, E.M. (1981) Social adjustment in victims of sexual assault. *Journal of Consulting and Clinical Psychology* **49**, 705–712.

Rothbaum, B.O., Foa, E.B., Riggs, D., Murdock, T. & Walsh, W. (1992) A prospective examination of posttraumatic stress disorder in rape victims. *Journal of Traumatic Stress* **5**, 455–475.

Russell, D.E.H. (1984) *Sexual Exploitation: Rape, Childhood Sexual Abuse and Work-place Harassment.* Sage, Beverly Hills, CA.

Schepple, K.L. & Bart, P.B. (1983) Through women's eyes: defining danger in the wake of sexual assault. *Journal of Social Issues* **39**, 63–81.

Schnicke, M.K. & Resick, P.A. (1990) Treating symptoms in adult victims of sexual assault. *Journal of Interpersonal Violence* **5**, 488–506.

Turner, S.W. & Lee, D.A (1998) *Measures in Post Traumatic Stress Disorder: A Practitioner's Guide.* Nelson, Slough.

Weiner, B. (1986) *An Attributional Theory of Motivation and Emotion.* Springer Verlag, New York.

Chapter 15

Sexual Health in Primary Care

Simon Barton and Paul Fox

A recent survey of sexual attitudes and life-style among over 18 000 British citizens has shown that only the minority of those reporting high-risk markers for the transmission of sexually transmitted infections (STIs) have ever attended a genito-urinary clinic (Pritchard & Robinson 1998). This finding emphasises the vital role of primary care in the management of STIs, many of which are undoubtedly going unrecognised. Unfortunately, there is a general lack of awareness of the minor symptoms which might indicate an STI (Mulvey *et al*. 1997). Furthermore, the asymptomatic acquisition and persistence of STIs, especially genital herpes, warts and chlamydia, has not reached general or public medical awareness (Bleker 1996). To add to the difficulties, this is an area of medicine in which barriers exist between patients and their doctors.

The nature of the doctor–patient relationship in matters concerning sexual health

The embarrassment which the majority of pa-tients feel in discussing matters relating to sex is the source of much ribald humour in our society. Doctors often feel as reluctant as their patients to broach issues which are intensely private and personal and which might necessitate an intimate genital examination.

The close and often life-long relationship between GP and patient may either promote or inhibit honesty when discussing sexual symptoms and practices. The patient is not likely to wish to inform an old friend about an extramarital affair. Conversely, the GP may not feel equipped to discuss sexual habits with a respected elder member of the community, particularly one of the opposite sex. Health care professionals are as subject to their own prejudices and sexual mores as all other members of society, and these can all too readily be detected by patients. Patients for their part will tend to assume that they are being judged unless it is made clear to them that this is not the case.

General practitioner training schemes place much emphasis on communication skills, but genito-urinary medicine (GUM) experience is rarely included, and obstetric and gynaecology training seldom extends to the area of sexual history taking. It inevitably takes practice to become adept at dealing with sexual topics, but helping patients through their sexual difficulties is both rewarding, and likely to put the doctor–patient relationship onto a very secure footing. Having been able to discuss the aspects of a person's life considered the most private then the possibility is opened up that on future occasions there can be considerably more openness and relaxation on both sides. Alternatively, those practitioners who do not feel equipped to handle sexual health issues could redirect the patient to a designated colleague who wishes to develop this expertise. The designated colleague could be either a fellow GP or a practice nurse.

Promoting sexual health awareness

Primary care offers many opportunities for promoting a positive outlook towards sexual health and screening for sexually transmitted infections. There is a widespread assumption that STIs are things that happen to *other* people, to very *promiscuous* people, and not to *nice* people such as ourselves. This has the unfortunate consequence of severely sapping self-esteem if an infection does occur. The 'well man' and 'well woman' clinic which usually has little to do with sexual health, except for providing cervical cytological examination in women, offers an ideal forum to enquire if the patient is sexually active and has ever had unprotected intercourse. If this is the case, a recommendation should be made that in view of the number of clinically silent STIs present in the community, they should consider having a sexual health screen. This may result in a rec-

ommendation to attend, or a formal referral to, the local GUM clinic. Those attending for travel vaccinations represent another group in which a sexual health discussion is pertinent. The dangers of acquiring STIs, particularly HIV, through unprotected intercourse abroad, should be mentioned, as in the relaxed atmosphere of the holiday high-risk sexual behaviour is more common than normal (Daniels *et al.* 1992).

Nor should the opportunity be missed at insurance or pre-employment medicals to educate patients about the advisability of screening and HIV testing when there have been multiple sexual partners. There is a good chance that the advice will not be heeded straight away, but at least the process of thinking about the issues will have been initiated. The opportunity may also have arisen during the consultation to correct any misapprehensions about what constitutes safer sex.

An important potential obstacle is the stigma attached to attending a GUM clinic. The principal anxiety is that of being recognised going in by friends, neighbours, and colleagues at work or even by their sexual partners. There is also a common misapprehension that information volunteered at such a visit will somehow enter into the public domain, and that information can be divulged to employers, insurance companies and the like without their consent. Individuals will sometimes go to great lengths to remain anonymous by providing false names and addresses, and by travelling to distant clinics where they are unlikely to be recognised.

There may also be a fear of the tests themselves: women who are frightened at the thought of a speculum examination, and men who have been told that a large 'umbrella' will be inserted into their penis. Simple reassurance on these matters can go a long way in helping to overcome the psychological obstacle of entering the portals of the 'special' clinic. Further encouragement could be provided by handing out a leaflet showing the location of the clinic, and by referring to a named doctor. Some personal contact between the primary care team and GUM services is also helpful in breaking down barriers for the patient, and will facilitate a shared understanding of difficulties that patients face, especially if it leads to joint protocols and joint clinical audit.

Most patients are ultimately pleasantly surprised by the user-friendly nature of the GUM clinic. The young are certainly making increasing use of GUM services, which might imply that amongst this group the clinics are becoming more acceptable (Pritchard & Robinson 1998).

The management of specific issues

Genital herpes simplex virus infection

Few aspects of sexual health are more potentially emotive than genital herpes simplex. Misconceptions about this STI have resulted in much psychological, psycho-sexual and relationship trauma, particularly in the environment of anger, guilt and mutual recrimination which so often follows a primary episode. The discovery that an individual's sexual partner has a history of HSV will not infrequently send them rushing off to seek medical advice in a state of high anxiety (Green & Kocsis 1997).

Genital herpes seems to have caught the popular imagination as a terrible, untreatable life-long affliction. It is vitally important to instil a much more positive and encouraging approach to the infection from the very beginning, as the expectation of prolonged suffering can turn negative thoughts into self-fulfilling prophesy. Poor coping skills have been related to frequency of recurrent episodes. The belief that herpes attacks can be precipitated by stressful life events has not so far been substantiated, but those with more frequent episodes do show greater levels of anxiety.

The first priority whenever a patient presents with herpes must be to commence antiviral therapy immediately, but that aside, it is pressingly important that the following information is imparted:

(1) Concerning prognosis: that it is by no means inevitable that recurrent episodes will occur; that subsequent episodes if they occur can be expected to be milder; and that the small percentage who get troublesome recurrences can be treated with prophylactic medication.
(2) Concerning aetiology: that 25% of apparent primary episodes are in people who have had the virus in their body for a much longer period without experiencing symptoms, in other words, they have not caught it from their current sexual partner; that they may have contracted the virus from a tiny cold sore on their partner's lip; and that their partner may have transmitted the virus from a tiny, more or less symptomless genital lesion without being aware that they were an infection risk. Primary attacks of herpes can occur in the context of very longstanding monogamous relationships.
(3) Concerning the risk of transmission to others: that their current or future part-

ners may have a high level of immunity to the virus without ever knowingly having been exposed to it, and may therefore not be at risk of infection; or if infected *may* not experience any troublesome symptoms; that the risk of transmission is in any case reduced if sex is avoided when lesions are present. The risk of transmission of a woman to her child during delivery, unless the HSV is symptomatic at the time, is also extremely low (Cassidy *et al.* 1997). Furthermore, in 34 cases of inadvertent vaginal delivery to women with symptomatic recurrent genital herpes none of the infants was infected (Green & Kocsis 1997). Herpes contracted *during* pregnancy is a quite separate issue, and remains extremely dangerous to mother and child.

Patients may be quite troubled because they fear that future potential partners will reject them if they are honest about the condition. We have indeed encountered patients who have been repeatedly rejected following *early* declaration within a relationship that they had the virus. The problem with this laudably honest approach is that partners tend to become irrational when the word 'herpes' is mentioned. The situation may be likened to the medieval leper compelled to shout 'unclean' when a healthy person came near. Partners who have not themselves been given the diagnosis assume that they are inevitably going to suffer. In the context of so many popular misconceptions one should advise circumspection. The issues should at the very least be carefully thought through before the partner is told. Those who argue that partners *must* be told are simply reinforcing pop-

ular paranoia and the feeling of guilt which some individuals carry unnecessarily on their shoulders. It should always be remembered that antibody to herpes simplex type 2 is found in 7% of UK blood donors, and antibody HSV-1 in a further 42% (Brown *et al.* 1991). These figures are higher in GU clinic attenders. Most people, around 80% in fact, are blissfully ignorant of their sero-status (Prober *et al.* 1987).

The unlucky few who experience frequent recurrences may find it more convenient to discuss the situation with their partners to explain why they are not able to engage in sexual activity at certain times. If the discussion about informing partners is entered into the doctor can circumvent a lot of psychological problems later on by offering to see both partners together in order to talk the issues through. Some form of psychological intervention should also be recommended as stress reduction has been shown to be beneficial in reducing both the number of episodes and in reducing their perceived severity. Hypnotherapy has shown some promise: the authors found an overall 38% reduction of episodes of genital herpes in a cohort of patients with frequent recurrences following a single episode of hypnosis (Fox *et al.* 1999). Those who responded showed a significant increase in a variety of immune parameters compared with those who did not respond.

Dealing with the issues of herpes is time consuming, and where more input is needed the services of the local genito-urinary clinic should be accessed, most particularly with frequent recurrences. It is self-evident that an erroneous diagnosis of herpes should be avoided at all cost, and where any doubt exists specialist advice should be sought.

Genital warts

Most patients are aware without being told that warts are a treatable condition, but it is worth mentioning that like all other types of wart the genital variety can resolve spontaneously, and that most treatments probably succeed ultimately by facilitating the destruction of the virus by the immune system. Destructive treatments currently used are cryotherapy, hyfrecation and laser ablation. The belief in a positive outcome helps to alleviate stress and is thereby likely to hasten recovery.

There are no data available on how long after apparent clearance of warts they might recur. Within this vacuum of information most clinicians when questioned tend to make up their own answers based on personal experience. In other words patients are often given conflicting advice, which in turn magnifies anxiety (Cowan *et al.* 1994).

There may be odd cases in which warts have apparently recurred years later, but to inform patients of this is not helpful, as it leads to needless worry, when in fact the great majority of patients will not experience recurrences after they have been clear for three to six months.

It should be remembered that perianal warts in the heterosexual male are quite common and do not imply anal intercourse. The patient should be asked about their sexuality as the issues of sexual health screening will need to be discussed, but if the patient is heterosexual it is important for the clinician to make it clear that he is in no way implying that the warts could only have got there through anal sex. In this way unnecessary embarrassment is avoided.

For the female patient a principal concern will be whether having warts means that they are at risk of cervical cancer. Since for many years the medical profession believed this to be the case it will take a long period of time before such fears die away. Reassurance can now be quite categorical: the types of human papillomavirus (HPV), specifically types 16 and 18, which produce carcinoma of the cervix, do not give rise to exophytic warts (Pecoraro *et al.* 1991; Ho *et al.* 1996). Conversely, the HPV types which produce exophytic warts are not implicated in cancer. There is no longer any indication for increased cytological surveillance in women who have had genital warts.

Warts can be treated very successfully by the primary health care team, podophyllotoxin cream producing a 75% cure rate within four weeks (Edwards *et al.* 1988), but the opportunity should never be missed to stress the urgency of a full sexual health screen, and thereafter discuss safer sex issues. The incidence of other STIs in association with HPV is perhaps as high as 30%, and many of them are asymptomatic (Kinghorn 1978).

Chlamydia trachomatis and pelvic inflammatory disease

Genito-urinary clinics have been unable to make any headway in reducing the prevalence of chlamydia infection within the community because most cases are asymptomatic and most asymptomatic cases are not being screened (Johnson *et al.* 1996a, b; Simms 1997). Only about 10% of cases come to the attention of a GU clinic. Moves are now afoot to screen at-risk women attending family planning clinics, but it is hoped that the GP clinic will play an increasing role in the future, perhaps by screening women when they attend for cervical cytology (CMO 1988).

To attempt *treatment* in the primary care setting without accessing the resource of the health adviser is unwise, because of the problem of contact tracing. Contact tracing is fraught with difficulty for the GP because for a variety of reasons, such as embarrassment and fears about confidentiality, most patients will be reluctant to provide a totally honest list of contacts. It is insufficient to ask the patient to notify her contacts, as she will need guidance on who exactly to tell and how to go about it. This is an area where the health adviser is truly invaluable, and in the future we hope that GPs will gain direct access to health advisers for the purpose of chlamydia contact tracing. Pilot studies are already under way. After being given a diagnosis patients will often divulge behaviour and sexual contacts to a health adviser that they initially felt the need to keep secret.

The key message to get across in the primary health setting is that complications such as infertility are relatively unlikely if the infection is treated before it becomes symptomatic, but that it is absolutely vital that all sexual contacts are treated before she resumes sexual intercourse.

Many doctors are unaware of the potential seriousness of asymptomatic chlamydia infection. Yet 40% of such women undergoing laparoscopy have no evidence of upper genital tract infection (Tait *et al.* 1997). Less than a third of such cases detected in the community are referred on. The remaining two thirds may not be given therapy that a specialist would consider adequate; while pressures of time and absence of support staff mean that contact tracing is frequently neglected (Mason *et al.* 1996).

Pelvic inflammatory disease, the consequence of undiagnosed and inadequately treated infections, is a condition which is both overdiagnosed in women with overt pelvic pain (Westrom *et al.* 1992) and much underdiagnosed in women with only minor symptoms. The danger in making an unsubstantiated diagnosis is that of causing needless anxiety about infertility and ectopic pregnancy, and of labelling someone with a stigmatising disease.

Concerns about fertility are often high following a diagnosis of PID, and need to be addressed swiftly. Follow-up of over a thousand woman with laparoscopically confirmed PID showed that of those with mild infection none became infertile, but for moderate and severe infections the combined prevalence was 13%. For two episodes the risk is 25%, and following three episodes there is a 75% risk of infertility (Westrom *et al.* 1992).

Urethral discharge in the male

The pressure brought to bear on the GP to treat a painful discharge with antibiotics may be considerable, especially out of hours when the facilities of a GUM clinic are not available. Married patients will want a quick-fix cure if they have had an extramarital liaison, so that they can go back to their partners and pretend that nothing has happened. All too often, however, they will also have had sex with their partners before symptoms developed. The fear of divulging the guilty secret to a spouse may be considerable. One man who attended our clinic with non-specific urethritis returned several months after successful treatment to discover if the infection was still present. He was hoping that by not telling his wife and then re-exposing himself through her he could thereby establish that she had not been infected. Inevitably he still had the infection, and she was beginning to get symptoms, with far more serious implications for the marriage.

Men will also sometimes tell their partners that they had 'thrush' rather than NSU, and that this was the cause of the discharge. This is sometimes an honest misunderstanding, but has the consequence of transferring the 'blame' to the female partner, who at the same time is not alerted to the possibility that she has an STI which needs treating as a matter of urgency. Candida is in fact an extremely rare cause of urethral discharge in men. Dysuria, without associated discharge, is likely to be assumed to be a urine infection rather than an STI. If urine sent by GPs which is negative for bacteria is examined for chlamydia by PCR, 6% of men are found to be positive (Kudesia *et al.* 1993).

Such salutary tales may be helpful in explaining to patients why they should see a specialist. Currently most cases of urethral discharge which present to the surgery are being treated there, and there is often little concern over treating their sexual partners (Ainsworth *et al.* 1996). It is commonly thought that men will object to being asked to go to a GUM clinic, and therefore few men are in fact asked to do. Yet surveys do suggest that only about one in 10 patients has any objection (Ross & Champion 1998). Urinalysis is customarily performed when men attend as new patients and at 'well man' clinics. These samples could easily be sent routinely for chlamydia testing, and in order to obtain permission for this an opportunity is generated to explore sexual health issues.

Psychogenic penile discomfort and even 'discharge' is extremely common in men who have reason to believe that they *should* have caught an STI, by having ill-advised unprotected intercourse with a casual partner, especially when they have suffered NSU or gonorrhoea previously. There is great danger of turning this into a chronic problem by reinforcement. This will occur if antibiotics are prescribed without taking steps to confirm the presence of infection. The patient becomes increasingly concerned if his psychogenic symptom is not relieved in this manner, and a chronic problem may have been initiated. Firm reassurance and access to microscopic evaluation of urethral smears is required to be able to give a categorical reassurance.

Vaginal soreness

In the busy surgery, the temptation to treat without examining can be great, as the doctor may well feel safe in the assumption that common things being common it will be a case of candida (Nunns & Mandal 1996). When symptoms then recur after antifungal treatment they are commonly attributed to treatment failure rather than exploring other possibilities. The woman may have other concerns but feel unable to ask for an examination, or possibly even feel a sense of relief that the internal examination was unnecessary. The temptation to assume that the cause is not an STI will be very marked in the case of a married woman: there may well be a natural reticence on the part of the doctor to enquire if there has been extramarital contact. If the family doctor is unprepared to examine and swab then he should have no hesitation in referring the woman for a specialist opinion.

As with penile irritation, vaginal soreness may be a psychogenic symptom in women who are concerned following a sexual encounter with a person whom they subsequently perceive as being an infection risk. Even in the absence of infection the fear of it may lead to frequent washing and consequent candidial vaginitis or bacterial vaginosis. The GUM clinic is ideally set up to exclude the several STIs and also the non-sexually transmitted infections which can lead to vaginitis and thereby offer instant reassurance.

Gay men's sexual health

Less than half of gay men are prepared to divulge their sexuality to their GP, although most are in fact registered (Fitzpatrick *et al.* 1994). They may fear rejection, hostility or perhaps only a lack of sensitivity and understanding. They may equally have concerns that the GP will have to divulge this information whenever the patient needs to be referred to the hospital, or whenever an enquiry is made by an insurance company. Many men who have sex with men still reflect the prevailing attitudes of society and feel a sense of shame about their sexual orientation. They will often go to great lengths to conceal their sexual orientation. That so many gay men will not discuss sexual issues with their GP is of some concern as about half have never attended a GUM clinic, despite the fact that their sexual practices do not differ from those who do attend (Hope & Macarthur 1997).

It is important that the huge trust a patient is putting in his doctor by revealing himself as being gay or bisexual is recognised by a show of support. The doctor should not be too effusive as this may suggest a lack of sincerity. The temptation to enquire about HIV testing

in the next breath should be resisted since this implies that the physician is suggesting all men who have sex with men are at risk of HIV infection. A helpful way of building up trusting relationship rapidly is to recognise potential fears about confidentiality and to diffuse them. Patients may well not be aware that both the BMA and the Royal College of General Practitioners have advised their members not to answer lifestyle questions in insurance reports.

An enquiry as to whether the patient has a partner offers the opportunity to establish rapport while at the same time gathering data to get an idea of risk. While many gay men are in monogamous relationships they are unlikely to take offence if asked whether they occasionally have 'extracurricular' encounters as to so do is such an accepted part of the gay lifestyle. A high percentage of gay men (like their heterosexual counterparts) occasionally have unprotected intercourse, not through ignorance of the potential consequences, but in the heat of the moment (Nardone *et al.* 1997; Ruiz *et al.* 1998). The easiest way to enquire about this is to ask if there have been any 'slip-ups' in the practice of safer sex. Psychological intervention, with emphasis on examining self-justifications (Gold & Skinner 1992) can and should be offered to reduce this risk-taking behaviour if the patient himself is concerned that this is putting him at risk of HIV infection. Such support is best accessed by direct referral to the health adviser at the local GUM clinic.

Sexual health of lesbians

Lesbian women are probably even less likely to

reveal their sexuality to their GP than are gay men, because they will not perceive a need on health grounds for their doctor to be aware. There is a widespread misconception that lesbians do not need to worry about STIs and cervical cytology. It is true that women adopting an exclusively lesbian lifestyle do have a lower incidence of STIs, but the risk of such infections should not be dismissed. Female to female transmission is possible, particularly of *Trichomonas vaginalis* and human papillomavirus. Bacterial vaginosis is also more common in lesbian women compared with heterosexuals, and may therefore be sexually transmissible (Skinner *et al.* 1996). Up to 90% of lesbians have reported having sex with men at some time during their lives, yet it is easy to fall into the trap of not asking about heterosexual encounters. Symptoms suggestive of possible STI in lesbians always warrant further investigation.

HIV testing

The majority of people who access HIV antibody testing in primary care fall into the low-risk category (Ross & Goldberg 1997), especially those people who are required to be tested for banks, insurance companies, sometimes employers, and for emigration purposes. Some will request testing because of a morbid fear of HIV. This group needs to be treated with circumspection since having the test may well fail to reassure, possibly even heightening anxiety. Others will want to be tested because they believe it the right thing for two individuals to do when beginning a new relationship.

In general most members of society would rather not think of HIV if at all possible, and especially not when they are pregnant. That some HIV-infected pregnant women are unaware of their status is something of a tragedy in the United Kingdom in view of the success of antiretroviral therapy in reducing vertical transmission (Madge & Singh 1998). It is time for primary care to grasp the nettle and promote testing for all women in early pregnancy, with targeted information emphasising the potential value of therapy to reduce the risk of maternal transmission and to increase maternal longevity.

GPs themselves can have considerable reservations about broaching the subject of HIV testing, and their concerns are greater when dealing with heterosexual men and women as distinct from the more established at-risk groups of gay men and intravenous drug users (Kellock & Rogstad 1998). Lower risk patients are often being actively discouraged from being routinely tested. The reluctance of the family doctor is clearly multifactorial. Time is one factor: time to take a good sexual history, time to have an adequate pretest discussion, time in having to pick up the pieces following a positive result (Wenrick *et al.* 1997). There may be uncertainties concerning how to approach the pretest discussion. In fact this need only be quite brief for low-risk individuals. If it is clear that a lengthier discussion is necessary then the patient can be referred to a specialist testing centre. Some GPs even feel that because of continued difficulties with insurance companies it is better that no mention of HIV should enter the case notes. A change in attitudes in primary care would go a long way to eliminating the gap between the prevalence of HIV revealed by anonymous screening and the known cases.

Those at high risk of infection usually have their test carried out in a specialist clinic (Fitzpatrick *et al.* 1994), perhaps with same-day testing facilities, and where full after-care is available in the event of a positive result. Here also the trauma of the long delay in waiting for a result can be kept to the minimum.

Managing the HIV positive patient

Unfortunately many patients still choose to keep their primary health care team in ignorance of their HIV seropositivity (Fitzpatrick *et al.* 1994; Shaw *et al.* 1996), although women with HIV seem to be more willing to involve their GP (Madge *et al.* 1998). Some newly diagnosed patients do depend on their local health centre for support as they go through all the phases of a traumatic experience: denial, anger, grief and acceptance. In order to minimise the trauma, as with giving any life-threatening diagnosis, the following positive aspects of current HIV management should be reinforced from the very beginning. Firstly, that in the era of combination antiretroviral therapy the infection is compatible with many years of healthy life, in which period more treatments are likely to emerge. We now anticipate that many people being diagnosed in their twenties and thirties will still be working in their forties and fifties. Secondly, that after the initial shock of diagnosis life can and should continue as normal. Life and travel insurance can now be obtained by HIV seropositive individuals. Thirdly, that it is quite possible to have children who are not infected.

Despite receiving sound advice at diagnosis some patients will inevitably become fixed in denial. We see them in the HIV or the GUM clinic and they then disappear, not returning

to the specialist clinic for vital aftercare, perhaps not for years until the onset of symptoms of advanced HIV. The stigma of infection is particularly felt by certain ethnic minority groups (Sherr *et al.* 1999), and in our experience can even prevent discussion of seropositive status between husband and wife. This leaves them isolated, unsupported and vulnerable.

At an early stage after diagnosis the implications for the patient's relationships will need to be thought through, and help with informing partners offered. The burden of guilt for the bisexual man whose wife is not aware of his double life, for the person who has had an extramarital liaison, perhaps while overseas, perhaps with a sex worker, or for the person who experimented with intravenous drugs in the past and did not tell their partner, can be tremendous. Even if the patient wants to inform his partner the words may not come out, and the longer the delay, the more difficult the task becomes. It is true that many relationships have been brought to an end as a result of the anger and suspicion which so often follows the diagnosis. It is useful to point out that a full disclosure of all the secrets at the outset is ultimately less damaging to the relationship than a gradual discovery over a protracted period of time. The relationship may well survive an initial shock when it would founder if more deceit came to light later on.

The consequences of not addressing this issue are really too appalling to contemplate. Individuals who cannot bring themselves to inform their partner may well continue to have unprotected sex, as to do otherwise might arouse suspicion. They will probably not be prepared to admit that they are so doing. The moral dilemma for the GP becomes all the more acute if, as is often the case, they are also looking after the partner or spouse, but at least this has the advantage in giving the doctor more leverage. The most helpful thing would be to offer to inform the partner on the patient's behalf.

Conclusion

Primary health care is being asked to become increasingly involved in sexual health issues, beginning with promoting awareness of asymptomatic STIs and identifying those patients in need of screening. The pressing issues of HIV infection in pregnant women, of steadily rising rates of HIV infection among heterosexuals, and the need to reduce high rates of asymptomatic chlamydia infection require the involvement of primary care if they are to be dealt with effectively. This means that GPs and their nurses will require a more in-depth knowledge of the psychology of sexual health and sexual history taking than traditional education provides them with. At least one member of the primary health care team should be specifically designated and trained to provide information and counselling on STIs. They will find the consultant and health adviser of their local GUM clinic very approachable for advice and support and as a point of contact if an individual patient requires more prolonged or specialised intervention. GUM as a speciality has recognised the importance of working more and more in partnership with primary care. It is hoped that the more relaxed approach towards the discussion of sexual matters which is increasingly evident within our society, and the redefinition of GUM clinics as 'sexual health centres',

will make it easier for patients to access these services.

Acknowledgements

We would like to thank Dr Nick Theobald, specialist in HIV community liaison, Debbie Vowles, Ceri Evans and Kathy Simpson, health advisers, for their helpful comments and for reviewing this chapter.

References

Ainsworth, J.G., Weaver, T., Murphy, S. & Renton, A. (1996) General practitioners' immediate management of men presenting with urethral symptoms. *Genitourinary Medicine* **72**, 427–430.

Barton, S.E. & Roth, P. (1992) Life insurance and HIV antibody testing. *British Medical Journal* **305**, 902–903.

Bleker, O.P. (1996) STD awareness today. *Genitourinary Medicine* **72**, 440–442.

Brown, Z.A., Benedetti, J., Ashley, R., Burchett, S., *et al.* (1991) Neonatal herpes simplex virus infection in relation to asymptomatic maternal infection at the time of labour. *New England Journal of Medicine* **324**, 1247–1252.

Cassidy, L., Meadows, J., Catalan, J. & Barton, S.E. (1997) Are reported stress and coping style associated with frequent recurrences of genital herpes? *Genitourinary Medicine* **73**, 263–266.

CMO (1988) *Chlamydia trachomatis.* Summary and conclusions of CMO's expert advisory group. Department of Health, London.

Corey, L. (1994) The current trend in genital herpes: progress in prevention. *Sexually Transmitted Diseases* **21**, 38–44.

Cowan, F.M., Johnson, A.M., Ashley, R., Corey, L. & Mindel, A. (1994) Antibody to herpes simplex virus type 2 as a serological marker of sexual lifestyles in populations. *British Medical Journal* **21**, S38–S44.

Daniels, D.G., Kell, P., Nelson, M.R. & Barton, S.E. (1992) Sexual behavior amongst travellers. A study of genitourinary medicine clinic attenders. *International Journal of STD and AIDS* **3**, 437–438.

Edwards, A., Atma-Ram, A. & Thin, R.N. (1988) Podophyllotoxin 9.5% v. podophyllin 20% to treat penile warts. *Genitourinary Medicine* **64**, 263–265.

Fitzpatrick, R., Dawson, J., Boulton, M., Mclean, J., Hart, G. & Brookes, M. (1994) Perceptions of general practice among homosexual men. *British Journal of General Practice* **44**, 80–82.

Fox, P.A., Henderson, D.C., Barton, S.E., *et al.* (1999) Immunological markers of frequently recurrent genital herpes simplex virus and their response to hypnotherapy: a pilot study. *International Journal of STD and AIDS* **19**, 730–734.

Gold, R.S. & Skinner, M.J. (1992) Situational factors and thought processes associated with unprotected intercourse in young gay men. *AIDS* **6**, 1021–1030.

Green, J. & Kocsis, A. (1997) Psychological factors in recurrent genital herpes. *Genitourinary Medicine* **73**, 253–258.

Ho, L., Terry, G., Cuzick, J., Wheeler, C. & Singer, A. (1996) Human papillomavirus genotype as a predictor of persistence and development of high grade lesions in women with minor cervical abnormalities. *International Journal of Cancer* **69**, 364–368.

Hope, V.D. & Macarthur, C. (1997) Acceptability of clinics for sexually transmitted diseases among users of the 'gay scene' in the West Midlands. *Genitourinary Medicine* **73**, 299–302.

Johnson, A.M., Wadsworth, J., Wellings, K. & Field, J. (1996a) Who goes to sexually transmitted disease clinics? Results from a national population survey. *Genitourinary Medicine* **72**, 197–202.

Johnson, A.M., Grun, L. & Haines, A. (1996b) Controlling genital chlamydia infection. *British Medical Journal* **313**, 1160–1151.

Kellock, D.J. & Rogstad, K.E. (1998) Attitudes to HIV testing in general practice. *International Journal of STD and AIDS* **9**, 263–367.

Kinghorn, G.R. (1978) Genital warts: incidence of associated genital infections. *British Journal of Dermatology* **99**, 405–409.

Kudesia, G., Zadik, P.M. & Riple, Y. (1993) *Chlamydia trachomatis* infection in males attending general practitioners. *Genitourinary Medicine* **70**, 356.

Madge, S., Mocroft, A., Olaitan, A. & Johnson, M. (1998)

Do women with HIV infection consult their GPs? *British Journal of General Practice* **48**, 1329–1330.

Madge, S. & Singh, S. (1998) The new imperative to test for HIV in pregnancy. *British Journal of General Practice* **48**, 1127–1128.

Mason, D., Kerry, S. & Oakeshott, P. (1996) Postal survey of *Chlamydia trachomatis* infection in English and Welsh general practices. *British Medical Journal* **313**, 1193–1194.

Mulvey, G., Temple-Smith, M.J. & Keogh, L.A. (1997) Sexually transmissible diseases: knowledge and practices of general practitioners in Victoria, Australia. *Genitourinary Medicine* **73**, 533–537.

Nardone, A., Mercey, D.E. & Johnson, A.M. (1997) Surveillance of sexual behavior among homosexual men in a central London health authority. *Genitourinary Medicine* **73**, 198–202.

Nunns, D. & Mandal, D. (1996) The chronically symptomatic vulva: prevalence in primary health care. *Genitourinary Medicine* **72**, 343–344.

Pecoraro, G., Lee, M., Morgan, D. & Defendi, V. (1991) Evolution of in vitro transformation and tumorigenesis of HPV16 and HPV18 immortalised primary cervical epithelial cells. *American Journal of Pathology* **138**, 1–8.

Pritchard, H. & Robinson, A.J. (1998) What evidence is given to patients with a new diagnosis of genital warts? *International Journal of STD and AIDS* **9**, 241–242.

Prober, C.G., Sullender, W.M., Yasukawa, L.L., Au, D.S., Yeager, A.S. & Arvin, A.M. (1987) Low risk of herpes simplex virus infections in neonates exposed to the virus at the time of vaginal delivery. *New England Journal of Medicine* **316**, 240–244.

Ross, J.D.C. & Champion, J. (1998) How are men with urethral discharge managed in general practice? *International Journal of STD and AIDS* **9**, 192–195.

Ross, J.D. & Goldberg, D.J. (1997) Patterns of HIV testing in Scotland: a general practitioner perspective. *Scottish Medical Journal* **42**, 108–110.

Ruiz, J., Facer, M. & Sun, R.K. (1998) Risk factors of HIV infection and unprotected anal intercourse among young men who have sex with men. *Sexually Transmitted Diseases* **25**, 100–102.

Shaw, M., Tomlinson, D. & Higginson, I. (1996) Survey of HIV patients' views on confidentiality and non-discrimination policies in general practice. *British*

Medical Journal **312**, 1463–1464.

Sherr, L., Barnes, J., Elford, J., Olaitan, A., Miller, R. & Johnson, M. (1999) Women with HIV disease attending a London clinic. *Genitourinary Medicine* **73**, 274–279.

Simms, I., Catchpole, M., Brugha, R., Rogers, P., Mallinson, H., & Nicoll, A. (1997) Epidemiology of genital *Chlamydia trachomatis* in England and Wales. *Genitourinary Medicine* **73**, 122–126.

Skinner, C.J., Stokes, J., Kirlew, Y., Kavanagh, J. & Forster, G.E. (1996) A case controlled study of the sexual health needs of lesbians. *Genitourinary Medicine* **72**, 277–280.

Tait, I.A., Duthie, S.J. & Taylor-Robinson, D. (1997) Silent upper genital chlamydial infection and disease in women. *International Journal of STD and AIDS* **8**, 329–331.

Wenrick, M.D., Curtis, J.R., Carline, J.D., Paauw, D.S. & Ramsey, P.G. (1997) HIV risk screening in the primary care setting. Assessment of physicians' skills. *Journal of General Internal Medicine* **12**, 107–113.

Westrom, L., Joesoef, R., Reynolds, G., Hagdu, A. & Sumner, E.T. (1992) Pelvic inflammatory disease and infertility. *Sexually Transmitted Diseases* **19**, 185–191.

Chapter 16

Personality Disorder and Sexual Health

Peter Scragg and Ron Alcorn

Introduction

Sexual health problems are greatly influenced by a patient's personality. Take for example two patients presenting with the same sexually transmitted disease. An obsessional patient may experience the illness in a very different way to a dramatic impulsive patient. They both may respond differently to standard advice and treatment; the obsessional patient may anxiously question every word of the clinician, following the treatment schedule to the letter, whereas the dramatic impulsive person may demand an unrealistic cure, throwing away the tablets angrily at the first hint of unwanted side effects.

The skilful clinician will find the right approach with each of these patients to avoid conflict and maximise the effectiveness of the treatment. This will be done without recourse to a great deal of formal analysis of personality factors. It is usually only the extremes of personality styles or repetitive problematic behaviour patterns in patients that cause us to stop and reflect on this issue. Extreme personality styles can lead to such maladaptive behaviour that the term 'personality disorder' is applied. In this chapter we aim to guide clinicians through this complex and controversial area.

Definition of the problem

Modern classification systems for psychological and psychiatric problems use more than one factor, or descriptor, in an attempt to capture more fully the multiple influences on a person's clinical presentation. It is not enough to say that someone is anxious or depressed. We need to understand the 'soil' in which such a problem takes hold and the 'climate' which will affect how it develops. The 'soil' in this analogy involves personality traits and developmental factors, and the 'climate' encompasses the current stresses in the person's internal and external environments (physical and social problems). *Personality traits* can be defined as 'enduring dimensions of individual differences in tendencies to show consistent patterns of thoughts, feelings and actions' (McCrae & Costa 1990, p. 23). Mischel and Shoda (1995) suggest that personality should be conceptualised as a stable system that mediates how the individual selects, construes and processes social information. Personality is distinguished from moods and emotional states which are transient.

What are personality disorders?

Personality *traits* become a personality *disorder* when they are found to be inflexible, maladaptive and cause significant impairment in social and occupational functioning (DSM-IV; American Psychiatric Association 1994). The diagnosis of personality disorder is made when an adult shows long-standing and pervasive impairments in their ability to work and cooperate with others (Cloninger *et al.* 1997). This negative impact on others is crucial to the diagnosis of personality disorder (Tyrer *et al.* 1993). However, it should not detract from the fact that patients with personality disorders usually have extremely poor self-esteem, a limited repertoire of life or coping skills and experience a great deal of emotional pain.

To make a diagnosis of personality disorder Cloninger *et al.* (1997) suggest that three dimensions of character will be quantifiably different in a personality disordered person as compared with a non-disordered person. The three dimensions are: self-directedness, cooperativeness and self-transcendence. On the first character dimension, self-directedness, personality disordered individuals would score low, as this dimension is concerned with accepting responsibility for control of one's goals and habits rather than blaming other

people or circumstances. Thus the personality disordered individual will show a blaming attitude, will have few goals, will appear to be helpless and lacking in resources and have poor self-esteem. On Cloninger *et al.'s* second dimension of character, cooperativeness, individuals with personality disorder will show low cooperativeness as indicated by being intolerant of others, lacking empathy, unhelpful, revengeful and unprincipled. Finally, Cloninger *et al.'s* last dimension of character, self-transcendence, refers to the extent to which a person feels like an integral part of the universe. Individuals high on this dimension are faithful, spiritual and idealistic, but are not self-absorbed (Cloninger *et al.* 1997). This last dimension does not seem as important in distinguishing personality disorder as self-directedness and cooperativeness.

DSM-IV (APA 1994) takes a *categorical* approach and ten categories, or personality disorders, are listed (plus two for further study in the appendix of the DSM-IV). These ten personality disorders are grouped into three clusters: Cluster A known as the odd or eccentric group (schizoid, schizotypal, paranoid); Cluster B known as the dramatic or erratic (borderline, antisocial, narcissistic, histrionic); and Cluster C known as the anxious and fearful cluster (avoidant, obsessive–compulsive and dependent). In research trials (or when clinicians use structured interviews) personality disordered patients typically meet the diagnostic criteria for more than one personality disorder. Dolan *et al.* (1995) suggest that when an individual has a number of personality disorder diagnoses this can be taken as a crude but useful measure of the range of psychopathology. They predict that the level of multiple diagnoses of personality disorder will be higher in settings that have more disturbed patients.

The problem of individuals meeting criteria for several personality disorders is one reason why some workers favour a dimensional or psychometric description of personality and personality problems. The five factor model is a well researched example of this approach (see Costa & Widiger 1993). Despite the strong psychometric arguments in favour of dimensional models of personality, they are not as popular in clinical practice probably because it is easier to communicate about patients in categorical form than discuss numerous dimensions. Therefore, for all their problems, the DSM-IV and ICD-10 personality taxonomies, which were founded in clinical observations, often prove more useful in understanding patients and predicting their responses to treatments.

Although a diagnostic label often provides for quick communication, for the purpose of clinical management description of the individual's main personality features is important (e.g. this patient has problems in the areas of). Then, in designing a treatment package the clinician should also know what conditions will trigger or modify these personality features.

In this chapter we will focus on Cluster B rather than Cluster A or Cluster C personality disorders. The reason for this selection is that individuals with this range of problems are more likely to present management problems for staff in sexual health services. However, this selective focus is not intended to imply that individuals with other types of personality disorders will not have psychological needs that affect their sexual health.*

Extent and nature of problem

Prevalence of personality disorders

Epidemiological studies show that the prevalence of personality disorder in the general population is between 10 and 13% (Weissman 1993). Casey and Tyrer (1986) examined the prevalence of personality disorder in an adult urban UK population using a structured interview and found a rate of 13%. Six of the personality disorders (i.e. paranoid, schizoid, schizotypal, antisocial, narcissistic and obsessive–compulsive) are more commonly diagnosed in males whereas three (i.e. dependent, histrionic and borderline) are more commonly diagnosed in females (DSM-IV: APA 1994).

Due to the fact that assessment of personality pathology is not made in routine clinical work, UK government figures of personality disorder (approximately 5%) almost certainly underestimate the prevalence of personality disorder (Hassiotis *et al.* 1997). Almost 50% of patients consulting psychiatrists meet criteria for personality disorder when it is formally assessed and 30% of primary care patients with conspicuous psychiatric morbidity meet the criteria for personality disorder (Casey *et al.* 1984).

Only a small number of studies provide data relevant to the prevalence of personality disorders in sexual health service settings. Descriptive studies from early liaison psychiatry involvement in venereal disease units highlighted the prevalence of personality disorders

---

*There is some statistical evidence that there are four natural clusters, not three, the fourth consisting of obsessional characteristics (see Tyrer *et al.* 1997).

in the range of problems referred (Bhanji & Mahony 1978). Most of the studies that use modern classification systems however have been carried out in HIV diagnosis and treatment centres with the exception of a study by Foster and O'Gorman (1995). They examined the rate of personality disorder amongst 50 patients attending an outpatient psychosexual services (for sexual dysfunction) and found that 38% met criteria for personality disorder. Ellis *et al.* (1995) recruited 61 homosexual and 57 heterosexual males, contacted through a genitourinary clinic, for a study on personality disorder and sexual risk taking. The subjects were either HIV negative or were unaware of their HIV status. They found a prevalence rate of personality disorder (assessed by structured interview) of 38% for the homosexual men and 28% for the heterosexual men.[†]

Perkins *et al.* (1993) found that there was a significantly higher prevalence of personality disorder in HIV-positive subjects (33%) than in their HIV-negative subjects (15%). All subjects in this study were gay men. Jacobsberg *et al.* (1995) reported on the prevalence of personality disorder (measured with a structured interview) among 220 volunteers who were seeking an HIV antibody test. A total of 18.6% of the subjects were subsequently found to be HIV positive and of these 37% met criteria for a personality disorder. The subjects who tested negative for HIV had a significantly lower rate of personality disorder: 20%. The HIV positive subjects differed from the HIV negative subjects in more frequently fitting the

dramatic/erratic personality cluster. When Axis I disorders were controlled for in the statistical analysis, borderline personality disorder (BPD) was more prevalent in the HIV positive than the HIV negative group. The fact that the presence of personality disorder was established in this study prior to the subject knowing their HIV status suggests an association between personality disorder and HIV risk (Jacobsberg *et al.* 1995).

With the exception of a study by Johnson *et al.* (1995), all studies examining the prevalence of personality disorder in HIV subjects have found that the rate is significantly higher than that found in HIV negative subjects (Golding & Perkins 1996). However it should be noted that the number of studies examining this question is limited to a handful and numbers of subjects are relatively small.[‡]

Personality disorders as predictors of psychiatric problems

Individuals with personality disorders have been shown to have poorer treatment outcome for a range of psychiatric syndromes (or Axis I disorders) (Reich & Green 1991). Furthermore, personality disordered individuals have also been shown to have a greater chance of developing an Axis I disorders. Quinton

---

[†]Possible sex bias in the diagnosis of personality disorder has been recently discussed by Widiger (1998).

[‡]Golding and Perkins (1996) suggest that the reason for Johnson *et al.*'s (1995) non-confirmation of a higher rate of personality disorder in HIV positive subjects compared with HIV negative subjects may be due to the fact that participants were recruited from an area with a very high rate of HIV infection. Furthermore their HIV status was known at the time of psychiatric examination.

et al. (1995) carried out a follow-up study of psychiatric patients 15–20 years after initial data was collected. Personality disorder predicted episodic psychiatric illness and was a particularly strong predictor of recurrent depression. Personality disorder predicted much poorer outcome on measures of role impairment. The course for those classified in the personality categories characterized by passive, avoidant or inadequate role functioning had a particularly poor outcome with all the individuals in this group showing pervasively poor social functioning at follow-up. The outcome for those individuals falling into the 'dramatic/erratic' personality disorder category was more varied. Half of this group showed poor functioning and 14% were rated as 'well' or 'predominantly well' on overall outcome. Quinton *et al.* (1995) note that personality problems in this cluster may be attenuated with age. Alnaes and Torgersen (1997) demonstrated that personality disorder predicted development and relapse of major depression whereas other co-morbid Axis I disorders appeared to be of no importance.

Personality pathology has been found to predict adjustment in non-clinical populations. For example, a recent study by Trull *et al.* (1997) provided 2-year follow-up data on young adults who scored 2 standard deviations above community norms on the Borderline Features Scale of the Personality Assessment Inventory, a psychometrically sound test of abnormal personality (Morey 1991). They found that individuals with borderline personality features were more likely to have academic difficulties over the succeeding two years. These individuals were also more likely to meet lifetime criteria for a mood disorder and experience more interpersonal dysfunc-

tion than their peers at the 2-year follow-up assessment.

In the context of sexual health a few recent studies have examined how personality pathology relates to Axis I disorders in HIV positive patients. Perkins *et al.* (1993) found the HIV positive subjects (all gay men) who met criteria for a personality disorder showed significantly greater mood and anxiety disturbances. This study also examined how individuals coped with being HIV positive. Individuals with a personality disorder showed significantly greater use of denial and a helpless coping style than subjects who did not have a personality disorder. Finally Perkins *et al.* (1993) reported that subjects with a personality disorder reported significantly more social conflict than the non-personality disordered subjects. Personality disorder was unrelated to the number of social supports or satisfaction with social support.

Johnson *et al.* (1995) found that HIV-positive subjects who had a personality disorder reported higher levels of psychiatric symptoms and poorer functioning than all participants without personality disorder. HIV-positive subjects were over six times as likely as the HIV negative participants without personality disorder to have a current Axis I disorder. Johnson *et al.* (1995) concluded that HIV infection and personality disorder may interactively increase the likelihood of clinically significant psychiatric symptoms. In a later paper Johnson *et al.* (1996) reported a logistic regression analysis that showed that personality disorder predicted onset of Axis I disorder, after controlling for HIV status and lifetime Axis I history. Cluster B personality disorders, rather than cluster A or C, were shown to be predictive of significant psychiatric symptoms.

Patients with personality disorder have a small but consistent tendency to complain more of physical health problems (Cloninger *et al.* 1997). This tendency often reflects mental processes (e.g. hypochondriasis) rather than actual health problems. Ellis *et al.* (1995) found that homosexual men with personality disorder tended to be frequent GUM clinic attendees. This was not observed for heterosexual men.

All this suggests that patients with personality disorders will be prone to multiple problems in their day-to-day life, difficulties in relating to clinical staff and emotional distress. These problems may well affect medical interventions and the way an individual manages illness. Interventions required for chronic or recurrent conditions, many with uncertain outcome such as genital herpes and HIV infection, may be particularly affected. These disorders require individuals to maintain long-term relationships with clinical teams, comply with difficult medication regimes and tolerate side effects. Even more crucially, people are called upon to adapt to new social, occupational and sexual realities. Individuals with personality disorder will find these changes challenging. Clinicians working in these settings may find the individual's difficulties with adaptation and cooperation similarly challenging.

Personality, personality disorder and the risk of sexually transmitted disease

When considering how personality may affect sexual and other risk-taking behaviours it is important to recognise that the expression and impact of personality factors can be constrained by social, educational and economic factors. The degree to which personality factors and personality disorder predict or relate to outcomes will vary across settings and populations. For example, one would not expect personality to be related to use of condoms in a population with restricted access to information about safer sex. However, in a population with access to condoms and knowledgeable about safer sex it can be predicted that personality would be a significant factor in the variance associated with consistent use of condoms.

A limited number of studies have examined how personality may influence safer sexual practices (for a review, see Pinkerton & Abramson 1995), although for many years it has been known that extroversion and sensation seeking is related to the desire for a greater number of partners. The correlation between sensation seeking and number of sexual activities and partners was recently confirmed in a gay male population (Schroth 1996). However, Schroth (1996) found no relationship between sensation seeking and unsafe sexual behaviour in his well-educated gay sample.

Sensation seeking and impulsivity are not the same thing although they are related (Zuckerman 1993). Thus mountain climbers are generally high sensation seekers but they are not impulsive in their climbing, planning carefully and checking their gear and conditions. According to Zuckerman (1993) the trait of impulsivity is primarily a failure of inhibition and anticipation of negative consequences. It would be surprising if impulsivity were not related to difficulties with safer sex and risky behaviour. Seal and Agostinelli (1994) used a questionnaire measure of personality and showed that impulsivity did correlate with unprotected sexual intercourse.

Impulsivity is an important feature of both antisocial personality disorder (APD) and borderline personality disorder (BPD).

Hull *et al.* (1993) found that 46% of women with BPD in their sample reported having entered impulsively into at least one sexual relationship with a partner they did not know well. Compared with the sample who did not have a history of impulsive sexual behaviour, these women were more likely to have problems with impulsivity in general. Personality testing showed that the patients with BPD who had impulsive sexual relationships were more extrovert and suffered less anxiety than the BPD patients who did not have this sexual history. The patients with a history of impulsive sexual behaviour were more likely to also meet the criteria for Histrionic Personality Disorder than the rest of the sample.

Ellis *et al.* (1995) investigated whether personality disorder placed sexually active men at risk for HIV infection. Failure to use a condom when having penetrative sexual intercourse with casual partners was associated with a diagnosis of personality disorder for both homosexual and heterosexual men. Multiple regression analysis indicated that APD was the main predictor of sexual risk-taking for the homosexually active men. For the heterosexually active men sexual risk-taking was predicted by both cocaine use and APD.

Brooner *et al.* (1993) examined the rate of HIV infection and APD in 272 intravenous drug users. Forty-four percent of the subjects met criteria for APD. Subjects with APD had a significantly higher rate of HIV infection than those without APD (18% vs 8%). This finding was not accounted for by ethnicity, gender or drug treatment. Brooner *et al.* noted that the finding of a relationship between a personality disorder and HIV infection is striking given that intravenous drug abusers, as a whole, have high HIV risk.

The diagnosis of APD is confounded in populations of substance misusers as many substances are illegal and antisocial behaviours are commonly adaptive features of this lifestyle. The *psychopathic personality* with its greater emphasis on personality style rather than criminal or antisocial behaviours was found by Tourian *et al.* (1997) to be more consistently related to HIV risk behaviour in methadone-maintenance patients than the DSM-IV diagnosis of APD. This is an important finding as it refines which aspects of antisociality are most important in HIV risk behaviour.

Borderline personality disorder and antisocial personality disorder

Individuals with BPD or APD more frequently present clinical challenges in sexual health service settings than the other personality disorders.

DSM-IV defines the central features of BPD as 'a pervasive pattern of instability of interpersonal relationships, self-image and affects, and marked impulsivity beginning in early adulthood and present in a variety of contexts'. Specific criteria are described in the DSM-IV which centre around impulsivity, mood instability, odd cognition (transient, stress related paranoid ideation or severe dissociative symptoms), and problematic interpersonal relationships.

Patients with BPD very often present in crisis on a background of repeated crises (the 'stable unstable person'). These presentations are often associated with very intense affect (often anger), which seems completely out of proportion to the event that they report to be troubling them. Often they will present following self-harm (e.g. wrist-cutting) or with suicidal ideation. The intention or motivation behind self-harming behaviour in BPD is commonly relief from emotional pain and there may not be an intention to die. Self-harming tends to be a chronic problem. Although the BPD patient discloses symptoms that suggest clinical depression there is usually a qualitatively different flavour to the depression as compared with patients with clinical depression. The 'depression' of BPD is characterised by emptiness, loneliness and a labile diffuse negative affectivity whereas patients with clinical depression will commonly evidence feelings of worthlessness and excessive guilt (Western *et al*. 1992). BPD patients have a strong effect on others. Millon (1987) writes 'both relatives and acquaintances feel "on edge" waiting for these patients to display a sullen and hurt look or become obstinate and nasty' (p. 356). Dramatic swings in relationships from someone being idealised to being devalued (often very quickly) are common.

Patients who have BPD present with very diverse problems and it is often this that can alert the clinician to the diagnosis. Bulimia, depression, substance misuse and varying interpersonal problems may alternate. There can be considerable overlap in the presentation of patients with post-traumatic stress disorder and BPD as both can present as desperate, impulsive, self-destructive and angry (Gunderson & Sabo 1993). Since a history of trauma (especially childhood abuse) is often found in BPD the clinician may have difficulty separating this condition from post-traumatic stress

disorder. Some patients may of course have both conditions.

APD is described in the DSM-IV as 'a pervasive pattern of disregard for and violation of the rights of others occurring since the age of 15 years'. Specific criteria are given in the DSM-IV and include unlawful behaviour, deceitfulness, impulsivity, aggressiveness and evidence of conduct disorder before age 15. Patients with APD proclaim that others are the source of their problems. They are non-conforming and act as they see fit regardless of how others judge them (Millon & Davis 1996).

In making an assessment of APD, the emphasis on the longitudinal nature of the problem should prompt evaluation of whether the DSM-IV criteria of childhood conduct disorder are satisfied. For example, while taking a history the patient can be asked, 'As a child did you get into many fights?' (Zimmerman 1994). This can be followed up with questions probing for whether the fighting was more serious than that normally seen in children and adolescents. The patient may be asked if he used weapons or if as a teenager he ever threatened anyone for money. Persistent truancy, early substance misuse and problems with a range of authority figures often feature in the history. The clinician should inquire about the patient's forensic history in order to ascertain if adult antisocial behaviour is present. It can be useful to ask the patient if it is easy for him to lie or hurt others. Perhaps surprisingly, some individuals will admit to such behaviours if asked. Concern for others in a range of scenarios is often limited or absent. Impulsivity can be examined by questions such as 'How often have you just walked off a job? or out of a relationship?' (Zimmerman 1994).

Developmental factors

Temperament in children and personality traits have a significant hereditary basis. However, there is also evidence from patients with personality disorders that childhood neglect and forms of abuse are important antecedents to personality problems (Herman *et al.* 1989; Luntz & Widom 1994). Modestin *et al.* (1998) studied the relationship between childhood traumatic experiences and parental attitudes as perceived retrospectively by patients with a range of personality disorder diagnoses. Their results showed that childhood traumatic experiences had an association with personality disorders from Cluster B (particularly BPD) and Cluster A (particularly Paranoid Personality Disorder). In Cluster C, only Dependent Personality Disorder seemed to be associated with childhood trauma. Interestingly Modestin *et al.* (1998) found differences between the sexes as to which aspects of childhood experience showed an association with personality disorder. In men, the paternal relationships (high control and low care) were related to personality disorder, whereas in women the relationship was with physical and sexual abuse.

Individuals with personality disorders can be conceived as having entrenched *overdeveloped* and *underdeveloped* interpersonal behaviour patterns. Cognitive therapy views the overdeveloped behaviours as *compensatory strategies* and the underdeveloped behaviours as *missing life skills* (Layden 1997). The overdeveloped behaviours are learned in childhood as strategies or coping skills, often in the context of abuse or other psychologically impossible situations. As Layden (1997) notes, these strategies are adaptive or *work* (at least

on occasions) and thus are reinforced. Unfortunately for the child who grows up to fulfil the criteria for personality disorder, living in such an abusive family or intolerable situation may result in not developing other strategies or having other compensatory life experiences. The environment deprives them of opportunities to see or try other strategies. New behaviours the child might attempt (that in later years could prove more adaptive) are not reinforced in abusive households where the family environment is full of threat or perverse incentives.

A common skill missing for patients with personality disorders is *judgment* of who to trust and who not to trust. For example, patients with BPD frequently appear to have a deficit in the capacity to judge which acquaintances or partners may turn out later to be abusive. They are blind to the cues or clues. This can usefully be viewed as a failure in learning. The clinician may hear a patient describe some new person they have met and picture the difficulties or hazards immediately. The patient, however, is missing the skills for reading cues or giving them meaning.

People tend to be attracted to the familiar and often select partners and friends who share characteristics of their parents. Cognitive therapy explains this observation with the concept of *schema maintenance*. It is posited that individuals find themselves seeking situations that confirm important schema and avoid situations that could disconfirm important schema (see Young 1994). Tacit schemas can lead an individual to know 'rationally' that a certain person is 'bad news' but, like an old pair of shoes, they feel right and they still fit even if they are so worn as to be causing back problems. The combination of schema maintenance processes and missing life skills described above can help clinicians understand how it is that personality disordered individuals continue to engage in such destructive behaviours. If the clinician can hold these notions in mind they may feel less frustrated and more flexible in the way they approach interactions with these patients.

What do patients tell us and key questions to ask

Patients rarely come into a consultation saying they need help with their personality problems. Nevertheless, patients do say things and behave in certain ways that raise this possibility. Cloninger *et al.* (1997) provide the following advice on recognising personality disorder. Firstly, individuals who impress others as irrational or highly emotional (interactions dominated by unregulated basic emotions of fear, anger and disgust) have a high likelihood of meeting criteria for a diagnosis of personality disorder. Secondly, a history of suicide attempts or psychiatric hospitalisation should prompt the clinician to review the individual's development and predominant personality style. Thirdly, individuals with a personality disorder often blame other people and external circumstances for their problems. They may say, for example, 'I'm always being used'.

Evidence from outside the clinician's consulting room is usually essential for establishing if the individual can be diagnosed as personality disordered. It is useful for the clinician to know whether other people find the patient uncooperative, difficult or blaming. Clearly, if such problems only arise with one clinician it is likely to be situationally governed. Past hospital notes, reactions of other staff, the experience of the individual's general practitioner or family and friends often clarify to what degree the patient's difficulties are persistent across a range of settings. It is equally important to establish that these features reflect life-long personality traits and are not recent developments.

Other factors that can confuse the appearance of personality problems include the effects of drugs or alcohol, the effects of medications, brain disorders (such as an emerging dementia) or other undiagnosed psychiatric problems such as long-standing depression. Comprehensive assessment, information from others and the longitudinal view are crucial in working through these possibilities. In this way personality disorder is most safely seen as a diagnosis of exclusion. However, reluctance to consider personality disorder may result in under-diagnosis, a phenomenon observed in many clinical settings.

A strong 'reaction' to a person may also be a clue to the problem of personality disorder. Here the clinician uses the information from their own emotions and responses to intervene sensitively and strategically. The clinician may feel himself or herself slipping into modes of behaviour that are uncharacteristic or 'against his or her better judgment'. Common amongst these is the urge to rescue, to respond back to the patient in an angry way, to proceed clinically in a way that he or she would not normally do (such as ordering more and more investigations or promising things one can't ultimately deliver) or to loosen his or her boundaries in the clinical sphere. These behaviours may unwittingly play into scenarios that confirm the patient's world view or maladaptive schema. They may also be experienced by the patient as intrusive, 'abusive' or rejecting. The principle that 'less may be more' is often important, especially for the inexperienced clinician. This is particularly so in dealing with BPD where one is tempted to try and solve the terrible range of presenting problems and pain. The risk of over-hospitalisation, over-investigation and personal over-involvement are well-known hazards.

Models of intervention

Personality disordered individuals as sexual health patients

In view of the paucity of controlled treatment trials in the field of personality disorder, the rest of this chapter is devoted to psychological principles and clinical observations that should help make consultations with individuals with personality disorders more successful.

A central tenet of interpersonal theory (Kiesler 1983) is that certain behaviours draw or elicit certain restricted classes of behaviour from others. Hence a patient will engage in behaviours that unwittingly provoke certain responses from the clinician. Interpersonal theory provides both a classification of personality and interpersonal transactions.

Interpersonal theory posits a geometric model where interpersonal behaviours form a circular order around two dimensions of power and affiliation (Leary 1957). The power dimension runs from dominance-to-submission and the affiliation dimension from hostile/cold-to-warm/friendly. Interpersonal behaviours form a circumplex around these dimensions. An individual's interpersonal behaviour may be plotted on the circumplex.

Someone with a dependent personality would fall at the submissive end of the power dimension and at the friendly end of the affiliative dimension. In contrast antisocial personality would consist of interpersonal behaviour that would be located at the dominant end of the power dimension and at the cold/hostile end of the affiliative dimension.

An individual's positions on the two interpersonal dimensions predict which behaviours will be elicited in others, including clinicians. For the power dimension interpersonal behaviour at one end will draw the opposite: dominant behaviour will provoke the other person to act submissively and submissive behaviour will elicit dominance. For the affiliation dimension interpersonal behaviour at one end of the dimension will draw similar behaviour: friendly behaviour will elicit friendly behaviour and hostile behaviour will provoke the other to be hostile. Returning to the examples above, a person who is dependent in personality (predicted to have interpersonal behaviours of both submission and friendliness), will elicit from the clinician friendly–dominant behaviour, whereas the individual whose interpersonal behaviour is dominant and hostile (antisocial personality) will likely provoke the clinician to exhibit (unwittingly) hostile–submissive behaviour.

By definition individuals with personality disorders exhibit relatively rigid interpersonal behaviour: they tend to exhibit behaviours from the same end of the interpersonal dimensions across different situations. Hence a 'difficult' patient (hostile–dominant interpersonal behaviour) may alienate a great many health care workers. The clinicians drawn into hostile–submissive interpersonal behaviour will likely be unable to provide effective counsel and care to the sexual health patient. For example, advice on sexual behaviour or anti-viral therapy from the clinician who is provoked into a hostile–submissive pattern will either not be attempted (the clinician may feel there is no point) or will be delivered in a manner that is unlikely to be accepted.

Understanding that a patient has a personality disorder should help the clinician predict what behaviours will be elicited. Thus if the patient is hostile–dominant the clinician will need to acknowledge to himself that he is likely to respond in a submissive–hostile manner, which would perpetuate the interpersonal dynamic. Clinicians must try to step outside this vicious cycle to provide effective counsel.

Cognitive therapy can also help a clinician understand the behaviour of personality disordered individuals. Beck *et al.* (1990) show that each of the personality disorders has a typical profile of beliefs and attitudes. For example, dependent personalities have a strong belief that they are helpless. Specific behavioural strategies follow logically from the characteristic belief. Thus the person who believes they are helpless seeks attachments. The person who believes that he will be rejected unless he is entertaining will be typically overly dramatic. These characteristic attitudes, according to the cognitive therapy view of psychopathology, are maintained by biased information processing. Interpersonal behaviour driven by strongly held attitudes will often result in actions that confirm the attitude. For example, the patient who believes he must be on guard will likely alienate others – perhaps the doctor – who in turn will try to steer clear or become defensive, thus confirming the need to be on guard.

Beck *et al.'s* work can be extremely helpful. If a clinician can ascertain the patient's personality disorder or type he or she will have a fair idea of the likely beliefs and attitude his or her patient holds including the attitude toward health care workers. The patient with a dependent personality is likely to be highly cooperative but will be made uncomfortable if attempts are made to force him or her to make decisions. Hence a dependent personality in treatment for HIV infection is likely to be made very anxious if asked to contribute to the decision-making of their treatment. The obsessive–compulsive personality who typically believes that details are important and that other people are too casual will be uncomfortable with clinicians who are informal. These patients will in all likelihood find decision-making difficult not because they see themselves as helpless but because they must leave no stone unturned in reaching a decision.

Anecdotal and unconfirmed experiences

Clinicians' experiences in dealing with clients with personality problems in sexual health settings highlight a number of common problems. Some problems can be predicted by an accurate diagnosis and review of the experiences of other people who have been involved with the patient. However, even the most skilled clinicians can encounter difficulties and need to know when to step back from the situation, take stock or ask for help.

Interventions by clinicians should be guided by an informed optimism. People with severe personality difficulties can and do change. There is no place for therapeutic nihilism.

However the clinician must be realistic; first, about the time frame of change (which is often over years, not weeks) and second, about the skills and setting required to undertake that work. Problems often arise when the patient is offered something that the clinician cannot realistically deliver. This can be something seemingly as simple as offering appointments or access to the clinician out of normal hours with the impression that this could be the norm. Something offered in good faith may then repeatedly be expected or abused. The concept of *boundaries* is therefore critical from the outset. Holding to these boundaries may appear punitive or withholding but can lessen the possibility of encouraging a false reality for the client.

Clinicians also need to be aware of the possibility of *splitting*. This is conceived of as a defensive move by the patient to enable them to cope with primitive anxieties. One of the most common scenarios is the inability of the patient with a personality disorder to *hold* psychologically or manage the ambivalence they feel towards a person or an organisation. The reality is that all clinicians have failings and faults and will ultimately disappoint some patients in some way. In order to ward off this reality the patient with a personality disorder may either see the clinician as all good or as all bad at different times. They may use different persons in the clinic, or indeed different clinics, to fulfil these *roles*. This is frequently an unconscious defence mechanism. It may also be used consciously by a patient who is attempting to gain power or privilege or wishes to punish a clinician or clinic. The chaos and confusion *splitting* can cause in a team can be observed when clinicians forcefully assert that the patient is misunderstood and needs much

more help (these may be the clinicians who have been exposed to the patient's idealisation) whereas other team members take the opposite view and are outraged about how manipulative the patient is being (these may be the clinicians who have been treated as 'all bad' by the patient). Adequate communication channels to enable clinicians to see and assess what is happening are vital. Breakdowns in well established networks and normal practice over an individual client need to 'set alarm bells ringing' and be carefully reviewed.

The organisation of STD and HIV clinics in some countries such as the UK are particularly prone to these problems. In the UK STD clinics are open access and anonymous. These features have their roots in highly admirable and practical concerns for the clients. However for the more chaotic patient with a personality disorder these organisational features are ideal for such things as: playing one clinic off against another; idealising one and denigrating the other; moving clinics when issues are starting to be confronted; and complicating treatment efforts with differing advice, investigations and interventions. These can have very serious ramifications for a person's medical or psychological management. Similarly staff at these centres can respond to difficulties with a particular patient by referring on inappropriately rather than working through issues or indeed discharging a client when this would be the more appropriate response.

Psychological terms such as *holding* (managing this range of psychological issues in a safe and consistent way) and *containment* (the keeping to therapeutic boundaries for therapeutic ends) have been coined and are highly relevant to the often very difficult and skilful task of managing patients with personality disorders. The value of a mature clinician who is consistent and does not respond inappropriately to seductive or hostile or varying presentations of the patient is inestimable.

If a clinician is having doubts over his or her work with a patient and personality pathology appears to be a factor, we recommend that the clinician seek guidance from a colleague and stick to what we will call the *here and now* (i.e. a focus on current psycho-social factors). Unstructured exploration of traumatic early experiences or psychological pain can easily overwhelm patients with personality disorder, causing an increase in disturbance.

The *here and now* approach does not dismiss these issues or deny their importance. The clinician must acknowledge these issues and their importance but orient the patient to what immediate and practical steps might be helpful. Patients with personality disorders often present at times of crisis or loss when they do not have the practical or psychological resources to cope with the additional anxiety or pain that an exploratory approach may generate. A structured *problem solving* approach is preferable in these circumstances, with therapy directed at uncovering trauma and ingrained conflicts being reserved for another time or setting. The *problem solving* approach will emphasise and *recruit* the more integrated, skilful parts of the patient's behavioural repertoire and enlist appropriate supports in the environment.

Safety is also a prime consideration in dealing with clients with antisocial or dramatic personality disorders. A few practical steps can help minimise risk of episodes of real or threatened self-harm or harm to others. Firstly, establish a list or *map* of the patient's network of supports, carers or involved professionals at the outset of treatment. This may include the GP, the probation officer or social worker, family members or local psychiatric services. This information will be critical for a coordinated response to a threat or incident of risk to self or others. Secondly, limits of confidentiality should be explained at the start of treatment or therapy with clear rules on what action the clinician will take if the person's behaviour becomes a risk to themselves or others. Thirdly, the clinician should ensure that an assessment of past risky behaviours is made including various types of impulsivity, deliberate self-harm, suicide attempts (and sequelae of these), forensic involvement and past efforts at help. The assessment should cover the prior context of risky behaviour including whether the individual was at the time in therapy or treatment. If the past dangerous or risky behaviour occurred in the context of therapy an assessment of what aspects of that intervention were problematic or useful will be helpful in treatment planning. Lastly, the clinician should think about the safety of the treatment setting. It would be unwise for example to be scheduling sessions with a client with a personality disorder at times when few people are around. Clinicians should be aware of need for a chaperone for physical examinations and that touch, however well meaning, may be easily misinterpreted by some clients.

References

Alnaes, R. & Torgersen, A.R. (1997) Personality and personality disorder predicts development and relapse of major depression. *Acta Psychiatrica Scandinavica* **95**, 336–342.
American Psychiatric Association (1994) *Diagnostic and*

Statistical Manual of Mental Disorders (DSM-IV). American Psychiatric Association, Washington, DC.

Beck, A.T., Freeman, A. & Associates (1990) *Cognitive Therapy of Personality Disorders*. Guilford Press, New York.

Bhanji, S. & Mahony, J. (1978) The value of a psychiatric service within the venereal disease clinic. *British Journal of Venereal Diseases* **54**(4), 266–288.

Brooner, R.K., Greenfield, L., Schmidt, C.W. & Bigelow, G.E. (1993) APD and HIV infection among intravenous drug abusers. *American Journal of Psychiatry* **150**, 53–58.

Casey, P.R. & Tyrer, P.J. (1986) Personality, functioning and symptomatology. *Journal of Psychiatric Research* **20**, 363–374.

Casey, P.R., Dillon, S. & Tyrer, P.J. (1984) The diagnostic status of patients with conspicuous psychiatric morbidity in primary care. *Psychological Medicine* **14**, 673–681.

Costa, P.T. & Widiger, T. (eds) (1993) *Personality Disorder and the Five-Factor Model of Personality*. American Psychological Association, Washington, DC.

Cloninger, C.R., Svrakic, D.M., Bayon, C. & Prezybeck, T.R. (1997) Personality disorders. In: *Washington University Adult Psychiatry* (ed. S.B. Guze), pp. 301–317. Mosby, London.

Dolan, B, Evans, C. & Norton, K. (1995) Multiple Axis II diagnosis of personality disorder. *British Journal of Psychiatry* **166**, 107–112.

Ellis, D. Collins, I. & King, M. (1995) Personality disorder and sexual risk taking among homosexually active and heterosexually active men attending a genito-urinary medicine clinic. *Journal of Psychosomatic Research* **39**(7), 901–910.

Foster, T. & O'Gorman, E. (1995) Prevalence of ICD-b personality disorder in a psychosexual outpatient population. *Sexual and Marital Therapy* **10**(1), 31–38.

Golding, M. & Perkins, D.O. (1996) Personality disorder in HIV infection. *International Review of Psychiatry* **8**, 253–258.

Gunderson, J.G. & Sabo, A.N. (1993) The phenomenological and conceptual interface between BPD and PTSD. *American Journal of Psychiatry* **150**(1), 19–27.

Hassiotis, A., Tyrer, P. & Cicchetti, D. (1997) Detection of personality disorder by a community mental health team: a study of diagnostic accuracy. *Irish Journal of Psychological Medicine* **14**(3), 88–91.

Herman, J.L., Perry, J.C. & van der Kolk, B.A. (1989) Childhood trauma in BPD. *American Journal of Psychiatry* **146**, 490–495.

Hull, J.W., Clarkin, J.F. & Yeomans, F. (1993) BPD and impulsive sexual behaviour. *Hospital and Community Psychiatry* **44**(10), 1000–1002.

Jacobsberg, L., Frances, A. & Perry, S. (1995) Axis II diagnosis among volunteers for HIV testing and counseling. *American Journal of Psychiatry* **152**, 1222–1224.

Johnson, J.G., Williams, J.B.W., Rabkin, J.G., Goetz, R.R. & Remien, R.H. (1995) Axis I psychiatric symptoms associated with HIV infection and personality disorder. *American Journal of Psychiatry* **152**(4), 551–554.

Johnson, J.G., Williams, J.B.W., Goetz, R.R., *et al.* (1996) Personality disorders predict onset of Axis I disorders and impaired functioning among homosexual men with and at risk of HIV infection. *Archives of Psychiatry* **53**, 350–357.

Kiesler, D.J. (1983) The 1982 interpersonal circle: a taxonomy for complementarity in human transactions. *Psychological Review* **90**, 185–214.

Layden, M.A. (1997) BPD. In: *Practicing Cognitive Therapy. A Guide to Interventions* (ed. R. Leahy). Jason Aronson, New Jersey.

Leary, T. (1957) *Interpersonal Diagnosis of Personality: A Functional Theory and Methodology for Personality Evaluation*. Ronald Press, New York.

Luntz, B.K. & Widom, C.S. (1994) APD in abused and neglected children grown up. *American Journal of Psychiatry* **151**, 670–674.

McCrae, R.R. & Costa, P.T. (1990) *Personality in Adulthood*. Guilford Press, New York.

Millon, T. & Davis, R.D. (1996) *Disorders of Personality: DSM-IV and Beyond*, 2nd edn. Wiley, New York.

Millon, T. (1987) On the genesis and prevalence of the BPD: a social learning thesis. *Journal of Personality Disorders* **1**, 354–372.

Mischel, W. & Shoda, Y. (1995). A cognitive-affective system theory of personality: reconceptualizing situation, dispositions, dynamics and invariance in personality structure. *Psychological Review* **102**(2), 246–268.

Modestin, J., Oberson, B. & Erni, T. (1998) Possible antecedents of DSM-III-R personality disorders. *Acta Psychiatrica Scandinavica* **97**, 260–266.

Morey, L.C. (1991) *Personality Assessment Inventory. Professional Manual.* Psychological Assessment Resources, Odessa, FL.

Perkins, D.O., Davidson, E.J., Leserman, J., Liao, D. & Evans, D.L. (1993) Personality disorders in patients with HIV: a controlled study with implications for clinical care. *American Journal of Psychiatry* **150**(2), 309–315.

Pinkerton, S.D. & Abramson, P.R. (1995) Decision making and personality factors in sexual risk-taking for HIV/AIDS: a theoretical integration. *Personality and Individual Difference,* **19**(5), 713–723.

Quinton, D., Gulliver, L. & Rutter, M. (1995) A 15–20 year follow-up of adult psychiatric patients: psychiatric disorder and social functioning. *British Journal of Psychiatry* **167**, 315–323.

Reich, J.H. & Green, A.I. (1991) Effects of personality disorder on outcome of treatment. *Journal of Nervous and Mental Disease* **179**(2), 74–82.

Schroth, M.L. (1996) Scores on sensation seeking as predictor of sexual activities among homosexuals. *Perceptual and Motor Skills* **82**, 657–658.

Seal, D.W. & Agostinelli, G. (1994) Individual differences associated with high-risk sexual behaviour: implications for intervention programmes. *AIDS Care* **6**, 393–397.

Tourian, K., Alterman, A., Metzger, D., Rutherford, M., Cacciola, J.S. & McKay, J.R. (1997) Validity of three measures of antisociality in predicting HIV risk behaviors in methadone-maintenance patients. *Drug and Alcohol Dependence* **47**, 99–107.

Trull, T.J., Useda, D., Conforti, K. & Doan, B. (1997) BPD features in nonclinical young adults: 2. Two-year outcome. *Journal of Abnormal Psychology* **106**, 307–314.

Tyrer, P., Casey, P.R. & Ferguson, B. (1993) Personality disorder in perspective. In: *Personality Disorder Reviewed* (eds P. Tyrer & O. Stein). Gaskell: Royal College of Psychiatrists, London.

Tyrer, P., Gunderson, J., Lyons, M. & Tohen, M. (1997) Special feature: extent of comorbidity between mental states and personality disorders. *Journal of Personality Disorders* **11**(3), 242–259.

Weissman, M.M. (1993) The epidemiology of personality disorder: A 1990 update. *Journal of Personality Disorder* (Suppl.), 44–62.

Western, D., Moses, M.J., Silk, K.R., Lohr, N.E., Cohen, R. & Segal, H. (1992) Quality of depressive experience in BPD and major depression. *Journal of Personality Disorder* **6**(4), 382–393.

Widiger, T.A. (1998) Invited essay: sex biases in the diagnosis of personality disorder. *Journal of Personality Disorder* **12**(2), 95–118.

Young, J.E. (1994) *Cognitive Therapy for Personality Disorders: A Schema-Focused Approach,* revised edn. Professional Resource Press, Sarasota, FL.

Zimmerman, M. (1994) *Interview Guide for Evaluating DSM-IV Psychiatric Disorders and the Mental Status Examination.* Psych Products Press.

Zuckerman, M.P. (1993) Impulsive sensation seeking and its behavioural, psychological and biochemical correlates. *Neuropsychobiology* **28**, 30–36.

Chapter 17

Managing the Sequelae of Childhood Sexual Abuse in Adults

Helen Kennerley

Introduction

In some instances, therapists do not need specialist skills to work effectively with adult survivors of childhood sexual abuse (CSA), the presenting problems are not complex and will respond to 'standard' therapies. However, the course of therapy with many survivors of abuse will be challenging: presenting problems will be multiple, the cognitive, emotional and behavioural sequelae will be dramatic and disturbing, interpersonal difficulties will undermine progress, therapists will despair.

This chapter aims to help therapists prepare for the particular treatment issues that can make it difficult to feel confident, competent or even safe, when working with this client group. It will address what we might mean by 'childhood sexual abuse', its prevalence and its sequelae. It will also present a generic model or heuristic for conceptualising the wide range of presenting problems in these persons with a common history. Finally, key issues and clinical recommendations will be discussed.

What do we mean by 'childhood sexual abuse'?

Both clients and therapists ask this question and the answer is of limited usefulness. There is no general agreement on definition and, for clinical purposes, the presenting problems of the adult often take priority. However, for research, audit or legal purposes, it is necessary to define CSA – and there are many definitions to choose from. For example, some specify minimum age differences between victim and perpetrator (Peters *et al.* 1986); some stipulate sexual maturity and intent on the part of the perpetrator (Baker & Duncan 1985); others distinguish between contact and non-contact abuse (Russell 1986).

In fact, abusive acts are as various as the abuser's imagination and range from contact (e.g. masturbation and penetration) to non-contact (e.g. forced witnessing of sex acts, being photographed for pornographic purposes); from wilful to negligent; the abuser may be close to the child (a parent or friend) or a stranger; the episodes of abuse may be single or repeated over years; the number of perpetrators can be several; the age and gender of a perpetrator can vary from victim to victim; the motives of the abuser might not be sexual; the victim can be a boy or a girl. Given the many forms of sexual abuse committed against children and young adults, it is important not to hold too narrow a view of CSA, and it is important to recognise that it is the interpretation of the event(s) which very likely determines the long-term consequences of the abuse and influences the prognosis of that person. Consider the personal meaning of the following cases.

Case examples

'Simon' was at boarding school. A gifted musician, he was awarded extra lessons with a widely respected teacher from a nearby music school. The music teacher sodomised Simon when he was eight, and threatened him with the police if he told. When the abuse recurred, Simon told his parents, who immediately informed his school and the police. They supported Simon throughout the police enquiry and then took a family holiday so that he might recover from his ordeal. His experience of abuse was never a taboo subject. As a young adult, Simon remembers the specific trauma but without shame or guilt. He also recalls a great sense of being cared for and protected by his parents.

'Suzy', at twenty, had great difficulty in trusting others – particularly men. She had not had a single close relationship and the thought of sex frightened her and left her feeling vulnerable. She related this to her step-father's pervasive sexual comments throughout her late childhood and adolescence. Whenever her mother was absent, he had made sexual suggestions to her,

had wandered into her bedroom when she dressed and undressed, refused to put a lock on the bathroom door and then took the opportunity to watch her bathing or going to the lavatory. She turned to her mother who dismissed Suzy's distress as fantasy and nonsense. As an adult, she felt responsible, threatened, unprotected and confused about sexual boundaries.

In each of these cases, an objective description of the sexual act, without reference to Simon or Suzy's interpretation and the reactions of their parents, would handicap the therapist in understanding and then meeting their psychological needs.

Although some definitions stipulate sexual intent on the part of the perpetrator, the motives of the abuser need not be sinister for the victim to suffer psychologically. Children can be victims of wilful or negligent sexual abuse, in the same way that they can be victims of active physical abuse or can be damaged by neglect. A mother might carelessly turn to her son as a sexual confidant; an older child might pressure a sibling into exploratory sex play; a brother might 'trade' his sister with his peer group, focusing only on the status that this gained him in the gang; a parent might turn a 'blind eye' to the abuse of a child. Each of these activities might have been carried out without realisation of the psychological consequences for the child, but such experiences could promote enduring emotional problems.

It is also important to recognise that *physical* and *emotional* abuse and neglect also contribute to marked psychological problems in adulthood, and these forms of abuse should not be considered less pernicious than sexual abuse (Mullen *et al.* 1993). Many survivors will have suffered physical, emotional and sexual trauma and the consequences of the former should not be underestimated and should be addressed.

With regard to prevalence, we are very uncertain. Disagreements in definition, the use of survey methods which differ widely, and the reluctance of individuals to report abuse all contribute to a very poor appreciation of prevalence. Drauker's (1992) statement on this is appropriately vague and is probably still our most relevant guide: 'Researchers now generally agree that the occurrence of child sexual abuse is much more frequent than originally believed.'

Summary

Although, for legal and evaluation purposes, a precise definition of sexual abuse may have to be emphasised, the therapist's emphasis will likely be the idiosyncratic needs of the client. While the sexual act and the motives of the perpetrator can be used to define the abuse, the survivor's perceptions will determine his or her therapeutic needs. We are still uncertain of the prevalence of CSA in both community and clinic populations.

What are the psychological sequelae and how do we understand them?

The long-term consequences of CSA vary. Outcome is influenced by the child's perception of the abuse, the family dynamics of that child and the reaction when CSA was disclosed. However, for some time, it has been accepted that there is a common set of correlates of CSA. Summit (1983) and Briere (1984) have used the phrases: 'CSA accommodation

syndrome' and 'post-sexual-abuse trauma' to describe the psychological sequelae of CSA. They list conduct disorders, depression, difficulty in dealing with anger, dissociation, somatisation and anxiety as early sequelae and substance abuse, promiscuity, suicidal ideas, sexual dysfunction and victimisation of others as later consequences.

Throughout the 1980s and 1990s, researchers have continued to investigate the possible sequelae of CSA and we have a clearer idea of its many correlates. 'Severity' is typically indicated by the age of onset of the abuse, the degree of sexuality of the act, the amount of force/violence used, and the number of perpetrators involved, and it has become apparent that, in general, the degree of adult psychopathology worsens with the severity of the abuse (Pribor & Dinwiddie 1992; Mullen *et al.* 1993). Swett *et al.* (1990) correlated childhood abuse with higher levels of psychiatric morbidity than in non-abused male patients, while Fromuth and Burkhart (1989) found a similar association when they studied male college students.

Childhood sexual abuse has been associated with all axes of DSM IV: the severity of CSA has been shown to correlate with DSM-IV axis I clinical disorders (American Psychiatric Association 1994) such as depression (Cheasty *et al.* 1998) and eating disorders (Waller & Ruddock 1993; Everill & Waller 1995). There is also an association with the development of personality disorders (DSM-IV: axis II): CSA has been linked with borderline personality disorder (Sheldon 1988; Fromuth & Burkhart 1989; Weston 1991) and with dissociative identity disorder (Putnam *et al.* 1986). Although fewer in number, studies have also linked Axis III and Axis IV disorders with CSA (e.g. Salmon & Caulderbank (1995) and Russell (1986), respectively).

From this, it is clear that CSA has been linked with a wide range of specific behavioural, affective, somatic, interpersonal and cognitive problems. Often, these overt difficulties provoke help-seeking and then serve as the focus of treatment.

Behavioural problems

Behavioural associations with CSA include adolescent turmoil (especially running away from home), alcohol and/or drug misuse and 'parentification' of the child (Herman & Hirschman 1981), eating disorders (Tice *et al.* 1989; Waller 1991), self-harm (Sedney & Brooks 1984; Briere & Zaidi 1989; Romans *et al.* 1995), increased seeking of surgical procedures (Salmon & Calderbank 1995); teenage pregnancies (Boyer & Fine 1992).

Affective problems

PTSD (Rodriguez *et al.* 1997) (see Chapter 14), clinical depression (Bilfulco *et al.* 1991; Cheasty *et al.* 1998) and suicidal behaviour (Briere & Zaidi 1989; Sedney & Brooks 1984; Jehu 1989b) have been associated with CSA. Emotional responses to abuse vary, but they are most frequently very negative, for example, Jehu (1989b) found the most common responses were guilt, shame and disgust, followed by fear, helplessness, anger and resentment.

Somatic problems

The apparent consequences of CSA are not limited to emotional and behavioural mani-festations; somatic correlates include somatisation and hypochondriasis (Salmon & Calderbank 1995), genito-urinary symptoms (Leserman *et al.* 1997), body shame (Andrews 1995), and dyspareunia (Jehu 1989a).

Interpersonal problems

Finkelhor & Browne (1985) developed a 'traumagenic dynamics model of CSA' which cites four dynamics influencing the interpersonal actions of survivors: stigmatisation, betrayal, powerlessness and traumatic sexualisation. Herman and Hirschman (1981) associated CSA with a history of repeated victimisation (battering/rape); it has also been linked with social isolation and discord in relationships (Donaldson & Cordes-Green 1994), difficulty in dealing with anger and difficulties in establishing and maintaining relationships (Bruck-er & Johnson 1987; Bifulco *et al.* 1991; Crowder 1995). Problems in sexual adjustment have been linked with CSA in women (Jehu 1989a; Cheasty *et al.* 1998) and in men (Dimock 1988; Fromuth & Burkhart 1989).

Cognitive problems

Finally, cognitive correlates can be considered as those of *process*, of *content*, and of memory (including flashbacks).

Cognitive processing in survivors may show patterns or biases: for example dissociation (Jehu 1989a; Vanderlinden 1993; Waller *et al.* 1995) and attentional bias for abuse (Waller & Smith 1994). With regard to *cognitive content or beliefs*, there is clearly a trend towards the negative. The self-image of survivors of abuse is poor (Herman & Hirschman 1981), with survivors holding negative personal constructs (Clarke & Llewelyn 1994). Jehu (1988) identified abused women's views of themselves as unusual, bad, worthless and blameworthy, while their concept of others was as untrustworthy and rejecting, and their notion of the future was hopeless: in summary, a negative cognitive triad of core beliefs. Kennerley (1995) carried out a simple factor analysis of the beliefs and assumptions of CSA survivors and discovered five 'clusters' of personal beliefs which reflected badness, helplessness, uncleanness, being a misfit, and being 'nothing' – a person with no personal identity or purpose.

It is accepted that *traumatic memories* are a sequel of trauma, but there has been much concern about the possibility of false memories for trauma: confabulated recollections of abuse which are believed, by the survivor, to be true. The most thorough review of this phenomenon was carried out by a working party of the British Psychological Society in 1995. The committee conclusion was that memory is largely accurate but can be distorted or elaborated; memories can be in error, but this is more likely to reflect incorrect rather than false memory; sustained pressure or repetition can create false memories in some; memory loss from trauma is reported and recall can occur within or independent of psychotherapy.

Flashbacks of the trauma are memories which the individual might experience as uncontrollable. Some experience flashbacks as no more than a 'sense' of a previous trauma, while others experience full sensory recall as if the event is being relived. The recollection can be intense, comprising visual, auditory, olfactory and/or tactile memories and, although the incident may be some time in the past, the experience for the client in flashback can be very immediate.

The memory can be triggered by sounds, the feel of a fabric, smells, certain words, being touched in a certain way, or any stimulus associated with the CSA. The triggers can be internal, such as the physical sensations of anxiety, or external, such as the smell of a certain aftershave. Flashbacks can be alarming and misinterpreted by the individual, as indicating madness, for example. The distress that they cause can then lead to compensatory behaviours to disrupt the flashback, such as self-mutilation, suicide attempts or substance misuse.

Accounting for the wide variation in problem presentation

Nearly every client will ask: 'Why me?', 'Why now?' and 'Why aren't things getting better?' So, therapists find themselves having to account for a widely varying presentation of problems in CSA survivors. The generic model, used by cognitive therapists, is a valuable framework in helping the clinician and the client understand this range of difficulties. The model is not one of pathology but of learning and information processing which, of course, is not exclusive to cognitive therapy and which underpins many of the psychotherapies.

Figure 17.1 illustrates this framework. At the first level (I) is the development of 'meaning' for the individual: namely, the sense that the individual makes of the world, the means of interpreting new experiences. The cognitive structure for this function is generally referred to as the schema and its nature is complex and has been extensively reviewed and revised over decades (Piaget 1948; Teasdale & Barnard

1993; Beck 1996). The model in Fig. 17.1 very much simplifies the concept of the schema.

'Meanings' or schemata are shaped through direct and indirect learning experiences which give the individual a sense of self and a perspective of others and the future. This may be at a conscious, subconscious or unconscious level: some 'meanings' are readily expressed by the individual, some are better described as 'felt-senses' whilst others do not readily map onto language at all (Layden *et al.* 1993; Teasdale 1996). Once established, schemata assimilate experiences in a conservative way, generally maintaining a person's view of self and the world.

The derivation of 'meaning' is influenced both by core beliefs and cognitive style. For example, consider a person with a fundamental sense of self as worthwhile, a view of others as essentially benign and an outlook which was reasonably optimistic. Contrast this with the person with a self-concept of worthlessness, a view of others as rejecting and hurtful and a sense of hopelessness about the future. Each would derive a different 'meaning' from a last-minute cancellation of a date. The former might see no menace in the act (reflecting his core beliefs) and would view the situation in context (reflecting his cognitive style). This is

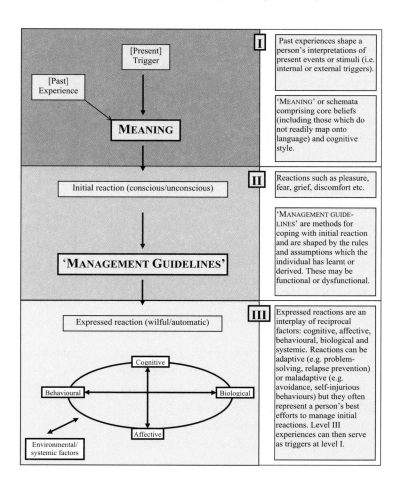

Fig. 17.1 Understanding the problem(s).

the first cancellation over several dates, so his conclusion might be that 'These things happen,' and his emotional response (his initial reaction) is one of disappointment.

In contrast, the 'meaning' for the second man might be that he was rejected because he was not good enough (reflecting his core beliefs). An inability to be circumspect (cognitive style) would mean that he would be unlikely to modify his extreme and hopeless interpretation. He might draw a final conclusion which leaves him feeling angry with himself and terrified of the future (his initial reaction).

This takes us to the second level (II) and 'management guidelines'. These are the rules and assumptions which a person uses to deal with the initial reaction. Some of these are taught to us ('look both ways before you cross the road'; 'nice girls don't do that'; 'don't cry'); some are inferred ('others like me so I can be open with them'; 'others hurt me so I must not trust anyone'; 'I can't handle this feeling – I must stop it'). The guidelines can be functional or dysfunctional.

In the example above, the first man might deal with his disappointment by drawing on functional guidelines such as: 'I can do something about this' and 'Give a person a second chance'. The second man, however, might be led by rules and assumptions such as: 'Don't trust: show the world that you don't need anyone,' and 'I can't handle this feeling – I've got to make it go away.'

Their reactions are then expressed at Level III. The first man might engage in some problem solving and decide to phone his friend and suggest another time for a date. In this way, the relationship is given a chance of surviving. In contrast, the second might withdraw socially and engage in heavy drinking to numb his feelings. In this way, the relationship is jeopardised and he never learns to manage his feelings.

Level III reactions are complexes of reciprocal factors: behavioural, affective, sensory, imaginal, cognitive, physiological and interpersonal (Lazarus 1973; Beck 1996). This dynamic complex has been usefully conceptualised in Padesky and Mooney's five-factor summary model (1991) which is illustrated at Level III. From this, both therapist and client can appreciate the interactive quality of these factors and the consequent wide range of problem presentations which can arise. Reactions at Level III can further serve as triggers at Level I.

Case examples

Briony (38 years) presented with an 11-year history of recurrent AGORAPHOBIA AND SOCIAL PHOBIA (Level III). As a child, she was raped by her father and told that she was wicked – she had internalised this. The trigger for the worsening of her problem, now, was the arrival of a new neighbour. The 'meaning' (Level I) of this event was: 'I am bad: she will realise that I am bad if she gets to know me.' This gave rise to an initial reaction of terror and the 'management guidelines' (Level II) which she turned to were essentially avoidant. She retreated to a single room within her home and avoided contact with all but her husband and her therapist.

Lawrence (34 years) attended the outpatient clinic with a DRIVING PHOBIA (Level III). When he was 7 years old, he had been homosexually abused by a neighbour. The trigger for his phobia was a minor road traffic accident, for which he was not responsible. The 'meaning' (Level I) which had been re-stimulated was: 'I am weak and can't control what happens to me' and his initial reaction to driving was fear (Level II). His 'management guidelines' were avoidant and his ability to drive was now very limited.

Jane (21 years) had a two-year history of DEPRESSION, SELF-HARM AND ANOREXIA with a concurrent diagnosis of BORDERLINE-PERSONALITY DISORDER WITH VISUAL HALLUCINATIONS (Level III). As a child, she had been repeatedly sexually abused by a family friend and this formed the content of her 'hallucinations'. She had begun to train as a nurse, but contact with patients who had been the victims of abuse triggered her own memories of abuse and revived her very negative self-concept. The 'meaning' (Level I) that she now derived from her day to day life was: 'I am bad, dirty and deformed: I don't matter and I can't do anything about it.' This gave her feelings of intense grief, fear and misery (Level II). She coped with this as best she could by trying to distract herself from the emotional pain through self-harm, self-starvation, avoidance of intimacy, but this only seemed to worsen her affect.

Summary

The sequelae of CSA vary widely, so therapists need to be able to explain a range of problems arising from childhood trauma. The model illustrated here enables the therapist to clarify how experience influences the sense a person makes of self and the world (Level I), how that, in turn, colours a person's reactions to certain triggers (Level II), and how this is ultimately expressed (Level III).

Therapeutic considerations

Although survivors of CSA (with or without physical and/or emotional abuse) will present with a range of clinical disorders, personality disorders and psycho-social problems, it is reasonable to anticipate that common guidelines can be relevant for the abused. From the point of meeting and assessing the client through to completing therapy, many of the fundamental processes and many key issues are similar across cases.

Initial contact

The revelation of a history of abuse does not indicate the need for therapy, and a relationship between CSA and a presenting difficulty should not be assumed. Not all those with a history of abuse will need help. Surveys indicate that some trauma survivors do not suffer from related psychological problems (West 1988; Sanford 1991): 'Simon' was such a person. There will also be those who experience difficulties, but who are able to cope without formal support. Some might present with mental health problems, somatic problems, social problems which are independent of a history of abuse and for which the abuse need not be directly addressed. Others will need a treatment which does address the CSA.

Whether the presenting difficulty is linked with CSA or not, the first step is to help clients make sense of their problem. Clients often make undermining assumptions about difficulties, for example: that chronic depression results from constitutional weakness; that repeated failed relationships reflect the inevitability of loneliness and hurt; that flashbacks are a sign of insanity. Therapists can help clients understand the development of problems by working through a shared conceptualisation. The client can then begin to appreciate how a problem makes sense in the context of experiences and a person's best attempts to cope.

Once a formulation has been derived, therapists can decide if intervention is appropriate. Some clients may benefit from simply disclosing their histories and understanding their problems; others may respond well to self-help literature (see Appendix); while some might benefit most from using community resources such as those support groups which the therapist feels confident in endorsing.

Where intervention is appropriate, therapists are faced with the decision: 'What kind of therapy?'

Choosing an appropriate intervention

Those who do present with a CSA-related problem, or multiple problems, will be at different stages of readiness or ability to use therapies. Some might be in the early stages of realising the extent and implications of their abuse and might do best with supportive counselling and gentle exploration; some might have systemic and social problems which need to be addressed before an Axis I problem can be tackled directly; those struggling with severe behavioural problems or personality disorders might benefit most from a behavioural intervention, such as Dialectic Behaviour Therapy (Linehan 1993), while others may require a preliminary period of motivational interviewing (Miller & Roll-

nick 1992) to help them engage in a focused therapy, such as CBT.

An augmented or specialised therapy is not necessary in all instances: many clients will benefit from a 'standard' therapy approach such as 'classic' cognitive therapy and this is often preferable as these methods frequently have superior empirical support. Jehu *et al.* (1986) report significant improvements in CSA survivors' negative beliefs using classic cognitive therapy and there is much empirical support for interventions which are specific to diagnosable problems associated with CSA, such as mood problems, eating disorders, PTSD, sexual difficulties.

For some complex presentations, more recently developed (but less well validated) approaches might, none-the-less, offer the best treatment for the client. Among these would be schema-focused cognitive therapy (Beck *et al.* 1990; Young 1990) and cognitive analytic therapy for complex cases (Ryle 1997). Of course, whatever the choice, the therapist should be able to justify that this is in the client's best interest.

Specific treatment protocols for CSA survivors do exist (Jehu 1988; Chard *et al.* 1997; Kennerley *et al.* 1998). However, such treatment 'packages' should be used cautiously as client needs vary and some needs will not be met by the elements of treatment protocols. Thorough, and extremely useful, reviews of psychological treatments used with survivors of abuse have been published by Cahill and colleagues (1991) and Jehu (1991). The authors explore a range of treatment options, including group and individual therapies.

In Oxford, we have developed an 18-session cognitive therapy programme for survivors of childhood trauma (Kennerley *et al.*

1998) which addresses issues which are common amongst survivors of abuse. The initial sessions are devoted to schema-based case conceptualisation (as outlined earlier) and the development of adaptive coping skills, including managing traumatic memories. The programme then focuses on salient issues for survivors, which are frequently schema-related. These include building self-confidence, developing trust, shifting blame, and managing relationships. The final sessions reinforce the relapse prevention skills which were introduced in the initial meetings. The programme is summarised in Table 17.1.

This is a cognitive therapy programme and, as such, will not suit all clients. Cognitive therapy is best used by those who can relate to psychological models; those who are able to develop a working alliance and those who are able to focus on particular difficulties, themes or issues. The Oxford programme has been used in individual, group and pair therapy. Group therapy is offered when the client will clearly benefit from sharing with those with similar histories and difficulties, but is limited to those who are socially skilled enough to work in a group and who are able to learn vicariously from other members. Pair therapy (that is, two matched clients working with a single therapist) seems to confer the benefits of sharing and is offered to those who are unable to use a group, for example, the socially inhibited.

A final, but important, consideration when beginning therapy with a person who has experienced CSA is the therapist's ability to take on the client: does s/he have the necessary support, clinical resources or emotional resilience at present? There may be times in a therapist's life or career when it would be unwise to offer

Table 17.1 Cognitive therapy programme for survivors of childhood trauma.

Session	Topic
1	Entering therapy
2	Developing coping strategies and skills to help you recover
3	Understanding your problem(s), your strengths and needs (1)
4	Understanding your problem(s), your strengths and needs (2)
5	Preparing and planning for the changes in your life
6	Improving your self-image and self-esteem
7	Remembering the past and dealing with flashbacks
8	Understanding the way you think
9	Understanding that you were not to blame (1)
10	Understanding that you were not to blame (2)
11	Anger: feeling it and dealing with it
12	Speaking out and dealing with confrontation
13	Dealing with your family
14	Dealing with intimacy
15	Dealing with sexual difficulties
16	Grieving and mourning: facing losses in the past and the present
17	Coping in the long term and preventing relapse
18	Ending therapy but continuing the work

formal intervention and this should be recognised.

The therapeutic relationship

In all cases, attention must be given to the therapeutic relationship. Raue *et al.* (1997) observe that, in both psychodynamic and cognitive therapies, 'a good alliance predicts client improvement'. We have already seen that interpersonal problems are common amongst the sexually abused and this is associated with a poorer therapeutic alliance (Muran *et al.* 1994). Thus, the therapist may have to allocate more time and/or emphasis to developing and maintaining a working relationship.

Common interpersonal issues which can limit progress are an inability to trust, the anticipation of rejection if the real self is revealed, the anticipation of hurt or harm. These interpersonal problems can, indeed, be fundamental to therapy. This is so for the psychodynamic psychotherapies and for certain cognitive therapies (Ryle 1990; Safran & Segal 1990).

It is not only the client who might struggle with issues relating to CSA. This is a particularly disturbing phenomenon which can also arouse strong feelings or revive issues in the therapist. Renshaw (1982) summarises unhelpful therapist responses as attack (e.g. exploitation), attraction (e.g. over-protection, arousal or over-identification) and/or avoidance (e.g. disbelief). This emphasises the need for therapists to process their own reactions and responses in relation to abused clients.

Sadly, therapists are not immune to further abusing the vulnerable client (Jehu 1994) or from being traumatised, themselves, by the work (Courtois 1994; Pearlman & MacIan 1995). The resolution of therapist issues will almost certainly be aided by good supervision and therapists will benefit from ongoing supervision to ensure therapeutic integrity and to ratify difficult therapeutic decisions.

An important task in establishing a good working relationship is making it a safe one, and therapists can take steps to make it easier for clients to engage and to build confidence. Simple measures can ease anxieties, such as negotiating the positioning of chairs, setting explicit 'ground-rules' or discovering what might trigger flashbacks in the session.

Several clinicians advocate a period of preparation for therapy for complex clients (Smith 1989; Layden *et al.* 1993; Courtois 1994; Kennerley *et al.* 1998) when clients learn basic mood management, stress management and relapse prevention skills. Thus, they are better equipped to handle the subsequent stresses of therapy.

Addressing common issues within therapy

Cognitive issues which are particularly pertinent to working with abuse survivors are: specific biases in information processing; the possibility of repressed memory and false memory; flashback management.

Biases in information processing will impinge on therapy: benign actions will be misconstrued, achievements will be minimised, ambiguity can terrify. Most psychotherapies can address this issue, although cognitive techniques can be particularly relevant as they address cognitive distortion directly and the therapy session provides opportunity for in-vivo work (Beck *et al.* 1979; Meichenbaum 1985). This approach is also effective in challenging the dysfunctional assumptions which give rise to problem emotions and behaviours.

For example, a common cognitive bias in patients is that of dichotomous thinking. The specific techniques of scaling (Pretzer 1990), which is also called the continuum technique (Padesky 1994), enables the client to develop a wider and more realistic range of perspectives, replacing the previous 'all or nothing' thinking style. The veracity of the new construction can then be tested within and outside the session.

Biases in processing often reflect the underlying schemata and, as such, some of the schema-change methods reviewed by Padesky (1994) and presented by Beck and colleagues (1990) will be very relevant to the therapist working with CSA survivors. Other therapies, such as CAT or systemic psychotherapies, which address fundamental belief systems can similarly effect schema change.

The concept of repression is controversial. Memory expert, Alan Baddeley (1996), has concluded: 'There is no doubt that cases of child abuse occur, and it seems probable that the memory of these is sometimes repressed' (p. 169). The BPS working party conclusion (1995) was that there are reports of trauma-related psychogenic amnesia which can remit and, given the danger of provoking 'false memories', the therapist should allow repressed recollections to emerge naturally and should not attempt to force recall and certainly should never offer leading or repeated interpretations.

Flashbacks, in some cases, respond well to cognitive-behavioural interventions. For some, exposure therapy, as advocated by Foa *et al.* (1991) will shift them, although this approach is not always helpful and is perhaps even traumatic. A recent study by Marks and co-workers (1998) indicated that exposure was no more effective than a cognitive re-appraisal in managing flashbacks. As the latter can be less anxiety provoking for both client *and* therapist, this finding has important implications for our practice.

Amongst others, Jaycox and Foa (1996) discovered that exposure therapy was not help-

ful for those who experience extreme anger, emotional numbing and overwhelming anxiety during the procedure. For these clients, the authors suggest modified exposure. An alternative approach which has been evaluated, is the imaginal re-structuring of Layden and co-workers (1993) which offers clients the opportunity to engage in a graded exposure to the traumatic images, combined with cognitive challenging and restructuring.

Affect-related issues which therapists need to keep in mind concern the powerful emotions which can be associated with re-processing or reviewing traumatic experiences. These can be very powerful – that is why the behavioural responses can be so dramatic. Affect has often been avoided through distraction in the form of dissociation, self-injurious behaviours and substance misuse and clients might find it helpful to learn emotion regulation skills (Linehan 1993). Some will then find it easier to get in touch with affect through graded exposure (Kennerley 1996).

Behavioural consequences of CSA can be extreme and it is not uncommon to see multi-impulsive and dangerous behaviours in this population. Therapists should be prepared, practically and emotionally, for dealing with suicide attempts, self-injury, substance misuse, engagement in unsafe sex, and of learning of ongoing abuse to the client or others associated with the client.

Some clients will experience repeated relapse and the shifting of problem behaviours. As one seems to come under control, another develops: self-mutilation is replaced by purging or alcohol misuse, for example. This can be demoralising for client and therapist alike and the introduction of relapse prevention (Marlatt & Gordon 1985) is often a necessary cognitive-behavioural cornerstone of the longer term therapies which are beset by relapse. When this pattern is persistent, it is usually necessary, if the conceptualisation indicates, to tackle the common underlying causes (at Level I and II) rather than persisting solely at Level III.

Systemic issues: Therapists need also attend to the 'system' in which the client lives – one should not assume that it is healthy. Clients continue to be abused in social, marital and work relationships and steps need to be taken to address this so that progress in therapy sessions is not constantly undermined or, at least, the therapist is aware of current trauma and can support and advise accordingly.

Clients have partners and children who also need to be considered. Progress in therapy, with its associated behavioural and emotional changes, can give rise to stresses in marriages; children can suffer, can be over-protected, can be neglected. Again, the therapist needs to keep the client's home life on the agenda and consider the relevance of involving significant others, involving other agencies and/or adopting a systemic approach.

The implications of change

Finally, the therapist must consider the implications of change for the client who has spent, perhaps decades, accommodating problems. All change is stressful and even the most positive changes can create stresses for which the client needs to be prepared. Whole systems and ways of life get thrown into upheaval and the client might actually be put at risk.

Behavioural change: The implication of shifting problem behaviours can be significant. For example, a woman who becomes more assertive towards an abusive partner, or family member, might risk antagonising a significant person in her life. At best, this could improve a poor relationship, but at worst, it could end an important one prematurely, or even put her at risk of physical harm. A man might reduce his alcohol misuse, only to become more depressed, even suicidal, because he is not as able to 'numb' himself to emotional pain.

Cognitive change: Therapists must also consider the impact of changing fundamental cognitions and not assume that the disappearance of a maladaptive belief is, necessarily, a good thing.

A common belief, as we have seen, is self-blame and shifting; this can put the client under tremendous strain. Consider the man whose self-blame exonerates his father ('He wasn't a bad man: I drove him to it'), enables the client to condone his mother's negligence ('She was a wonderful woman but I was to blame, so of course she didn't protect me') and gives him a comforting view of the world ('Bad things happened to me because I was to blame. If I weren't bad, these things would not have happened to me'). Perhaps only now does he have to recognise that his father was an active paedophile, that his mother did not protect him and that terrible things happen that are beyond our control. Shifting a single core cognition shatters his inner world.

A further example is the woman who, in middle age, successfully challenges the assumption: 'Men cannot be trusted'. Although she has gained the ability to form intimate relationships, she might now have to face the grief of having 'lost' her childbearing years.

Recovery sometimes comes with startling revelations and clients should be prepared for a possible worsening of affect and acute grief. A period of 'grieving' might be necessary before clients can move on in therapy. For those who have spent a lifetime dissociating from intense affect, recognising the meaning of their abuse and linking this with emotion can be traumatic in itself.

Summary

As with all client groups, therapists can promote insights and plans for recovery, and a good conceptualisation will guide the therapist in this. The foundations for recovery should be made as sound as possible; well validated approaches should be used, as far as possible, and augmented with caution; therapy should be paced so that change is manageable and therapists should never assume but should always verify meanings with the client.

Conclusion

Although we are unclear about the definition and prevalence of CSA, it is recognised as a real phenomenon and one which merits clinical discussion and research. Various therapeutic interventions will be relevant in helping the abused and therapists should recognise the skills that they can bring to the work and not be deterred by a belief that CSA work requires exclusive skills. Whatever a therapist's orientation, steps can be taken to better accommodate client needs, namely, setting up supervision, exploring therapist reactions, creating safety both within and outwith sessions, and preparing for adverse reactions which might never occur.

Appendix: literature for clients

Ainscough, C. & Toon, K. (1993) *Breaking Free: Help for Survivors of Childhood Sexual Abuse.* Sheldon, London. A self-help guide which is structured so as to take the reader through a programme of recovery. This will be over-ambitious for some clients who might benefit from using it as an adjunct to therapy.

Bain, Q. & Sanders, M. (1990) *Out in the Open: A Guide for Young People who have been Sexually Abused.* Virago. An introduction to coming to terms with having been sexually abused. Addresses many of the questions that youngsters pose and offers guidelines for recovery.

Gil, E. (1983) *Outgrowing the Pain.* Dell. An excellent introduction to coming to terms with physical, emotional and sexual abuse. Readable and sensitive without too many vignettes, which can sometimes distress clients more than they help.

Gil, E. (1992) *Outgrowing the Pain Together.* Dell. A book for the partners or family of the abused. Again, clear and helpful.

Gilbert, P. (1997) *Overcoming Depression.* Robinson. Most relevant for those suffering from depressed mood, but particularly pertinent because of its sections on shame management.

Lew, M. (1990) *Victims No Longer: Men Recovering from Incest and other Sexual Abuse.* Perennial. A hopeful text which addresses issues that are pertinent to men who were sexually abused by other men or by women.

References

American Psychiatric Association (1994) *Diagnostic and Statistical Manual of Mental Disorders,* 4th edn. (DSM IV). American Psychiatric Association, Washington DC.

Andrews, B. (1995) Bodily shame as a mediator between abusive experiences and depression. *Journal of Abnormal Psychology* **104**(2), 277–285.

Baddeley, A. (1996) *Your Memory: A User's Guide.* Prion, London.

Baker, A.W. & Duncan, S.P. (1985) Child sexual abuse: a

study of prevalence in Great Britain. *Child Abuse and Neglect* **9**, 457–467.

Beck, A.T. (1996) Beyond belief: a theory of modes, personality and psychopathology. In: *Frontiers of Cognitive Therapy* (ed. P. Salkovskis). Guilford, New York.

Beck, A.T., Rush, A.J., Shaw, B.F. & Emery, G. (1979) *Cognitive Therapy of Depression*. Guilford, New York.

Beck, A.T., *et al.* (1990) *Cognitive Therapy of Personality Disorder*. Guilford, New York.

Bifulco, A., Brown, G.W. & Adler, Z. (1991) Early abuse and clinical depression in adult life. *British Journal of Psychiatry* **159**, 115–122.

Boyer, D. & Fine, D. (1992) Sexual abuse as a factor in adolescent pregnancy and child maltreatment. *Family Planning Perspective* **24**, 4–11.

Briere, J. (1984) The effects of childhood sexual abuse on later psychological functioning: defining a post sexual abuse syndrome. Paper presented at *The Third National Conference on Sexual Victimization of Children*, Washington DC.

Briere, J. & Runtz, M. (1987) Post sexual abuse trauma: data and implications from clinical practice. *Journal of Interpersonal Violence* **2**, 367–397.

Briere, J. & Zaidi, L.Y. (1989) Sexual abuse histories and sequelae in female psychiatric emergency room patients. *American Journal of Psychiatry* **146**, 1602–1606.

British Psychological Society (1995) *Recovered Memories; The Report of the Working Party of the British Psychological Society*. BPS, Nottingham.

Brucker, D.F. & Johnson, P.E. (1987) Treatment of adult male victims of childhood sexual abuse. Social casework. *Journal of Contemporary Social Work* **68**, 81–87.

Cahill, C., Llewellyn, S.P. & Pearson, C. (1991) Treatment of sexual abuse which occurred in childhood: a review. *British Journal of Clinical Psychology* **30**, 1–12.

Chard, K.M., Weaver, T.L. & Resick, P.A. (1997) Adapting cognitive processing therapy for child sexual abuse survivors. *Cognitive and Behavioural Practice* **4**(1), 312–352.

Cheasty, M., Clare, A.W. & Collins, C. (1998) Relationship between sexual abuse in childhood and adult depression: a case controlled study. *British Medical Journal* **316**, 198–201.

Clarke, S. & Llewellyn, S. (1994) Personal constructs of survivors of child sexual abuse receiving cognitive analytic therapy. *British Journal of Medical Psychology*

67, 273–289.

Courtois, C. (1994) Treatment of incest and complex dissociative traumatic stress reactions. In: *Innovations in Clinical Practice: A Source Book* (eds L. Vandercreek, S. Knapp & T.L. Jackson), Volume 13. Professional Resource Press, Saratosa, FL.

Crowder, A. (1995) *Opening the Door: A Treatment Model for Therapy with Female Survivors of Sexual Abuse*. Brunner/Mazel, New York.

Dimock, P.T. (1988) Adult males sexually abused as children. *Journal of Interpersonal Violence* **3**, 203–221.

Donaldson, M.A. & Cordes-Green (1994) *Group Treatment of Adult Incest Survivors*. Sage, CA.

Drauker, C.B. (1992) *Counselling Survivors of Sexual Abuse*. Sage, CA.

Everill, J. & Waller, G. (1995) Disclosure of sexual abuse and psychological adjustment in female undergraduates. *Child Abuse and Neglect* **19**, 93–100.

Finkelhor, D. & Browne, A. (1985) The traumatic impact of child sexual abuse: a conceptualisation. *American Journal of Orthopsychiatry* **55**, 530–541.

Foa, E.B., Rothbaum, B.O., Riggs, D.S. & Murdock, T. (1991) Treatment of PTSD in rape victims: a comparison between cognitive-behavioural procedures and counselling. *Journal of Consulting and Clinical Psychology* **59**, 715–723.

Fromuth, M.E. & Burkhart, B.R. (1989) Long term psychological correlates of childhood sexual abuse in two samples of college men. *Child Abuse and Neglect* **13**, 533–542.

Herman, J. & Hirschman, L. (1981) *Father–Daughter Incest*. Harvard University Press, Cambridge, MA.

Jaycox, L.H. & Foa, E.B. (1996) Obstacles in implementing exposure therapy for PTSD: case discussions and practical solutions *Clinical Psychology and Psychotherapy* **3**(3), 176–184.

Jehu, D. (1988) *Beyond Sexual Abuse: Therapy with Women who were Victims in Childhood*. Wiley, Chichester.

Jehu, D. (1989a) Sexual dysfunction among women clients who were sexually abused in childhood. *Behavioural Psychotherapy* **17**, 53–70.

Jehu, D. (1989b) Mood disturbances among women clients sexually abused in childhood: prevalence, etiology, treatment. *Journal of Interpersonal Violence* **4**, 164–184.

Jehu, D. (1991) Clinical work with adults who were sexually abused in childhood. In: *Clinical Approaches to Sex Offenders and their Victims* (eds C.R. Hollin & K. Howells). Wiley, Chichester.

Jehu, D. (1994) *Patients as Victims: Sexual Abuse in Psychotherapy and Counselling.* Wiley, Chichester.

Jehu, D., Klassen, C. & Gazan, M. (1986) Cognitive restructuring of distorted beliefs associated with childhood sexual abuse. *Journal of Social Work and Human Sexuality* **4**, 49–69.

Kennerley, H. (1995) A schema questionnaire for survivors of childhood trauma: preliminary findings. *International Cognitive Therapy Newsletter* **9**(2), 1.

Kennerley, H. (1996) Cognitive therapy of dissociative symptoms associated with trauma. *British Journal of Clinical Psychology* **35**, 325–340.

Kennerley, H., Whitehead, L., Butler, G. & Norris, R. (1998) *Recovering from Childhood Trauma: A Therapy Workbook.* Oxford University Press, Oxford.

Layden, M.A., Newman, C.F., Freeman, A. & Byers-Morse, S. (1993) *Cognitive Therapy of Borderline Personality Disorder.* Allyn & Bacon, Needham Heights, MA.

Lazarus, A.A. (1973) Multi-modal behaviour therapy: treating the 'BASIC ID'. *Journal of Nervous and Mental Disease* **156**, 404–411.

Leserman, J., Zhiming, L., Drossman, D.A., Toomey, T.C., Nachman, G. & Glogau, L. (1997) Impact of sexual and physical abuse on health status: development of an abuse severity measure. *Psychosomatic Medicine* **59**, 152–160.

Linehan, M.M. (1993) *Cognitive-Behavioural Treatment of BPD.* Guilford, New York.

Marks, I., Lovell, K., Noshirvani, H., Livanou, M. & Thrasher, S. (1998) Treatment of posttraumatic stress disorder by exposure and/or cognitive restructuring: a controlled study. *Archives of General Psychiatry* **55**, 317–325.

Marlatt, G. & Gordon, J. (1985) *Relapse Prevention: Maintenance Strategies in the Treatment of Addictive Behaviours.* Guilford, New York.

Meichenbaum, D. (1985) *Stress Inoculation Training.* Pergamon, Oxford.

Miller, W.R. & Rollnick, S. (1992) *Motivational Interviewing: Preparing People to Change Addictive Behaviour.* Guilford, New York.

Mullen, P.E., Martin, J.L., Anderson, J.C., Romans, S.E. & Herbison, G.P. (1993) Child sexual abuse and mental health in adult life. *British Journal of Psychiatry* **163**, 721–732.

Muran, J.C., Segal, Z.V., Samstag, L.W. & Crawford, C.E. (1994) Patient pre-treatment interpersonal problems and therapeutic alliance in short-term cognitive therapy. *Journal of Consulting and Clinical Psychology* **62**(1), 185–190.

Padesky, C. (1994) Schema change processes in cognitive therapy. *Clinical Psychology and Psychotherapy* **1**(1), 21–27.

Padesky, C. & Mooney, K. (1991) Clinical tip: presenting the cognitive model to clients. *International Cognitive Therapy Newsletter* **5/6**, 3–4.

Pearlman, L.A. & MacIan, P.S. (1995) Vicarious traumatisation: an empirical study of the effects of trauma work on trauma therapists. *Professional Psychology Research and Practice* **26**(6), 558–565.

Peters, S.D., Wyatt, G.E. & Finkelhor, D. (1986) Prevalence. In: *A Source Book of Childhood Sexual Abuse.* (ed. D. Finkelhor), pp. 15–89. Sage, Beverley Hills, CA.

Piaget, J. (1948) *The Moral Judgement of the Child* (Translated: M. Gabain). Freepress, Glencoe, IL.

Pretzer, J. (1990) Borderline personality disorder. In: *Cognitive Therapy of Personality Disorders* (eds A.T. Beck *et al.*). Guilford, New York.

Pribor, E.F. & Dinwiddie, S.H. (1992 Psychiatric correlates of incest in childhood. *American Journal of Psychiatry* **149**(1), 285–293.

Putnam, F.W., Guroff, J.J., Silbermann, E.K., Barban, L. & Post, R.M. (1986) The clinical phenomenology of multiple personality disorder: a review of 100 recent cases. *Journal of Clinical Psychiatry* **47**, 285–293.

Raue, P.J., Goldfried, M.R. & Barkham, M. (1997) The therapeutic alliance in psychodynamic interpersonal and cognitive-behavioural therapies. *Journal of Consulting and Clinical Psychology* **65**(4), 582–587.

Renshaw, D. (1982) *Incest: Understanding and Treatment.* Little Brown, Boston.

Rodriguez, N., Ryan, S.W., Van der Kemp, H. & Foy, D.W. (1997) Posttraumatic stress disorder in adult female survivors of childhood sexual abuse: a comparison study. *Journal of Consulting and Clinical Psychology* **65**(1), 53–59.

Romans, S.E., Martin, J.L., Anderson, J.C., Herbison, G.P. & Mullen, P.E. (1995) Sexual abuse in childhood and deliberate self-harm. *American Journal of Psychiatry* **152**(9), 1336–1342.

Russell, D.E.H. (1986) *The Secret Trauma: Incest in the Lives of Girls and Women.* Basic Books, NY.

Ryle, A. (1990) *Cognitive Analytic Therapy.* Wiley, London.

Ryle, A. (1997) *Cognitive Analytic Therapy for Borderline Personality Disorder.* Wiley, London.

Safran, J.D. & Segal, Z.V. (1990) *Interpersonal Process in Cognitive Therapy.* Basic Books, New York.

Salmon, P. & Calderbank, S. (1995) The relationship of childhood sexual abuse to adult illness behaviour. *Journal of Psychosomatic Research* **40**(3), 329–336.

Sanford, L.T. (1991) *Strong at the Broken Places.* Virago, London.

Sedney, M.A. & Brooks, B. (1984) Factors associated with a history of childhood experience in a non-clinical female population. *Journal of American Academy of Child Psychiatry* **23**, 215–218.

Sheldon, H. (1988) Child sexual abuse in adult female psychotherapy referrals: incidence and implications for treatment. *British Journal of Psychiatry* **152**, 107–111.

Smith, G. (1989) The traumatic response cycle: working with adult survivors of childhood sexual abuse. *Clinical Psychology Forum* **22**, 38–42.

Summit, R. (1983) The child sexual abuse accommodation syndrome. *Child Abuse and Neglect* **7**, 177–193.

Swett, C., Surrey, J. & Cohen, C. (1990) Sexual and physical abuse histories and psychiatric symptoms among male psychiatric outpatients. *American Journal of Psychiatry* **147**(5), 632–636.

Teasdale, J.D. (1996) Clinically relevant theory: integrating clinical insight with *cognitive* science. In: *Frontiers of Cognitive Therapy* (ed. P Salkovskis). Guilford, New York.

Teasdale, J.D. & Barnard, P.S. (1993) *Affect, Cognition and Change: Re-modelling Depressive Thought.* Lawrence Earlbaum Associates.

Tice, L., Hall, R., Beresford, T., Quinones, J. & Hall, A. (1989) Sexual abuse in patients with eating disorders. *Psychiatric Medicine* **7**(4), 257–267.

Vanderlinden, J. (1993) *Dissociative Experiences, Trauma and Hypnosis: Research Findings and Clinical Applications in Eating Disorders.* Eburon, Delft.

Waller, G. (1991) Sexual abuse as a factor in the eating disorders. *British Journal of Psychiatry* **159**, 664–671.

Waller, G. & Ruddock, A. (1993) Experience of disclosure of childhood sexual abuse and psychopathology. *Child Abuse Review* **2**, 185–195.

Waller, G. & Smith, R. (1994) Sexual abuse and psychological disorders: the role of cognitive processes. *Behavioural and Cognitive Psychotherapy* **22**, 299–314.

Waller, G., Quinton, S. & Watson, D. (1995) Dissociation and the processing of threat-related information. *Dissociation* **8**, 84–90.

West, D. (1988) Incest in childhood and adolescents: long term effects and therapy. *British Journal of Hospital Medicine,* **40**, 352–360.

Weston, D. (1991) Cognitive-behavioural interventions in the psychoanalytic psychotherapy of borderline personality disorder. *Clinical Psychology Review* **11**, 211–230.

Young, J.E. (1990) *Cognitive Therapy for Personality Disorders: A Schema-Focussed Approach.* Practitioner Resource Exchange, Sarasota, FL.

Chapter 18

Psychological Aspects of Fertility, Reproduction and Menopause

Anne Walker and Myra Hunter

Introduction

Fertility, reproduction and menopause are embodied experiences, associated with apparent and hidden, physical and physiological processes. They are also experiences which have psychological and cultural meanings, and which occur within the framework of particular material social circumstances. For this reason, reproduction, like sexuality, has been the site of considerable theoretical debate within and between psychology, psychoanalysis, sociology, medicine and feminism in recent years (Ussher 1997). For this reason too, it is difficult to draw generalisations about psychological aspects of reproductive experiences. People differ not only in their physical manifestations of fertility, but also in the cultural and social situation in which they encounter those experiences and in their personal cognitive and emotional reactions to them. These sociocultural and psychological factors also imply that similar experiences can have vastly different meanings at different times in the same person's life. For example, the onset of menstruation may be greeted quite differently by a 17-year-old who has risked conception than by the same woman seeking to conceive in her late thirties.

The reproductive problems which we are concerned with here fall largely into the category of gynaecological disorders. Men also experience physical and psychological problems associated with reproduction (Gannon 1995), although these have received far less attention within the medical and scientific literature. In this chapter, the discussion will be restricted to experiences for which people seek help (e.g. menstrual problems, or difficulties with conception), or which are commonly thought to be troublesome (e.g. menopause). The sections below describe psychological approaches to infertility, menstrual problems, premenstrual syndrome, postpartum depression and menopause. For women, interactions with health professionals in any of these circumstances may require an intimate examination or procedures which may themselves be traumatic, hence psychological aspects of gynaecological procedures will also be discussed.

Over the last century, several broad features have characterised the major part of scientific interest in reproduction. First, there has been a predominant focus on the physiological mechanisms underlying reproduction, with a strong emphasis on medical diagnosis and treatment of problems. The research and development activity surrounding reproductive technology and assisted conception is a good example of this. Relatively little attention has been paid to reproductive experiences from a lifespan developmental or normative perspective. Second, research and treatment has almost always been concerned with women, reflecting the long-held cultural assumption that reproduction is 'women's work' (Martin 1989). The capacity to have children is often seen as the 'essence' of femininity, and assumed to be linked directly to women's emotional experiences and cognitive capacities; hence, the attention paid to premenstrual syndrome, 'menopausal syndrome' and 'postnatal depression'. In contrast, pain and discomfort associated with menstruation have been historically considered 'normal', and many gynaecological problems have received relatively little research attention (e.g. chronic pelvic pain, endometriosis, menstrual disorders, pelvic inflammatory disease, uterine and ovarian cancers). Third, reproduction has been viewed until recently through the lens of heterosexual sexuality, resulting in a neglect of the gynaecological problems experienced by lesbian women and the fertility issues of people who are not in heterosexual relationships.

In recent years, biopsychosocial models have come to replace essentialist biomedical or psychosomatic theories of reproductive experiences (Ussher 1992). These models address the need to examine the complex relationships between psychological, social and biological influences and explain individual differences. These models take into account an individual's psychosocial and cultural context as well as their experience of physical changes, in determining the meaning and impact of reproductive problems. Cognitive factors such as symptom attributions or illness representations are often positioned centrally in biopsychosocial models and the model can be expanded and tailored to individual clients in clinical settings.

Gynaecological procedures

Gynaecological procedures can range from relatively minor examinations, such as cervical screening or IUD insertion, through more invasive procedures, such as dilatation and curettage (D&C) or colposcopy, to major surgery, e.g. hysterectomy or pelvic floor repair. Surgery usually occurs in hospital, but other procedures can occur in a variety of settings, including family planning or 'well woman' clinics and GP surgeries as well as specialist gynaecology clinics. The overwhelming majority of women will experience at least one vaginal examination during their lifetime, and other procedures are also common. For example, one in five women in Britain will have had a hysterectomy by the age of 65. Some procedures are more common for some groups of women, however. A representative study of hospital admissions in Britain found significant differences in the frequency of hysterectomy, D&C and hospital admission rates according to social class and educational qualification, with all procedures being more frequent amongst the less advantaged groups

(Kuh & Stirling 1995). Studies like this suggest that, whilst there may be similarities across women, there will also be differences – which will be mediated by inequalities in health care and clinical assumptions about what is in a particular woman's interest.

Almost all gynaecological procedures involve an internal vaginal examination, which can be a stressful experience for several reasons. It involves exposure and examination of parts of the body which are usually kept secret; it can mimic penetration during heterosexual intercourse; and the woman herself has no control over the examination. For the majority of women, a vaginal examination is stressful, and symptoms of post-traumatic stress disorder have been identified following gynaecological investigations (Menage 1993). Many women express a preference for a female doctor (Ivins & Kent 1993).

In addition to the stresses associated with any gynaecological consultation, particular procedures also arouse anxiety, because of concerns about what an investigation may show or the long-term consequences of treatment. It is difficult in these situations to disentangle the psychological effects of particular diagnoses (especially those which might imply cancer) and the stress of the procedure itself. For example, women who undergo treatment following an abnormal cervical smear test result experience considerable distress during the process of diagnosis and treatment, although the treatment itself may not have measurable psychological costs over and above the effect of diagnosis (Palmer *et al.* 1993).

Hysterectomy, removal of the uterus, is one of the most common major surgical operations in many countries. In many cases, the woman's ovaries are removed at the same time to prevent ovarian cancer. In premenopausal women, hormone replacement therapy (HRT) is usually prescribed if the ovaries are removed, to counteract the effect of a premature menopause. A hysterectomy can be conducted abdominally (in which an incision is made and the uterus removed), or vaginally. Both procedures require general anaesthesia and hospital admission. Post-operative recovery usually takes about eight days in hospital and then six weeks or so to convalesce. Early studies suggested a high rate of psychiatric disorder following hysterectomy; however, carefully controlled studies have refuted this. In recent studies, rates of psychological distress are lower after surgery than before (Gath *et al.* 1995). The effect of hysterectomy on sexual activity and enjoyment is less clear, with wide variation between women, some experiencing an improvement in their sex lives after surgery, and others (approximately 1 in 5) a deterioration (Nathorst-Boos *et al.* 1993). Women whose ovaries have been removed are more likely to be dissatisfied with sex after the operation, often describing difficulties with sexual arousal and vaginal lubrication, regardless of HRT use. The best predictors of satisfaction with sex after surgery are measures of satisfaction before the operation and feelings towards a sexual partner, suggesting that for some women relationship or sexual counselling may be helpful (Helstrom *et al.* 1993).

Endometrial ablation (EA) is a surgical technique to remove or reduce the endometrium (lining of the uterus) without removing the uterus itself, and has become a popular alternative to hysterectomy for women with menorrhagia. EA requires a general anaesthetic but can be undertaken in day-care units and post-operative recovery time is short. A proportion of women, however, experience a return of their symptoms at some point after the procedure, and may go on to have a hysterectomy. Hence, many women are faced with a difficult choice between EA and hysterectomy. A recent randomised controlled trial of EA and hysterectomy found that both significantly reduced anxiety and depression, with no differences in mental health between the two groups 12 months after surgery (Alexander *et al.* 1996).

Psychological interventions can effectively reduce the anxiety associated with gynaecological procedures (Rafferty & Williams 1987). These interventions are usually presented as part of the preparation for either medical (usually screening) or surgical procedures. Five main types have been investigated: information, behavioural instructions, relaxation, modelling and cognitive coping training. Most of these strategies have been tested in relation to cervical screening, colposcopy or hysterectomy, and their efficacy assessed in terms of 'hard' outcomes, such as use of analgesia or length of stay in hospital postoperatively as well as mood and well-being. Reviews of these studies suggest that, whilst information alone can be beneficial, the best outcomes are obtained from interventions which include aspects of reassurance, relaxation or cognitive coping, enabling women to use whatever type of preparation best fits with their own coping styles (Johnston & Vogele 1993).

Menstrual problems

Menstruation, the shedding of the lining of the womb, is one part of a cycle of physiological changes involving the hypothalamus, pituitary and ovaries as well as the uterus itself. In western societies, most women experience menstruation for the first time between 10 and 16, and will have around 400 menstrual periods before the menopause. Despite the textbook description of a 'clockwork' 28-day menstrual cycle, only one in eight cycles is exactly 28 days long. In fact, although individual women tend to have their own menstrual patterns, menstrual cycles in general vary considerably both between women and across the lifetime of an individual woman, in terms of cycle length, the number of days on which menstruation occurs and the amount of blood and fluid lost during menstruation. This variability means that menstrual disorders are difficult to define, and epidemiological studies are problematic. However, menstrual disorders are among the ten most common complaints seen in primary care settings, and since many women do not seek help from physicians (Scambler & Scambler 1993) it is likely that large numbers of women experience menstrual problems at some time in their life, and that most of these women develop their own ways of coping with them.

The most common menstrual problem is dysmenorrhoea, or pain before and during menstruation. In studies of non-patient populations as many as 70% of women report some pain associated with menstruation, and 5–10% regularly experience pain which is severe enough to be incapacitating for between an hour to three days each month (Golub 1992). Other common complaints are excessive menstrual bleeding (menorrhagia), and absence of menstruation (amenorrhoea). Menorrhagia is usually defined as loss of over 50 ml of blood in one menstruation, a level which may put women at risk for anaemia (Rees

1987), and approximately 5% of women between 30 and 49 will seek help from a doctor for it. There are many organic causes of menorrhagia, for example, uterine fibroids, thyroid dysfunction or intrauterine contraceptive devices. For as many as half of the women complaining of heavy periods, however, no organic cause can be found. Recent research suggests that some of these women may have inherited blood disorders (Kadir *et al.* 1998). The most likely medical investigation is a D&C, followed by hormonal or surgical treatments, usually hysterectomy or endometrial ablation.

Primary amenorrhoea is defined as the absence of menstruation by the age of 16, whilst secondary amenorrhoea is the cessation of periods among women who have experienced menstruation. Primary amenorrhoea may be associated with particular genetic characteristics (e.g. Turner's syndrome) or it may be caused by organic disease (e.g. pituitary tumour). The most common cause of secondary amenorrhoea is pregnancy. However, the close physiological interaction between body weight, psychological and physical stress and reproductive function means that both primary and secondary amenorrhoea may be associated with low body weight or intense physical training. Secondary amenorrhoea may be a symptom of an eating disorder, although the precise mechanism for this is not clear (Weltman *et al.* 1990).

The psychological component of menstrual problems is best viewed through a biopsychosocial lens. For example, dysmenorrhoea is generally associated with high levels of prostaglandins in the uterus, and 80% of women obtain effective pain relief with non-steroidal anti-inflammatory drugs (NSAIDs) which have an anti-prostaglandin effect. However, women who experience severe period pain are more likely to be depressed or anxious during menstruation than women who do not, and quickly develop a learned anticipatory fear response to menstruation. Similarly, a range of behavioural and environmental factors, such as smoking, a diet which is low in fish oils, high levels of stress and some occupational hazards, increase the risk of dysmenorrhoea. These factors suggest that psychological interventions may have a role to play in helping women to deal with aspects of their lives which increase dysmenorrhoea, or to manage negative reactions to it. Similarly, studies have suggested that almost two-thirds of women who seek help for heavy periods are also at least mildly depressed (Greenberg 1983), and a relationship has been found between recent life events and help-seeking (Harris 1989). Heavy menstruation is difficult to cope with at a practical level, and may cause disruption in close relationships or interfere with work, as well as being associated with the risk of anaemia. Hence, it is not surprising that women who seek help are mildly depressed, or that they tend to seek help at times when recent life events may have exhausted their ability to cope with heavy periods. Cognitive coping interventions may also prove beneficial for these women, although they have not yet been evaluated. Psychological interventions for women with amenorrhoea are rarely specific to the menstrual problem itself, but are more likely to be concerned with other difficulties which are associated with it, for example anorexia.

Premenstrual syndrome

Surveys suggest that around 95% of women in

western cultures experience minor changes in their physical or emotional well-being in the days before some or all of their menstrual periods, and that a small proportion (around 5–10%), experience debilitating symptoms which disrupt their lives. Almost two hundred possible premenstrual signs and symptoms have been identified. Individual women vary in terms of how many of these they experience, in what combination, how intense they are, and whether they occur in every cycle or less frequently. Most of the documented signs are usually considered to be unpleasant, e.g., irritability, depressed mood, breast tenderness, swelling of the abdomen, backache and fatigue. However, epidemiological studies suggest that for around 5–15% of women the premenstrual phase of the menstrual cycle is associated with 'positive' experiences, such as high energy levels, creativity or feelings of well-being (Walker 1997).

Unpleasant premenstrual experiences which are relieved within a few days of the onset of menstruation were defined as 'premenstrual syndrome' (PMS) by Greene and Dalton (1953). Such an all-encompassing definition can acknowledge the huge range of experiences which women complain of, but is problematic, because it can be used either to imply that almost all menstruating women are 'ill' and incapacitated for days or weeks of each month, or that PMS is common and therefore 'normal'. Considerable effort has been made in both gynaecology and psychiatry to produce a definition which discriminates between women whose experiences warrant clinical intervention and those who do not, whilst at the same time allowing for the diversity of premenstrual experiences, so far with limited success. The best known, and most contro-

versial recent definition is that of 'premenstrual dysphoric disorder' (PMDD) in DSM-IV (Gold & Severino 1994). PMDD, as its name implies, refers principally to emotional experiences in the days before menstruation, and is controversial because it implies that premenstrual experiences constitute a psychiatric disorder. It has been argued that there are a number of different 'premenstrual syndromes', of which PMDD may be one, but empirical support for this is mixed (Jorgensen et al. 1993). It has also been argued that PMS is an idiosyncratic syndrome, which is expressed differently in different women (Gotts et al. 1995).

Theories about the cause of PMS range from physiological to social constructionist, and none have been well supported in research studies. Currently, biopsychosocial models of PMS are the most widely advocated. For example, Bancroft (1993) hypothesises that PMS results from the interaction between a 'timing factor', related to the hormonal fluctuations of the cycle, a 'menstruation factor', involving processes leading up to menstruation, and a 'vulnerability factor', characteristics of the woman which make her vulnerable – such as personality, a predisposition to depression or stress. Others see PMS as the result of interactions between physiological, psychological, socioeconomic and cultural processes (Ussher 1992). The interactions between these systems are proposed to be so complex and intricate that PMS is effectively an idiosyncratic syndrome with different causes and different symptoms in different women.

Management of PMS should begin with careful assessment of the nature, timing and context of the woman's complaints. It is usually recommended that, following a thorough history, the woman should keep a daily symptom chart or diary for two menstrual cycles, to monitor the pattern of changes she experiences (O'Brien 1993). Some women find diary keeping therapeutic in itself, and it can form the basis for cognitive-behavioural work as well as helping to identify more chronic conditions. Three broad approaches have been taken to interventions for PMS: changes in diet and lifestyle; control of the menstrual cycle; and management of specific symptoms. Reviews of different surgical, pharmacological, dietary and psychosocial treatments for PMS have suggested that many of these are effective for at least some premenstrual symptoms but none can 'abolish' PMS without simultaneously abolishing the menstrual cycle (Rivera-Tovar *et al.* 1994). In addition, all of the surgical and pharmacological treatments have associated risks and side effects (Mortola 1994). Careful trials are essential in PMS research because of the high initial placebo effect, which is usually greater than 50%, and can be as high as 94%.

A number of studies have now been conducted of a variety of psychological interventions, including support groups, relaxation and cognitive-behavioural type therapies with individuals or groups. All of these can be effective and several studies of CBT have demonstrated a beneficial effect over placebo, which is at least as powerful as progesterone treatment. It is not clear whether these effects relate specifically to premenstrual experiences or whether the woman is generally 'happier' or more able to cope. What is clear is that enabling women to develop their own coping strategies and skills can be as effective as the majority of current drug therapies (Stout 1995).

Fertility problems

Infertility, defined as the inability to conceive following twelve months of regular sexual intercourse without contraception, is estimated to affect 10–15% of couples of childbearing age (Greenhall & Vessey 1990). Fertility problems can be separated into primary, i.e. never having conceived, and secondary, in which the couple have at least one child. It is generally estimated that 40% of infertility can be attributed to male factor problems, such as deficient sperm production or impaired delivery of sperm, and about 40% to female factor problems such as ovulatory and hormonal as well as pelvic problems, i.e. endometriosis, adhesions or tubal blockages. However, in a substantial number of cases no specified cause can be identified (Snowden & Snowden 1984).

Psychological factors have been considered in early studies as potential causes of fertility problems. Attempts to identify specific psychological characteristics of infertile women have largely been unsuccessful, although the possibility remains that stress may affect some aspects of reproduction, such as ovulation. It is now recognised that the experience of fertility problems and the process of treatment itself is often associated with considerable emotional distress (Edelmann & Connolly 1987; Slade *et al.* 1992), although individual reactions are highly variable (Jones & Hunter 1994). Commonly reported negative effects include reactions of grief, self-blame, depression, anxiety, lowered self-esteem, disturbed sexual functioning (often caused by anxiety, feelings of failure as well as pressure to have intercourse at specific times) and difficulties in achieving adequate support in relationships where both partners might be dealing with distress in different ways. The costs of some treatments, such as in vitro fertilisation (IVF) social and cultural pressures to conceive, and the cycles of hope and disappointment that can characterise repeated treatment attempts are frequent sources of distress. In addition, waiting times for treatment appointments, communication about investigation and treatments, and provision for the emotional aspects of infertility during investigation and treatment have been pinpointed by couples as areas that warrant improvement (Greenhall & Vessey 1990).

Medical treatments include ovulation induction, surgery, intra-uterine insemination and the newer reproductive treatments such as IVF, gamete intra-fallopian tube transfer (GIFT), intra cytoplasmic sperm injection (ICSI), donor insemination (DI) and egg donation. IVF is regarded as the only hope of treatment for many couples, particularly those with tubal damage, but is associated with high levels of anxiety and distress and relatively moderate outcomes (approximately 15–20% of treatment cycles result in a live birth). DI is a simpler procedure and is often more successful. However, there are many social and ethical issues associated with a couple having a child who is genetically and 'socially' the woman's, but only 'socially' the man's; the reverse would be the case for a woman using egg donation. The issue of secrecy versus openness in terms of telling the DI child remains controversial. Many couples at the treatment stage opt for secrecy, while concerns for the rights of the child to know his or her biological origins and the difficulties of maintaining secrecy when some people know have led to arguments for greater openness (Daniels & Taylor 1993).

Few psychological interventions for individuals and couples with fertility problems have been developed or evaluated. However, adequate information, realistic expectations about the processes and outcomes of treatments and the opportunity to weigh up possible options – both with and without a child – would seem to be reasonable aims of counselling (Glover et al. 1998). Adjustment to infertility has been compared to a bereavement process – the loss of a future child – which can be facilitated by psychological support. Individual, group, couple or psychosexual therapy may also be helpful in some cases. In an earlier study, Domar and colleagues (1992) developed a ten-week group cognitive-behavioural intervention for couples undergoing fertility treatments. Although no control group was included there were significant reductions in anxiety and depression following the intervention. The need for psychological support for people with fertility problems has been reinforced by the Human Fertility and Embryology Act (1990) which recommends that counselling (implications, supportive and therapeutic) be made available for all people seeking licensed treatments, i.e. IVF or treatments involving donated gametes. Psychologists might also be involved in interventions to modify behavioural and psychosocial factors such as smoking and unsafe sexual practices, that might influence infertility.

Postnatal depression

Postnatal depression (PND), defined strictly as persistent depression with one or more other symptoms, is estimated to affect approximately 10–15% of women within a year following childbirth (Cox & Holden 1993). However, depressed mood per se is reported by up to 30% of women postnatally. While it is not certain whether PND is essentially different from depression at other times of life, or whether the levels of depression at this time represent a significant increase, it can be differentiated from the 'maternity blues' and postnatal psychosis, which affect 50–75% and 0.2% of mothers respectively. Nevertheless, PND may have a greater potential impact than depression at other times. There is an increasing body of evidence suggesting negative long-term outcomes for the mother (Philips & O'Hara 1991) and the child (Murray et al. 1993), for example, in terms of mother-child attachment, and the child's behavioural and cognitive functioning where the mother has PND.

Theories about PND have again been polarised between medical models which have sought to define a clinical syndrome with a hormonal or neurochemical substrate, and psychosocial models, which view childbirth as a significant life event, with the same potential for precipitating depression as other major events. While reproductive hormone levels do change dramatically after childbirth, no association has been demonstrated between such changes and PND, although the possibility of a hormonal contribution to PND cannot be ruled out. Stronger associations have been found between psychosocial factors and PND, in particular, previous history of depression, anxiety or depression during pregnancy, a poor relationship with a partner and inadequate social support (Eliot 1989). In addition, financial and housing problems, a history of childhood sexual abuse, neglect or difficult early relationships, past pregnancy loss

or cot death and/or bereavement during pregnancy are commonly associated with PND.

From the woman's point of view, the experience of motherhood with tiredness, sleepless nights, isolation, anxieties about mothering skills and possibly feeding difficulties, can fall short of idealised media images. A qualitative study of women's experiences of childbirth suggested that, apart from the physical adjustment and initial insecurities, the degree and quality of support in the early months of mothering was probably the most crucial factor accounting for emotional distress. In addition, the women described the potential loss of former identity, sometimes including loss of occupation, contacts with friends and change of role within the family (Nicolson 1990). However, it is not uncommon for women to have ambivalent feelings which may, for example, be positive about the child but more complex about being a mother. A focus upon postnatal problems has tended to emphasise the negative and overlook the positive experiences following childbirth (Green & Kafetsios 1997).

PND is difficult to acknowledge and remains undetected in many cases, partly because women feel ashamed or fear the consequences of the involvement of psychiatrists and social services, and also because it is often difficult to know when to label feelings as 'abnormal' in the context of a dramatically changed and unfamiliar new lifestyle (Holden et al. 1989). Similarly, health professionals may be reluctant or lack the training to identify PND. A screening questionnaire, the Edinburgh Postnatal Depression Questionnaire (EPDS) (Cox & Holden 1993) has been developed which is short and easy for health visitors to use at the six-week postnatal visit and can be used to evaluate interventions. However, consideration should be given to training and supervision of staff who are to carry out the screening.

Interventions for PND include antidepressants, hormone therapy and psychological treatments. Ideally, multidisciplinary systems should be used to co-ordinate treatments, including health visitor, midwife, general practitioner, clinical psychologist, obstetrician, psychiatrist and community resources. Additional services for women considered to be at risk of developing PND have been provided antenatally, in order to offer increased support for women in small groups, with promising results (Eliot 1989). Psychological interventions for those identified as being at risk using the EPDS, which have proved successful in reducing levels of PND, include group treatments using cognitive models (Eliot 1989) and postnatal non-directive listening visits (up to eight) offered by health visitors to women who scored above a cutoff point on the EPDS at their six-week postnatal visit (Holden *et al.* 1989). Training and supervision of health visitors is recommended for this type of service, as is support for such interventions by the many professional systems involved. There is some evidence that as well as reducing depression, treatments can have positive effects for the well-being of the child. For example, in a recent British study three types of psychological intervention for women identified as having PND were compared in a primary care setting: non-directive counselling, cognitive-behaviour therapy focusing on mother-child interactions and dynamic therapy called 'mother-child therapy'. The three therapies proved equally effective in reducing depression and the rate of maternal reports of mother-child

relationship problems (Copper & Murray 1997).

The menopause

The menopause, a woman's last menstrual period, occurs on average between the ages of 50 and 51 (typical age range 45 to 55) and is preceded by a gradual decrease in production of oestrogen by the ovaries and reduction in the frequency of ovulation. The most commonly used classification in medical practice and research is based on menstrual criteria, defining women as postmenopausal if no menstruation has occurred during the previous twelve months. On average it takes four years from the first noticeable change in the pattern of menstruation until twelve months after the last menstrual period (McKinlay *et al.* 1992). However, there is marked variation between women with respect to its timing and duration. Menopause can also result from surgery (oophorectomy), medical treatment or disease, and is considered to be premature if it happens before the age of 40.

Hot flushes and night sweats, also called vasomotor symptoms, are the only definite symptoms of the menopause, and affect between 60 and 70% of women. Nevertheless, a wide variety of symptoms have been attributed to hormone changes during the menopause, such as irritability, headaches, depression, anxiety, weight gain, aches and pains, poor memory and concentration, and loss of libido – experiences often included under the broad term 'menopausal syndrome'. The dominant medical model posits the menopause as an oestrogen deficiency disease, a cluster of physical and emotional symptoms that can be treated by hormone replacement therapy (HRT). This view has been challenged by social scientists and feminist researchers who advocate biopsychosocial or social constructionist perspectives, which are less likely to pathologise the menopause.

From a woman's perspective the menopause has acquired complex social and cultural meanings, being inextricably linked to age and often coinciding with life changes (Hunter & O'Dea 1997). Concepts such as 'empty nest', physical decline, loss of femininity, loss of sexuality, involutional melancholia and vaginal atrophy have contributed to varied but generally negative stereotypes of menopausal women in western cultures. In general, women living in non-western societies appear to report fewer symptoms at the menopause than those living in the west. However, it is likely that material differences, such as dietary and reproductive practices and levels of exercise, contribute to cross-cultural differences, as well as cultural values and the social position of mid-aged and older women.

Controversial issues in menopause research and practice focus upon the relationship between menopause and depressed mood and the promotion of HRT for a broad range of 'symptoms'. Do women become depressed during the menopause, and should HRT be offered as treatment for emotional problems? Epidemiological and treatment studies provide evidence to address these issues.

In the 1980s, several prospective studies (Hunter 1996) were carried out in North America and Europe, using general population samples in order to clarify what changes occurred and whether any changes were associated with stage of menopause, ageing or psychosocial factors. The studies followed women for between three and five years across the menopause transition. Overall, the results suggest that the menopause is not associated with psychological symptoms or depressed mood. Similarly, there is no substantial evidence to support the view that psychiatric disorder is more prevalent during the menopause (Pearce et al. 1995). Vaginal dryness increases in prevalence in postmenopausal women and there appears to be a small but significant decrease in reported sexual interest across stages of the menopause transition, but not in ratings of overall satisfaction with sexual relationships. Depressed mood was predicted mainly by past depression together with low socio-economic status, not being employed outside the home, as well as negative beliefs. In general, psychological problems were associated with psychosocial factors to a greater extent than stage of the menopause. For example, life stress, particularly losses such as bereavements, have been found to be associated with emotional and physical symptoms, especially if they occurred in the context of additional stresses. Similarly, reduced sexual interest after the menopause was associated with prior sexual interest, marital satisfaction and stress, as well as partner's sexual functioning.

HRT is increasingly promoted for the prevention of osteoporosis and cardiovascular disease, as well as relief of hot flushes and, more recently, for improvements in quality of life. HRT has also been advocated as a treatment for depression. However, correlational studies do not support an association between oestrogen levels and mood, and treatment studies do not provide conclusive evidence that HRT alleviates depressed mood – over and above placebo effects and the secondary relief from hot flushes (Hunter 1996). HRT does, however, improve hot flushes and relieve vaginal dryness, which can in turn lead to improvements in sexual relationships.

Psychological interventions for women who do seek help for various problems during the menopause are beginning to be developed. Preliminary studies have been carried out focusing on prevention, ways of enhancing doctor-patient communication and dealing with emotional problems reported by women who seek help. For example, the effects of providing 45-year-old women with balanced information, the opportunity to discuss beliefs and expectations and health education is currently being evaluated (Liao & Hunter 1998). Interventions are also being set up to empower women in order to facilitate decision-making during medical consultations, and to overcome barriers such as lack of information and stigma of the menopause, differing agendas, gender differences and power relationships between women and health professionals (Hampson & Hibbard 1996). Psychological interventions have been developed for the treatment of hot flushes and night sweats including behavioural treatments, particularly deep breathing and relaxation. In a recent study, a cognitive-behavioural intervention, including relaxation, was found to be as effective as HRT in reducing hot flush frequency (Hunter & Liao 1996). Psychological therapies are likely to be helpful for women who attend clinics with emotional and physical problems. Individual or group therapy can help women to clarify the causes of distress in their lives and seek appropriate solutions.

Conclusions

Gender differences in psychological distress and emotional well-being have often been attributed to hormonal changes occurring across the reproductive cycle. The examples described in this chapter show that, for the majority, reproductive processes do not have major psychological sequelae. Emotional problems are more likely to be associated with psychosocial factors, such as social support and stressful life events, than hormonal changes. Similarly, the meaning of reproductive events is inevitably influenced by the woman's psychological, social and cultural context which will impact upon her experience of bodily changes. Biopsychosocial models, that give equal weight to cultural, psychosocial and biological factors, are advocated in order to lessen the likelihood of dualistic thinking and polarised views about women's health problems.

The focus in this chapter has been centred on women who do have problems and seek medical help. However, these problems need to be understood in the context of normal developmental processes and individual variation in reproductive experiences; differences in socioeconomic status, ethnicity, sexuality and age should also be acknowledged. Appreciation of these factors may help to counter assumptions and unhelpful stereotypes about female problems. The aim is to develop approaches that address women's needs for help without overly medicalising, psychologising or trivialising the difficulties that some women have, often for complex reasons.

Good communication is central to clearer understandings of reproductive problems in health care settings (Hunter 1994). A woman's beliefs, or cognitive representations, of her problems are at the core of the biopsychosocial model, and it is her own theory or model, based on a range of influences, which is crucial and which may or may not be communicated to the health professional. Differing understandings or illness representations, between doctor and patient, can lead to dissatisfaction with communication and inappropriate treatment decisions. Therefore, it is important that an environment is created that is non-judgemental so that different explanations of problems can be explored. Women are increasingly being faced with complex reproductive health decisions and treatment choices, for example, relating to antenatal and perinatal care, fertility treatments and hormone replacement therapy. Further research is needed to develop optimum procedures that facilitate informed decision-making, particularly in this area of women's health, where there is a long history of polarised views and myths about the impact of reproductive events.

Interventions have been described that include medical treatments and psychological approaches. The value of psychological interventions has been demonstrated in many areas of reproductive health, such as preparation for surgery, alleviation of pelvic pain, treatment and prevention of postnatal depression and is promising in the areas of menstrual problems, menopause and infertility. Individual and group interventions have been used, that have been carried out by clinical psychologists as well as other trained health professionals, such as health visitors. From the research outlined above, such treatments need to maintain an awareness of social and cultural aspects of reproductive problems, and to help women to develop useful theories about their difficulties which not only help them to cope but also enable them to make changes that address some of the psychosocial diffi-

culties in their lives that are commonly reported. There is a gap between research findings and the clinical application of these findings in health care settings. For optimum service delivery multidisciplinary teams need to be set in place and a biopsychosocial framework used as the basis for discussion of clinical problems. Staff training in communication skills and exploration of stereotypic beliefs relating to fertility, reproduction and menopause are essential for services that aim to provide good communication and an appropriate range of treatments.

References

Alexander, D., Naji, A., Pinion, S., *et al.* (1996) Randomised trial comparing hysterectomy with endometrial ablation for dysfunctional uterine bleeding: psychiatric and psychosocial aspects. *British Medical Journal* **312**, 280–284.

Bancroft, J. (1993) The premenstrual syndrome, a reappraisal of the concept and the evidence. *Psychological Medicine* (Suppl.) **24**.

Copper, P.J. & Murray, L (1997) The impact of postnatal depression on infant development: a treatment trial. In: *Postpartum Depression and Child Development* (eds L. Murray and P.J. Cooper). Guilford Press, London.

Cox, J.L. & Holden, J. (eds) (1993) *Prevention of Depression after Childbirth: Use and Abuse of the Edinburgh Postnatal Depression Scale*. Gaskell Press, London.

Daniels, K.R. & Taylor, K. (1993) Secrecy and openness in donor insemination. *Politics and Life Sciences* August, 155–170.

Domar, A.D., Zuttermeister, P.C., Seibel, M. & Benson, H. (1992) Psychological improvement in infertile women after behavioural treatment: a replication. *Fertility and Sterility* **58**(1), 144–147.

Edelmann, R.J. & Connolly, K.C. (1987) The counselling needs of infertile couples. *Journal of Reproductive and Infant Psychology* **5**, 63–70.

Eliot, S.A. (1989) Psychological strategies in the prevention and treatment of postnatal depression. *Bailliere's Clinical Obstetrics and Gynaecology* 3, 879–903.

Gannon, K. (1995) Andrology: men and reproduction. In: *The Psychology of Reproduction: Reproductive Potential and Fertility Control* (eds C.A. Niven & A. Walker), pp. 92–108. Butterworth-Heinemann, Oxford.

Gath, D., Rose, N., Bond, A., Day, A., Garrod, A. & Hughes, S. (1995) Hysterectomy and psychiatric disorders: are the levels of psychiatric morbidity falling? *Psychological Medicine* 25, 277–283.

Glover, L., Hunter, M., Richards, J.M., Katz, M. & Abel, P.D. (1999) Development of the Fertility Adjustment Scale. *Fertility and Sterility* 72, 623–628.

Gold, J. & Severino, S. (eds). (1994) *Premenstrual Dysphorias: Myths and Realities*. American Psychiatric Press, Washington DC.

Golub, S. (1992) *Periods: From Menarche to Menopause*. Sage, California.

Gotts G., Morse, C. & Dennerstein, L. (1995) Premenstrual complaints: an idiosyncratic syndrome. *Journal of Psychosomatic Obstetrics and Gynaecology* 16, 29–35.

Green, I. & Kafetsios, K. (1997) Positive experiences of early motherhood – predictive variables from a longitudinal study. *Journal of Reproductive and Infant Psychology* 15, 141–157.

Greenberg, M. (1983) The meaning of menorrhagia: an investigation into the association between the complaint of menorrhagia and depression. *Journal of Psychosomatic Research* 27, 209–214.

Greene, R. & Dalton, K. (1953) The premenstrual syndrome. *British Medical Journal* 1, 1007–1014.

Greenhall, E. & Vessey, M. (1990) The prevalence of subfertility: a review of the current confusion and a report of two new studies. *Fertility and Sterility* 54, 978–983.

Hampson, S.E. & Hibbard, J.H. (1996) Cross-talk about the menopause: enhancing interactions about menopause and hormone replacement therapy. *Patient Education and Counselling* 27, 177–184.

Harris, T.(1989) Disorders of menstruation. In: *Life Events and Illness* (eds G. Brown & T. Harris). Unwin Hyman, London.

Helstrom, L., Lundberg, P., Sorbom, D. & Backstrom, T. (1993) Sexuality after hysterectomy: a factor analysis of women's sexual lives before and after subtotal hys-

terectomy. *Obstetrics and Gynecology* 81, 357–362.

Holden, J., Sagovsky, R & Cox, J. (1989) Counselling in a general practice setting: a controlled study of health visitors intervention in treatment of postnatal depression. *British Medical Journal* 298, 223–226.

Hunter, M.S. (1994) *Counselling in Obstetrics and Gynaecology*, pp. 60–86. BPS Books, Leicester.

Hunter, M.S. (1996) Editorial: Depression and menopause. *British Medical Journal* 313, 1217–1218.

Hunter, M.S. & Liao, K.L.M. (1996) Evaluation of a four session cognitive-behavioural intervention for menopausal hot flushes. *British Journal of Health Psychology* 1, 113–125.

Hunter, M.S. & O'Dea, I. (1997) Menopause: bodily changes and multiple meanings. In: *Body Talk* (ed. J.M. Ussher), pp. 199–222. Routledge, London.

Ivins, J. & Kent, G. (1993) Women's preferences for male or female gynaecologists. *Journal of Reproductive and Infant Psychology* 11, 209–214.

Johnston, M. & Vogele, C. (1993) Benefits of psychological preparation for surgery: a meta-analysis. *Annals of Behavioural Medicine* 15, 245–256.

Jones, S. & Hunter, M. (1994) The influence of context and discourse on fertility experience. *Journal of Reproductive and Infant Psychology* 14, 93–111.

Jorgensen, J., Rossignol, A. & Bonnlander, H. (1993) Evidence against multiple premenstrual syndromes: results of a multivariate profile analysis of premenstrual symptomatology. *Journal of Psychosomatic Research* 37, 257–263.

Kadir, R., Economides, D.L., Sabin, C.A., Owens, D. & Lee, C.A. (1998) Frequency of inherited bleeding disorders in women with menorrhagia. *Lancet* 351, 485–489.

Kuh, D. & Stirling, S. (1995) Socioeconomic variation in admission for diseases of female genital system and breast in a national cohort aged 15–43. *British Medical Journal* 311, 840–843.

Liao, K.L.M. & Hunter, M.S. (1998) Preparation for the menopause: prospective evaluation of a health education intervention. *Maturitas* 29, 215–224.

Martin, E. (1989) *The Woman in the Body: A Cultural Analysis of Reproduction*. Open University Press, Milton Keynes.

McKinlay, S.M., Brambilla, D.J. & Posner, J. (1992) The normal menopause transition. *Maturitas* 14(2),

103–116.

Menage, J. (1993) Post-traumatic stress disorder in women who have undergone obstetric and or gynaecological procedures. A consecutive series of 30 cases of PTSD. *Journal of Reproductive and Infant Psychology* **11**, 221–228.

Mortola, J. (1994) A risk-benefit appraisal of drugs used in the management of premenstrual syndrome. *Drug Safety* **10**, 160–169.

Murray, L., Kemppton, C., Woolgar, M. & Hooper, R. (1993) Depressed mothers' speech to their infants and its relation to infant gender and cognitive development. *Journal of Child Psychology and Psychiatry* **34**, 1083–2001.

Nathorst-Boos, J., van Schultz, N. & Carlstrom, K. (1993) Elective ovarian removal and estrogen replacement therapy, effects on sexual life, psychological well-being and androgen status. *Journal of Psychosomatic Obstetrics and Gynaecology* **14**, 283–293.

Nicolson, P. (1990) Understanding postnatal depression: a mother-centred approach. *Journal of Advanced Nursing* **5**, 689–695.

O'Brien, P. (1993) Helping women with premenstrual syndrome. *British Medical Journal* **307**, 1471–1475.

Palmer, A., Tucker, S., Warren, R. & Adams, M. (1993) Understanding women's responses to treatment for cervical intra-epithelial neoplasia. *British Journal of Clinical Psychology* **32**, 101–112.

Pearce, J., Hawton, K. & Blake, F. (1995) Psychological and sexual symptoms associated with the menopause and the effects of hormone replacement therapy: a review. *British Journal of Psychiatry* **167**, 163–173.

Phillips, L.H.C. & O'Hara, M.W. (1991) Prospective study of postpartum depression: A 2 year follow up of women and children. *Journal of Abnormal Psychology*

100, 151–155.

Rafferty, P. & Williams, S. (1987) Psychological aspects of gynaecological procedures. In: *The Psychology of Reproduction: Reproductive Potential and Fertility Control* (eds C.A. Niven & A. Walker). Butterworth-Heinemann, Oxford.

Rees, M. (1987) Menorrhagia. *British Medical Journal* **294**, 759–762.

Rivera-Tovar, A., Rhodes, R., Pearstein, T. & Frank, E. (1994) Treatment efficacy. In: *Premenstrual Dysphorias: Myths and Realities* (eds J .Gold & S. Severino). American Psychiatric Press, Washington DC.

Scambler, A. & Scambler, G. (1993) *Menstrual Disorders*. Routledge, London.

Slade, P., Raval, H., Buck, P. & Lieberman, B.E. (1992) A three year follow up of emotional, marital and sexual functioning in couples who were infertile. *Journal of Reproductive and Infant Psychology* **10**, 233–243.

Snowden, R & Snowden, E. (1984) *The Gift of a Child*. Allen & Unwin, London.

Stout, A. (1995) Cognitive behavioural treatment of premenstrual syndrome and chronic gynecologic pain. *Depression* **3**, 60–65.

Ussher, J. (1992) Research and theory relating to female reproduction: implications for clinical psychology. *British Journal of Clinical Psychology* **31**, 129–151.

Ussher, J. (ed.) (1997) *Body Talk: The Material and Discursive Regulation of Sexuality, Madness and Reproduction*. Routledge, London.

Walker, A. (1997) *The Menstrual Cycle*. Routledge, London.

Weltman, E.A., Stern, R.C., Doershuk, C.F., Moir, R.I., Palmer, K. & Jaffe, A.C. (1990) Weight and menstrual function in patients with eating disorders and cystic fibrosis. *Paediatrics* **85**, 282–287.

Chapter 19

Cognitive-behavioural Group Interventions to Initiate and Maintain Safer Sex

Andrew Billington and Shamil Wanigaratne

Introduction

This chapter describes a small group intervention targeted at gay men and developed and run in a London sexual health clinic. The intervention was aimed at reducing the risk of HIV and STD infection, and facilitating sexual behaviour change.

The question of whether to intervene or not has to be asked when faced with demands for behaviour change. The pressure to intervene is so strong when faced with an epidemic such as HIV that individuals have rushed to do so, armed with very little else other than intuition and belief that they could not sit on the sidelines and watch the pandemic unfold. Millions of pounds have been spent on HIV prevention interventions that have never been successfully evaluated (Oakley *et al*. 1995). Some of these interventions have undoubtedly been innovative and creative and may well have made significant difference. On the other hand they may have been nothing but well-intentioned attempts to do something that have actually come to nothing. The concept of evi-dence-based practice (Sackett *et al*. 1997) provides a framework to prevent such wastage.

Groupwork with gay men

Gay men have been shown to form the group with the highest prevalence of HIV in the United Kingdom (AIDS/HIV Quarterly Surveillance Tables, 1998). Despite recent dramatic progress in the management of HIV infection, there is still no cure for HIV. Therefore there is still an emphasis on HIV prevention.

Early prevention work with gay men was undertaken mainly by voluntary organisations from within the gay community such as the Terrence Higgins Trust (King 1993) and led to the wide-scale adoption of safer sex by gay men in the mid-1980s. Later work then focused on notions of 'relapse', although this was and remains a controversial term in this context, with implication of pathologising gay men who do not always practise safer sex. The 're-gaying' of AIDS in the early 1990s (King 1993) saw a growth of gay community prevention organisations, such as Gay Men Fighting

AIDS (GMFA), alongside statutory sector initiatives such as the appointment of gay men's HIV prevention workers within health authorities and social service departments.

Studies have repeatedly shown that approximately one third of gay men have had at least one or more incidents of unprotected sex in the last year (Weatherburn *et al.* 1992), whilst HIV prevalence amongst gay men has remained stable. Much of the focus of prevention work therefore continues to be in developing interventions which support gay and bisexual men in initiating and maintaining safer sex. This is the nature of the group work described in this chapter, which aims to facilitate changes that encourage the adoption and maintenance of safer sex.

Why groupwork?

Groupwork has a number of factors in its favour which make it a suitable vehicle for an HIV prevention intervention.

Studies have shown that peer group approval and support is an important factor in the successful adoption and maintenance of safer sex (Kelly *et al.* 1990). Groupwork can provide a forum in which this support and approval can be expressed and focused. Furthermore the peer group, in this case, gay men, can educate each other and problem-solve together in order to help facilitate change. Difficulties in adopting and maintaining safer sex are normalised within a group where all are facing a similar problem. In doing this the stigma which gay men can face from peers if not practising safer sex is lessened, thereby increasing the likelihood of building self-esteem and encouraging the individual to make sustained changes.

The 'group processes' (Tuckman 1963) can also be used to encourage the adoption and maintenance of safer sex. The adoption of a safer sex norm by the group may strengthen the notion of peer approval. Participants and facilitators can model relationships, which may encourage safer sex practice.

Groupwork is also an efficient use of resources in the sense that it enables an intervention to be targeted at more than one individual. This makes it a more cost-effective intervention than one-to-one work. Cognitive-behavioural group interventions have proved effective in the maintenance and adoption of changes in other areas of behaviour (Roth & Fonagy 1996).

The groupwork described here, when initially developed, was aimed at gay men who expressed difficulties with practising safer sex. It used cognitive behavioural techniques as the key elements to facilitate change.

Theoretical background

Psychological interventions in the early period of the pandemic may have fallen into the category of well-intentioned interventions. In the absence of 'evidence' of what works, psychologists and other behavioural scientists delved into existing broad theoretical frameworks on which to base their interventions. In psychology the broad theoretical frameworks include psychodynamic approaches, humanistic approaches and cognitive-behavioural approaches. Individual, couple and group interventions based on these approaches or an amalgam of them were developed and applied. Evidence for their efficacy in other areas was often used to justify interventions. It must also be said that contributions from different branches of psychology, such as social psychology and cognitive and theoretical models developed within these areas such as the Health Belief Model (Becker 1974) and the Theory of Reasoned Action (Fishbein & Ajzen 1975) have influenced interventions.

The intervention described in this chapter adopted an integrative approach using elements from the frameworks and models described above, in conjunction with models developed in the area of addictions, namely the Prochaska and DiClemente model of change (1986) and the Marlatt and Gordon (1985) model of the relapse process. It also incorporated aspects of group psychology (Yalom 1975) and Buddhist philosophy.

Background to the group

The group was started in 1990 in a central London sexual health clinic where the largest group of clinic attenders was gay men. Genito-urinary medicine (GUM) clinic attenders have been shown to be a high-risk group in terms of HIV transmission (Johnson *et al.* 1994) and thus gay men attending such a clinic are a prime target for HIV prevention work. In addition staff anecdotally reported high levels of knowledge of the mechanics of HIV transmission amongst the gay male attenders who were still facing difficulties maintaining safer sex. This seemed to indicate the need for a psychologically-based intervention, as opposed to one based on information-giving alone, an approach which would focus on psychological and emotional factors associated with failure to maintain safer sex (Wanigaratne *et al.* 1997). The group continues to be run within the clinic and to be funded jointly by the GUM and Health Promotion Services.

In early groups recruitment of participants came entirely from referrals made by clinic staff. Subsequently, however, participants have also been recruited through advertisements in the gay press, leaflets promoting the group left in London GUM clinics and through leaflets distributed in HIV services and gay bars and clubs.

All participants were required to attend a pre-group interview to ensure that the group was appropriate to their needs. The interview was also used to gather the basic details about the clients and to assess their level of motivation.

The group intervention lasts for 14 hours excluding all breaks. Initially this took place over a period of eight evening sessions. After two years, during which the group was reviewed regularly, the present format was adopted. This consists of two weekend days of five hours (including two 15-minute breaks but not including an hour lunch break) and two evening sessions of two hours each (including one 15-minute break). Feedback from participants has demonstrated that this is the most popular format and the attrition rate has proved considerably lower than that of the early groups.

Three to four groups are run each year. Psychologists, health advisers or social workers, all of whom have had extensive experience in groupwork and cognitive-behavioural work in a clinical setting, have facilitated the groups. The facilitators received supervision after each session from a clinical psychologist or from another facilitator with experience of running the groups.

The key aims and objectives of the group are as follows:

- To prevent the spread of HIV infection amongst gay men by helping participants change their personal sexual practices to safer ones and enhance the probability of maintaining these changes.
- To support and develop a greater understanding of HIV infection and its transmission.
- To support and develop a greater sense of command and choice over sexual behaviour.
- To develop and enhance sensual and sexual exploration and fun.
- To increase self-esteem, confidence and overall satisfaction with daily life.
- To explore strategies for negotiation and change.

The intervention

The intervention is described below in detail with outlines of the theoretical rationale.

Session 1 (2 hours): Setting the frame

Facilitators explain the goals and aims of the group and the use of cognitive-behavioural techniques within the group. Facilitators give a simple description of cognitive-behavioural therapy. Explaining the rationale of treatment to clients is a basic principle in cognitive-behavioural therapy (Beck *et al.* 1979).

Participants list what they hope to achieve in attending the group at this point in time, and what their main anxieties are.

Ground rules are set by facilitators and participants. These always include agreements on confidentiality, on respect for others' opinions and on timekeeping.

Participants set their 'Personal Sexual Goals'. These are the aims they wish to work towards in their sex lives and on which they will focus during the group. They are encouraged to think of their aims in terms of the changes they would have to make to achieve them. Participants are encouraged to think which of the goals they have listed are realistic, achievable and measurable.

The facilitators demonstrate how large and thus seemingly unachievable goals can often be broken down into a succession of smaller more achievable goals. Participants are introduced to the idea of each small goal being one step on the route to achieving a larger one. They are introduced to the notion of self-motivation by measuring achievements.

Session 2 (5 hours)

1. Motivation to change

Participants are introduced to the 'Decision Balance Sheet' (Janis & Mann 1977) and asked to complete it using one of their previously stated aims. The sheet analyses the aim in terms of both the personal gains and losses participants feel they would experience should the change finally come about. The sheet aims to increase participant motivation and allow the individual to assess if they are ready for change.

2. Recognising and coping with stress and anxiety

Coping with stress and anxiety session in which participants define what they mean by anxiety and name the physical, emotional and behavioural symptoms of anxiety. The entire group then shares methods of coping with anxiety using a problem-solving approach. The intervention is based on the model of Stress Inoculation Training (Meichenbaum 1977).

Participants are introduced to the basic cognitive-behavioural model of thoughts, feelings and actions (Barlow 1988; Rachman & De Silva 1996) using examples focusing on anxiety to explain the model. Participants then start to outline ways in which they can cope with stress and anxiety by changing anxious thoughts, feelings or actions. Participants are encouraged to focus on any links between sex, stress and anxiety, for example, either as a source of anxiety or as a coping mechanism.

3. Eroticising safer sex

- 'What turns me on?' exercise in which participants in two groups make a list of as many possible things they can think of which they find sexually arousing. This encourages participants to talk more explicitly about sex by desensitising the subject. It also demonstrates to participants that most sexual activities are unlikely to transmit HIV.

4. High-risk situations

- 'High-risk situational hotspots' exercise in which participants are asked to name situations in which they are more likely to end up having unsafe sex or in which sex can be problematic for them. The aim of the exercise is to encourage participants to realise that they may be able to anticipate these situations and thus can plan ways of either coping with them or avoiding them (Marlatt & Gordon 1985; Wanigaratne et al. 1990).
- 'High-risk or "Hotspot" situation report' (Roffman et al. 1988) exercise in which participants are given a High Risk Situation Report to complete for homework. The report requires them to select a situation

where they had unsafe or problematic sex and to complete in as much detail as possible what they remember of the experience under the following headings:
(1) Date, day and time.
(2) External situation.
(3) Were drugs and alcohol involved and, if so, in what quantities?
(4) What was your mood and how were you feeling?
(5) Had anything happened earlier that was related to the event?
(6) What was the outcome? How did you feel about it and about yourself?
(7) Could anything have been done differently that would have changed the outcome?
(8) How might you cope better in the future?

The report aims to help participants identify any particular 'triggers' for their behaviour which may lead to them having unsafe sex and to recognise any patterns associated with this behaviour. It aims also to help participants start to think about how they may go about starting to change any patterns or triggers.

5. Self-esteem and 'body image'

- Body image exercise. Participants work in pairs drawing an outline of each other's bodies and then individually marking on this outline things they like, dislike and wish to change about their bodies. They then discuss this in pairs, focusing on positive feedback. A group discussion then focuses on the relationship between body image and sex.

Body image and self-esteem are closely linked and self-esteem has been shown to be a factor in difficulties in adopting and maintaining safer sex (Horn & Chetwynd 1989). Hence low self-esteem arising from perceptions of poor body image becomes a high-risk situation according to the Marlatt and Gordon (1985) model. This exercise allows participants to discuss their feelings about their body image and the part it plays in sex and encourages them to think about any changes in relation to body image that may be possible. Participants are also encouraged to challenge one another on any of the negative views of their bodies that they express.

- Relaxation exercise.

Session 3 (5 hours)

1. High-risk situations II

The High Risk Situation Report that was given out during the previous session is discussed in pairs, then in the large group.

2. Safer sex knowledge

Participants list any questions they have linked to safer sex, HIV or STDs. These are then divided out amongst small groups of participants and answered so they remain anonymous, with input as necessary from the facilitators.

3. 'Cognitive aspects of unsafe sex' – presentation by facilitator

Participants are encouraged to consider thoughts they have before and during a situation that ends in unsafe sex. They are introduced to the following as patterns of thinking that can be linked to having unsafe sex:

- 'Denial' – denying that the underlying thought is one of wanting to have sex/unsafe sex.

- 'Seemingly irrelevant decisions' – thoughts, which although they played a part in subsequent sexual behaviour, were not recognised by the individual as playing any role in decision making.
- 'Rule violation effect' – referring to the process whereby an individual sets a goal, fails to achieve this goal on one occasion and then takes this as proof that it can never be achieved.

4. Negotiation of safer sex

In small groups participants devise a scenario to appear in an imaginary video – 'Good Sex Guide' on the subject of 'negotiating enjoyable and safe sex'. This is followed by a discussion. Participants are thus able to model successful negotiation skills and share techniques for effective communication with prospective or current sexual partners.

5. Lifestyle balance

Lifestyle balance is the way in which everyday stressors are balanced with pleasurable stress-relieving activity. It is seen as a critical factor in maintaining change over a period of time according to the Marlatt and Gordon model. Participants complete a grid which divides their life into up to nine areas on which they place emphasis. They then analyse how much emphasis they feel they place on each area and what changes they wish to make to ensure they have the type of balance between each area that they wish for.

- Relaxation exercise.

Session 4 (2 hour evening session)

- Evaluation – verbal and written.
- Discussion on future work and referral.
- Relaxation exercise.

Session 5 (2-hour follow-up session 3 months after last session)

• Discussion on how members have coped over last 3 months and focus on personal sexual goals.

Lessons learnt from running the groups

Important lessons concerning cognitive-behavioural groupwork interventions with gay men were learnt during the life of the 'Getting the Sex You Want' group. These concerned primarily the referral criteria, the pre-group interview, the content of the group, the facilitation, confidentiality and participants' safety in the group, the feedback and evaluation process that identifies the changes that need to be made. Some of the lessons learnt are outlined below.

Referral

Referral criteria need to focus on problems in maintaining rather than changing to safer sex

In 1990 many gay men were still changing to safer sex and many were finding difficulties in doing so. Referral criteria for the group reflected this and demanded that potential participants must currently be having problems in changing to or adopting safer sex. However, by 1995 the issue for most gay men was no longer changing to safer sex but maintaining it or adopting a sexual strategy that minimised risk of HIV transmission but did not include condom use, i.e. unprotected intercourse between partners who have tested HIV negative. Thus referral criteria were changed to allow for those men who, although currently practising safer sex, occasionally did not do so or who wished for support in maintaining safer sex or their own personal sexual strategy.

Referral criteria need to be broad enough to include those with issues that have been linked by research to problems with maintaining safer sex

Reported failure to maintain safer sex has been linked to a number of factors. These include: problems with communication skills in a sexual situation; dissatisfaction with sex with a regular partner; low self-esteem issues linked to sex; numbers of sexual partners; infection with STDs other than HIV; lack of assertiveness in sexual situations (Thornton & Catalan 1993). Many individuals were referred to the group or self-referred for help with one or more of these issues, although they disclosed no difficulty in maintaining safer sex. Referral criteria were broadened to allow these individuals to attend. Evaluation indicated that these participants felt helped by the group and thus felt more able to maintain safer sex in the future. Furthermore, during the group, a large number of these individuals disclosed occasional unsafe sex, presumably at a point when they felt comfortable enough to do so.

The broadening of the criteria had helped to ensure that as many men as possible who needed help in maintaining safer sex were able to access the group.

Referral criteria need to be linked to the aims of those attending

The broadening out of the referral criteria was reflected in the aims which participants listed in the first session of the group. In early groups most aims were directly related to adopting and maintaining safer sex. The following were typical:

- 'To find safer sex as exciting as unsafe sex'.
- 'To always use a condom'.
- 'To have a better understanding of why I practise unsafe, anonymous sex'.

Later groups, post 1995, saw participants being primarily concerned less with unsafe sexual behaviour and more with thoughts and feelings around sex:

- 'To overcome fears and guilt about sex.'

Many participants who described incidents of unsafe sex did not see this as their principal concern but focused more on emotional and psychological issues linked to sex, as illustrated here:

- 'To feel more relaxed with myself so I can say no to sex I don't want'.
- 'To work out how I can stay with my partner and cope with his sexual needs'.

These aims were thus in keeping with the broadened referral criteria.

Recruitment

Recruitment is most effective when it can identify individuals who are motivated to change

Given that cognitive-behavioural work relies heavily on the client's wish to change it was important that participants who attended the group had reached a level at which they were motivated to make a change. This was often marked by the fact that they either self-re-

ferred or agreed to be referred by a professional. The majority had attended an agency, seeking help, or had seen the group's promotional material. Exercises in the group also clarified this motivation further (c.f. the Decision Balance Sheet). It would thus seem that the group adopted a useful method of recruitment that successfully identified those individuals who were at the correct motivational stage.

Content

It is important to maintain a core of exercises focused on sexual change that are always delivered in the same format

Feedback and evaluation over the years has indicated that most participants found the majority of the exercises in the group useful and helpful in facilitating change (Wanigaratne *et al.* 1997). The exercises that formed the core of the group have always been delivered in the same format. They are the 'skeleton' of the intervention and introduced participants to cognitive-behavioural methods of change. They were: setting personal sexual goals; the decision balance sheet; high-risk situations and the 'hotspot report'; cognitive aspects of safer sex; the lifestyle balance exercise; safer sex knowledge; relaxation exercises.

Exercises can be adapted to reflect changing society and the nature of the epidemic

As practising safer sex became more of a social norm amongst gay men the HIV prevention technique of 'eroticising safer sex', which had been widely used in HIV prevention initiatives, started to lose its impact. The aims of the 'eroticising safer sex' session in the group was thus changed to one of encouraging men to voice their sexual needs and to practise talking about sex, thus remaining in keeping with the cognitive-behavioural approach of the group.

A simple approach to an exercise using the participant's own experience can help to convey complex ideas

The 'Recognising and Coping with Stress and Anxiety' session proved a useful way of introducing the groups to a basic cognitive-behavioural model of functioning and demonstrated how the individual can facilitate change using this model. Participants found the model easy to understand when put in the context of a stressful situation they could recognise and when encouraged to identify their own methods of coping and view these as cognitive-behavioural techniques, when appropriate. Participants often fed back that this helped them to see how they could regain control in their lives.

A communications skills session works best when an interactive format is used

The 'Negotiating Safer Sex' session originally took the form of the group watching a video illustrating successful and unsuccessful communication techniques followed by a discussion. However, feedback called for a more interactive session. In the current session, which has been positively evaluated, participants are encouraged to practise communication skills with each other and to share knowledge and experience whilst imagining that they are making their own video which illustrates successful and unsuccessful negotiation skills.

Using other models and approaches alongside the cognitive-behavioural model can be highly effective

The self-esteem and body image session has often been that most positively evaluated by participants. It has also often been the session which many participants have found the most challenging. Participants supportively challenged any irrational and negative beliefs they held about their own and others' self-image. They were also encouraged to problem-solve in relation to making changes to their bodies. Frequently, however, there were issues not linked to sex which arose during this session which could not be dealt with within the confines of the group. Facilitators then had to use their skills to direct participants sensitively to other areas for help. This session often demanded a detailed discussion and a 'debrief' after it.

There is need for a substantial amount of time to be allotted for discussion and problem solving in the large group

Overall, time allotted to tasks completed individually and in small groups had to be shortened to allow for more time in discussion and problem solving in the large group. This led to less of an emphasis on the exercises and more of a focus on individuals' own emotional and psychological issues. The increase in time for group discussion was in direct response to participant feedback over the years. Indeed many participants rated 'sharing difficulties' and the group problem solving approach as being the most useful aspect of the intervention (Wanigaratne et al. 1997).

An eclectic approach has proved most useful to improve the quality of the intervention

Although cognitive-behavioural exercises remain at the core of the group, other models and approaches have also proven useful and effective when included. Also, because of more interaction between participants in the large group, group processes have played an increasingly greater role in the functioning of the group.

Facilitation

Gay men demonstrate a preference for gay male facilitators

Participant evaluations consistently stated a preference for the facilitators to be gay men, although an early group was facilitated by a woman and was positively evaluated.

Facilitators must be highly skilled and experienced in counselling and groupwork to run groups focused on sexual change

All the facilitators had experience in groupwork and qualifications in counselling and often in groupwork. Some had initially attended the group as a participant. Some facilitators were participants in an randomised controlled evaluation of a one-day version of this intervention (The Behavioural Intervention with Gay Men (BIG) Project; Imrie & Stephenson 1996; Wanigaratne 1996) and had had training and experience of running this brief intervention.

Given the structured nature of the group, facilitators had to ensure that all the topics and exercises were completed but also had to allow time for group discussions. It was also rec-

ognised that different groups are more focused on different issues and thus facilitators allowed the groups to spend more time on whatever issues they found most useful.

Facilitators also had to ensure that participants did not lose the cognitive-behavioural focus of the group in order to encourage them to acquire the techniques that would, it was hoped, facilitate change. There was often a tension between some participants, who would want to look at issues other than sexual behaviour change, or would wish to operate more in a psychodynamic framework, and the facilitator who had to keep the group broadly on its cognitive-behavioural course.

Facilitators had also to cope with difficult situations that can often arise in groups. Some of these are situations which are more likely to arise in a group which is concerned with sex than in other groups. During the eight years of 'Getting the Sex You Want' these situations have included: issues relating to confidentiality; disclosure of sexual abuse; sexual attraction and sexual tension between group members. Facilitators must thus be highly skilled and experienced to cope successfully with all the above pressures and expectations.

Facilitators must have access to high quality supervision

To help facilitators cope with difficult situations that may occur they had access to skilled supervisors with knowledge of groupwork. Supervisions took place immediately after each group session to permit most effective feedback. Supervisors also played a key role in the feedback process as they were often able to comment on issues that the facilitator, as part of the group, was not able to identify.

Confidentiality and group safety

Establishing safety in groups is key to the success of the group

Participants have consistently fed back that a major positive factor in their experience of the group was their ability to 'share with other gay men' anxieties about sex without fear of censure. Ensuring that participants feel safe and relaxed early on in the group has thus been one of the prime concerns for the facilitators.

Identifying ground rules is one of the first steps to establishing a safe group

Group members and facilitators always established rules around confidentiality at the beginning of the first session. These included not identifying participants to others outside the group and decisions on contact between participants outside of the group. Some group members have chosen not to acknowledge each other outside of the group. No group has chosen to set specific rules around limiting sexual contact.

It is important to agree rules regarding confidentiality

If two or more participants acknowledged that they were already acquainted with each other one was offered a place on a future group, if either felt uncomfortable with the other's presence.

Facilitators stated they would never acknowledge a group member outside of the group unless the participant did so first.

Participants were not required to give their full names and addresses although the majority had done so. Those who had not done so at the start of the group often did so at the end

to allow facilitators to contact them regarding the follow-up session.

Exercises should be structured to ensure participants feel safe to disclose personal information

The exercises were mostly structured to allow participants to record information alone, then share it in a pair or small groups, then finally discuss it in the large group. They could thus choose a 'level' of disclosure. Participants have repeatedly fed back the usefulness of this process in that it allowed them a choice in what and to whom they disclose. Sessions that involved possible disclosure of very personal information occurred later in the group when it was most likely that a culture of trust and safety would have been established.

Pre-group interview

A pre-group interview helps ensure a low attrition rate

The first group run in 1991 involved no pre-group interview. A large number of men attended and the attrition rate was extremely high. A pre-group interview was therefore introduced. This ensured facilitators knew who would be attending the group and that the applicant was appropriate for the group and vice versa. It also enabled facilitators to obtain basic referral information from the client or to refer them elsewhere if they were not appropriate for the group. This interview was seen as the first stage of the intervention since it involved some disclosure and goal setting on the client's part as they were required to give examples of the personal sexual goals they wished to achieve from the group.

Since the introduction of the interview, attrition rates have run at an average of one per eight participants. Most participants who left did so after the initial session, in which case they were not subsequently contacted. Facilitators only contacted those who dropped out after later sessions.

Evaluation

Evaluation and participant feedback has indicated that this focused groupwork is beneficial in promoting and maintaining safer sexual behaviours (Wanigaratne *et al.* 1992; 1997).

Evaluation is key not only to demonstrating effectiveness but also in developing the content of the group

The importance of sound mechanisms and structures for evaluation lies not only in the need for demonstrating the effectiveness of the intervention in changing the behaviour of participants but in its role of re-shaping the intervention over the years to make it more responsive to, and thus more effectively meet the needs of, the participants. As the nature of the HIV epidemic evolves so do gay men's responses to it and the social context in which this is happening. Thus all the changes made to the group, from referral criteria to individual exercises, were a direct response to participant feedback.

Conclusions

The aspects of the group which have proved crucial to its success are a tight referral process, content and structure which responds to participants' needs, skilled facilitation that en-

sures participants' safety and an evaluative process that ensures effective development of the group. A flexible and imaginative approach has been adopted when redesigning certain aspects of the group. The group has always been structured around cognitive-behavioural techniques and exercises but these have been altered according to feedback on their usefulness for participants. Other exercises and approaches have been adopted if they have proved useful, have complemented the cognitive-behavioural approach and have been positively evaluated.

The future

'Getting the Sex You Want' will continue to develop and change according to client and facilitator evaluation and retain its dynamic approach to the delivery of a groupwork intervention. There are clearly some restrictions on how it can develop. It will remain essentially a cognitive-behavioural intervention. It is also limited by practical concerns, mainly resources. For example, participants have frequently fed back the need for 'support meetings' once the group has finished. Such meetings would be appropriate to the model since they correspond to the notion of 'top up'. Indications are that maintenance of change is most effective with support or top-up sessions following an initial intervention. However, other than the three-month follow-up meeting, lack of resources has prevented this happening. It may be that a structured programme of support could prove successful if it were carefully built in to the intervention.

There may clearly be other formats and ways of running similar groups which may maximise the impact of this form of groupwork. Two other projects, both randomised controlled trials examining the effectiveness of cognitive-behavioural style group interventions, are currently under way. One is a community based 12-hour intervention lasting over three weeks ('Gay Men Fighting AIDS'; 'Hard Times' Project) and the other a one-day 5-hour clinic based intervention (University College London's 'Behavioural Intervention with Gay Men (BIG) Project'; Imrie & Stephenson 1996; Wanigaratne 1996) both based on the content and approach of 'Getting The Sex You Want'. These will prove a chance to examine the effectiveness of the intervention within two different settings and time frames.

Many questions still remain as to how to deliver this intervention most effectively. Given the complexity of the reasons why gay men have unsafe sex and difficulties involved in facilitating behaviour change, there is still a need for sensitive and accurate measures for evaluation which can better gauge the effectiveness of such a group. This needs to be coupled with yet more accurate ways of gathering feedback from clients so that the group can be even more responsive to current changes in the epidemic and its effect on gay men.

References

Barlow, D.H. (1988) *Anxiety and its Disorders.* Guilford Press, New York.

Beck, A.T., Rush, A.J., Shaw, B.F. & Emery, G. (1979) *Cognitive Therapy of Depression.* Guilford, New York.

Becker, M. (ed.) (1974) *The Health Belief Model.* Slack, Thorofare, NJ.

Fishbein, M. & Ajzen, I. (1975) *Belief Attitude, Intention and Behaviour: An Introduction to Theory and Research.* Addison Wesley, New York.

Horn, J. & Chetwynd, J. (1989) *Changing sexual practices among homosexual men in response to AIDS: who has changed, who hasn't, and why?* Department of Health, Auckland, New Zealand.

Imrie, J.C.G. & Stephenson, J., for the BIG Project Study Group (1996). Is groupwork based intervention within an STD clinic a feasible and appropriate intervention for high risk gay men? A pilot study. *XI International Conference on AIDS,* Vancouver.

Janis, I.L. & Mann, L. (1977) *Decision Making.* The Free Press, New York.

Johnson, A.M., Wadsworth, J., Wellings, K. & Field, J. (1994) *Sexual Attitudes and Lifestyles.* Blackwell Scientific Publications, Oxford.

Kelly, J.A., Lawrence, J.S., Brasfield T.L., *et al.* (1990) Psychological factors that predict AIDS high risk versus AIDS precautionary behaviour. *Journal of Consultation in Clinical Psychology* **58**, 117–120.

King, E. (1993) *Safety in Numbers.* Cassel, London.

Marlatt, G.A. & Gordon, J.R. (1985) *Relapse Prevention: Maintenance Strategies in the Treatment of Addictive Behaviours.* Guilford, New York.

Meichenbaum, D. (1977) *Cognitive Behaviour Modification: An Integrative Approach.* Plenum, New York.

Oakley, A., Fullerton, D. & Holland, J. (1995) Behavioural interventions for HIV/AIDS prevention. *AIDS* **9**, 479–486.

Prochaska, J.O. & DiClemente, C.C. (1986) Towards a comprehensive model of change. In: *Treating Addictive Behaviors: Process of Change* (eds W.R. Miller & N. Healther). Plenum, New York.

Public Health Laboratory Service (1998) *AIDS Centre AIDS/HIV Quarterly Surveillance Tables* **41**, 98/3.

Rachman, S. & De Silva, P. (1996) *Panic Disorder. The Facts.* Oxford University Press, Oxford.

Roffman, R.A., Gordon, J.R. & Craver, J.A. (1988) *AIDS Risk Reduction: Preventing Relapse to Unsafe Sex* (unpublished manuscript). University of Washington, Seattle.

Roth, A.D. & Fonagy, P. (1996) *What Works for Whom? A Critical Review of Psychotherapy Research.* Guilford Press, New York.

Sackett, D.L., Richardson, W.S., Rosenburg, W. & Haynes, RB. (1997) *Evidence-based medicine: How to Practice and Teach EBM.* Churchill Livingstone, London.

Thornton, S. & Catalan, J. (1993) Preventing the sexual spread of HIV infection – what have we learned? *International Journal of STD and AIDS* **4**, 311–316.

Tuckman, B.W. (1963) Development sequence in social groups. *Psychological Bulletin* **63**, 384–399.

Wanigaratne, S., for the BIG Project Study Group (1996) The BIG Project – A randomised controlled evaluation of a cognitive behavioral group intervention aimed at initiating and maintaining safer sex behaviours in gay men at high-risk of HIV infection attending a London sexually transmitted disease clinic. *Annual Conference of the British Association for Behavioral and Cognitive Psychotherapies*, Southport.

Wanigaratne, S., Wallace, W., Pullin, J., Keaney, F. & Farmer, R. (1990) *Relapse Prevention for Addictive Behaviours: A Manual for Therapists.* Blackwell, Oxford.

Wanigaratne, S., Aroney, R. & Williams, M. (1992) Initiating and maintaining safer sex: Description and evaluation of groupwork with gay men. *Abstracts, VIII International Conference on AIDS*, Amsterdam.

Wanigaratne, S.D., Billington, A. & Williams, M. (1997) Initiating and maintaining safer sex: evaluation of groupwork with gay men. In: *The Impact of AIDS* (eds J. Catalan & B. Hedge). Harwood Academic Publications, London.

Weatherburn, P., Hunt, A., Hickson, F. & Davies, M. (1992) *The Sexual Lifestyles of Gay and Bisexual Men in England and Wales.* Project SIGMA, London.

Yalom, I.D. (1975) *The Theory and Practice of Group Psychotherapy,* 2nd edn. Basic Books, New York.

Chapter 20

Psychological Management of Pain Syndromes in a Sexual Health Setting

Micheline Byrne and Paula Christmas

Genital pain arises as a consequence of many different aetiologies and ranges from acute to chronic in nature. In a proportion of cases it can be difficult or indeed impossible to identify a cause and this can make treatment problematic.

Chronic pain

Chronic pain has been defined as pain which persists past the time when healing is expected to be complete. This varies from 1 to 6 months.

Female

The terminology with regard to chronic vulval pain is confusing and there is no one uniformly accepted definition. The term 'vulvodynia' was introduced in 1991 by the International Society for the Study of Vulval Diseases (ISSVD) in an attempt to define chronic vulval pain. As defined by the ISSVD 'vulvodynia is chronic vulvar discomfort, especially that characterised by the patient's complaint of burning, stinging, irritation or rawness'. However, no guidance is given as to how long the pain needs to be present before it can be defined as chronic. Pain present for less than a month is likely to have a different cause to that which persists for a month or longer. Therefore duration of pain is a useful indicator in guiding the practitioner to the diagnosis.

It is important to appreciate that vulvodynia is a *symptom*; no one factor can be identified as a cause of vulvodynia. The ISSVD committee on vulvodynia recognised that there are subsets of vulvodynia with different clinical presentations and responses to therapy that may be defined by certain diagnostic criteria (Tables 20.1 and 20.2).

These subsets may occur alone, simultaneously or sequentially; treatment for one condition may affect the onset of another. Most work on psychological approaches to working with women with vulval pain revolves around the diagnosis of vulvar vestibulitis, and these approaches are presented here. However, these

Table 20.1 Common causes of acute vulval pain.

Category	Condition
Infection	Thrush
	Genital herpes
	Abscess
Trauma	Surgery
	Injury
Dermatoses	Eczema
	Lichen sclerosus
	Lichen planus (erosive)
	Bullous disorder e.g.
	Pemphigus vulgaris
Neoplasia	Squamous cell carcinoma
Systemic disease	Behçet's disease
	Crohn's disease
	Apthous ulceration

Table 20.2 Subsets of vulvodynia.

(1) Vulvar dermatoses
(2) Cyclic vulvitis
(3) Squamous papillomatosis
(4) Vulvar vestibulitis
(5) Essential (dysaesthetic) vulvodynia
(6) Idiopathic vulvodynia

approaches are not exclusive to vulvar vestibulitis, and could be applied to many vulval conditions.

1. Vulvar dermatoses (Table 20.3)

The dermatoses are classified as non-neoplastic epithelial disorders of the skin which lead to chronic inflammation. They are morphologically distinct, usually easy to diagnose and amenable to medical treatment. Symptoms can be remarkably variable but a proportion will have persistent chronic pain.

Table 20.3 Common dermatoses.

- Eczema
- Lichen sclerosus
- Lichen simplex
- Lichen planus
- Psoriasis
- Pemphigus vulgaris
- Cicatricial pemphigroid

2. Cyclic vulvitis

This group of patients report symptoms that seem to follow a pattern, for example exacerbations at the same time during each menstrual cycle. It is noteworthy, however, that they describe periods of symptom-free days or weeks.

Although *Candida* infection may be related to cyclic vulvitis, this remains to be proven.

3. Squamous papillomatosis

Papillomatosis is a descriptive term for the presence of multiple papillae seen in the vestibule and the labia minora that may cover the entire mucosal surface. In the 1980s it was occasionally suggested that mucosal papillomatosis may represent subclinical human papillomavirus (HPV) infection and give rise to the pain symptoms but a consistent association has not been proven. Furthermore, as papillomatosis is seen in clinically asymptomatic normal women it is now considered to be a normal anatomic variant. Colposcopic examination and biopsy may be helpful as it remains very unclear to date what is appropriate treatment for these women.

4. Vulvar vestibulitis syndrome

Vulvar vestibulitis syndrome (VVS) is not necessarily a new entity as a similar condition was originally described by Skene in 1889. Since then a number of authors have used different names to describe a group of similar conditions. In 1987, Friedrich coined the term 'vulvar vestibulitis syndrome' in an attempt to standardise the description of this disorder. According to Friedrich the term VVS should be applied to those women who present with the following constellation of criteria:

(1) Severe pain on vestibular touch or attempted vaginal entry.
(2) Tenderness to pressure localised within the vulvar vestibule.
(3) Physical findings confined to vestibular erythema of various degrees.

Clinically, it is important to establish or indeed refute the diagnosis of VVS and in most cases this is not difficult with a little expertise. Some women may not necessarily fulfil all the criteria at a first visit, however, and at the first consultation it may not always be possible to clinch the diagnosis beyond doubt.

If all the criteria for VVS, as we understand them, are not met, other causes of vestibulitis (i.e. inflammation of the vestibule), need to be considered in order to avoid misdiagnosing VVS.

The principal problem for patients with VVS is that of pain during sexual intercourse (dyspareunia). This can be severe enough to preclude intercourse. For a small proportion of women the pain can also be triggered by tampon insertion or removal, wearing tight clothes, horse-riding, cycling and by sitting in certain positions.

In many cases the condition has been present for some considerable time before the diagnosis is eventually made.

Management of VVS

Establishing a diagnosis. Many women with a diagnosis of VVS have suffered with vulval pain for some time, and despite repeated visits to doctors and clinics, have been given contradictory information, and often, very few answers. Therefore, one of the most helpful interventions which we can offer is to give a firm diagnosis, some information about the condition and reassurance that it is not a psychosomatic condition. The value of this should not be underestimated.

Furthermore, the *manner* in which the doctor diagnoses, explains, and manages this condition can have a profound effect on the patient's ability to cope with the symptoms. Although there has been no research on doctor–patient communication in vulvar vestibulitis, we can extrapolate some themes from other research, which might also be applicable in a vulval clinic (e.g. Grace's (1995) qualitative research into the difficulties of communication between patients and doctors in a chronic pelvic pain service):

(1) Patients report that if doctors fail to listen to the patient's own experience of her pain and its meaning to her, it reduces her confidence that she could take responsibility for her condition and find ways to cope in the context of her lifestyle. This may leave patients feeling that their vulva has become 'a symptom area' (rather than a potentially 'sexual area') and that their fate is in the hands of doctors, rather than within their own control (such as through pain management strategies, strategies for avoiding unnecessary exacerbation of pain, strategies for being creative about sexual functioning).

(2) Patients in gynaecological settings have found that there may be more emphasis given to those symptoms which were visible/detectable (through examinations or tests) than to the other symptoms the patient had (including pain). This makes it difficult for the patient to interpret her whole experience of the condition and she may start to doubt her own ability to perceive or report her symptoms. An example of this is a patient who may say 'The doctor tells me the vestibulitis is getting better, as it is less red, but it doesn't feel any better.'

(3) A doctor's diagnosis of 'pain without a known cause' can lead patients to fear that the doctor is actually diagnosing neurosis or psychological problems. It is important to remember that many women who are initially getting their diagnosis of VVS may have attended clinics on many occasions, when doctors have been unable to find anything physically wrong with them, and they have been left with a feeling that doctors and/or partners believe that the pain is 'all in their heads'. 'Pain without a known cause' must therefore be explained with care.

Medical treatment:
- Simple measures e.g. avoid use of irritants, aqueous cream
- Topical steroids
- Anti-fungals
- Anaesthetic gels
- Low dose tricyclic antidepressants.

Surgical treatments:
- Laser ablation
- Vestibulectomy.

Diet:
- Calcium citrate tablets plus low oxalate diet.

Psychological approaches. Psychological interventions with women with a diagnosis of VVS include cognitive-behavioural pain management, and psychosexual work. These are usefully started at an early stage and done in combination with medical treatments. The primary focus tends to be on sexual functioning, for two important reasons:

(1) Sexual functioning is usually impaired, or even prohibited, by this condition. VVS invariably affects penetration but often also impacts on many other acts of sexual intimacy, including oral sex and masturbation. Most women attending the clinic report that they would like to be able to reinstate some sexual activity.

(2) Chronic sexual difficulties tend to create repercussions on other significant areas of functioning: for example women often report a strain on their regular relationship, loss of confidence in their ability to find new partners, concerns about ability to conceive naturally. The factor which may underpin all of these is that VVS can cause a change in how women define and identify themselves as a sexual person.

There are some data on the extent to which sexual functioning is impaired in women with a diagnosis of VVS. Meana *et al.* (1997) reported that women with VVS showed lower frequencies of intercourse, lower levels of desire and arousal, and were less successful at achieving orgasm through oral stimulation and through intercourse than controls. The VVS group also showed more negative attitudes towards sexuality. However, these differences seem to be exclusive to measures of sexual functioning: on general scales of psychological symptomatology (including depression and anxiety) women with VVS often do not show higher levels than controls.

On a more positive note, Goetsch (1991) interviewed 31 gynaecology patients with a diagnosis of VVS and found that more than half thought that they had found a way to accommodate their difficulties and still maintain a satisfactory sexual relationship, or that the problems were so minor that their relationship was not disturbed. At the other end of the spectrum, several subjects attributed failed relationships or significant stress to having vestibular pain. Some of these subjects wondered whether they had a hidden emotional aversion to sex. The psychological approach to sexual dysfunction in these patients can incorporate a number of interventions, depending on the particular difficulties they experience. It can be useful to present these interventions (which are primarily behavioural) in a context of discussing theoretical models of chronic pain and pain management interventions. Explaining Melzack and Wall's Gate Control Theory of Pain (Melzack & Wall 1996; Wall & Melzack 1999) can facilitate the process of helping patients to generate cognitive and behavioural strategies which may either reduce their pain, or diminish its significance for them.

Self-examination

For most women, it can be useful to give them some written material on the anatomy of the genitals, and the changes which occur during sexual excitement and during different stages of the menstrual cycle. If given in combina-tion with self-examination exercises, women can be encouraged to gather as much information as possible on variations in their pain experience. Through these exercises some women have identified, for example, a relationship between levels of stress/tension and pain, or have identified several discrete tender locations with separate sensations associated with touching these areas.

Vaginismus

Some women develop a vaginismus response to painful intercourse. The treatment for vaginismus is a straightforward, home-based programme of gradual dilation, whilst maintaining relaxation. It is preferable to ask women to attempt the dilation using their fingers rather than dilators, partly because this seems to de-mystify the process, but also because the women get useful feedback from the fingers on the extent to which they are managing to relax the muscles of the vaginal wall. In addition, finger penetration can form part of the information-gathering task, and can increase understanding of the extent to which she can tolerate being touched in the vulval area without triggering pain. A programme of gradual dilation can be useful if the patient describes a history of vaginismus but is not currently in a sexual relationship, since it can be very helpful in restoring confidence in sexual functioning.

Kegel exercises

For some patients it may be worth recommending Kegel (pelvic floor) exercises. These exercises were developed as a means of enhancing sexual responsiveness, and have been used in therapy for women with low sexual arousal or anorgasmia. Their value in treating female sexual dysfunction has been widely debated, however they have been suggested to have a potential role in the treatment of vulval pain. Anecdotally, they appear to be of particular benefit for patients who feel they have no control over their pain or over their physical response to their pain. The exercises promote awareness of different vaginal/vulval sensations, in addition to facilitating relaxation in the muscles of the pelvic floor.

Since it is postulated that Kegel exercises may be an effective treatment for low sexual arousal (through the mechanism of focusing the patients' attention upon sensations in the genital areas), Kegel exercises may have a role to play in restoring desire and arousal in women who report that, as a consequence of their vulval pain, they no longer have desire for sex and are unable to become aroused during sex.

Desire

A common problem for women with VVS is that of having little, or no sexual desire. This seems to engender high levels of concern and distress, and a frequently cited fear is that sexual interest will never return.

The literature on low sexual desire in women recognises that it is an extremely complex problem to evaluate and treat. Several hypotheses have been proposed to explain the mechanisms by which desire may wane, and then may be maintained at a low level. It seems possible that in VVS, desire may be extinguished in the first instance by the association of pain and attempted sexual intercourse. It may be that low sexual interest becomes maintained by a combination of factors including the persistence of pain, the absence of any pos-

itive reinforcers for any sexual contact, and potentially, depression.

Facilitating penetration

For women who are in a sexual relationship and wanting to attempt penetrative intercourse, there are a number of practical issues which it can be beneficial to discuss, to identify strategies for achieving penetration with the minimum of aggravation to the trigger points in the vulva. This might include trying different sexual positions (notably, encouraging the patient to adopt a superior position, thus allowing her greater control over the angle, depth and speed of penetration). It can also be helpful to discuss options such as the use of lubricant gels to reduce friction in the vulval area (which is additionally useful if the patient is also working to overcome vaginismus). The use of anaesthetic gels can be discussed, in order to give temporary relief (however, these need to be used with caution, since patients sometimes describe a temporary relief from pain, followed by subsequent severe pain since the vulval spots were not guarded/avoided in the usual way).

It is useful to encourage women with VVS to communicate fully and openly with their partner prior to attempting penetration – particularly if there has been a long period of abstaining from intercourse. It can be particularly helpful for a woman to know that she can initiate sexual contact without it necessarily having to lead on to penetration; that she can interrupt proceedings during intercourse, if necessary, without fear of a negative reaction; that she can include her partner in activities which may help her to feel more comfortable or relaxed about penetration (such as the partner sharing in the activity of dilation with fingers prior to penetration) and very importantly, for the partner to be aware of and involved in the active task of reinforcing and maximising desire.

Of course, work on communication may form part of a broader piece of work with the couple, if the sexual difficulties have become a part of more general problems within the relationship.

Cognitive-behavioural approaches to pain management might include identifying and challenging the woman's unhelpful beliefs about VVS and the limits it imposes on her life. Many women with VVS also have significant concerns about their future, which can be addressed.

Case example: Sarah

Sarah is a 31-year-old woman with a two-year history of VVS. She had previously had successful sexual relationships, with no pain. When she was referred to the psychologist she had just started a new sexual relationship after a period of being single. She was being treated with low-dose amitriptyline, and since she had begun her new sexual relationship she felt that the medication had decreased the intensity of her pain during penetrative intercourse, and had decreased the length of time for which she was in pain after sex (from two days to one day). She also used a local anaesthetic gel during penetration, and found this to be very helpful in blocking out some of the pain. She wanted to be able to have penetrative sex, and was able to do so for a period of time, but found that the pain would invariably begin after some minutes of penetration, and once she felt pain she became distracted, and unable to enjoy sex.

Sarah described her relationship with her new partner as very positive, and felt that she was able to have very open constructive conversations with him about adapting sexual activities in order to avoid triggering/aggravating the vulval pain. However, she had two main concerns:

(1) She was concerned about vaginismus, which she had had since the onset of vestibulitis two years ago, and which was still present with the new partner.
(2) She was worried that in their attempts to compensate for the difficulties with penetration, oral sex might become more central to their sexual repertoire. She was very happy to give oral sex but was not at all happy for her partner to perform oral sex on her.

There were several different components to the psychological work with Sarah:

(1) A programme of dilatation and relaxation was suggested for the vaginismus.
(2) We discussed ways of minimising/avoiding pain whilst attempting penetration. She found that penetration was less likely to trigger pain if she adopted the female superior position. Liberal use of lubricant in addition to the local anaesthetic cream was also very helpful.
(3) We discussed ways in which she could continue with love-making if she was beginning to feel some pain through penetration, and the ideas we generated included, having a pause once she began to feel pain, adjusting her position, and possibly engaging in some sensual activities such as holding, caressing, kissing, in order to facilitate arousal.
(4) We talked about the value of her having a broad sexual repertoire, which

was not entirely dependent on penetration for successful, satisfying love-making. We therefore spent some time talking about the concerns she had about receiving oral sex, which included feeling that she did not look 'right'. We devised various tasks for her to try at home, which included encouraging her to re-discover the sensuality of her body, and the pleasure of touch on her body, which had fallen by the wayside since her diagnosis of VVS and her conceptualisation of her genitals and her vulva as 'faulty'. She was encouraged to develop fantasies about oral sex, including in them the variables that would need to be met in order for her to be comfortable (which included feeling clean, loved and relaxed). Finally she was given the task of completing some genital sensate focus exercises with her partner, with adjustments to provide her with a progressive desensitisation to oral sex.

---

5. Essential (dysaesthetic) vulvodynia

The term essential (or dysaesthetic) vulvodynia is applied to a group of women who complain of constant, diffuse, unremitting burning of the vulva. Rarely this may extend into the thigh, or buttock. In the past a number of other terms, such as 'non-pathogenic vaginitis', 'psychosomatic vulvovaginitis', and the 'burning vulva syndrome' have been used.

This condition tends to affect an older age group than those with VVS. The discomfort may be aggravated by sitting, and be worse towards the end of the day. Women may complain of pain during intercourse, but this seems to be of less consequence than the burning. There are no abnormal physical findings on clinical examination of the vulva, and it has

been suggested that the problem arises as a result of neural dysfunction rather than there being pathology of the skin.

Based on evidence that tricyclic antidepressants are effective treatments for other pain syndromes, tricyclics have been used empirically in essential vulvodynia with some success.

6. Idiopathic vulvodynia

Inevitably there are patients with vulval pain who do not fulfil any of the diagnostic criteria discussed. Although not currently recognised as a subset of vulvodynia by the ISSVD we have classified these under the subset of 'idiopathic vulvodynia'. This may be a function of the evolving diagnostic classification of vulval conditions. For these women, the time spent listening and doing careful examination, and emphasising the absence of any serious underlying condition, can be therapeutic. Many patients have a fear that their symptoms are those of cancer, or an infection.

Pain in the male

There is little literature on chronic genital pain in men, and arguably, the process of distinguishing the symptoms into diagnostic classifications is still under way. Harris (1999) clearly summarises the various conditions which may cause genital pain, and the associated diagnostic investigations. Luzzi and O'Leary (1999) identify that a syndrome of chronic perineal and penile pain, often labelled as chronic prostatitis, is probably highly prevalent. They point out that for non-bacterial forms of this condition the cause is unknown, there is no definitive diagnostic test, and no generally agreed clinical definition which brings together the symptomatic features and investigative findings.

The National Institutes of Health proposed a new classification system for chronic prostatitis in 1995, with new diagnostic criteria. This proposed classification system (which is similar to the previous system) identifies four conditions:

- Acute bacterial prostatitis
- Chronic bacterial prostatitis
- Chronic pelvic pain syndrome (inflammatory)
- Chronic pelvic pain syndrome (non-inflammatory).

Aetiology

The aetiology of inflammatory chronic pelvic pain syndrome is unknown. Proposed mechanisms have included *Chlamydia trachomatis* infection, bladder neck dysfunction, tension myalgia of the pelvic floor, and autoimmunity. The cause and significance of inflammation is unclear. The aetiology of non-inflammatory chronic pelvic pain is similarly unclear. (These patients have symptoms of discomfort or pain in the genital area and on examination there is no obvious clinical sign of any abnormality to explain such a symptom.) Markers of inflammatory activators have been detected in non-inflammatory chronic pelvic pain, which suggests that inflammation may occur in both conditions.

Some have noted that chronic pain is often seen in male patients who have been involved in sexual activity which has subsequently made them feel guilty, or ashamed or confused. These patients may interpret their symptoms

as evidence of the presence of an infection, which cannot be detected with examinations or investigations.

Treatment

Treatment of chronic bacterial prostatitis is with antibiotics which are suitable for the organism cultured from urine or prostatic secretions, preferably an antibiotic with good prostatic penetration. Treatment is usually for a month initially, but up to a third of patients may relapse and need prolonged courses or suppressive antibiotic treatment.

There are no published large-scale randomised treatment trials for chronic pelvic pain syndrome. Small controlled trials have suggested the benefit of selected antibiotics (which Luzzi & O'Leary (1999) suggested may act by non-antimicrobial mechanisms, such as by anti-inflammatory effects), alpha blockers, transurethral microwave thermotherapy, and allopurinol (a xanthine-oxidase inhibitor, which reduces the production of uric acid). New approaches to treatment include cognitive behavioural pain management, and low dose tricyclics.

The psychological approach for working with men with chronic genital pain has clear parallels with the approaches discussed for female pain. Sexual functioning interventions can be useful for men who have developed problems with desire secondary to the pain, in addition to problems such as erectile disorder. Pain management approaches can be invaluable, helping patients to minimise their focus on their symptoms, and to maintain a normal, balanced lifestyle.

As with women with chronic genital pain, other issues may emerge such as relationship difficulties or communication problems, depression or anxiety. However our understanding of chronic pains in men, and their optimal management, is patchy and unsatisfactory. It is an area which clearly needs much more careful systematic research if we are to make progress.

References

Appendix 1: 1–5 (www.niddk.nih.gov/health/urolog/pubs/cpwork/cpwork.htm)

Friedrich, E.G., Jun. (1987) Vulvar vestibulitis syndrome. *Journal of Reproductive Medicine* **32**, 110.

Goetsch, M. (1991) Vulvar vestibulitis: prevalence and historic features in a general gynaecologic practice population. *American Journal of Obstetrics and Gynecology* **164**, 1609–1616.

Grace, V.M. (1995) Problems women patients experi-ence in the medical encounter for chronic pelvic pain: a New Zealand study. *Health Care for Women International* **16**(6), 509–519.

Harris, J.R.W. (1999) Male genital pain syndrome. *Sexually Transmitted Diseases* **16**(4), 779–782.

ISSVD (1991) Committee on Vulvodynia. Vulval vestibulitis and vestibular papillomatosis. *Journal of Reproductive Medicine* **36**(6), 413–415.

Luzzi G. & O'Leary, M. (1999) Chronic pelvic pain syndrome. *British Medical Journal* **318**, 1227–1228.

Meana, M., Binik, Y.M., Khalife, S. & Cohen, D.R. (1997) Biopsychosocial profile of women with dyspareunia. *Obstetrics and Gynaecology* **90**, 583–589.

Melzack, R. & Wall, P. (1996) *The Challenge of Pain*. Penguin, London.

National Institutes of Health (1995) *Executive Summary: Chronic Prostatitis Workshop*. National Institute of Diabetes and Digestive and Kidney Diseases.

Wall, P. & Melzack, R. (1999) *Textbook of Pain*. Churchill Livingstone, London.

Chapter 21

Unconventional Sexual Lifestyles

Robin Bell

Introduction

There is immense variability in human sexual behaviour. Many people lead unconventional sexual lifestyles. The ways they conduct their sex lives are different from conventional views within their society about how people usually behave sexually.

However behaving differently from other people is not in itself abnormal. Unconventional sexual lifestyles are clearly not a 'problem' needing psychological intervention in their own right. Nonetheless, it is instructive to consider the additional issues that may arise in offering psychological care in a sexual health setting to people with unconventional sexual lifestyles. The boundaries for the consideration of this chapter are admittedly arbitrary. Sexual activity that lies outside the law is not the focus here, this being the proper field of forensic psychology.

Formal medical and psychiatric literature has very little to say about these variations in human sexuality. The more extreme variations occur as isolated case reports, or in the context of legal cases or in people who develop physical complications as a result of unconventional sexual activities. This can lead the unwary reviewer into assuming that these sexual variations are rare, and associated with a high frequency of complications. It can appear that people who lead unconventional sexual lifestyles are usually distressed about those lifestyles or that they are likely to want desperately to change them. This is probably not the case, but rather an artefact of selection bias in those few cases that make it to the formal literature. Few people go to a physician to say how happy they are with their sex life.

For convenience, the topic has been broken down into three sections. These are unconventional patterns of partners, unconventional content of sexual acts and unconventional meanings of 'sex'.

Patterns of partners

The conventional pattern of partner change in the western world is at variance with role models taught by the major religions. Monogamy with one partner until parted by death is an ideal that is no longer the most practised pattern. Serial partnerships ending in separation, often with other partnerships overlapping in time, have become the social norm, and this 'serial monogamy', with or without adultery, will not be considered here as an unconventional form.

The two main issues that unconventional patterns of partners present for the professional are:

(1) Being comfortable oneself in tackling the work in a non-pejorative way.
(2) Adapting standard tools, often developed for 'couple work', to fit unexpected circumstances.

If professionals are aware that they are uncomfortable dealing with clients with such alternative lifestyles, they would be well advised to refer the client on to someone with greater experience with such clients. Sometimes, of course, that is not possible. It is very important for the professional not to import their own prejudices or moral outlook into the interaction with the client, however difficult that might be on occasion. A client who feels that a health professional is judging them adversely is unlikely to engage with, or benefit from, treatment.

Perhaps as important, though less obvious, is the need for the professional dealing with unfamiliar lifestyles to spend time trying to understand from the client what that lifestyle involves and how the client sees it. It is easy to make assumptions which turn out to be wrong and which at best lead to confusion and at worst undermine the client's faith in the health professional. This is an area where it is usually best to admit one's own ignorance and encourage the client to explain.

Case example

Mary

Mary was raised in a strictly Catholic household. She now lives with her partner John and together they are active in a circle of friends for whom sex is a sport not limited by the boundaries of who is 'attached' to whom. In a discussion about contraception she was talking about how important it was to her to know that John would be the father of her child and the difficulties of this when she was having sex with more than one man. When she mentioned 'going out dogging' the professional with whom she was talking had no idea what it meant. Rather than remain in ignorance, and at risk of misinterpreting the whole discussion, the professional said that she did not know enough about this sort of sex, but would like to know more, and asked Mary to explain.

Mary seemed quite happy to expound on the subject, explaining that she and John would drive together to a secluded but 'notorious' wooded area in their van. They would leave the rear door open and start to have sex, being joined by other anonymous men in the area who would 'use' her for sex, while John either looked on or joined in. It was clear from the explanation that Mary enjoyed this, and would often initiate the trips. With the extra information the professional could offer Mary better care and more appropriate contraceptive advice.

Recognition and awareness of the existence and frequency of alternative lifestyles is fundamental to such basic sexual health functions as contact tracing from an index case of a sexually transmitted disease. Clients are very good at telling professionals what they think they want to hear, and if the interviewer makes it clear that they want a first name to identify the 'extra' partner, the unspoken message is that there was one other partner and that the relationship, however fleeting, was intimate enough for names to have been exchanged and remembered. The client who has actually attended a 'swinging' party and had multiple anonymous partners is unable to answer the first question put to her, and unless feeling very confident, will not correct the implicit assumption that there was *a* partnership of some form. If the true situation is understood, a single phone call to the host of the evening (with the client's agreement of course) may ensure full and discreet contact tracing, rather than a strained interview which fails to achieve anything.

It is important to be clear with the client why information about their sex life is being elicited. This is, of course, generally true in sexual health work. However it is doubly true when dealing with a client with an unconventional sexual lifestyle who will be aware that their lifestyle is unusual and may well be on the look-out for signs of disapproval from the professional. They may be uncomfortable answering detailed questions until they are sure of the reaction of the professional. In terms of the psychological care of the individual it is often better to leave probing questions until a later interview if the client is uneasy. If there is a pressing reason for eliciting the information, that reason can be explained to the client, who may then see why they are being asked, and not feel as threatened by the apparent intrusion.

Case example

Philip

Philip attended a genito-urinary clinic with gonorrhoea. He was rather vague about his recent sexual partners. In order to try to work out who should receive a contact tracing slip (a slip which the patient gives to contacts explaining how to get treatment and carrying a code for the index case's infection), questions along the line of 'whom did you last have sex with?' were abandoned. The nature of, and reasons for, contact tracing were explained and he was then asked how many contact slips he would like to take away to pass to recent contacts whom he felt would benefit from being contacted. When the question was put in this way he was able to ask for a dozen slips. He explained that he was married, but had attended a 'private party' where he had had sex with several other people. He felt that he could contact not only his direct sexual contacts from that night, but also the other people who had attended and were also at risk. He still did not seem at ease, and did not want to talk about it further. Over the next week eight people were seen in the clinic bringing in his contact slips. One was his wife. The other seven were gay men who had attended the same party.

When Philip next attended he was asked if he would like vaccination against hepatitis A and B since these were routinely offered to men who had men as sexual partners. He noticeably relaxed at this point, as he realised that his bisexuality would not adversely alter the quality of care he received. He was thereafter able to discuss his sex life as a bisexual man and appropriate discussions with regard to safer sex and other sexual health matters were easily conducted. He said that if he had been 'pushed' to disclose more on the first visit he would probably have lied and not returned for follow-up.

Being ready to adapt their style and approach to the information given by the client is a basic skill that most professionals have. It is doubly important to make use of that skill with a group of clients who are concerned about the possible reaction of the health professional and who may be embarrassed to discuss their sex lives frankly as a consequence.

Perhaps the easiest trap to fall into for the health professional is to concentrate on what is unfamiliar and therefore striking about unconventional relationships and to fail to see that they obey the usual rules of sexual interaction, albeit within an unfamiliar context. Usually the standard tools and approaches of psychology still apply, and just need a little adjustment to novel circumstances.

Case examples

George

George was 47 and attended requesting help for erectile dysfunction. On the basis of his history this was thought probably to be psychological in origin, since he was able to maintain an erection with no problems for masturbation and morning erections were unaffected. When asked if his wife would attend with him for 'couple work' he looked most uncomfortable; gentle enquiry revealed that his domestic arrangements were more complex than the 'married' response on the booking form suggested.

He had left his home town in Ireland to live in London because of his domestic arrangements. He had fallen in love with his wife and her sister when he was a young man in Ireland. The two sisters were aware of what was happening and after some discussion they had settled to live together as one family unit. In order to avoid the limitations of living in a small town they

had moved to London, and now lived with the three adults and a total of five children in one house. Although he had a full relationship with each of the sisters he was shocked when asked if they all had sex together, since he saw that as abnormal. He simply slept with the sisters on different nights. The erectile dysfunction had started at the same time with both the sisters. After several visits that he attended on his own he brought his wife with him, and a standard Masters and Johnson sensate focus programme was successfully used. Through this time he continued trying sex with the other sister, and reported a gradual return of erectile function with her as well, even though no exercises were done between them.

Jean-Paul

Jean-Paul and his Japanese wife and English boyfriend all lived together. They usually slept in one bed, but there were three bedrooms in their flat, and each of them thought of one room as being their own. Their sex life was varied, each on occasion having sex with the other two, or sometimes they all had sex together. It was an open arrangement, and additional partners were commonly brought home, sometimes to be shared.

Jean-Paul initially came to the clinic for a 'check-up', he was well informed about sexual issues and had already been vaccinated against hepatitis A and B. His screen for sexual infection was negative, but he then asked if there was someone that he could talk to about sexual function. He had been having difficulties with his erections at home, both with his wife and boyfriend, though there was no problem if a fourth person was involved, or if he had gone back to someone else's home for sex with only two people present. He had attended for a checkup when he had noticed that his boyfriend was having similar problems, and thought that must mean it was being caused by something that was catching. After an initial consultation where he agreed that because the erectile dysfunction was situational it was likely to be psychological, he re-attended with his wife and boyfriend.

Some communication work was needed before they were ready to address the sexual difficulties, but once they were clear that they all wanted to stay together, a modified Masters and Johnson programme of sensate focus was implemented, which they carried out as a threesome. Each of them took turns to be still, while the other two were 'constructively selfish' in taking pleasure from the third person's body. The usual progression from non-genital exercises was followed. The biggest problem was the increased concentration needed in the feedback sessions to make sure that the balance between the three of them was maintained. After seven sessions they felt that they had recovered their sexual function, and were communicating better, not only sexually, but also in regard to the other domestic arrangements (such as who should empty the dishwasher). They cancelled their three-month follow-up appointment with a postcard that said all was well and that they didn't need a final visit.

David
David had a regular male partner with whom he had been living for the past five years. Their relationship had always been open and, on occasions, they would bring a third man home to join them in sex. They were having sex together less often than they used to. David was concerned that he was seeking out anonymous sexual contacts as a balance to the lack of sex at home. He was reassured that this pattern of sexual life, with a reduction in sex with a long-term partner is common, and that if it suited them both, making up the difference elsewhere is not 'abnormal'.

As is often the case, the problem then more or less reformulated itself. There were problems at home with his partner having formed a relationship with a younger man. David was now feeling insecure in his primary relationship. The increased sexual encounters away from home were a problem to him because they were an attempt to reaffirm his sexual prowess that he felt was threatened, and not an expression of his natural sexuality. After several sessions he came to a clearer view of his present situation and was able to discuss his fears with his partner. The perhaps orthodox expectation would be for the relationships to resolve at this stage into a couple and one man left on his own, depending on whether his partner chose David or the younger man. In fact this couple had an alternative solution. As David said 'Our emotional bed was big enough, so we all got on to it together.' The younger man moved in and they all slept in the same bed, with sex for David again being based at home for most of the time, but now as part of a threesome.

Embarrassment or fear of the reaction of the professional are potent reasons for non-disclosure or partial information being given by a client. The client may be hypervigilant for any sign of disapproval from the professional. It is easy even if the professional is not prejudiced for the choice of words or the setting of the interview to lead the client to expect a prejudiced response to disclosure.

Case example

Julia
Julia was 23 and worked for an advertising company. She attended on a Monday morning requesting the 'morning after

pill'. She had no regular partner, and once that had been established became very reluctant to discuss her sex life further. The whole interview seemed to have become highly fraught. The doctor realised that he was losing the trust of the patient, and explained his difficulty to Julia. He produced the tablets and left them on the table, saying that he would not cause her any problems in obtaining them, but that he did want to make sure that she was all right and they were a suitable method of contraception for her.

Julia seemed to relax, and explained that she had no regular partner, but had been to a club on the Saturday night. She had used recreational drugs. She usually relied on condoms both for contraception, and for protection against sexual infection. On the Saturday night/Sunday morning she had gone home with a new man, and they had not had any condoms to hand. She was not sure that they had had penetrative sex, but was concerned that since she was at the fertile phase of her menstrual cycle she might become pregnant by a man whom she hardly knew.

She was comfortable with her current lifestyle, so no attempt to judge it nor to alter it was made. Post-coital contraception was given, and a 'check-up' for sexual infection was performed, which was normal, and a repeat screen at two weeks was offered to exclude bacterial infections still within their incubation period. Discussion of future contraception was brief because she was well informed and she was sure that this one episode without a condom was unusual for her. She was happy to continue using condoms for contraception and protection from infection.

Content of 'sex'

The term 'sex' covers a vast range of behav-iours. What is perceived as part of 'sex' by a client may not be the same as the professional expects. If in doubt it is always wise to check with the client. This is particularly true in SM (sado-masochism) where a consensual act may be overtly sexual, but if it was not consensual would be an assault and not part of sex at all.

Presentation with difficulties relating to the content of sexual activity has three main types:

- that which is incidental to the presenting problem;
- that which causes difficulties to the client;
- that which causes difficulty to the client's partner.

Sadly we are all aware of professionals who have focused on the unconventional aspect of a client's life and not addressed the problem for which the client had sought help.

Case example

Robert
Robert was 27. He had sought help from several agencies for an unsatisfactory sex life. He is 'into' CP (corporal punishment) and enjoyed being beaten with a belt before more traditional sex. His professed problem was a difficulty making friends and keeping them. Previous agencies had concentrated on the 'problem' of the CP. Robert did not see this as a problem at all, and was somewhat mystified by the focus that others had placed on it. Putting the content of the sex on one side and listening to him revealed other problems. The biggest difficulty in his making and keeping friends turned out to be a quite severe obsessional compulsive disorder (OCD) that meant he was very unreliable at keep-

ing appointments, since he was taking up to half an hour (up to two hours if going away for a weekend) in checking rituals before he could leave home.

Cognitive behavioural work on the OCD freed him from the difficulties of leaving home, and allowed him to make and keep friends. His sexual life continued with the same content, but became more fulfilling since now it could be in the context of a relationship.

Clients who have partners often become concerned about how their sexual activities can be encompassed within the relationship. If the content of sexual activity is causing concern to the client this can often best be addressed by seeing the client on their own. Particularly where clients come as members of couples it is important to see each member of the couple individually so that they may speak frankly. Otherwise key information may be missed. Sometimes the concern of the client is about fantasy rather than about activity. Often all that is required in such cases is reassurance that the unusual content of their sexual fantasies is not 'abnormal' or 'damaging'. Surprisingly often unfulfilled sexual fantasies that cause concern to the client can be accommodated by their partner without any problems, although the issue of such fantasies does need to be approached with care with partners since their reaction cannot be guaranteed.

If the client is single, they may just need help to accept the nature of their desires and possibly some practical advice on finding others with similar interests. 'Coming out' into a sexual minority interest has many similarities with 'coming out' as gay, and psychological support is similarly useful. It should not need stating that the aim is for the client to achieve their own goals, and not for the professional to impose their own.

Case example

Mark

Mark took a job in the UK having been raised in the USA with British parents. He had discovered while at college that he had a sexual interest in SM. He preferred his partner to be female, but he had discovered that although he did not like gay sex, it was easier to find partners prepared to treat him as he wanted on the 'gay scene'. He attended a clinic for a routine STD screen, and mentioned his sexual difficulties in passing. Giving him a resource list of heterosexual contact points allowed him to find his feet in a new city, and in a new sexual world he was subsequently able to fulfil his sexual life with women, in a way he had not previously been able to.

Sometimes a client will present with the explicit request to lose a set of sexual fantasies. Although there are techniques for adjusting sexual needs, they are unlikely to fundamentally change a deep-seated sexual longing. Psychotherapeutic work is usually better centred on making sexual choices, and addressing a cognitive framework in which the desire is placed. Often the development of other sexual interests can lead to some satisfaction, while the unwanted fantasy may remain, but unfulfilled, to the satisfaction of the client. A bisexual man may ask to be 'made heterosexual'. In practice there is a lot that he can gain from psychological work, though changing his orientation is probably neither possible nor desirable.

Case examples

Luis

Luis was 26. He attended the clinic initially for an HIV test, being very concerned at a limited homosexual experience some three months before. The rest of his sexual life had been heterosexual and he was living with his girlfriend. He was asked if he thought he might have sex with a man again in the future, in order that he could be offered hepatitis vaccinations. He looked rather distressed and asked for help to stop him from 'being so weak' again. In a series of visits over six months he explored the nature of his sexual life, both in reality and in fantasy and was finally able to recognise that he was bisexual, and that he could choose which modes of sexual expression he would practise. Whilst it was his expressed intent only to have sex with women in the future, he had recognised and integrated the possibility of further homosexual experiences, which, if they occurred, he now saw as part of his being human and not a sign of weakness.

Philip

Philip was referred by his GP complaining that he seemed to have become obsessed with women's shoes. He was living with his long-term female partner, and had not felt able to discuss the situation with her. He was now suffering from erectile dysfunction with her. When he tried to have sex he noticed that his thoughts were moving to shoes when he was having sex. Once he noticed that this had happened he felt guilty and lost his erection. After discussion he decided to tell his girlfriend why his erections were not as strong as they had been. Her reaction was to ask him which of her shoes he preferred and then for her to wear them in the bedroom. Sex returned to normal and he found the intrusive ideas were usually absent. His girlfriend found the whole thing mildly amusing and would wear whatever footwear was requested but the requests became less frequent and Philip said that he had 'got it out of his system'.

If the sexual content of the client's fantasies is causing problems for the partner then seeing the couple together – after careful separate interviewing of the partners – has obvious advantages. Often there has been a gradual increase in the fetishist content of sexual activity. When the content was only a little unusual the partner may well have been quite happy to accommodate it, but if it becomes more extreme it may cross the partner's boundaries of what is acceptable. Withholding the permission to indulge the fetish may also sometimes be part of power play within the relationship. Once the nature of sexual interaction has become an issue, communication on other matters may also break down. Simply being able to talk together about 'the problem' may be enough to resolve the situation. If not, then structured bargaining of sexual content for other wants of the partner can be very useful.

Case example

Michael and Joanna

This couple came for help when Michael's rubber fetish led him to want to wear Wellington boots in bed for sex. Joanna had quite enjoyed the 'naughtiness' of his previous rubber paraphernalia, and was quite happy dressing up in it herself for 'special occasions'. When Michael had first appeared with Wellington boots on she had tried to go along with it, but found that she kept being kicked by him. Thinking that this was part of what he wanted was too much for her, and she refused to play again if he was wearing the boots. This had become a major issue between them.

On the first session in clinic they described what had happened and Michael was upset to discover that he had kicked her. This was not part of his sexual need, and he was upset that she had not told him what the problem had been. It became apparent that communication had not been very effective for some time, and most of the time in the clinic was devoted to communication skills. Eventually the Wellington boots were used as a subject for a 'negotiated settlement' in the safety of a clinic setting. The temporary solution was that she would allow him to wear the boots, as long as they didn't get onto the bed. Initially this led to him standing by the bed for sex, but as they became more confident of their communication they tried sex in other rooms of the house. Joanna found that the boots were not a problem if she could keep out of their way. As part of their negotiation, Joanna also asked for some sex without any rubber, and was surprised that Michael was happy to do this if he could do it 'his way' on other occasions.

There are of course occasions when the client's sexual desires fall outside of the range of activity that a partner will tolerate. It is important not to be seen to be taking sides when seeing such couples, and the temptation to act as an arbitrator of 'what is acceptable' should be avoided.

Case example

Dennis and Margaret
Dennis and Margaret had been married for fourteen years. Their sex life had been fairly conventional and, Margaret thought, very satisfying. Difficulties had started to arise when Dennis had brought back from

a holiday abroad a pornographic video. Having watched it together he asked Margaret to perform oral sex on him, which had not been part of their sexual repertoire up until this time. Margaret reluctantly agreed but was not willing to let him perform the same on her. When Dennis suggested that they try anal sex she was outraged, refused and withdrew from all sex with him. By the time they arrived for help there was a marked strain in the relationship. In the first session she expressed her satisfaction with how their sex life had been for fourteen years. He expressed his dissatisfaction with it, and a sense of frustration that he had been unable to experiment. It was also clear that he was angry that he had 'lost' his younger years and good looks when finding an alternative partner for sex would have been easier.

At the end of the first session nothing had been resolved although each had a clearer idea of what the other wanted. They re-attended together two weeks later. Margaret was upset that their sex life had not been satisfying him through all their years of married life. She was questioning how it could have gone on so long without her knowing. Dennis was adamant that all that he wanted was 'normal sex' as shown in the video, and that he had been denied too long. Margaret looked to the professional for confirmation that the 'dirty' things in the video were wrong. Side-stepping that, the professional got them to discuss it between themselves. It was clear that they held very different beliefs about what was acceptable sexually.

At the next visit Dennis attended alone to say that they had agreed to differ, and agreed to separate to give him the freedom to experiment and not make her address sexual activity that she found abhorrent.

Meaning of 'sex'

Sexual acts have many meanings. Sex can be, at one end of the spectrum, a consummation of a loving relationship or, at the other end of the spectrum, as impersonal as playing a stranger at squash.

If sex means different things to the people involved then strains may appear in a relationship. Sex outside the primary relationship may be perceived very differently by the partners, where one may perceive it as of little significance while the other perceives it as a betrayal, devaluing the sex occurring within the primary relationship.

Cognitive work, addressing the different types of relationship, and their special rewards and responsibilities, can be very useful, but it does presuppose that the therapist is able to work in a field where there is no clear 'orthodox' model for running a relationship. The possible 'types' of relationship encountered tend to be generated afresh by the individual client, and often do not conform to any 'template'.

Dissatisfaction for an individual may occur if they have not realised that sex can mean different things at different times. A fairly common presentation in clinics is the man or woman who has mastered the 'art' of casual sex, but is aware that they are missing out on the intimacy and the quality of sex that can occur with a regular partner. Moving from wanting casual relationships to wanting longer-term relationships over time is not uncommon but for some people it presents real difficulties.

A 'regular' sex partner is not necessarily the same thing as a boy or girlfriend. These carry implications of a relationship extending beyond the purely sexual. However many people have regular sexual partners with whom their relationship is more or less purely based on sex and uncluttered by the other responsibilities of a relationship. Sometimes this is simply a matter of preference. Sometimes they may find it difficult to 'deepen' a relationship beyond the purely sexual.

For the cognitive-behavioural components of moving from a series of more or less casual relationships to settling down with a partner, there are a series of steps to make, rather than one large leap. The first is a realisation that this is not always a choice between one and the other, depending on the attitude of the partner. Recognising that one is 'missing out' on the rewards of a longer term relationship is not the same as wanting to give up on the gratification achieved by casual sex. Achieving a long-term relationship is not always easy. Over a sexual career, out of many potential sexual partners most people would only want to have sex with a few and of those only a few would be potentially suitable for a committed long-term relationship.

The behavioural approach to moving from casual sex to having an ongoing relationship is therefore a matter of breaking down the problem into easy stages. First to master the transition of getting from a one-night stand to talking over breakfast, then to arranging to see a partner once more, and then maybe a relationship can develop. Looked at this way, no big changes are needed, and 'homework' tasks become less threatening.

Case example

Paul

Paul asked for help because he was dissatisfied with his sex life. He was a gay man, and although getting lots of sex he hardly ever took anyone home, and felt his encounters were 'shallow'. He was scathing of the idea that he should 'want' a boyfriend, seeing it as pandering to a heterosexual model of fidelity that he would not accept. Early clinic sessions were based on looking at what a relationship meant, and what sex meant. Intellectually he could see the differences between various forms of relationships, and was relieved when he realised that he did not have to make a lifetime choice between them, but rather adapt his behaviour to allow other forms to have a chance to develop. His first homework exercise was simply to have sex indoors, rather than in a public park. This he achieved quite easily by way of a series of one-night stands. He reported a change in his feeling about the sex when it was occurring in a bed and when the partner stayed overnight and they slept together.

Once he was comfortable with this, he was set the exercise of trying to arrange to see one of the one-night stands again, either for sex or for a social occasion. He was very nervous of trying this, since it left him open to a rejection that he felt he might find hard to accept. After working through his fears and contemplating the worst that could happen, he began trying to 'keep in touch' with people if he had enjoyed their company. Some of these partners became friends, and some regular casual partners who he saw more or less exclusively for sex. Time in the sessions was spent on 'working at relationships' and the need to invest in them, and to become more tolerant of the other person if you wanted to get the rewards of them being accepting of you.

Paul realised that his social life was changing almost without him having really tried and that he was having less casual sex simply because he was busier doing other things. Eventually he met a man and they got to know each other without having sex first. After eight clinic visits Paul was settled into this relationship, which was providing him with the 'missing' elements of his previous life. He continued to have anonymous sex for its own rewards.

Sex in which power play is to the fore may cause problems with boundaries. When this has happened, some formal method of 'deroleing' becomes important. This can either be a statement used between the participants that the roles are no longer operative, or an agreement that the roles only apply once over the threshold of the bed or play room.

For example, someone who is masochistic sexually may then find it difficult to assert him- or herself in other areas of the relationship, or even in related fields such as work. Issues of boundaries in sex which involves 'role playing' can raise particular problems. It is one of the truisms of SM sex that the 'bottom' or subservient participant is actually the one with greatest control. A realisation of this is very useful when discussing safer sex issues in the context of power play.

Case example

Gareth

Gareth was referred to the clinic for concerns over safer sex. It was apparent that he knew all the relevant information, but that he felt disempowered to implement safer sex strategies when playing 'bottom' (masochist). Over a series of visits he explored the differences between 'surrendering control' as part of sexual role play and actually being helpless. Whilst recognising that the standard advice of negotiating the content of a sex session with a new partner was seldom possible ('If you've talked it all through in detail there is not much point left in doing it') he did develop ways of telling a partner that although they were 'in charge' it was within the safer sex boundaries that he would be comfortable with. He found that in practice once this had been agreed he was better able to surrender to the role he was playing and that this enhanced the experience for him, as well as reducing his fears of HIV transmission.

One of the difficulties in offering psychological support to people practising alternative forms of sex like SM, with complex cultures of their own, is that there is a limit to how often the professional can ask to have the context explained. Trying to bluff or plough on in ignorance is not a realistic option. Where possible, referral on to a more informed professional is recommended if the practitioner is aware that they are needing to clarify too much too often with a client.

Conclusion

People with unconventional sexual lifestyles are driven by the same basic social and sexual forces as everyone else. What they do may be unconventional but the process by which they got to those behaviours is not. It follows from this, of course, that the psychological treatments which work in other people will work as well in them; it is simply a matter of adaptation and flexibility of approach. It is easy to become centred on the unfamiliarity of unconventional sexual behaviours and assume that they must therefore represent the operation of some peculiar psychological process in the individual, rather than being unconventional activities developed from conventional processes.

Suggested further reading

Patterns of sexual behaviour

Wellings, K., *et al.* (1994) *Sexual Behaviour in Britain.* Penguin Books, London.
Michael, R., *et al.* (1995) *Sex in America.* Warner Books, New York.
Coxon, A. (1996) *Between the Sheets.* Cassell, London.

Sexual content

Morn, J. (1986) *Anal Pleasure and Health.* Yes Press, San Francisco.
Henkin, B. (1996) *Consensual Sadomasochism. How to Talk About It and How to Do It Safely.* Daedalus, Los Angeles.
Townsend, L. (2000) *The Leatherman's Handbook,* Silver Jubilee edn. Lt Publication, Los Angeles.

Chapter 22

Pregnancy, Pregnancy Loss and Induced Abortion

Anne Walker

Introduction

Pregnancy is central to human life and sexual health, whether or not it is a first-hand experience (Morrell 1994). Like other reproductive experiences (see Walker & Hunter, this volume), pregnancy has psychological and cultural meaning, and it occurs within the context of particular social and material circumstances. A pregnancy may be longed for, planned and wanted, unplanned and accepted or unplanned and unwanted. It may be undertaken joyfully as an active choice or result from physical or social coercion. It may end in the birth of one or more children, or prematurely, through miscarriage or induced abortion. It can be a joyful experience, a great adventure, a traumatic and nerve-wracking roller coaster or an unmitigated personal disaster.

The main aim of this chapter is to consider the experience of induced abortion. Abortion is a contentious social issue (Denious & Russo 2000). It is regulated throughout the world, and access to safe and effective abortion facilities varies hugely for different groups of women. Debates about access to abortion focus around the morality of terminating a pregnancy, often in terms of the 'right to life'. What they often fail to recognise is that life is not an inevitable consequence of pregnancy. Not all pregnancies end in the birth of a healthy child, and the experience of pregnancy loss is common although rarely discussed (Cecil 1996). For this reason, the experience of induced abortion is probably best understood in the context of pregnancy itself and its other possible outcomes – childbirth, miscarriage, stillbirth and neonatal death.

Pregnancy and birth

Pregnancy or gestation is the period of time from conception to the delivery of a child (or children). Full-term normal pregnancies can range from 37 to 43 weeks, with the majority of births occurring between 39 and 41 weeks. In the United Kingdom and many other developed countries, birth rates have fallen over the last century, while infant and maternal survival rates have increased. Pregnancy and child-birth are easier and safer now in the west than they have ever been, with maternal mortality rates of about 10 per 100 000 live births and a lifetime risk of dying as a result of pregnancy of between 1 in 4000 and 1 in 10 000. This is not the case in many other parts of the world, however. More than half a million women die each year of pregnancy-related causes world-wide, with a lifetime risk of 1 in 15 in some developing countries (Doyal 1995).

The epidemiology of pregnancy has changed over time, and is dramatically influenced by economic, social and political factors that determine the amount of control women have over their fertility. For example, the pro-natalist policies introduced by the Ceaucescu government in Romania in 1966 effectively doubled birth-rates within two years (Baban 1999). In the UK, the mythical average contemporary woman will be pregnant for around three years of her life, compared to as much as 15 years in the late nineteenth century (Oakley 1993). Currently, in the UK, around three-quarters of a million babies are born each year and, despite increasing numbers choosing to remain child-free, around 80–90% of women will have at least one child. The most popular age to have a baby is between 25 and 35, with the average age for a first baby falling in the late twenties (Central Statistical Office 1996).

Pregnancy is usually a happy time, associated with considerable physical, social and psychological changes. Serious health problems, such as hypertension and pre-eclampsia, toxaemia, gestational diabetes or obstetric cholestasis, can occur but they are relatively uncommon. Nonetheless, in industrialised cultures the most common view is that pregnancy and childbirth are biological and medical events, or potentially problematic 'health states' (Woollett & Marshall 1997). In other words, pregnancy has been medicalised (Tew 1990; Barker 1998). The implication of this view for women is that they are assigned simultaneously passive and active roles. They are passive containers for their growing babies, but they are expected to actively monitor their own health and behaviour and to ensure their child's future health (Gross 2000). The implication of this view for psychological research is a tendency to focus on the problems that can occur, rather than on pregnancy as a developmental transition (Smith 1999) or biopsychosocial process (Scott & Niven 1996). Descriptions of psychological well-being during pregnancy need to be considered with this in mind.

Empirical research suggests that pregnancy is a time of mixed emotions for most women. Joy and excitement combine with anxiety, stress and occasionally depression. Which of these mood states predominates varies between women and across different stages of pregnancy. A survey of a large, representative sample of women living in England found that 74% felt happy in early pregnancy, while 46% felt anxious (Green et al. 1990). Levels of reported anxiety tend to be associated with events during pregnancy, and can generally be regarded as normal reactions to them (Gross 2000). In straightforward pregnancies, anxiety levels tend to be low in the middle trimester, but higher in early pregnancy and near to the expected date of delivery (Wolkind & Zajicek 1981; Gross & Pattison 1995). This pattern is different for women who undergo prenatal diagnostic testing (e.g. amniocentesis or chorionic villus sampling). In this group, anxiety levels are high as they await the test and its results, but fewer symptoms tend to be reported during the last weeks of pregnancy than in comparison women who have not undergone prenatal testing (Marteau *et al.* 1992; Hewison *et al.* 1996). Women who have had problems in previous pregnancies or other reproductive difficulties may experience high levels of anxiety throughout the pregnancy (Van den Akker *et al.* 1990). Partners of pregnant women may also experience changes in their emotional state as the pregnancy progresses. Raised levels of anxiety, irritability and depression have been found among fathers-to-be (Condon 1987), and men express concerns about the risks their partners are facing and the effect of the pregnancy and birth on their relationship (Lewis 1986).

Depression during pregnancy is less common than anxiety, but there is growing evidence that depressed mood during pregnancy predicts postnatal depression (Fergusson *et al.* 1996; Green 1998; Nicolson 1998). A recent study of 9000 women in the UK has shown that rates of depressive symptoms are higher in the later stages of pregnancy than after birth, and that the majority of women who are depressed postnatally were also depressed or very anxious during their pregnancy (Fergusson *et al.* 1996). Hence, it seems that while childbirth may be a catalyst for depression in some women, for many others it is a positive event that improves emotional well-being (Thorpe & Elliott 1998).

Pregnancy occurs in a social and personal context. The reactions of family members and the level of resources available to women can have profound effects on the experience of pregnancy. For example, women whose partners are unsupportive or reject the pregnancy have poorer well-being than those with supportive families (Collins *et al.* 1993). Similarly,

the material resources available during pregnancy affect the ability to cope. When employment rates are low, or where there is no partner, vulnerability to poverty is high during pregnancy (Scott & Niven 1996).

The visibility of pregnancy makes women public property, with significant impact on their social identity and self-perception (Baker 1989). Some women feel less attractive during pregnancy (Slade 1977; Oakley 1980), while others may feel 'normal' (Wiles 1990). At this time, women's bodies tend to be viewed as 'functional' rather than 'ornamental' (Price 1988), and become the focus for comments and advice from all comers (Gross 2000).

For the majority of pregnancies, childbirth is the ultimate outcome. Birth practices vary immensely across cultures: it can be a private or public event; the labouring woman can be seen as powerful or defiled; she may be attended by other women, male partners or specialised attendants (e.g. midwives and obstetricians); and the attendants can administer a wide range of remedies to facilitate delivery and prevent complications (Raphael-Leff 1991). In Britain, childbirth currently occurs most commonly in a hospital setting with specialised attendants and often the father present, and with varying degrees of technological involvement. In questionnaire surveys, the majority of women express high levels of satisfaction with the birth, although this global assessment can disguise quite high levels of dissatisfaction with specific aspects of the process (Quine *et al.* 1993; Green *et al.* 1998). Levels of satisfaction are related not only to events occurring during labour (e.g. pain, complications, interventions), but also to the expectations that women have of labour beforehand. Women having their first baby are generally less satisfied with the experience than more experienced mothers, and women who wanted to be in control of the process but were not able to be also express high levels of dissatisfaction (Green *et al.* 1998).

Emotional well-being after childbirth is related to a number of different factors, as noted earlier. However, it is worth noting that apart from postnatal depression, a proportion of women do experience post-traumatic stress type symptoms following labour (Niven 1988; Menage 1993; Ballard *et al.* 1995). These include intrusions, avoidance and hyperarousal, at levels equivalent to those found in sufferers of combat trauma (Menage 1993). The prevalence of post-traumatic symptoms six weeks after giving birth to a normal healthy baby is estimated to be 3% (Czarnocka & Slade 2000), that is about 21 000 women per year in the UK, not all of whom experience postnatal depression. Predictors of severe post-traumatic symptoms include perceived low levels of social support from partner and staff, blaming staff for difficulties during the delivery, and low perceived control over labour. Factors such as the length of labour, type of delivery or nature of interventions do not seem to be important (Czarnocka & Slade 2000).

Psychological interventions during pregnancy are generally designed to facilitate decision-making or reduce anxiety associated with procedures such as antenatal screening; to relieve pain or anxiety during childbirth; to prevent poor emotional well-being after the baby is born; to treat ongoing psychological problems; or to improve the health of the baby. Traditional antenatal classes are the most common form of psycho-educational intervention during pregnancy. A number of studies have evaluated the effects of these classes on pain experiences during labour, with mixed findings. The only consistent finding is that women who attend classes tend to use less pain medication, however, it is not clear whether this is because they are using the coping strategies taught in the classes or for other reasons. However, antenatal classes do appear to increase women's knowledge about childbirth and their confidence in coping with labour (Slade 1996). Counselling and/or non-specific social support during pregnancy have been shown to result in beneficial outcomes for both mothers and babies (Flint & Poulengris 1987; Oakley *et al.* 1990). More recently, monthly support group meetings from mid-pregnancy until six months after birth have been shown to significantly reduce rates of postnatal depression amongst first-time mothers at risk (Elliott *et al.* 2000).

Pregnancy loss

Spontaneous abortion, or miscarriage, is the involuntary loss of a baby in the early stages of pregnancy. In the United Kingdom, a pregnancy that is lost before 24 weeks of gestation is described as a miscarriage. Anything later than this is defined medico-legally as a still-birth. The proportion of pregnancies that are lost varies widely between different countries and cultural groups (DeLuca & Leslie 1996). Studies using hormone assays to detect pregnancy from its earliest stages suggest that around 30% of pregnancies are lost in western societies, with the vast majority of these losses occurring within the first weeks after fertilisation, before the woman is aware that she is pregnant (Wilcox *et al.* 1988). Approximately

10–20% of recognised pregnancies in the UK end in miscarriage or stillbirth. The majority of women who conceive again after the miscarriage will have a normal healthy pregnancy. However, some will miscarry again, and a diagnosis of recurrent miscarriage is usually made if women have lost two or more pregnancies in this way (Gannon 1994).

The usual symptoms of a miscarriage are uterine cramps, followed by bleeding (The Boston Women's Health Book Collective 1998). As the miscarriage proceeds, cramps become more intense and the bleeding becomes heavier until the foetus and afterbirth are expelled. This process can last for a few hours. Once the foetus has been lost, bleeding continues but gradually diminishes. What is lost during a miscarriage will vary considerably depending on the stage of pregnancy that had been reached. It may be a well-formed baby, a very tiny foetus, parts of a baby or foetus, or blood and tissue without identifiable parts (Kohner 1992). The majority of women who miscarry are seen in hospital, where the care is concerned with minimising blood loss and the risk of infection. Most will undergo a dilatation and curettage procedure (D & C) to ensure that the uterus is empty, and then stay in hospital for around 24 hours (Cecil & Slade 1996). In most hospitals, investigations into the cause of the miscarriage will only be undertaken if a woman has experienced one or two miscarriages in the past.

The reasons why a particular pregnancy has miscarried are often obscure, and it is relatively unusual for a specific diagnosis to be given. The most common cause of miscarriage in general, however, is a chromosomal abnormality in the foetus. Studies of foetuses that have been miscarried suggest that about half of them have some sort of chromosomal abnormality, compared with around one in 20 stillborn babies, and one in 200 liveborn babies (Simpson & Bombard 1987). Viral or bacterial infections in early pregnancy can also be associated with a higher probability of miscarriage, in particular, viral infections such as German measles, chickenpox, mumps, measles or influenza, bacterial infections such as listeria, and contact with farm animals infected with brucellosis or chlamydia (Charles & Larsen 1987). Uterine anomalies (McDonald 1987), hormonal deficiencies (Horta et al. 1977) or immunological factors (Carp et al. 1990) may also be involved in some miscarriages. Psychological factors, especially personality, have been investigated as potential causes of recurrent miscarriage. However, despite the generally poor methodological quality of this research, there is little empirical support for the hypothesis that psychological factors play a causal role in recurrent miscarriage (Gannon 1994). The absence of a specific reason for the miscarriage can make it particularly difficult for parents to come to terms with the loss of a wanted baby (Tunaley et al. 1993).

Beliefs and practices surrounding pregnancy loss vary considerably between cultures (Cecil 1996). However, many societies lack shared rituals or practices to mark the loss of a pregnancy, or for disposal of the baby's body or remains (Chalmers 1992). In the UK, the Stillbirth and Neonatal Death Society (SANDS) recommends that the needs and preferences of the parents should be taken into account in decisions about disposal procedures, and cremation or burial facilities should be available (SANDS 1991).

Miscarriage involves the loss of a child (or children), and the majority of psychological studies assume that a bereavement model is the most appropriate for understanding responses to it. However, it is also a traumatic physical experience, suggesting that models of reactions to stress may be helpful (Cecil & Slade 1996). Women's responses to miscarriage vary widely, from relief to profound depression (Graves et al. 1987). In the first month after miscarriage, between 20% and 50% of women are significantly depressed (Prettyman et al. 1993; Cecil & Slade 1996). High levels of anxiety are also common (Prettyman et al. 1993; Cecil & Leslie 1993), as are intrusive experiences such as nightmares, flashbacks and unwanted memories (Cecil & Slade 1996), and feelings of guilt (Leppert & Pahlka 1984). The timecourse of these symptoms is still unclear. Some studies suggest that the majority of women who were depressed are feeling 'back to normal' within three months of the miscarriage (Prettyman et al. 1993). Others suggest that it takes longer than this (Garel et al. 1992; Neugebauer et al. 1992), and that symptoms may recur at various points for a year or more afterwards (Robinson et al. 1994). As long as two years later, a quarter of women still think about their miscarriage often, and around one in eight experience significant distress when they think about it (Cordle & Prettyman 1994). Not surprisingly, women who have had a miscarriage tend to be anxious and concerned about the possibility of miscarrying in subsequent pregnancies (Statham & Green 1994).

It is difficult to predict which women are most at risk of negative emotional experiences after miscarriage (Slade 1994). Demographic factors such as age, being in a stable relationship, having children already or social class are not consistent predictors, neither are the length of the pregnancy or the extent to which it was planned (Friedman & Gath 1989; Tharpar & Tharpar 1992; Prettyman et al. 1993). A past history of psychiatric or emotional problems is a significant predictor (Prettyman et al. 1993; Toedter et al. 1988; Friedman & Gath 1989). The impact of previous fertility problems or miscarriages is unclear, with inconsistent findings reported (Garel et al. 1992; Friedman & Gath 1989; Jackman et al. 1991). Women's personal views of the meaning of the experience are likely to be important in determining their reaction to it, however, few studies have investigated cognitions about miscarriage. Those which have suggest that women who blame themselves, or feel blamed, for the miscarriage are more likely to be depressed or anxious (Madden 1988; Robinson et al. 1994), and those who have developed their own explanation for the miscarriage are less anxious (Tunaley et al. 1993). Feeling in control of the outcome of a subsequent pregnancy is associated with high levels of anxiety and depression (Madden 1988; Tunaley et al. 1993). This contrasts with studies of depression in general, which usually find that feelings of control are associated with positive well-being (e.g. Steptoe & Appels 1989).

It is not only women who are affected by miscarriage. Although there have been few studies of male partners, the evidence that exists suggests that they also experience grief in the weeks following a miscarriage (Puddifoot & Johnson 1997, 1999). In contrast to women, men tend to be less demonstrative in showing their grief, but express high levels of difficulty in coping and despair. Like women, the duration of the pregnancy does not seem to make a difference, but men who have seen an ultrasound scan of their baby are more distressed than those who have not. Further research is needed to investigate the longer term impact of miscarriage for partners and the wider family (Cecil 1994).

Miscarriage involves considerable pain, loss of blood and emergency hospitalisation, yet few studies have considered whether the nature of the experience or the quality of care received have an impact on how women feel afterwards. Some studies have shown an association between high levels of depression and low satisfaction with hospital care (Garel *et al.* 1992; Cecil & Slade 1996), however, as mood influences memory, these findings need to be treated with caution. Further research is needed to investigate whether aspects of care influence the process of adjustment.

The potential psychological impact of miscarriage has only been acknowledged in recent years, and very few studies have investigated the effectiveness of interventions to help women and their families come to terms with it. Neugebauer *et al.* (1992) found that women who participated in a detailed telephone interview about the miscarriage were less likely to be depressed six months afterwards than women who did not. The opportunity to develop a personal meaning for the miscarriage, either through counselling or from information about likely causes given by hospital staff, is likely to be beneficial but awaits systematic investigation.

Stillbirth and neonatal death

Stillbirth and neonatal death are rare but tragic events in western societies. The majority of stillbirths are unexpected, and occur during labour. In some cases, the death is foreseen before labour, and both obstetric staff and the mother may know for a period of time that the baby has died (Kirkley-Best & Kellner 1982). In these cases, labour is usually induced, and the mother may be given some time before the birth to come to terms with it. Even so, the evidence suggests that most parents, and obstetric staff, continue to 'hope for the best' until the baby is finally born (Mander 1994).

Shock is often the initial reaction to stillbirth, especially if it is totally unexpected (Hutchins 1986). Disbelief and confusion are common reactions (Littlewood 1992). Almost always, this is followed by intense and complex feelings of grief (Littlewood 1996). The strength of these feelings may be frightening for some parents and difficult to describe. The expectation of a joyful birth and the hopes and dreams invested in the new baby make the loss particularly hard to accept, as does the difficulty of trying to say 'hello and goodbye' at the same time (Hutchins 1986). In addition, many women feel guilty for surviving when their baby died (Mander 1994). Anger and outrage are common responses, and may last for years following the death (Littlewood 1996). Overall, as Littlewood (1996) says, 'the death of a baby is uniquely difficult to cope with' (p. 153).

Responses to the death of a baby in the first few days or weeks of life (neonatal death) can be similar. Anger, guilt, disbelief and a sense of unreality are common. Neonatal death is generally less of a shock than stillbirth, however, and parents have had at least some time to get to know their baby. The staff who cared for the baby can also be helpful in providing support to the parents and validating his or her existence as a separate individual (Littlewood 1992, 1996).

Professional practice surrounding stillbirth and neonatal death has changed over the last 20 years. Prior to that, it was characterised by Mander (1994) as 'rugby tackle management', focusing on removal of the body as quickly as possible, institutional disposal, and discouraging parents to see or talk about the baby. In response to initiatives by self-help organisations (SANDS 1991), supported by government agencies (HMSO 1992), practice has changed rapidly in the UK. Parents are now encouraged to see and hold their baby, to take photographs and keep mementoes, such as a lock of hair or the baby's name tag, to talk about the baby, and to dispose of the body as they wish (Mander 1994; Littlewood 1996).

The desire to have another child is often strong after a baby has died (Littlewood 1996). The experiences of parents who embark on another pregnancy have received little attention, however, it seems likely that they will need sensitive support from health professionals.

Induced abortion

It is estimated that 22% of all pregnancies worldwide are terminated by elective abortion (Alan Guttmacher Institute 1999). However, rates of abortion vary widely across countries and continents, and are not necessarily dependent on the legal status or accessibility of abortion. For example, rates of abortion in Western Europe are lower than in Latin America, despite the fact that abortion is highly restricted in Latin American countries (Denious & Russo 2000). In Britain, about 195 000 abortions were conducted in 1999, a rate of around 12 per thousand women of reproductive age (Information and Statistics Division for the National Health Service in Scotland 2000; Office for National Statistics 2000). Trends in abortion rates in Britain vary by the age of the woman. Since the 1960s, abortion rates have risen in all age groups, but most notably among women between 16 and 24. About 45% of all abortions are performed on women in this age group.

Abortion, procured by abortifacient drugs or instrumental means, is one of the oldest and most widely practiced methods of preventing the birth of unwanted children (Williams 1987). Currently, in countries with legal and unrestricted access to good abortion facilities, it is a safe and straightforward medical procedure. This applies to almost all countries in Europe, the former Soviet Union and North America – covering about 40% of the world's female population. However, unsafe abortion is a major cause of death and disability for women of child-bearing age worldwide. Approximately 20 million unsafe abortions are conducted annually worldwide, and estimates of the numbers of women who die from unsafe abortions range from 70 000 to 200 000 (The Boston Women's Health Book Collective 1998). Mortality rates are 119 per 100 000 abortions in Latin America, and 680 per 100 000 in Africa (Alan Guttmacher Institute 1999).

The most common methods of abortion are suction termination or medical abortion using mifepristone and prostaglandin. Medical abortion is at its most effective in the earliest stages of pregnancy (< 7 weeks from last menstrual period) but can also be used later (Henshaw & Templeton 1998), and is now used in about 45% of early abortions in the UK (Information and Statistics Division for the National Health Service in Scotland 2000). Conventional suction termination under local or general anaesthetic is most effective between 7 and 15 weeks (Kaunitz *et al.* 1985). Women having abortions in early pregnancy value the opportunity to choose between these two methods, and are more satisfied with their care if they have received their preferred procedure (Howie *et al.* 1997; Slade *et al.* 1998). Dilatation and evacuation (D & E) procedures are generally used for abortions that are performed beyond 15 weeks, and should only be undertaken by trained specialists who have a sufficient case-load to maintain their skills (Royal College of Obstetricians and Gynaecologists 2000). From a medical point of view, abortion is safer than continuing a pregnancy to term, and complications are uncommon (Royal College of Obstetricians and Gynaecologists 2000). Mortality rates vary between 0.6 and 1.2 per 100 000 abortions in countries where abortion is practised legally by qualified practitioners (Alan Guttmacher Institute 1999), compared to between six and 25 maternal deaths per 100 000 live births in the same countries. There are no proven associations between induced abortion and subsequent infertility or problems during pregnancy in countries where abortion is legal (Royal College of Obstetricians and Gynaecologists 2000).

A woman may choose to terminate her pregnancy for any number of psychological, practical and social reasons. In a study of 1900 abortion clients (Torres & Forest 1988; Russo *et al.* 1992), the reasons women gave could be categorised into two broad types. Personal/ internal reasons were to do with the woman's own personal qualities at the time, e.g. feeling too young or immature for the responsibility

of a baby. External reasons were to do with the situation in which the woman found herself. For example, her economic status, her relationships with others, the health of the foetus/ baby or commitments to education, work or existing children. Both external and internal reasons were important for all the women studied, but 75% of the women under 18 years of age felt that their own psychological immaturity was the major reason for their decision.

The decision to have an abortion may be made very quickly, even before a woman is sure that she is pregnant (Smetana & Adler 1979; Allen 1981; Cohan *et al.* 1993; Holmgren 1994). After the event, the vast majority of women continue to feel that abortion was the right decision for them at that time. In a recent study of 368 women attending 10 hospitals across Scotland, 91% felt that they had made the right decision (Penney *et al.* 1994). Deciding to have an abortion is not stressfree, however, and for some women is a very difficult decision (Adler *et al.* 1990). Women may be convinced that they are 'doing the right thing' but still feel confused, or even positive about the pregnancy (Boyle & McEvoy 1998).

Carol Gilligan (1982) has placed abortion decision making within a developmental context. Her in-depth study of 24 pregnant women, who were undecided about abortion at the time of the first interview, considered the process within the theoretical context of moral development. All of the women in this study were experiencing conflict over whether to end the pregnancy or not, and their resolution of the real-life dilemma was compared to the resolution of an artificial moral dilemma. The resolution of the real-life dilemma both depended on and reflected the stage of moral development that the woman had reached. At the earlier stages of development, women gave priority to self-preservation. With increasing maturity, responsibility for others (at the expense of personal safety) became more important. At the most mature stage, women were able to balance responsibility for others with a responsibility for themselves. The conflict experienced by an individual woman, and the way she resolves it, depends on her perception of what is right at that particular stage. This study makes the important point that abortion decision making is not independent of other psychological and developmental processes.

The majority of psychological research around abortion has focused on the well-being and mental health of women afterwards. There are a number of problems with research into psychological responses to abortion, however (Boyle 1997; Boyle & Ussher 2000). First, assertions about the presence or absence of psychological problems following abortion (or 'post-abortion syndrome') are widely used in debates about access to abortion (e.g. Adler 1992; Stotland 1992; Hopkins *et al.* 1996; Boyle 1997). As Boyle points out, knowing that the findings of research may be used in this way makes it difficult for researchers to focus on the full range of positive and negative psychological reactions to abortion, and limits the picture of women's experience. Second, most of the research has used standardised measures of psychological distress, which tend to focus on the presence or absence of a fairly narrow range of experiences. Third, the research is difficult to conduct and fraught with methodological problems (Walker 1996). For example, women seeking abortions and abortion providers are often reluctant to participate in research, biasing the study sample; control or comparison groups are difficult to identify; and the timing of post-abortion assessment varies from 24 hours to several months.

Do women experience depression, regret or traumatic experiences after elective abortion? Despite all the problems with research in this area, the simple answer to this question in the vast majority of cases is no. Meta-analysis of 24 studies comparing psychological well-being before and after abortion found that overall women feel better afterwards than they did before (average effect size 0.6) (Posavac & Miller 1990). Levels of well-being differ by less than one tenth of a standard deviation of the measures used between women who have had an abortion and comparable women who have not (Posavac & Miller 1990). So consistent are these findings that the development of significant psychological problems following abortion has been described as 'minuscule from a public health perspective' (Adler 1992). Some women do experience high levels of anxiety and depression after abortion; in most cases though, these are a continuation of problems that they were experiencing before the pregnancy (Dagg 1991; Russo & Denious 2000). In a secondary analysis of data from a national survey in North America, Russo and Denious (2000) found that women who had had an abortion were much more likely to have experienced childhood abuse and/or abuse from a partner than women who had not. Both of these types of experience are high risk factors for both unwanted pregnancy and high levels of depression and anxiety. When the researchers separated out the contributions of childhood abuse and partner abuse, having an abortion no longer made any significant contribution to the level of depression.

The experience of women who have an abortion because there is a high risk that their baby will be 'abnormal' is different from those who have abortions for other reasons in a number of ways (Boyle 1997). The pregnancy is more likely to be wanted and planned. The abortion itself may occur at a later stage in pregnancy, and both women and their partners may have had the opportunity to see an ultrasound scan of their baby. Finally, the social context in which the abortion occurs is very different. The overwhelming majority of the British population support the availability of pregnancy termination if there is a strong concern that the baby may be 'handicapped' (Green *et al.* 1993) or have a foetal 'defect' (Jowell *et al.* 1991), and the majority of pregnant women agree (Green *et al.* 1993). Despite the feeling that ending the pregnancy is 'the right thing to do', feelings of grief and loss, similar to those following miscarriage, are common amongst this group of women and their partners (Haslam 1996). Rates of psychiatric morbidity are also much higher among women who have terminated a desired pregnancy in the second trimester because of a foetal abnormality than among those who chose to end their pregnancy at an earlier stage for different reasons (Iles & Gath 1993).

Men's experiences of abortion are difficult to research and very few studies have been conducted (Boyle 1997). The men that have participated in research tend to be in stable, supportive relationships with their partners, are generally white and middle-class and are willing to talk about the experience (Shostack *et al.* 1984; Neustatter 1986). Interviews with these men suggest that many of them are uncertain about the role they should play in the abortion – both in the decision to terminate

the pregnancy and in the process itself. Similar uncertainty was expressed about how best to support their partners after the abortion or how to talk about the experience with her (Haslam 1996). A feeling of being excluded from the decision is common, whilst acknowledging that whether or not to terminate the pregnancy must ultimately be the woman's choice. These men experienced grief after a termination for a foetal abnormality but, unlike women in this situation, seemed less able or willing to express it (Black 1991; Boyle 1997). These studies suggest that, at least for some men, abortion is a meaningful experience. However, they are concerned with a very specific, and possibly atypical, subgroup of men.

Conclusions

It is clear from this discussion that reactions to pregnancy and its outcomes are strongly mediated by gender, social context and the meaning that the pregnancy has for the individuals concerned. For the majority of women and men, pregnancy is a joyful time and results in the safe delivery of a healthy baby. Some women enter pregnancy with existing psychological and social difficulties to contend with, and a proportion become depressed or anxious during pregnancy and continue to be so after birth. If a pregnancy is lost, then emotional problems are more likely to occur if it was desired and then lost, no matter whether that loss occurs through miscarriage, stillbirth or induced abortion. Losing an unwanted pregnancy through induced abortion does not cause psychological problems for the majority of women, although it may do in exceptional cases. It is also clear that, although grief is the socially expected response to the loss of a pregnancy, it is not the only emotion that women or men experience. Shock, anxiety, relief, confusion and many other feelings are reported. Similarly, although joy is the socially expected response to the birth of a baby, it is not the only emotion that women experience. The psychological picture is more complex, rich and variable than social expectations suggest in both cases.

Psychological interventions have been found to be valuable in helping people to cope in many areas of reproductive health (see Walker & Hunter, this volume). This is far less true for pregnancy and pregnancy loss. The interventions that have been considered are mostly concerned with the alleviation of postnatal depression or anxiety associated with prenatal testing. In both cases, they have been found to be helpful. Given the importance of developing a personal understanding of pregnancy loss, psychological interventions might be expected to have beneficial effects in these areas too, but still await evaluation.

Acknowledgements

The Health Services Research Unit is funded by the Chief Scientist Office of the Scottish Executive Health Department. The opinions expressed in this chapter are those of the author and may not be shared by the funding body.

References

Adler, N. (1992) Unwanted pregnancy and abortion: definitional and research issues. *Journal of Social Is-sues* **48**, 19–35.

Adler, N., David, H., Major, B., Roth, S., Russo, N. & Wyatt, G. (1990) Psychological responses after abortion. *Science* **248**, 41–44.

Alan Guttmacher Institute (1999) *Sharing Responsibility: Women, Society and Abortion Worldwide.* Alan Guttmacher Institute, New York.

Allen, I. (1981) *Family Planning, Abortion and Sterilisation Services.* The Policy Studies Institute, London.

Baban, A. (1999) Romania. In: *From Abortion to Contraception. A Resource to Public Policies and Reproductive Behaviour in Central and Eastern Europe from 1917 to the Present* (ed. H.P. David), pp. 191–221. Greenwood Press, Westport, CN.

Baker, D. (1989) Social identity in the transition to motherhood. In: *The Social Identity of Women* (eds S. Skevington & D. Baker). Sage, London.

Ballard, C.G., Stanley, A.K. & Brockington, I.F. (1995) Post-traumatic stress disorder (PTSD) after childbirth. *British Journal of Psychiatry* **166**, 525–528.

Barker, K.K. (1998) A ship upon a stormy sea: the medicalization of pregnancy. *Social Science and Medicine* **47**, 1067–1076.

Black, R.B. (1991) Women's voices after pregnancy loss: couple's patterns of communication and support. *Social Work in Health Care* **16**, 19–36.

Boyle, M. (1997) *Re-thinking abortion.* Routledge, London.

Boyle, M. (2000) The experience of abortion: a contextualist view. In: *Women's Health: Contemporary International Perspectives* (ed. J. Ussher), pp. 339–355. BPS Books, Leicester.

Boyle, M. & McEvoy, J. (1998) Putting abortion in its social context. Northern Irish women's experience of abortion in England. *Health* **2**, 283–304.

Carp, H.J.A., Toder, V., Mashiach, S., Nebel, L. & Serr, D.M. (1990) Recurrent miscarriage. A review of current concepts, immune mechanisms and results of treatment. *Obstetrical and Gynecological Survey* **45**, 657–669.

Cecil, R.I. (1994) I wouldn't have minded a wee one running about. Miscarriage and the family. *Social Science and Medicine* **38**, 1415–1422.

Cecil, R. (1996) (ed.) *The Anthropology of Pregnancy Loss.* Berg, Oxford.

Cecil, R. & Leslie, J.C. (1993) Early miscarriage: preliminary results from a study in Northern Ireland. *Journal of Reproductive and Infant Psychology* **11**, 89–95.

Cecil, R. & Slade, M.P. (1996) Miscarriage. In: *The Psychology of Reproduction: 2. Conception, Pregnancy and Birth* (eds C.A. Niven & A. Walker), pp. 87–100. Butterworth-Heinemann, Oxford.

Central Statistical Office (1996) *Social Trends 1996.* HMSO, London.

Chalmers, B. (1992) Terminology used in early pregnancy loss. *British Journal of Obstetrics and Gynaecology* **99**, 357–358.

Charles, D. & Larsen, B. (1987) Infectious agents as causes of spontaneous abortion. In: *Spontaneous and Recurrent Abortion* (eds M.J. Bennett & D.K. Edmonds). Blackwell, Oxford.

Cohan, C., Dunkel-Schetter, C. & Lydon, J. (1993) Pregnancy decision making: predictors of early stress and adjustment. *Psychology of Women Quarterly* **17**, 223–240.

Collins, N., Dunkel-Schetter, C., Lobel, M. & Scrimshaw, S. (1993) Social support in pregnancy: psychological correlates of birth outcomes and postpartum depression. *Journal of Personality and Social Psychology* **65**, 1243–1258.

Condon, J. (1987) Psychological and physical symptoms during pregnancy: a comparison of male and female expectant parents. *Journal of Reproductive and Infant Psychology* **5**, 207–213.

Cordle, C.J. & Prettyman, R.J. (1994) A two-year follow-up of women who have experienced early miscarriage. *Journal of Reproductive and Infant Psychology* **12**, 37–43.

Czarnocka, J. & Slade, P. (2000) Prevalence and predictors of post-traumatic stress symptoms following childbirth. *British Journal of Clinical Psychology* **39**, 35–51.

Dagg, P. (1991) The psychological sequelae of therapeutic abortion – denied and completed. *American Journal of Psychiatry* **148**, 578–585.

DeLuca, M.A. & Leslie, P.W. (1996) Variation in risk of pregnancy loss. In: *The Anthropology of Pregnancy Loss* (ed. R. Cecil), pp. 113–131. Berg, Oxford.

Denious, J. & Russo, N.F. (2000) The socio-political context of abortion and its relationship to women's health. In: *Women's Health: Contemporary International Perspectives* (ed. J. Ussher), pp. 431–440. BPS

Books, Leicester.

Doyal, L. (1995) *What Makes Women Sick? Gender and the Political Economy of Health.* Macmillan Press, Basingstoke.

Elliott, S.A., Leverton, T.J., Sanjack, M., *et al.* (2000) Promoting mental health after childbirth: a controlled trial of primary prevention of postnatal depression. *British Journal of Clinical Psychology* **39**, 223–341.

Fergusson, D.M., Horwood L.J. & Thorpe, K.J. (1996) Changes in depression during and following pregnancy. *Paediatric and Perinatal Epidemiology* **10**, 279–293.

Flint, C. & Poulengris, P. (1987) *The 'Know Your Midwife' Scheme.* Report Published by Authors, London.

Friedman, T. & Gath, D. (1989) The psychiatric consequences of spontaneous abortion. *British Journal of Psychiatry* **155**, 810–813.

Gannon, K. (1994) Psychological factors in the aetiology and treatment of recurrent miscarriage: a review and critique. *Journal of Reproductive and Infant Psychology* **12**, 55–64.

Garel, M., Blondel, B., Lelong, N., Papin, C., Bonenfaut, S. & Kaminiski, M. (1992) Réactions dépressives après une fausse couche. *Contraception, Fertility and Sterility* **20**, 75–81.

Gilligan, C. (1982) *In A Different Voice: Psychological Theory and Women's Development.* Harvard University Press, Cambridge, MA.

Graves, W.L. (1987) Psychological aspects of spontaneous abortion. In: *Spontaneous and Recurrent Abortion* (eds M.J. Bennett & D.K. Edmonds). Blackwell Scientific Publications, Oxford.

Green, J. (1998) Postnatal depression or perinatal dysphoria? Findings from a longitudinal community-based study using the Edinburgh Postnatal Depression Scale. *Journal of Reproductive and Infant Psychology* **16**, 143–156.

Green, J., Coupland, V. & Kitzinger, J. (1990) Expectations, experiences and psychological outcomes of childbirth: a prospective study of 825 women. *Birth* **17**, 15–24.

Green, J., Coupland, V.A. & Kitzinger, J.V. (1998) *Great Expectations: A Prospective Study of Women's Expectations and Experiences of Childbirth.* Books for Midwives Press, Hale.

Green, J., Snowden, C. & Statham, H. (1993) Pregnant

women's attitudes to abortion and prenatal screening. *Journal of Reproductive and Infant Psychology* **11**, 31–39.

Gross, H. (2000) Pregnancy: a healthy state? In: *Women's Health: Contemporary International Perspectives* (ed. J. Ussher), pp. 296–302. BPS Books, Leicester.

Gross, H. & Pattison, H. (1995) Cognitive failure during pregnancy. *Journal of Reproductive and Infant Psychology* **13**, 17–32.

Haslam, D. (1996). *Coping with a Termination*. Mandarin, London.

Henshaw, R.C. & Templeton, A.A. (1998) Antiprogesterones. In: *Progress in Obstetrics and Gynaecology* (ed. J. Studd), pp. 259–277.

Hewison, J. (1996) Prenatal screening. In: *The Psychology of Reproduction: 2. Conception, Pregnancy and Birth* (eds C.A. Niven & A. Walker) pp. 74–86. Butterworth-Heinemann, Oxford.

HMSO (1992) *Health Committee (2nd Report) Maternity Services*, Vol. 1. HMSO, London.

Holmgren, K. (1994) Repeat abortion and contraceptive use: report from an interview study in Stockholm. *Gynecological and Obstetric Investigations* **37**, 254–259.

Hopkins, N., Reicher, S. & Saleem, J. (1996) Constructing women's psychological health in anti-abortion rhetoric. *Sociological Review* **44**, 539–564.

Horta, J.L.H., Fernandez, J.G., Delcon, B.S. & Cortes-Gallegos, V. (1977) Direct evidence of luteal insufficiency in women with habitual abortion. *Obstetrics and Gynaecology* **49**, 705–708.

Howie, F.L., Henshaw, R.C., Naji, S.A., Russell, I.T. & Templeton, A.A. (1997) Medical abortion or vacuum aspiration? Two year follow up of a patient preference trial. *British Journal of Obstetrics and Gynaecology* **104**, 829–833.

Hutchins, S.D. (1986) Stillbirth. In: *Parental Loss of a Child* (ed. T. Rando). Research Press, Champaign, IL.

Iles, S. & Gath, D. (1993) Psychiatric outcome of termination of pregnancy for foetal abnormality. *Psychological Medicine* **23**, 407–413.

Information and Statistics Division for the National Health Service in Scotland. (2000) *Health Briefing 00/11: Abortion Statistics Scotland 1998 and 1999.* ISD, Edinburgh. (www.show.scot.nhs.uk/isd/publications/).

Jackman, C., McGee, H. & Turner, M. (1991) The experience and psychological impact of early miscarriage. *Irish Journal of Psychology* **12**, 108–120.

Jowell, R., Witherspoon, S. & Brook, L. (1991) *British Social Attitudes: 7th Report*. Gower, Aldershot.

Kaunitz, A.M., Rovira, E.Z., Grimes, D.A. & Schulz, K.F. (1985) Abortions that fail. *Obstetrics and Gynecology* **66**, 533–537.

Kirkley-Best, E. & Kellner, K. (1982) The forgotten grief: a review of the psychology of stillbirth. *American Journal of Orthopsychiatry* **52**, 420–429.

Kohner, N. (1992) *A Dignified Ending*. SANDS, London.

Leppert, P.C. & Pahlka, B.S. (1984) Grieving characteristics after spontaneous abortion: a management approach. *Obstetrics and Gynecology* **64**, 119–122.

Lewis, C. (1986). *Becoming a Father*. Open University Press, Milton Keynes.

Littlewood, J. (1992) *Aspects of Grief: Bereavement in Adult Life*. Routledge, London.

Littlewood, J. (1996) Stillbirth and neonatal death. In: *The Psychology of Reproduction: 2. Conception, Pregnancy and Birth* (eds C.A. Niven & A. Walker), pp. 148–158. Butterworth-Heinemann, Oxford.

Madden, M.E. (1988) Internal and external attributions following miscarriage. *Journal of Social and Clinical Psychology* **7**, 113–121.

Mander, R. (1994) *Loss and Bereavement in Childbearing*. Blackwell Scientific Publications, London.

Marteau, T., Kidd, J., Cook, R., *et al.* (1992) Psychological effects of having amniocentesis; are these due to the procedure, the risk or the behaviour? *Journal of Psychosomatic Research* **36**, 395–402.

McDonald, I.A. (1987) Cervical incompetence as a cause of spontaneous abortion. In: *Spontaneous and Recurrent Abortion* (eds M.J. Bennett & D.K. Edmonds). Blackwell Scientific Publications, Oxford.

Menage, J. (1993) Post traumatic stress disorder in women who have undergone obstetric and/or gynaecological procedures. *Journal of Reproductive and Infant Psychology* **11**, 221–228.

Morrell, C. (1994) *Unwomanly Conduct: The Challenges of Intentional Childlessness*. Routledge, New York.

Neugebauer, R., Kline, J., O'Connor, P., *et al.* (1992) Depressive symptoms in women six months after miscarriage. *American Journal of Obstetrics and Gynecology* **166**, 104–109.

Neustatter, A. (1986) (with Newson G.) *Mixed Feelings: the Experience of Abortion*. Pluto Press, London.

Nicolson, P. (1998) *Postnatal Depression*. Routledge, London.

Niven, C.A. (1988) Labour pain: long term recall and consequences. *Journal of Reproductive and Infant Psychology* **6**, 83–87.

Oakley, A. (1980) *Women Confined*. Martin Robertson, Oxford.

Oakley, A. (1993) Promoting the health of childbearing women. In: *Essays on Women, Medicine and Health*, pp. 95–107. Edinburgh University Press, Edinburgh.

Oakley, A., Rajan, L. & Grant, A. (1990) Social support and pregnancy outcome. *British Journal of Obstetrics and Gynaecology* **97**, 155–162.

Office for National Statistics (2000) *Health Statistics Quarterly 08*. ONS, London. (www.statistics.gov.uk).

Penney, G.C., Glasier, A. & Templeton, A. (1994) A multi-centre, criterion based audit of the management of induced abortion in Scotland. *British Medical Journal* **309**, 15–18.

Posavac, E. & Miller, T. (1990) Some problems caused by not having a conceptual foundation for health research: an illustration from studies of the psychological effects of abortion. *Psychology and Health* **5**, 13–23.

Prettyman, R.J., Cordle, C.J. & Cook, G.D. (1993) A three-month follow-up of psychological morbidity after early miscarriage. *British Journal of Medical Psychology* **66**, 363–372.

Price, J. (1988) *Motherhood: What It Does to Your Mind*. Pandora, London.

Puddifoot, J.E. & Johnson, M.P. (1997) Legitimacy in grieving – the partner's experience of miscarriage. *Social Science and Medicine* **45**, 837–845.

Puddifoot, J.E. & Johnson, M.P. (1999) Active grief, despair and difficulty coping: some measured characteristics of male response following their partner's miscarriage. *Journal of Reproductive and Infant Psychology* **17**, 89–93.

Quine, L., Rutter, D. & Gowen, S. (1993) Women's satisfaction with the quality of the birth experience. *Journal of Reproductive and Infant Psychology* **11**, 107–115.

Raphael-Leff, J. (1991) *Psychological Processes of Childbearing*. Chapman & Hall, London.

Robinson, G.E., Stirtzinger, R., Stewart, D.E. & Ravelski, E. (1994) Psychological reactions in women followed for one year after miscarriage. *Journal of Reproductive and Infant Psychology* **12**, 31–36.

Royal College of Obstetricians and Gynaecologists. (2000) The care of women requesting induced abortion. RCOG, London. (www.rcog.org.uk/guidelines/abortion).

Russo, N. & Denious, J.E. (2000) Violence in the lives of women having abortions: implications for public policy practice. *Professional Psychology: Research and Practice*

Russo, N., Horn, J. & Schwartz, R. (1992) US abortion in context: selected characteristics and motivations of women seeking abortions. *Journal of Social Issues* **48**, 183–202.

SANDS (1991) *Guidelines for Professionals: Miscarriage, Stillbirth and Neonatal Death*. Stillbirth and Neonatal Death Society, London.

Scott, G. & Niven, C.A. (1996) Pregnancy: a bio-psycho-social event. In: *The Psychology of Reproduction: 2. Conception, Pregnancy and Birth* (eds C.A. Niven & A. Walker), pp. 41–56. Butterworth Heinemann, Oxford.

Shostack, A., McLouth, G. & Seng, L. (1984) *Men and Abortion: Lessons in Love*. Praeger, New York.

Simpson, J.L. & Bombard, A. (1987) Chromosomal abnormalities in spontaneous abortion: frequency, pathology and genetic counselling. In: *Spontaneous and Recurrent Abortion* (eds M.J. Bennett & D.K. Edmonds). Blackwell Scientific Publications, Oxford.

Slade, P. (1977) Awareness of body dimensions during pregnancy: analogue study. *Psychological Medicine* **7**, 245–252.

Slade, P. (1994) Predicting the psychological impact of miscarriage. *Journal of Reproductive and Infant Psychology* **12**, 5–16.

Slade, P. (1996) Antenatal preparation. In: *The Psychology of Reproduction: 2. Conception, Pregnancy and Birth* (eds C.A. Niven & A. Walker), pp. 101–113. Butterworth-Heinemann, Oxford.

Slade, P., Heke, S., Fletcher, J. & Stewart, P. (1998) A comparison of medical and surgical termination of pregnancy: choice, emotional impact and satisfaction with care. *British Journal of Obstetrics and Gynaecology* **105**, 1288–1295.

Smetana, J. & Adler, N. (1979) Decision making regarding abortion: a value X expectancy analysis. *Journal of Population* **2**, 348–355.

Smith, J.A. (1999) Identity development during the transition to motherhood: an interpretative phenomenological analysis. *Journal of Reproductive and Infant Psychology* **17**, 281–300.

Statham, H. & Green, J. (1994) The effects of miscarriage and other 'unsuccessful' pregnancies on feelings early in a subsequent pregnancy. *Journal of Reproductive and Infant Psychology* **12**, 45–54.

Steptoe, A. & Appels, A., eds (1989) *Stress, Personal Control and Health*. John Wiley, Chichester.

Stotland, N. (1992) The myth of the abortion trauma syndrome. *Journal of the American Medical Association* **268**, 2078–2079.

Tew, M. (1990) *Safer Childbirth?* Chapman & Hall, London.

Tharpar, A.K. & Tharpar, A. (1992) Psychological sequelae of miscarriage: a controlled study using the general health questionnaire and the hospital anxiety and depression scale. *British Journal of General Practice* **42**, 94–96.

The Boston Women's Health Book Collective (1998) *Our Bodies Ourselves for the New Century*. Touchstone, New York.

Thorpe, K. & Elliott, S. (1998) The well-being of mothers. In: *The Psychology of Reproduction: 3. Current Issues in Infancy and Parenthood* (eds C.A. Niven & A. Walker), pp. 107–136. Butterworth-Heinemann, Oxford.

Toedter, L.J., Lasker, J.N. & Alhedeff, J.M. (1988) The perinatal grief scale. *American Journal of Orthopsychiatry* **58**, 435–449.

Torres, A. & Forest, J. (1988) Why do women have abortions? *Family Planning Perspectives* **20**, 169–176.

Tunaley, J., Slade, P. & Duncan, S.B. (1993) Cognitive processes in psychological adaptation to miscarriage: a preliminary report. *Psychology and Health* **8**, 369–381.

Van den Akker, O., Sweeny, V. & Rosenblatt, D. (1990) Psychological factors associated with pregnancy and the postnatal period in women at risk for preterm labour/delivery. Paper presented at SRIP conference.

Walker, A. (1996) Psychological aspects of elective abortion. In: *The Psychology of Reproduction: 1. Reproductive Potential and Fertility Control* (eds C.A. Niven & A Walker), pp. 139–153. Butterworth-Heinemann, Oxford.

Wilcox, A.J., Weinberg, C., O'Connor, J.F., *et al.* (1988) Incidence of early loss of pregnancy. *New England Journal of Medicine* **319**, 189–194.

Wiles, R. (1990) I'm not fat, I'm pregnant. The impact of pregnancy on fat women's body image. In: *Women and Health: Feminist Perspectives* (eds S. Wilkinson & C. Kitzinger), pp. 33–48. Taylor & Francis, London.

Williams, J. (1987) *Psychology of Women: Behaviour in a Biosocial Context*, 3rd edn. WW Norton, New York.

Wolkind, S. & Zajicek, E. (1981) *Pregnancy: A Psychological and Social Study*. Academic Press, London.

Woollett, A. & Marshall, H. (1997) Discourses of pregnancy and childbirth. In: *Material Discourses of Health and Illness* (ed. L. Yardley). Routledge, London.

Chapter 23

Conclusion

John Green and David Miller

In this book we have sought to show the diversity of sexual health issues which are subject to psychological enquiry. Inevitably sexually transmitted diseases are a prominent part of the book. We are, after all, in the midst of a global AIDS epidemic which is having devastating consequences for many countries and bringing untold misery to millions. In the shadow of AIDS are the epidemics of other sexually transmitted diseases: syphilis, gonorrhoea, chlamydia and wart virus infections. If AIDS miraculously disappeared tomorrow we would still have many other challenges to face.

Without a clear understanding of the prevalence of sexually transmitted diseases and the available methods of control it is next to impossible to mount effective sexual health programmes. As Michael Adler's chapter shows, there are formidable problems in controlling sexually transmitted infections globally. Mounting effective control procedures is not simply a matter of choosing the most effective strategy in scientific terms – difficult though this is – there is also a need to change

social attitudes towards those affected, to mobilise the political will of governments to act effectively and to ensure that adequate resources are available and are properly deployed. The latter is a particular problem in countries where there are many competing priorities and few resources available. Control of sexually transmitted diseases is as much a social, economic and political issue as it is a medical and psychological one.

Even where the political will is present and there are resources to deploy, understanding how to deploy them optimally is not easy. As Green's chapter shows there is much that we do not understand about what drives sexual behaviour and how it can be modified to help people to keep themselves safer. Basic public knowledge of sexually transmitted diseases is poor. While knowledge alone is not sufficient to lead people to change their behaviour, without at least some basic awareness that a problem exists people are hardly likely to change their behaviour. However, lack of knowledge by the public is only one problem. The models which have been developed to explain sexual risk behaviour are incomplete and we do not understand fully how people react to, and think about, sexually transmitted diseases.

Nonetheless, despite the current limitations of what we know and understand, as Dubois-Arber and Carael show, theory can successfully influence positive behaviour change. To be of use, theory needs to encompass an understanding of the psychosocial and cultural context of sexual behaviours. Sexual behaviour does not occur *in vacuo* but in the context of people's everyday lives and interactions. It is not simply internally driven and cannot be understood without consideration of its background.

Richens examines how cultural belief systems can impact upon public health efforts, and vice versa. Mobilising the community and seeking to create a social climate supportive to individual behaviour change is crucial to the success of intervention with individuals. As Davidson and colleagues show, a 'one-size fits all' approach to sexual health is an inadequate response. Populations in every country are not homogeneous but are made up of diverse groups. Creating an appropriate climate and setting up appropriate services means considering diversity, the different cultural groups within a population, and working with them to make sure that what we do is appropriate to each of those groups.

Interventions need to be effective, but they also need to be practicable and applicable by non-specialists in everyday clinical work. There simply are not enough STD specialists in the world to deal with the level of morbidity. Barton and Fox's chapter shows how good practice can be applied in a primary care setting and how general and specialist services can work effectively together. Another ap-

proach to seeking to make the best use of scarce resources is to seek to intervene with groups rather than individually. Billington and Wanigaratne describe such an intervention designed to help initiate and maintain safer sex in gay men in the UK. The approach is one which might be modified to be applicable in a range of settings and across a range of populations.

Easton and colleagues identify many of the barriers in our thinking which, if we are not on our guard against them, interfere with appropriate action. Their chapter brings out a key theme in this book: if we artificially pathologise sexual behaviour, seeing risky sexual behaviour for example as a reflection of some peculiar failing in the individual rather than as the result of the operation of common and general psychological processes, then we make finding a proper understanding of risk behaviour impossible. Robin Bell's chapter illustrates the sheer variety of human sexual behaviour and how it results from such general processes. The sad history of attempts to control sexually transmitted diseases shows how pathologising sexual behaviour can lead governments and professionals into coercive control strategies which ultimately prove self-defeating.

A good example of the complexities of implementing effective control strategies is partner notification. As Chippindale's chapter shows, partner notification is not a straightforward matter of instructing patients to tell their partners or a health care professional going out and doing it for them. Partner notification can only be effective in a context of greater social tolerance where there are meaningful options for the index patient.

Reducing the psychology of sexually transmitted diseases to an issue of infection control would be a caricature. People also need help in addressing the psychological and personal problems which arise from sexually transmitted disease. As the chapter by Petrak and Miller shows, HIV presents particular, but by no means unique, difficulties for the individual. Addressing only transmission issues does not add up to proper management of the patient; there is also a need to provide an integrated approach to a complex set of problems. As Catalan's chapter shows, frank psychiatric problems are common in people with HIV disease and these problems are best addressed through an effective multidisciplinary approach. To provide services only aimed at restricting spread is to fail properly to help the patient.

Scragg and Alcorn provide a detailed examination of personality disorder and its manifestations in sexual health settings. Their chapter is a reminder that even for the specialist in sexual health problems a wider awareness of psychological issues is indispensable.

The problems associated with dealing with sexually transmitted diseases represent only one, albeit important, aspect of sexual health. For many people in the world the regulation of fertility is at least as important. Gupta and Elstein demonstrate how the history of fertility regulation is every bit as controversial as the history of STD management, and as crucial for sexual health. As with STDs, the regulation of fertility occurs within a social, cultural and political context which has to be understood if we are to act effectively to improve people's sexual health.

Walker and Hunter's review of menstruation, fertility problems and menopause picks up and extends many of these issues. The authors make a convincing case for addressing these issues from a biopsychosocial frame-

work, and identify the danger of pathologising natural processes.

Of all sexual health issues, perhaps the most common in the population is that of sexual functioning problems. At any one time up to a third of people are likely to have some degree of difficulty in functioning sexually. As the chapter on taking a sexual history and the following chapter by Hiller and Cooke show, there is much that can and needs to be done in this area. Again there is a wider political context. Psychosexual problems are very distressing, can often be treated effectively, and yet they are often seen by governments, and sometimes by individual health practitioners, as somehow outside the remit of the health care system. They are seen as private matters to do with 'lifestyle' and personal pleasure rather than as legitimate health needs. Unless we identify sexual health issues as worthy of intervention then we will not act to deal with them. Health care in sexual health does not just concern issues which have an economic impact on countries; it is also about the well-being of individual members of the population.

Lee's chapter on assault shows the complexity of the sequelae of rape and how people who have been the victims of sexual assault can be best helped – an area in which compelling psychological theory is matched to treatment intervention and a model of what might be achieved elsewhere. Kennerley's chapter on sexual abuse and its consequences complements this chapter. Together they illustrate the importance of strong theoretical thinking, proper testing of models and systematic development and evaluation of interventions – something which is needed across the whole of the psychological aspects of sexual health if we are to make progress.

Byrne and Christmas's chapter picks up perhaps one of the central themes of this book. There is no sharp divide between mind and body and, in sexual health, there is no sharp divide between psychological interventions and medical interventions. Best practice in all areas of sexual health comes from combining complementary approaches.

What of the future? Speculation is always a risky business, but we can at least look forward to what we would hope to see in the next ten or twenty years. In the Introduction, we mentioned the syndromic management of STDs. Syndromic management is a response to lack of resources, lack of trained staff and lack of proper diagnostic facilities. While the benefits of such an approach may seem clear, they are rarely perfectly achieved, and may have substantial costs over time in terms of increased and broadly based drug resistance. While we would like to believe that global wealth will have trickled down to the extent that everyone in the world will get the sort of medical facilities found in the wealthiest countries within the next twenty years, we do not believe it likely. We would hope, however, that cheaper and technically simpler diagnostics combined with clear treatment protocols, including proper protocols for the psychological management of the patient, will be available to most people in the world by that time.

We would also hope to see major developments and innovations in voluntary counselling and testing (VCT) approaches in HIV/AIDS. It is disturbing how little progress there seems to have been in thinking about patient management, which remains pretty similar to the approach which we described in 1985 (Miller et al. 1985). At that time there were no effective drug treatments for HIV disease and

no methods of preventing vertical transmission. While we still believe that the principles of informed consent and confidentiality which informed our model at that time are cornerstones of good practice, treatment advances have significantly tipped the balance of advantage towards the benefits of being tested for most patients, at least in those parts of the world where treatment is available. Models must adapt and change to meet the requirements of their target populations, and the times in which they are being implemented. In ten years' time we would hope to see VCT models which reflect current treatment possibilities being the norm. That assumes, of course, that the current situation where most of the world has no access to treatment has changed, something we fervently hope will have happened.

We would also like to see the various components of VCT examined in a systematic way. Basing approaches to clinical practice on clinical experience is unavoidable early in the experience of a disease; later however one hopes to see experience being replaced as a guide by evidence. It is not so much the need for outcome trials of VCT, although more such trials are vital, it is work on the components of VCT which needs to be carried out, so that we can understand how to provide better VCT models.

Adherence to treatment is a key area which needs further development. Given the costs of health care relative to the per capita spending on health in many countries and the risks of drug resistance with incomplete adherence, the importance of developing effective models for ensuring full adherence to treatment regimes cannot be overestimated. The same can be said of the challenges in providing access to, and ensuring compliance with, condom use in males and females.

Increasingly, the cost–benefits of advances in treatment regimes and psychological management approaches must be determined if the key elements – especially in communication – are to be invested in. Clarifying the costs and benefits associated with particular interventions such as counselling or nationalised prescription costs for life-threatening diseases can influence policy – as in the case of the Brazilian government providing antiretroviral treatment for those with HIV disease. Costings bring into stark relief the relative benefits of action versus inaction.

We also anticipate that the area of genetics will take on increasing importance. There are a few diseases which are more or less purely genetically determined, like cystic fibrosis and sickle cell disease. Far more diseases are likely to turn out to be the result of complex interactions between genes and environment. As more and more genes are identified which play some part in the development of disease and rapid cheap screening techniques for genetic disorders are developed, as seems inevitable, then genetics and sexual health will start to converge. Already we might offer people screening for, say, sickle cell trait and the opportunity to find out if they are carriers of the recessive gene. Indeed such screening is already offered in some areas. Couples are, in principle, in a position to find out that they are both carriers of the recessive gene for sickle cell disease and that each of their children has a one in four chance of having the disease.

As the number of potentially identifiable genes playing a part in disease rises, will we find couples choosing not to have children together as a result of their shared genes? Will

people start to look at the genetics of potential partners before deciding to settle down together? How will they decide which alleles are worth worrying about, which can be lived with? Where behaviour change can reduce the influence of genes, for instance by modifications of diet or regular screening for disease, how will we help people to achieve such changes? Which genetic problems are likely to be regarded by people as so serious that they might influence who they have children with? How can we best advise them and how can we deal with the psychological sequelae of such decisions? These issues are currently a mystery but no doubt within the next 10–20 years we will start to discover the answers and, if experience in other areas is anything to go by, we will have to start looking systematically at the psychological aspects of the various issues in much more detail and on a much larger scale.

Perhaps one of the greatest challenges in developing a psychology of sexual health is to ensure access to psychological care to all those with sexual health problems who need it. Elaborate interventions which prove effective are not likely to be affordable in many places. When interventions are developed they need to be practicable. Partly that is a matter of designing them so that they can be delivered by non-specialists; partly the issue is a more general problem of shortage of funds for health care worldwide, and this needs to be addressed.

Great progress has been made in helping people to regulate their fertility, but there is a long way to go before the aim of ensuring that everyone in the world can control their fertility as they wish is achieved. The problem is not limited to developing countries. The UK for instance has a poor record on unwanted teenage pregnancies. Reducing coercion in sex and providing proper services and support to those who are its victims, of whatever age, is a priority. Better access to treatments for sexual dysfunction would improve the lives of many.

As we write, there is a massive worldwide epidemic of HIV, and yet 95 percent of those with HIV do not know they have it. Most countries in the world cannot afford to provide treatment for most of their citizens who need it. Even if they could afford the drugs, which are currently wildly more expensive than most developing countries can afford, the other costs associated with treatment including simple blood tests and reasonable standard hospital care are unaffordable. The only way to get on top of the costs is to get the infection rate down. In the absence of an effective vaccine, behaviour change is the only way to achieve that. We should be putting far more resources into researching better ways to help people to reduce risk. However we already know enough to be able to make a difference and we cannot wait for further research before

acting. We need to put more resources into services to deliver what we already know, however imperfect. In this area, as in so many others in health, you pay now or you pay later, but pay you inevitably will.

Ultimately it comes down to resources and the allocation of resources is vital, whether they be for drug treatments for HIV, better condoms, a male contraceptive pill, or whatever the latest technical advance might be. These are tangible benefits, but the advantages of psychological treatments are a lot less salient to governments and policy-makers. However that doesn't make them any less important. If fear of the pox is the beginning of wisdom, then wise resource allocation may be the final judge of the wisdom of all our efforts.

Reference

Miller, D., Green, J. & McCreaner, A. (1985) Organising a counselling service for AIDS-related problems. *Genitourinary Medicine* **62**, 116–122.

Index